D0843862

Hindu-Christian Dialogue

FAITH MEETS FAITH

An Orbis Series in Interreligious Dialogue

Paul F. Knitter, General Editor

In our contemporary world, the many religions and spiritualities stand in need of greater intercommunication and cooperation. More than ever before, they must speak to, learn from, and work with each other, in order to maintain their own identity and vitality and so to contribute to fashioning a better world.

FAITH MEETS FAITH seeks to promote interreligious dialogue by providing an open forum for the exchanges between and among followers of different religious paths. While the series wants to encourage creative and bold responses to the new questions of pluralism confronting religious persons today, it also recognizes the present plurality of perspectives concerning the methods and content of interreligious dialogue.

This series, therefore, does not want to endorse any one school of thought. By making available to both the scholarly community and the general public works that represent a variety of religious and methodological viewpoints, FAITH MEETS FAITH hopes to foster and focus the emerging encounter among the religions of the world.

Already published:

Toward a Universal Theology of Religion, Leonard Swidler, Editor
The Myth of Christian Uniqueness, John Hick and Paul F. Knitter, Editors
An Asian Theology of Liberation, Aloysius Pieris, S.J.
The Dialogical Imperative, David Lochhead
Love Meets Wisdom, Aloysius Pieris, S.J.
Many Paths, Eugene Hillman
The Silence of God, Raimundo Panikkar
The Challenge of the Scriptures, Groupe de Recherches
    Islamo-Chrétien
The Meaning of Christ, John P. Keenan

FAITH MEETS FAITH SERIES

Hindu-Christian Dialogue

Perspectives and Encounters

Harold Coward, Editor

ORBIS BOOKS

Maryknoll, New York 10545

Second Printing, April 1990

The Catholic Foreign Mission Society of America (Maryknoll) recruits and trains people for overseas missionary service. Through Orbis Books, Maryknoll aims to foster the international dialogue that is essential to mission. The books published, however, reflect the opinions of their authors and are not meant to represent the official position of the society.

Copyright © 1989 by Harold Coward
Published by Orbis Books, Maryknoll, NY 10545
All Rights Reserved
Manufactured in the United States of America

Library of Congress Cataloging-in-Publication Data

Hindu-Christian dialogue : perspectives and encounters / Harold
    Coward, editor.
        p.   cm. — (Faith meets faith series)
    Includes bibliographical references.
    ISBN 0-88344-634-0. — ISBN 0-88344-633-2 (pbk.)
    1. Christianity and other religions — Hinduism.   2. Hinduism —
Relations — Christianity.   I. Coward, Harold G. II. Series: Faith
meets faith.
BR128.H5H55   1990
261.2'45. — dc20   89-29673
                                                           CIP

To my children
David, Kenneth and Susan
and the different dialogues each is living

CONCORDIA UNIVERSITY LIBRARY
PORTLAND, OR 97211

Contents

Part Three
FUTURE PERSPECTIVES ON HINDU-CHRISTIAN DIALOGUE

Foreword

The Ongoing Dialogue

RAIMUNDO PANIKKAR

This book does not engage in dialogue. It is *about* dialogue. It describes "the state of the art," and provides knowledge and insights that are indispensable for proceeding further and deeper in the encounter between these two major traditions of the world.

Dialogue is more than a casual or merely well-intentioned conversation. The Hindu-Christian dialogue, in its present state, demands both a deep experience of one's own tradition and a sufficient knowledge of the other one. We do not begin anew. This dialogue is not of yesterday. It requires a certain knowledge of what has already happened. The history of this encounter has a loaded karma.

Hindu-Christian Dialogue: Perspectives and Encounters provides a useful service by giving us a fair picture of the situation. Harold Coward is to be congratulated on putting together this kind of sociological introduction that is far from being of merely theoretical interest. Many of those writing here are renowned scholars who have already contributed to this field, as has Coward himself in his excellent book, *Pluralism: Challenge to World Religions* (which represents lectures he gave at the University of Madras). The present volume offers a brilliant confirmation of that earlier effort. "For in such dialogue lies the future of religions."

In the present book a group of experts presents us with enough information to allow me to speak of a fourth phase in the dialogue; and in order to do so, I would like to present the *Sitz im Leben* of this important contribution.

The context of the Hindu-Christian dialogue, as well as of any interreligious dialogue, is not the narrowly specific "religious" field, but the arena of life, the daily struggle for justice, peace, happiness. We meet the true 'other' not in an artificial milieu, but as fellow-traveler in the concerns of real life. But today people meet in the streets of cities, in their places of work and entertainment, and normally exchange only information of superficial feelings, having put a mask on their true personalities. A book of this kind may help readers not only by furnishing them with information, but also by providing them an occasion for deepening human communication, enhancing their own lives. True dialogue takes place not only in life; it is an exchange of life, a dialogue of life.

Some twelve million Hindus live today in the West and their number is multiplying. Not all of them are 'orthodox' Hindus. Yet the archetypes still come from the Indic traditions. An increasing number of Westerners also have close ties with the Indic subcontinent. Not all of them are 'orthodox' Christians. Yet the archetypes still come from the Christian tradition. Mutual interactions are inevitable. Understanding between people belonging to those two religions is imperative for peace in the world. The way to peace is neither isolation nor competition, but through dialogue. It should be clear here that Hinduism is not reducible to orthodox Vedanta, and Christianity not identical with the orthodox versions of it. Religions today, as in times gone by, are living entities. They are moving and changing realities—labels notwithstanding. Only from the outside do we have a static view of a religion. If we live a religious faith consciously and sincerely, we experience at the same time the freedom to transform it precisely by living it. The Hindu-Christian dialogue of the present cannot be limited to discussing frozen doctrines of the past. And yet the past is still effective in the present. We cannot neglect it.

The pages of this book resonate in me, not as mere ideas, but as bits and pieces of my own life and experience. Perhaps my best qualification for introducing these enriching and illuminating essays is that I have played practically all the roles described in them. I have gone in pilgrimage to distant places in the north and south of India; I have been lost among the crowds and in danger often in my life. I have lived the simple life of the masses and have also been an academic, taking part in the more intellectual aspects of the dialogue. I have found myself sincerely carrying on the dialogue from both ends of the spectrum. I have played the role of the Hindu, feeling obliged to respond out of a sense of justice and self-respect when Christians misunderstood the Hindu tradition or made a caricature of it. I have also felt called upon to play the role of the Christian, when Hindus also misunderstood the Christian tradition or made a caricature of it. And each time, I emphasize, without being insincere, syncretistic, or condescending. My reactions were not those of the merely informed expert; they were rather those of the enlightened believer. I have been shunning labels all my life. No one label can define who a person is, for one's 'circumstance,' one's environment (*Umwelt, circumstancia*) is as much a part of oneself as is one's individualized substance. In saying this, am I already too Hindu? Or too Indian? Actually, I am describing a universal existential reality.

I have spontaneously identified myself with both sides—Hindu and Christian—without preconceived strategies. Over thirty years ago I discovered myself timidly saying that I was both a Hindu and a Christian without being an eclectic. Trying to justify this original insight, this spontaneous feeling and unreflected experience, I subsequently discovered that I was not the first, and that the dialectics of either/or do not apply so easily to an Asian mentality. Do I belong to my father or to my mother? Is my Hindu karma not a Christian one? Does not the Gospel tell me to respect my *dharma?*

There is another less existential and more academic aspect of this situation. I am assuming that we are all searchers after truth and not mercenaries at the service of some ideology or institution. We are all convinced of our own beliefs, have thought about them, studied and analyzed them. Psychologically one could say that we are full of our own convictions. In a sincere dialogue situation we show more interest in the unknown—intriguing and even somewhat unconvincing as it is—than in what we believe we already know. The exotic, in its etymological sense, triggers our curiosity and even perhaps the desire intelligently to rebuke it. But this is true also for the other side. The result is that we become more interested in the arguments and ideas of the *pūrvapakṣin* (the opponent), to use Sanskrit scholastic terminology, than in our own, already held convictions. Instinctively, when the dialogue is genuine, we cease to perform mere monologues. Each one of us struggles to understand the partner. In this exchange we discover points or perspectives lacking in our own beliefs, and something similar happens to the other partner. Then we discover that we have perhaps gone too far and try to retreat to our previous positions, but it is too late for both sides. Something has changed in each, although it sometimes goes unconfessed to the other party. We do not want to lose face. But we both have lost ground.

This book describes many situations in which I myself have shared. I have duly performed Hindu ceremonies (at Guruvayur, one of the most orthodox Hindu temples, for instance) and celebrated the Christian mysteries (in Shillong Cathedral, one of the most "orthodox" Roman Catholic churches, for example). I have been dialoguing in Europe, America, and India; sitting in ashrams, gurukuls, universities, and bishops' houses; living in presbyteries and temples. Karma-*bhakti* and *jñāna-yoga* are not unknown or foreign to me; the Vedas and the Bible are holy books for me and I have spent long years in practice, study, and meditation of both (*śravaṇa, manana, nidhidhyāsana*). Finally, let me assert that through all of this I kept my freedom because I have renounced any type of power. I begin every time all over again!

I present my credentials here because I intend to do something more risky than merely introducing these authors, or summing up the argument of the book. To do the first is unnecessary when the writers are already so well known. To do the second would be redundant, when they have reached such examplary clarity. We cannot, and should not, engage in dialogue if we are not spiritually, intellectually, and humanly equipped for it, most of the authors tell us. But instead of insisting on all this, let me try to situate the book as a whole and venture a hypothesis.

The book as a whole is an enlightening introduction to the "state of the art." In spite of what the non-specialized reader may expect, the Hindu-Christian dialogue is as old as the religions themselves. The chapters of this work give us a fair idea of that constant symbiosis between the two religions. This is a typical feature of India. We may recall that the census of 1911 still had a large category of "Mohammedan Hindus," or remember that as late as the middle of the last century the common name for God used by the Muslims in rural Bengal was Íśvara (and not Allâh). If literacy means putting labels on things, then some aspects of this living interaction among popular religions may have been repressed. It is for this very reason that the description of the encounter and mutual influences between these two religions on the popular level is so important.

While some will stress the difficulties in academic dialogue, others will say that only Christians are interested in it. It all depends on what we understand by dialogue. Indeed dialogue on Western terms interests mostly only Westerners or Westernized Indians. But one of the lessons of this book is that dialogue has many meanings and is carried out on many levels.

Those many levels may be bewildering for the neat minds of certain 'intellectuals,' but I submit that they have a deeper reason than sociological considerations may lead us to believe. In point of fact, both Hinduism and Christianity are two abstract labels. Hinduism does not exist; there are only living and separated traditions, *sampradāyas* and such. Christianity also is non-existent; there are thousands of churches, doctrines, and groups that, seen from the outside, appear as baroque and overwhelming as Hinduism may appear to the outsider. There is not one Hindu-Christian dialogue. There are scores of them, and this very book is a beautiful example of the variety of such encounters. This is another reason to reinforce the recurrent idea in the book that we need to be knowledgeable, and to have done our homework, before engaging in dialogue.

This book reflects both the doctrinal and the institutional difficulties standing in the way of a fruitful dialogue, and the necessity of taking those difficulties into account. They form a great part of the very contents of the dialogue. The obstacles are part of the way. The Hindu-Christian dialogue is not a merely theoretical issue. It belongs to the life of the peoples of the world, and of the Indic subcontinent in particular. Many historical movements today are not only incomprehensible, but they would have been impossible without this mutual fecundation between religions, Hinduism and Christianity in this case. History is not only an account of wars. Che Guevera and Martin Luther King, Jr., are impossible without Gandhi, who is indebted to Tolstoy, who in turn is the product of an Eastern Christianity that has one of its roots in Eastern spiritualities of an extra- and pre-Christian nature. The great names of the school of Alexandria were strongly influenced by Indic doctrines. Pantaenus went to India; Ammonius Saccas, whatever his origin, was conversant with oriental religions. . . . There is a *mala*, a rosary of living names, East and West, Hindu and Christian, which forms the warp and woof of real human history. In short, the Desert Fathers and the Hindu mystics as much as the British viceroys and the Hindu rajas or Muslim nawabs are latent partners in the present-day encounters.

John Webster reminds us that Mahatma Gandhi, when addressing a group of Christians in 1927, told them to use Hindi instead of English and to give the spinning wheel priority over literacy in uplifting the masses; Gandhi thus touched on two of the most fundamental pillars for dialogue: *language* and *praxis*.

Dialogue, to begin with, has to be *duo-logue*. There have to be two *logoi*, two languages encountering each other, so as to overcome the danger of a double monologue. One has to know the language of the other, even if one has to learn it precisely from the other, and often in the very exercise of dialogue. Dialogue engages the intellect, the *logos*. The academic study of religion is not a luxury.

At the same time, it has to be *dia-logue*, that is, a piercing of the *logos*, an overcoming of the mere intellectual level, a going *through* the intellect into an encounter of the whole person. It has to proceed from praxis and discover the symbolic power of action.

The dialogue comes from the heart of the people, and is situated in the middle of life. The spinning wheel is the symbol of Gandhi's challenge to technocracy and the way of saying that the Hindu-Christian dialogue has to proceed starting from both sides. Many present-day dialogues set the stage according to the terms of one of the parties alone. To assume that Christocentrism — or Theocentrism, for that matter — can offer a basis, is as unsatisfactory as to presume that *apauruṣevatva* (that which is not man-made, such as 'scriptures') — or *karman* for that matter — are proper starting points. But there is a much more subtle partner for fruitful and unbiased dialogue: modernity.

The modern kosmology (*sic*), which assumes that time is linear, that history is paramount, that individuality is the essence of Man (*sic*), that democracy is an absolute, that technocracy is neutral, that social Darwinism is valid, and so on, cannot offer a fair platform for the dialogue. The basis for the dialogue cannot be the modern Western myth. As I have explained elsewhere, we face here a "conflict of kosmologies." Religions are not only doctrines. And even doctrines have roots in the respective myths that make the doctrines plausible. Modern Science has permeated the modern world to such an extent that it is difficult to avoid taking it as the basis of the dialogue. Both Hinduism and Christianity have to come to grips with Modern Science, but it would not be fair to Hinduism to consider Modern Science as the neutral starting point. Though Modern Science is not Christianity, both share many common myths extraneous to the Hindu traditions. One can understand a certain Hindu resistance to an apparently neutral dialogue based on the assumptions of a scientific kosmology.

In other words, a complete *dialogos* should be at the same time a *dia-mythos*. The respective *logoi* are bearers of meaning and life only within their respective *mythoi*. And it is by means of dialogue that we reach the myth of the other and create a climate of communication. To mention the *mythos* belongs certainly to a prologue introducing the *dialogue*. The *mythos* is that which goes before the *logos* and makes it possible. The *pro-logue*, the foreword, belongs to the *mythos*. The Unsaid, which is taken for granted . . .

How often have academics forgotten, if not despised, the spinning wheel! How often have communal riots and cold wars persisted through the ages because people have forgotten, if not despised, learning the language of the other! Language here means, of course, more than Hindi, and the spinning wheel more than *khadi.*

I would like to stress here a not-so-insignificant result of the Hindu-Christian dialogue. In spite of misunderstandings, difficulties, and draw-backs, it has an unavoidable effect: It changes not only our opinion of the religion we study and dialogue with; it also changes our stand and inter-pretation of our own religion. It undermines, as it were, the very basis on which one stood when beginning the dialogue. The dialogue, even if im-perfectly undertaken, backfires. We may not convince the partners; we may even get irritated at the others; they may be impervious to our opinions. Nevertheless, we ourselves imperceptibly change our stance. The interre-ligious dialogue triggers the intra-religious dialogue in our own minds and hearts. Indeed, the dialogue backfires. . . . I would like to expand briefly on what this implies.

What follows is not intended as a contribution to the third part of the book, dealing with the future of the dialogue. It offers only a non-futuristic thought, first from a psychological and then a sociological perspective.

A good number of factors have changed in the present-day historical constellation:

1) Both Hinduism and Christianity have lost political power. India is no longer dominated by a Christian empire. Nor is she legally controlled by Hindu institutions. Both Hindus and Christians still have to overcome mu-tual suspicions and heal wounds of the past, but the meeting can take place without direct political interference.

2) Both Hinduism and Christianity are undergoing an institutional crisis, and this creates fellowship when the Hindus sense that the same difficulties and struggles are also felt by the Christians, and vice-versa.

3) Both religions are also facing a similar challenge from the technocratic complex. The challenge is not the same nor is it seen in the same way, but nevertheless it is there. Traditional religions are not the most exciting as-pects of modern life, for the burgeoning middle class at least. This puts people interested in traditional religions in the same boat, as it were. I am not saying that we strengthen our links by recounting our mutual woes and

fears, or that we should be crusading against a common opponent. I am saying that the platform for the dialogue is changing.

4) Something similar could be said regarding Marxism or Humanism.

5) Due to many reasons, at least some of them having to do with the above-mentioned points, both religions are on the brink of a mutation, different as the two mutations may be. Perhaps the key word here is *secularity*. At any rate, there is a re-interpretation of tradition and a reformulation of the main tenets of both religions, or, as I have said, of those bundles of religions that we gather under these two generic names. This puts the dialogue in a very peculiar and fruitful position. Unless we are going to discuss, say, what Śaṅkara and Aquinas wrote, that is, unless we are engaging in merely historical and exegetical research, when we come together ready for a dialogue we do not know much. Not only do we not know what the other is going to say, we don't even know what we ourselves are going to be elicited to articulate. The dialogue does not take place from two firm and well-delimited trenches; rather, it is an open field. How often one has heard the criticism from the other side: "But you as a Hindu (or a Christian) should not be saying this." And yet we are saying it. I am not saying that dogmas do not exist. I am affirming that dogmatism is not needed, and that even dogmas are on the move. Saying this, I am at the same time uncovering for the dialogue a task beyond the already important tasks of understanding each other or dispelling misunderstanding. I am ascribing to the dialogue the important role of building a new self-understanding of both traditions. This can be helped by such a descriptive book on the Hindu-Christian dialogue.

I foresee a new and fundamental function of dialogue in the encounter of religions. The first aim was to better know each other, to dispel fears and misinterpretations. A second role was that of mutual influence and fecundation. I envisage now a third function: that of positively contributing to the new self-understanding of both sides. If this is the case, the dialogue will become an indispensable element in the very formation of the new identity of each religious tradition. We shall no longer sit facing each other, but sitting at a truly round table, or squatting side-by-side (following the two physical ways of sitting), we will discuss together the deepening of our insights. The revolution this would accomplish should be apparent to all.

Let me underline, once again, the same ideas in a more systematic way.

Kerala Christians, Francis Xavier, Akbar, British Rāj, Hindu Renaissance and present-day situations are described in these pages as the necessary background for what I have called the fourth phase of the Hindu-Christian dialogue.

The first phase could be described as the period in which Hindus were the dominating power. All too often the history of Kerala Christians has been judged from the perspective of the second phase, that in which Christians had the power, although they were not in the majority. All too often, also, the Hindu reactions to an overwhelming Christian domination have not been sufficiently underlined.

I am saying that the Hindu-Christian dialogue has never been a round-table conference, not a merely theoretical exercise in *brahmodya* (theological disputations). It is embedded in particular socio-political circumstances and takes place within a certain elusive myth.

The first phase was that of a tiny minority finding its own identity: Christians dialoging with the Hindu majority in order to establish their own identity. No wonder the dialogue was not one of the great theological speculations, as it has been noted. It was the *Christian* dialogue with Hinduism.

The second phase reverses the roles. Demographically, the Hindus were the majority, of course, but the power was on the other side. Hinduism had to establish its identity, and awaken from an alleged slumber that had permitted first the Muslim and later the Christian conquests. The so-called Hindu Renaissance is witness thereof. It was a *Hindu* dialogue with Christianity.

I insist on mentioning these two more existential phases of the dialogue in order to underline the importance of the historical chapters of the book, and to prevent an exclusive doctrinal interpretation of the dialogue.

The third phase is the prevalent one today in religious and academic circles. It could only flourish after the colonial period. It is the *Hindu-Christian* dialogue. Christians, to be sure, have taken most of the initiative, and it has been a predominantly *Christian-Hindu* dialogue; but Hindu voices are also present and many of the Christians have adopted an unpartisan stance. It has been a predominantly doctrinal dialogue. Christian doctrines have been deepened, enlarged, or perhaps also stretched thin for the sake of the dialogue. Hindu doctrines have been awakened so as to show that there was also 'science,' 'rationality,' service of neighbor, and the like in Hindu lore. Comparative studies of great value have appeared. Śaṅkara and Aquinas; Krishna and Christ; Hindu and Christian pilgrimages; the notion of grace; scriptures, God, and so forth, are today well-studied topics. But comparative studies are only implicit dialogues.

This third phase has eliminated clichés of superiority, exclusivism, and absolutism from both sides—exceptions notwithstanding. Schopenhauer and Hegel, for example, read all the available Hindu materials of their times. Yet their knowledge of Hinduism today seems insufficient. Vivekananda and Aurobindo, similarly, had sympathy for Christianity and were somewhat informed. Yet their knowledge of Christian theology was rudimentary. It is to the credit of this third phase that it has created a more conducive climate for dialogue. And here one has to acknowledge the great services of academic studies.

Many of the contributions here encourage me to present the fourth phase I am trying to envisage. We learn from one another, we respect each other, we come to know ourselves better by means of the other, we dispel misunderstandings of the past and the present. All of this is a result of the encounters of the three previous phases.

But I envision a distinctive fourth phase. Many of the contributors indicate that the present-day situation seems a little anemic. Great fights are over, big misunderstandings are overcome, a certain tolerance is reached, and from both sides emerge fundamentalisms that seem to threaten the progress made so far.

The fourth phase stresses the third word of the title of the book. It is, simply, *dialogue.*

The fourth phase, I submit, challenges the fixed identity of both parties. The fecundation of the previous phases has produced its effects. The fourth phase is a genuine dialogue among people who happen to be Hindus and Christians. It is the *religious dialogue* among Hindus and Christians. Let me elaborate on this.

"As a Hindu, I have never found it difficult to identify with the person of Jesus," writes Anantanand Rambachan in typical fashion. To which I personally could add: As a christian (and I insist on the lower case), I have no difficulty in identifying myself with the Hindu *dharma.*

Colleagues from both sides will rightly remark that it all depends on what we understand by Jesus and *dharma.* Jesus, whose "person," according to the first Christian councils, is not human but divine? The Risen Christ, as St. Paul believes? What Jesus? *Dharma,* as Manu describes it? Or, as the *svadharma* of the Gîtâ? The Sanâtana *Dharma* of neo-Hinduism?

But here the problems begin and do not end. What does it mean to be a Hindu? Or a Christian? Is it a doctrine, an interpretation? A church or *sampradâya*? A historical tradition? Is it party line? What makes one a Hindu? Or a Christian? Who decides? And even if we say a community, which one? And according to which criteria? Have we to prescribe once and for all what it is to be a Hindu or a Christian? Are all the meat eaters bad Hindus? And all the non-churchgoers bad Christians?

The Hindu-Christian dialogue is not exhausted with the comparison between Râmânuja and Bonaventure — important as those and similar studies are.

As some contributors suggest, the dialogue has to be secular, it has to descend to the areas of mutual concern, it has to enter into the human and political arena of our times. But the understanding of the *saeculum* does not need to be the Christian notion of secularization. We need to unearth the underlying kosmologies.

The fourth phase starts a dialogue in which neither a politically dominating Hinduism nor an established and powerful Christianity has the upper hand or provides the framework in which the dialogue takes place. Nor is the dialogue purely dialectical or simply doctrinal. The dialogue has gone deeper, on the one hand, and more external, on the other. Deeper, for we discuss personal issues and beliefs with immense consequences for our lives. More external, for we do not involve large communities or speak from the definite position of a church or *sampradāya*. Both sides seem to be confronted with a similar technocratic civilization, even in the remote corners of the countryside.

It would amount to a superficial stance, and possibly to a betrayal of one's deepest convictions, were we to deal with modern problems of technocracy, peace, justice, hunger, or simply business and work in such a way that we make abstraction of religious beliefs or relegate them to the private sphere. The Hindu and Christian contexts are different; they are religious and personal, but at the same time political, economic, secular, and they inform ordinary life. Do we need an Ayatollah Khomeini to remind us brutally that one side alone does not set the rules of the game? The fourth phase of the dialogue is a burning issue. The quick rise of an Indian middle class apparently successful in the rules of a competitive society in a technocratic system is not an alien problem to the Hindu-Christian dialogue. It becomes a necessary part of dialogue—perhaps even for survival.

This fourth phase is, first of all, dialogue. It is a dialogue among experts or common people, merchants or industrialists, intellectuals or artists who happen to more or less love their traditions, but who are not tied to them to such an extent that they defend any fixed orthodoxy. The archetypes may play a more important role than the explicit ideas. To be sure, any authentic dialogue is a search for truth, and therefore it runs the 'risk' of finding itself 'outside' the fold. But in this emerging fourth phase there are no non-negotiable topics, no 'classified' materials or hidden agendas, not because previously people were not sincere, but because the very notion of orthodoxy has become flexible, dynamic, and not merely intellectual.

It would be a setback in the dialogue if this fourth phase were to be lured into the trap of superficiality. The chapters of this book prevent us from falling into well-intentioned but barren sentimentalisms, into facile irenic positions, or purely political or social discussions.

The fourth phase is a new step. It is creative not only in interpreting the 'other.' It is also innovative in understanding 'oneself.'

I could put it in terms of depth psychology. Should not a Christian, after twenty years of studying Hinduism—and a Hindu, after a similar period of struggling with Christianity—assume that in an imperceptible way the studied subject matter has made inroads into their respective psyches, just as one spontaneously imitates the gestures and idioms of the persons one lives with? Should we not suspect also that one may one day fall in love with the person with whom one is constantly dealing? Cultural symbiosis is also a phenomenon happening among religious traditions. We also know that the constant encounter with each other may generate hatred and disgust. Fundamentalist reactions are also possible. And again one feels thankful for the chapters of this book, which instruct us with the lessons of history and lead us into a phase that is the prelude to overcoming religious nationalisms *pari pasu* so that we may walk toward a healthy pluralism.

Acknowledgments

This book is a research project of the Calgary Institute for the Humanities, University of Calgary. The Institute is to be thanked for sponsoring the research and preparing the manuscript for publication. In particular, thanks are due to Gerry Dyer, the Institute's administrator, for her efforts in bringing the scholars together and in preparing the manuscript for publication.

The costs involved in assembling the scholars were borne by grants from the Social Science and Humanities Research Council of Canada, the Department of Religious Studies and the Dean of Humanities of the University of Calgary, the Hindu Society of Calgary, the United Church of Canada, the Anglican Church of Canada, and the Roman Catholic Church in Canada. Grateful thanks are due to all of these organizations for their financial support.

As usual the staff at Orbis, especially Eve Drogin and Catherine Costello, were encouraging and helpful from the start of the project. The general editor of the Faith Meets Faith series, Paul Knitter, offered criticism that has strengthened the book.

Finally, however, gratitude must be extended to Raimundo Panikkar who helped formulate the idea for the project, and has written a most thoughtful Foreword to the volume.

In addition to this book, a continuing product of the research seminar is the *Hindu-Christian Studies Bulletin*, co-edited by Harold Coward and Anand Amaladass and co-published from Calgary and Madras. The 1988 and 1989 issues have appeared, and the *Bulletin*, which contains academic articles, viewpoint essays, book reviews, and items of news from around the world, will continue to be published on an annual basis in June of each year.

Harold Coward,
Director,
The Calgary Institute
for the Humanities

Hindu-Christian Dialogue

Introduction

HAROLD COWARD

Hindu-Christian dialogue has had a long and checkered history. Up until the beginning of this century most Hindu-Christian interaction took place in India. The first half of this century saw the expansion of Hindu-Christian discussion to Europe and North America. Worldwide pluralism in the decades since the fifties has resulted in a gradual intensification of this interaction at both the lay and scholarly levels. But there has been no broad and sustained Hindu-Christian dialogue.

Recent scholarship has shown that there was considerable trade and intellectual contact between India and the Graeco-Roman world during the first few centuries after Christ.[1] Hindu thought seems to have influenced the Neo-Platonists and is specifically commented upon by Clement of Alexandria (200 C.E.). During the Medieval period, however, this early interaction deteriorated into a Christianized myth based on biblical allegories that painted India as a land of griffons, monsters and demons lying somewhere east of the terrestrial paradise.[2] There is much speculation regarding early Christian activity in India. According to the fourth-century Christian historian Eusebius, St. Thomas was allotted a mission territory reaching across northwest India as far as the Indus, although no definite trace of Christianity can be found in that region. Tradition, however, continues to connect Thomas with India. Gregory, Bishop of Tours (ca. 580 C.E.), mentions that Thomas's relics rest in an elaborate church in South India, and Marco Polo (ca. 1290) locates this church in Mylapore, just south of Madras. There is definite evidence of a Persian, perhaps Nestorian, Christian community in southern India in the seventh or eighth century, but there seems to have been little Christian impact upon Hinduism.[3]

It was with the arrival of the British and Portuguese traders in India in the seventeenth century that the way was paved for Christian missionaries from Europe. As early as 1573 the Emperor Akbar summoned Jesuit Christians from Goa to appear before him and take part in theological debate, but it was not until the Moghul empire collapsed and the British took control to protect their trading interests that the Christian missionaries arrived in force. British rulers wanted to govern the Hindus according to Hindu law and religion, so they established the Asiatic Society of Bengal

1

for the study of Indian philosophy and literature. Christian missionaries also began taking an interest in Hindu thought—mainly to be able to criticize it and gain converts.[4] Some, however, learned Sanskrit and became serious scholars of the Hindu texts. The cumulative effort of these and other activities produced the Hindu Renaissance, which aimed at rationalizing and reforming Hinduism.

Rāmmohun Roy (1772-1833) set out to recover from obscurity the ideas of Vedic Hinduism, which had become neglected in favor of shallow idol worship. Roy was deeply interested in the new religious teachings of the Christian missionaries. He read the New Testament and extracted those ethical teachings that he felt were universally consistent with the laws of nature. These he translated into Sanskrit as *The Precepts of Jesus* so as to improve the hearts and minds of his fellow Hindus.[5] Because he had rejected the divinity of Christ, Roy caused an uproar among the Calcutta Christian missionaries. After more than three years of debate with the Christians, Roy began to write "Vindication of the Hindu Religion Against the Attacks of Christian Missionaries."[6] In public letters he effectively argued that Hinduism is not inferior to Christianity (as the missionaries were suggesting), but that the mysteries of each religion equally transcend human understanding so that one cannot be preferred to the other.[7] In order to defend Hinduism against the Christian charges that it was a pagan and idolatrous religion, Roy and his colleagues set out to reform it. For this purpose the Brāhmo Samāj was formed. Its goal was to "purify Hinduism and immunize it against the Christian ideas and practices."[8] This strategy initiated by Rāmmohun Roy was passed to Keshub Chunder Sen, and then to Dayānanda Sarasvatī. But before moving on it is worth noting the role played by Roy in the introduction of English into Hindu education, an action that has certainly encouraged Hindu-Christian dialogue.

Roy believed that the only way to modernize Hindus was through the introduction of English language education. He opposed British attempts to introduce traditional Sanskrit education, and instead argued effectively for modern Western learning through the medium of English.[9] The subsequent emphasis on English and lack of stress on Sanskrit has had an impact on Hinduism that has yet to be evaluated. Certainly it turned the minds of young Indians to the West and Christianity, and away from the traditional wisdom of Hindu Sanskrit texts.

Keshub Chunder Sen was willing to go much further than Rāmmohun Roy in appropriating Christianity. Indeed, in the last years of his life he did something reminiscent of Akbar—he experimented in synthesizing elements from the major world religions. "Although he borrowed devotional and yogic practices from Hinduism, he drew even more heavily on Christian teachings and practices."[10] Sen went so far that he was virtually excommunicated from Hinduism, and his conversion to Christianity was constantly expected. Whereas Roy had accepted only the ethical teachings of Jesus, Sen embraced Christ as the fulfillment of Hinduism's devotional strivings.

He argued for the Asiatic nature of Christ, the apostles and the gospel and concluded "in Christ, Europe and Asia, the East and the West, may learn to find harmony and unity."[11] Keshub thought that not only Christianity and Hinduism could coalesce, but also Islam. He thought that the resulting new religion would both sustain India and lead the world into a worldwide spiritual brotherhood. The Hindu religious genius in continuity with the Old and New Testament revelations would, he felt, be able to reconcile all religions by absorbing "all that is good and noble in each other."[12]

While Sen was preaching the one extreme of a Christian-Hindu universal religion in Bengal, an opposing viewpoint was put forth by a stern, ascetic Hindu in Northern India. Dayānanda Sarasvatī (1824-1883) was also an ardent reformer, but he wanted to go in the opposite direction from sympathetic dialogue. "Standing foursquare on the authority of the Vedas, he fearlessly denounced the evils of post-Vedic Hinduism."[13] He was taught complete reverence for the Vedas and a disdain for all later texts. He devoted his life to lecturing on the exclusive authority of the Vedas. Because of the fervor of his reforms and preaching, he was called "the Luther of India." His followers are grouped together in the Arya Samāj, which became especially strong in Punjab, and that now, with the emigrations from India to many countries, has spread around the world. Dayānanda's approach to other religions and other groups within Hinduism was aggressive and militant. This marks a considerable change from the traditional Hindu attitudes of passive tolerance for all other beliefs. Dayānanda's approach to Christianity was to engage a minister in debate and to demonstrate the logical inconsistencies of Christian belief.[14] A very "Christian-looking" system of religiously-sponsored schools was established (from preschool to university), along with the creation of a class of specially educated paid preachers (*updeshaks*) for proselytization purposes.[15] The introduction of these new modes of communication served to heighten the communal tensions, which had traditionally existed in the Punjab among Hindus, Muslims and Sikhs. This unfortunate result of Hindu-Christian interaction has left a legacy that still haunts us today.[16]

In sharp contrast to the confrontational thrust of Dayānanda and his followers was the statesmanlike oratory of Vivekananda, who appeared on the world stage when he addressed the First World Parliament of Religions at Chicago in 1893. He subsequently toured North America and England preaching the spiritual riches that Hinduism had to contribute to the modern West. Since most of his listeners were Christians, this preaching mission was an early instigator of dialogue between Hindus and Christians in the West.[17]

Vivekananda's inspirational preaching was followed up by Sarvapelli Radhakrishnan's sophisticated and scholarly presentation of Hinduism to the modern West. The seeds for Radhakrishnan's approach were sown by A. G. Hogg, missionary to India and principal of Madras Christian College, where Radhakrishnan took his first university degree. Hogg gave careful consideration to points of contact between Hindu and Christian thought.[18] Following the lead of Hogg, Radhakrishnan appealed to the universalist aspects of Christianity that would show contiguity with the Vedantic teachings of Hinduism. Radhakrishnan represents the approach of orthodox Hinduism toward dialogue with Christianity. Hinduism and the Vedas are still the ultimate truth of religion, but a truth which may be shown to encompass the highest Christian teachings and thus be universally acceptable.[19] Certainly his appointment to the Spalding Chair of Eastern Religions and Ethics at Oxford and his lectures there from 1936–38 significantly raised the profile of Hindu-Christian dialogue in the English-speaking West.

In Radhakrishnan Rāmmohun Roy's goal is realized. Through its various dialogues with Christianity, Hinduism revived and reformed itself. And now, in the twentieth century, Hinduism presents itself to Christianity as *guru* or spiritual guide to the future. This is especially seen in the way Gandhi's life and teachings have been studied and emulated by such Western Christian leaders as Martin Luther King, Jr. In a quieter but more widespread way the dialogue with Christianity has continued in the West in universities and colleges where courses on Hinduism are taught. The preaching approach of Vivekananda continues through the Ramakrishna Missions distributed throughout Britain and North America and through the more recent International Society for Krishna Consciousness movement.[20]

World War II and its aftermath marked a hiatus in activities, but the past two decades have seen a gradual revival of interest in Hindu-Christian dialogue through publications and conferences, especially in India. Writing in the mid-sixties, Wilfred Cantwell Smith gave notice to Christian theologians that all future theology will have to be worked out in dialogue with theologians of other religions.[21] Major initiatives in this direction came from Indian Christians. For example, Dr. P. D. Devananda's efforts as director of the Christian Institute for the Study of Religion and Society, Bangalore, were aimed at establishing Hindu-Christian dialogue at a deeper level than had previously existed. In India, he observed, "Most interreligious meetings ... are still full of 'parallel monologues.' "[22]

In the Institute's hosting of conferences and through its journal, *Religion and Society*, Devananda's hope has been at least partially realized. The Institute has played a major role, especially during the seventies, in initiating serious Hindu-Christian dialogue. Especially notable in this regard was the Institute's "Consultation on the Praxis of Inter-Faith Dialogue" in 1978, which brought together leading scholars on dialogue from all over India. Several of the papers from this Consultation were published in volume 26 of *Religion and Society* and provide a good evaluation of the state of Hindu-Christian dialogue within India. One weakness of the Consultation, however, was that Hindu scholars did not have equal representation with Christian scholars. The Consultation emphasized that Hindu-Christian dialogue should transform the existing religious ideas of clean-unclean and sacred-profane in both religions because they militate against the realization of an inclusive human community in India. A particularly good paper by A. M. Abraham Ayrookuzhiel,[23] which focuses on popular Hindu experience, argues that it is misleading to frame Hindu-Christian dialogue strictly in terms of the classical Hindu philosophical systems. Several of the Consultation papers reported on the practical experience of Christian ashrams dedicated to Hindu-Christian dialogue. Sara Grant's report offers a delightful solution to the problem of how to handle the desire of Hindu colleagues to participate in the Eucharist.[24] Her report also conveys the necessity for Hindus and Christians to live together in community if real dialogue is to develop. Another issue dealt with in these reports is the seeming conflict between the approach of dialogue and the traditional Christian conception of missionary evangelism.[25]

A number of Western scholars have also made helpful recent contributions to the revival of the dialogue. In 1966 Ninian Smart's *The Yogi and the Devotee* explored the Hindu tradition from the context of the Christian notion of natural theology.[26] Smart found several points where Hindu thought could bring illumination to Christianity. Based on his experience as bishop of Madras, Lesslie Newbigin, in *The Finality of Christ*, stressed that the Christian dialogue must include not only intellectual understanding of Hinduism, but also an attempt to enter into the feelings and experiences that underlie Hindu teachings. Newbigin also notes that although the commitment to Christ is something that can never be left behind, still the Christian must expect his or her own religion to be corrected as a result of dialogue with Hinduism.[27]

The classic work of the sixties was Klaus Klostermaier's *Hindu and Christian in Vrindaban*, which was published in German and English and read widely in both Catholic and Protestant circles.[28] Residing in Vrindaban, a North Indian pilgrimage center for devotees of Lord Krishna, Klostermaier lived a life of dialogue for two years. Dialogue began by joining his Hindu colleagues on pilgrimage, understanding their devotional practice, developing a deep friendship with them, and only then entering into theological dialogue in which the differences between Hinduism and Christianity were explored. The subtle but influential factor of the influence of climate and country is powerfully explored in a chapter titled "Theology at 120°F." With his "Hindu brother" Swami Yogananda Tirtha, Klostermaier read the Gospel According to John and explained it line by line in *guru*-student style. Klostermaier's experience is a dialogue of everyday life and of experiments in faith in India. It is a dialogue based in friendship, but with a deep and underlying scholarly quest.

Lacking Klostermaier's existential involvement, but still of value is the abstract academic comparison of Hindu Vaiṣṇavism and Christianity by Professor N. K. Devaraja, published in 1969.[29]

A good but rather narrow focus is presented by Sisir Kumar Das in a

1973 study of how the Hindu-Christian dialogue in Bengal produced the "Bengal Renaissance" in literature and religion.[30]

Another historical study worthy of note is Eric Sharpe's *Faith Meets Faith: Some Christian Attitudes to Hinduism in the Nineteenth and Twentieth Centuries*. Sharpe suggests that the lack of progress in the dialogue of the preceding decades (prior to 1975) was largely due to "the progressive disintegration of Christian theological thought, and the rapid changes which have taken place in that external world in which the encounter of faiths has to be played out."[31]

During the past decades discussion on the methodology of Hindu-Christian dialogue has become popular. M. M. Thomas suggests that Hindu syncretism, from the Christian perspective, is unavoidable. Just as the Christian sees the work of the "hidden Christ" in Hinduism, so Hindus, like Radhakrishnan, see in Christianity aspects of "hidden Vedanta."[32] In the modern transformation of every religion, says Thomas, the meeting with another religion plays an important part—as for example in the role played by Christianity in the Hindu Renaissance.[33]

Hinduism, following its traditional method in the debating of differing views, is teaching Christian theologians that the first and necessary step in the process is the mastering and restating of the opposing position.[34] Only from the ground of a shared basic knowledge of each other can Hindu-Christian dialogue successfully proceed.

A Hindu scholar living in the United States, Bibhuti Yadav examines Radhakrishnan's ontology of religious tolerance and then observes that what it requires from Christianity is the giving up of its notion of a "special revelation" in Christ. To claim special revelation, says Yadav, is to kill the Absolute and to enthrone oneself and one's own religion as Absolute. This, he argues, is methodologically unacceptable. Following the Vaisnava Hindu theology of Vallabha, Yadav says the proper methodology is to see God as speaking through the scriptures of all religions and dialogue as the necessity of discussion among God's various words. "Interreligious dialogue is the method of establishing communion between the Words of God, of recognizing that God is specially immanent in and larger than them all."[35]

A methodologically similar but opposing move is made by a Christian thinker, James Redington, S.J. Redington focuses on the Christian thesis that "God wills to save all people" and sees dialogue as directed toward the understanding of how God is doing so in Hinduism.[36] But in his or her study of Hinduism, cautions Redington, the Christian must not make the mistake of choosing a preferred type of Hinduism (e.g., Advaita Vedanta) and act as if this is the only valid one. "This would be the Hindu sectarian mistake (and a Hindu in dialogue could make the corresponding mistake of holding out strongly for one Christian sect over all others)."[37] One of the fruits of dialogue may be to teach us how to live tolerantly with the different divisions within our own religion, be it Hindu or Christian.

Aside from the above methodological considerations, recent thinkers also see a most important result of Hindu-Christian interaction as the development of "Inner Dialogue." The notion of inner dialogue is picked up by John A. T. Robinson from Murray Rogers and is developed in Robinson's book, *Truth Is Two-Eyed*.[38] Inner dialogue includes both the impulse that leads one to desire outer or interreligious dialogue and the effects of the outer dialogue on one's own faith. A detailed description is given by Raimundo Panikkar: "an inner dialogue within myself, an encounter of the depth of my personal religiousness, having met another religious experience on that very intimate level."[39] Panikkar's earlier book *The Unknown Christ of Hinduism*[40] and Robinson's *Truth is Two-Eyed* are excellent examples of such inner dialogue from a Christian perspective. The aim is an inner reflection upon the teachings and practices of the different religions, which leads to new insights and integrations in the experience of one's own religion.

The past two decades have seen a marked increase in Hindu-Christian dialogue. Advances have been made in methodology as well as in recognition of the inner impact of dialogue. This has been particularly true of the Christian side of the dialogue, with significant leadership being provided by Indian Christians. Today Western Christian theologians are more and more doing their theologizing as an inner dialogue in which the other world religions, including Hinduism, have an impact. With a few notable exceptions (for example, Yadav) contemporary Hindu thinkers do not seem to be engaged with Christianity in the way their predecessors were at the turn of the century (for example, Roy, Sen, Dayānanda and Radhakrishnan).

The following chapters represent a state-of-the-art assessment of Hindu-Christian dialogue. Part One offers various historical perspectives on Hindu-Christian dialogue of the past, mainly in India. In Part Two a variety of approaches are taken in examining the current status of the dialogue in India, Canada and America. In addition, the influence the dialogue is having on the spiritual practice of each religion is examined. Part Three looks to the future of Hindu-Christian dialogue in relation to academia, scripture, the World Council of Churches and its coming impact on India. These chapters are not intended to be the last word on the subject, but to provide a foundation and stimulus for future scholarship.

NOTES

1. Donald F. Lach, *Asia in the Making of Europe*, vol. 1 (Chicago: University of Chicago Press, 1965), pp. 12-19.

2. Ibid., p. 20.

3. The above summary is based on "Note on Christianity in India" in N. G. Barrier, *The Sikhs and Their Literature* (Delhi: Manohar, 1970), pp. 521ff.

4. P. T. Raju, "The Development of Indian Thought," *Journal of the History of Ideas* 13:540.

5. W. T. De Bary, *Sources of Indian Tradition*, vol. 2 (New York: Columbia University Press, 1969), pp. 23-25.

6. Ibid., p. 26.

7. Rāmmohun Roy, "Letter to the Editor of the Bengal Hurkanu" (May 23, 1823), reprinted in De Bary, p. 28.

8. De Bary, p. 51.

9. Rāmmohun Roy, "Letter on Education," in De Bary, pp. 40-43.

10. De Bary, p. 64.

11. Keshub Chunder Sen, "Jesus Christ: Europe and Asia," in De Bary, pp. 68-69.

12. Keshub Chunder Sen, "We Apostles of the New Dispensation" in De Bary, p. 75.

13. De Bary, p. 76.

14. The above summary is based on De Bary, pp. 76-81.

15. G. R. Thursby, *Hindu-Muslim Relations in British India* (Leiden: E. J. Brill, 1975), p. 13. See also J. F. T. Jordens, "Dāyananda Sarasvati and Christianity," *Indian Church History Review* 15 (1981): 34-47.

16. Kenneth W. Jones, "Communalism in the Punjab," *The Journal of Asian Studies* 28 (1968): 39-40. See also Richard Fox Young, *Resistant Hinduism* (Vienna: The De Nobili Research Library, 1981).

17. De Bary, pp. 94-107.

18. See, for example, A. G. Hogg, *Karma and Redemption* (Madras: Christian Literature Society, 1909).

19. S. Radhakrishnan, *Eastern Religions and Western Thought* (Oxford: Clarendon Press, 1939).

20. A good example of a serious attempt at dialogue from the Hare Krishna movement is found in *Christ and Krishna*, Swami Bhaktipada (Moundsville: Bhaktipada Books, 1985). The author is the son of conservative Baptist parents.

21. Wilfred Cantwell Smith, *The Faith of Other Men* (New York: Harper and Row, 1972), p. 123.

22. P. D. Devananda, *Preparation for Dialogue* (Bangalore: The Christian Institute for the Study of Religion and Society, 1964), p. iii.

23. A. M. Abraham Ayrookuzhiel, "The Living Hindu Popular Religious Consciousness and Some Reflections on It in the Context of Hindu-Christian Dialogue," *Religion and Society* 26 (1979): 5-25.

24. Sara Grant, "Reflections on Hindu-Christian Dialogue in an Ashram Context," *Religion and Society* 26 (1979): 42-58. Grapes and flowers were placed on the altar table and offered to the Hindu participants.

25. See "Consultation Working Group Reports," *Religion and Society* 26 (1979): 110.

26. Ninian Smart, *The Yogi and the Devotee* (London: Allen and Unwin, 1968).

27. Lesslie Newbigin, *The Finality of Christ* (London: SCM Press, 1969), p. 21.

28. Klaus Klostermaier, *Hindu and Christian in Vrindaban* (London: SCM Press, 1969). See also Klostermaier, "A Hindu-Christian Dialogue on Truth," *Journal of Ecumenical Studies* 12 (1975): 157-71.

29. N. K. Devaraja, *Hinduism and Christianity* (Bombay: Asia Publishing House, 1969).

30. Sisir Kumar Das, *The Shadow of the Cross: Christianity and Hinduism in a Colonial Situation* (New Delhi: Munshiram Manoharlal, 1973).

31. Eric J. Sharpe, *Faith Meets Faith* (London: SCM Press, 1977), p. 132.

32. M. M. Thomas, "A Reply to Guru Dutt," *Journal of Religion and Society* 23/3 (1976): 61.

33. M. M. Thomas, *The Acknowledged Christ of the Indian Renaissance* (London: SCM Press, 1969).

34. Kana Mitra, "A Hindu Self-Reflection," *Journal of Ecumenical Studies* 17 (1980): 121-22.

35. Bibhuti S. Yadav, "Vaisnavism on Hans Küng: A Hindu Theology of Religious Pluralism," *Journal of Religion and Society* 27 (1980): 60.

36. James D. Redington, S.J., "The Hindu-Christian Dialogue and the Interior Dialogue," *Theological Studies* 44 (1983): 587.

37. Ibid., p. 595.

38. John A. T. Robinson, *Truth Is Two-Eyed* (Philadelphia: Westminster Press, 1979), p. 7. Robinson cites Murray Rogers, "Hindu and Christian — A Moment Breaks," in *Inter-Religious Dialogue*, ed. H. Jai Singh (Bangalore: C.I.S.R.S., 1967), pp. 104-17.

39. Raimundo Panikkar, *The Intra-Religious Dialogue* (New York: Paulist Press, 1978), p. 40.

40. Raimundo Panikkar, *The Unknown Christ of Hinduism*, rev. ed. (Maryknoll, NY: Orbis Books, 1981).

PART ONE

Historical Perspectives on Hindu-Christian Dialogue

1

Dialogue between Hindus and the St. Thomas Christians

ANAND AMALADASS

Dialogue is taking place at different levels in discussions, symposiums, colloquiums, conferences, consultations, seminars and workshops in which an attempt is made to study or understand the views or traditions of religions other than one's own and in that process also to analyze, articulate and even evaluate (though not always critically) one's own position. Slowly an awareness is created in such meetings that there are other points of view and perspectives that are validly held by well-meaning people. Listening to others who communicate the truth and participating in discussions on appropriate occasions are factors leading to right understanding and the removal of ignorance.

But one might still wonder whether there is real dialogue taking place at all in these meetings. Dialogue understood as "a reciprocal relationship in which every party 'experiences the other side' so that their communication becomes a true address and response in which each informs and learns"[1] may not be realized in all these meetings. But an orientation toward this goal seems to be emerging gradually, as seen in the changing attitudes toward some specific issues and in fresh initiatives.

In the Indian context dialogue with Hinduism is taking place in another form. In the garb of inculturation, Ashram movements and social awakening through action-groups an openness is being created among Christians to come together on a common platform, to study other religious phenomena and adopt their names and customs, while remaining within one's own religious framework. During the last two decades the dialogue initiative has gained momentum in India: various centers of dialogue have been established and publications on dialogue are on the increase. This is true of different Christian churches in India. This chapter tries to highlight specifically the contributions made by St. Thomas Christians to the process of dialogue with the Hindus. Hence an identity of this particular Christian community in India has to be established in order to assess its role in this process of dialogue.

THE IDENTITY OF ST. THOMAS CHRISTIANS

There are two views among historians concerning the origin of Christianity in India: one group traces it back to St. Thomas, the apostle, or even to two apostles, St. Thomas and St. Bartholomew; the other ascribes it to the enterprise of merchants and missionaries of the East-Syrian or Persian church. According to Indian tradition St. Thomas came by sea and first landed at Cranganore about the year 52 A.D. He converted high-caste Hindu families in Cranganore, Palayur, Quilon and some other places. Then he crossed over to China and preached the gospel and returned to India and organized the Christians of Malabar under some guides (priests) from among the leading families he had converted. He also erected a few public places of worship before he was martyred.[2]

The sources vary with regard to the total number of St. Thomas Christians during the sixteenth and seventeenth centuries. The annual letters of the Jesuits in Goa to their superiors in Rome in the years 1648 and 1654 speak of eighty thousand Christians; in 1644 there were ninety-two churches; and it is said that St. Thomas Christians lived in the territories of about twenty rajas and a multitude of petty chieftains. About half of them were to be found in the three kingdoms of Cochin, Vadakkumkur and Kottayam.[3]

St. Thomas Christians today are divided into different groups.[4] In fact, the divisions and formations of different churches are far too complex to be treated here. We can only identify the major groups among them and list the different churches without going into the causes for their divisions. The 1653 revolt against the Portuguese ecclesiastical rule split the community for the first time as Syrian Catholics and Syrian Orthodox. (Syrian Orthodox are also known as Jacobites—named after a renowned sixth-century ecclesiastic of Syria—and Puthenkur, which means the new party.)

At present there are about four and a half to five million St. Thomas Christians in India. The largest group is in communion with Rome. Among these Catholics there are now three groups in Kerala: 1) the Syro-Malabarians (also called the Romo-Syrians), who follow the East Syrian rite; 2) the Syro-Malankarians, who came into communion with Rome in 1930 led by Mar Ivanios, the pioneer of this reunion movement; and 3) the Latin rite Christians. There are many Thomas Christians working in the religious congregations of the Latin church. They are not included in our study here since they do not work as members of the Oriental churches.

The non-Catholic St. Thomas Christians are the Jacobites, who after the split in 1653 adopted the West Syrian rite. Many other denominations separated themselves from the Jacobites: 1) the Anjurians (the Church of Thozhiyur), which separated in 1772 under the leadership of bishop Mar Kurilos; 2) the Syrian Anglican church (1864); 3) the Mar Thoma Church (1889)[5]; 4) the Evangelical Church of St. Thomas, which separated in 1961 under the leadership of John Varghese, a priest of Mar Thoma Church; 5) the Church of the East (Chaldeans), which in its present form came into existence as a result of the visit by Mar Elias Mallus, who was sent in 1874 by the Nestorian Patriarch of Iran to India to establish his jurisdiction over the Malabar Christians. The Mallusians gave up the Syro-Malabar or the Latinized East Syrian Rite and adopted the East Syrian rite of the foreign Nestorians; 6) the Society of St. Thomas (Christavashram) Manganam (1934); 7) the Church of South India, which contains a number of Syrian Christians. And there are also some Syrian Christians in the Salvation Army, the Pentacostals and other small groups. All these churches claim their Christian origin from the preaching of the apostle St. Thomas. Their integration with the rest of the society in Kerala is characteristic of St. Thomas Christians in general, in spite of their continuing links with their church of origin outside India.

ST. THOMAS CHRISTIANS BEFORE THE SIXTEENTH CENTURY

Dialogue among the members of different religions as it is understood today is of recent origin, and one cannot expect it among the early Christian communities or among the St. Thomas Christians in India. We do not have any document of doctrinal or theological nature relating to the St. Thomas Christians prior to their contact with the West in the sixteenth century; even the records available to the Portuguese writers of the sixteenth century were destroyed. We can only infer from the lifestyle, customs and traditions the type of theology that might have shaped their thinking and religious outlook.

Today Oriental theologians, mostly under the influence of Western theology, have begun to articulate the implicit theology of the St. Thomas Christians before the sixteenth century. Dr. A. M. Mundadan sums up this search into three basic trends among the early Christian community in India: a) their attitude toward indigenous culture, a sort of "incarnational theology," though not a systematized one; b) a special idea of the individual church in which an autonomous status was preserved through the local assembly of lay leaders though governed by metropolitans and archdeacons; and c) their attitude toward other religions — everyone can be saved in his or her own religion — and all laws are right — which was condemned by the Synod of Diamper.[6] Antony Mookenthottam, for example, comes to the conclusion that "their identification with their socio-cultural milieu was so thorough. . . . This oneness with their socio-cultural milieu implies an implicit incarnational theology lived, an awareness that Christ in becoming man assumed everything human and redeemed all social and cultural values."[7]

Such an assessment needs to be carefully evaluated. There seems to be an overenthusiasm to read late twentieth-century theological reflection into the early Christian community in India. The type of theology that ruled the church at that time, which derived from the East-Syrian Christians of Persia on whom the St. Thomas Christians depended very much and the lack of theological training for these Christians, does not warrant such a conclusion. In fact, Paul Thenayan observes that "living in isolation and in the midst of an overwhelming majority of Hindus and separated from other Christian communities, the Thomas Christians were not aware of or concerned with the theological disputes in the other parts of Christendom."[8]

But St. Thomas Christians had an identity of their own. The socio-cultural environment was predominantly Hindu, and it affected their lifestyle, their customs and traditions, but this influence was only external. Their faith life, form of liturgy and theology remained that of East-Syrian Christians of Persia. And that led to the oft-quoted description of them as "Hindu in culture, Christian in faith and Syrian in worship."[9]

It is true that St. Thomas Christians were proud of their religion, but they were poorly instructed. So European missionaries tried to change some practices such as belief in fatalism and transmigration, and witchcraft. However, at times the missionaries were inclined to see superstition where there was none.[10] The Synod of Diamper in 1599 forbade a number of customs and practices the Portuguese considered "pagan" (Hindu). Some of the practices that were restricted at that time are now being reintroduced (after Vatican II) in the name of inculturation. For example, it is said in the sources that up to about the year 1570 Christian churches were built after the fashion of the local Hindu temples. Royal umbrellas (*muthukūḍa*), musical instruments, torches and so forth were used in both Christian and Hindu processions. An imitation of the Hindu *prasād* in the offerings of eatables, money, fowls, sweets and so on made to the church and returned to the people; the Hindu marriage custom of tying a *thāli* (chain or yellow thread) around the neck of the bride by the bridegroom; the administration of the temple properties by a *yogam* (assembly) are some of the instances of Hindu influence on the life of the St. Thomas Christians.[11]

In fact, the St. Thomas Christians had a respectable social status, which enabled them to be in harmony with their predominantly Hindu neighbors. We could call that a dialogue in life. Dr. A. M. Mundadan concludes that "these prohibitions and restrictions imposed by the Synod are a witness to the communal harmony and cordial relations that existed between Christians and Hindus. Their communal harmony and spirit of tolerance should be considered a typical Indian contribution to the Christian vision."[12] As a matter of fact, their social status helped them to keep their faith. In the words of E. R. Hambye, "Being a minority in a closed milieu and not always well-trained and instructed, it is remarkable that they kept the faith together with their social status."[13]

While listing the factors that contributed to the survival of this Christian community in India Paul Thenayan includes also the large-heartedness and spirit of tolerance of their Hindu neighbors, and the caste system which did not allow one to change religions.[14] This is an important observation. The tolerant Hindu neighbors were not exclusivistic in their approach to other religions, even if they did not have an articulate theology of dialogue or of pluralism at that time. And the Hindu neighbors did not find the Christians a threat since the Christians were a minority and did not increase their number by conversion, which is a bone of contention today in India. On the one hand the St. Thomas Christians were accused of lacking missionary consciousness,[15] and on the other hand this very fact enabled them to survive. They accepted their status and did not seek converts from other castes.

One has to raise a few questions with regard to the relation between Hindus and Christians before the arrival of the Portuguese. Did the Christian faith bring about a change in the outlook and attitude of the early Christian community in India? Did they see any conflict between their Christian identity and the social customs they shared with the Hindus? First of all, there is no documentary evidence that might answer these questions. Given their situation and the period of history in which they lived one cannot attribute any theological vision concerning these issues. But in fact they did not see any contradiction between their faith and the social practices they shared with their Hindu neighbors, since they were already part of that social milieu. It would be different for a person coming from another milieu who has to make an effort to find out the implications of these practices before accepting them. St. Thomas Christians did not conceptualize their living situation since nobody challenged them and no justification was needed at that time. Secondly, one has to interpret their situation in the context and culture of the people of India of that time. What the European missionaries of the sixteenth century did and their outlook on the religion of their neighbors need not be the model to interpret the early Christian history in India. The exclusivistic thinking of the Christian churches of the sixteenth century coupled with the conquerors' attitude (of the colonizers) is not to be equated with that of Hinduism of that time.

Hinduism has gone through the process of accommodating other religions and thus learned to exist side by side with other religious groups. Encounter between religions was a common phenomenon in Indian history;[16] at least sociologically, different religious groups existed side by side even without a conscious theological conviction about the complementarity of religious perspectives. Within the framework of the Hindu worldview there were different religious affiliations. At the beginning the Hindu approach might have been more of an existential dialogue, a process of attraction and repulsion of other religions in the life of every person.

Often one hears of the tolerant attitude in Hinduism. Unless one explains it carefully, the word *tolerance* itself is not an adequate expression. As P. Hacker puts it, it is more of an inclusivistic tendency that accommodates other religious groups by absorbing their basic beliefs as one's own.[17] Even if one cannot use a modern expression of pluralism in religion, theology of dialogue and so on, one has to admit that this problem was faced by Hinduism and the answer given highlights the specific contribution of Hinduism. This counters the repeated claim that dialogue is a Christian initiative and that Hindus do not respond to it favorably.[18]

THE PROTESTANT MISSIONS AND ST. THOMAS CHRISTIANS

Dialogue could also be understood as the meeting of two different ideologies or worldviews. There could be confrontations at the beginning due to opposing values or accommodation with varying degrees of perception of the values involved; this could lead to a transformation gradually affecting the belief and practice of the partners concerned. Such a process is not uncommon in history. Duncan B. Forrester[19] presents the question of caste in India and the attitudes of Christians to caste down through the centuries as an instance where the change of attitude seems to have emerged as a result of Christian values challenging the caste values.

The Roman Catholic missions in India from the time of the Portuguese seem to have regarded the caste system as a neutral social structure within which the evangelization process could be accommodated. Of course there were challenges and criticism to the methods of De Nobili within the Catholic Church and also papal decrees, which denounced untouchability as alien to Christianity. However accommodation seems to have had a long history within the Catholic tradition.[20] The Protestant missionaries — especially the Anglo-Saxon missionaries — appear to have been far more outspoken in their opposition to caste in India.

The Syrian Christians had inserted themselves within the Indian caste society for centuries and were regarded by the Hindus as a caste occupying a high place within their caste hierarchy. They were distinguished from other castes by the peculiarity of their cult and also by their priesthood and episcopate, which were necessarily linked with the church outside India. "In brief, the caste system seems to have made it possible for Christianity to survive in Kerala, but on condition that it observed the norms of the system, in particular the prohibition on recruitment from 'other castes' and the acceptance of the rules of a radically hierarchical society. The Syrian Christians, like the Jews of Cochin and the Bene Israel of Bombay, survived and indeed flourished because they accepted the social system within which they found themselves and observed its norms."[21] The Syrian Christians as a whole form one community, though there is an internal division among them as Northists and Southists. "Every Christian is either a Northist or a Southist, no matter what his ecclesiastical allegiance may be."[22] The basis for this division need not detain us here, since the various stories concerning this do not conclusively establish anything; such parallels also exist among the Hindu communities.

For several centuries before the arrival of the Portuguese St. Thomas Christians did not baptize those of low castes lest they lose their social position. When the Portuguese arrived, they used to send them to the Portuguese for baptism but after baptism they still would not admit them to their churches or have any relations with them.[23] That explains the formation of a separate church for the new Christians in Kerala (the Latin Christians).

The first Protestant to display much interest in the Syrian Christians was Dr. Claudius Duncan, who visited Kerala in 1806. In the same year the London Missionary Society started to work in South Travancore encouraged by Colonel Colin Macaulay, and John Munro appealed to the Church Mission Society (CMS) to send missionaries to work for the reformation of the Jacobite Syrians. Thus the Mission of Help was established in 1816 to assist the Syrians in restoring the "primitive doctrine and missionary energy" in them. But gradually tension built up between the Mission of Help and the Syrian Church. The missionaries resented the restriction of direct evangelism among the Hindus. The relationship broke down in 1836. A few Syrians came with the CMS, and they turned to the Ezhavas and the hill tribes. But the missionaries had their own problems and were deeply divided on the issue of baptizing a sizable number of Pulayas. Not until 1854 was the first Pulaya baptized in the CMS. Even then they had to tolerate separate congregations for Syrians and low-caste converts.

The Mar Thoma church was formed under the influence of the CMS Mission of Help, and one of the issues involved was the question of evangelism among non-Syrians. Even here converts were rarely given equal treatment with Syrians.[24]

All this emphasizes that caste attitudes were strong among the Syrians. The expectations of the new Christians for equality of treatment clashed with the older attitudes among the Syrian Christians. Conversion was seen as a way of overcoming the caste barrier. The new converts claimed to be Syrians, which was ridiculed by the Syrians. Forrester speaks of a sort of "Syrianization" among the Christians like that of the Sanskritization of M. N. Srinivas.[25] This instance of caste versus Christianity shows the process of dialogue between two worldviews: the Hindu caste system, and the Christian value of equality. The missionary impact disturbed the settled Christian community and even now poses a challenge and leaves the Syrian Christians with uneasy consciences concerning social disparities and Christian ideals. The Syrian response varied through the centuries, but significant changes did take place over a period of time.[26]

THE PRESENT SITUATION

After the arrival of the Portuguese the history of the Catholic Syrian Christians became one of struggle for identity and autonomy. This struggle made them preoccupied with their own local problems; without freedom there was no scope to theologize or to make any creative contribution in liturgical form. The process of Latinization was resented by the Orientals, and the resentment remains among many. On 20 May 1887 autonomy was restored again with the establishment of two vicariates in Trichur and Kottayam in Kerala. Now among the Catholics (Syrian) there are eleven Syro-Malabar and three Syro-Malankara dioceses. In 1962 Kottayam Seminary was established; this is another stage where awareness about identity became an object of theological reflection and missionary activity. Trained by the Latins, there was not much leadership emerging among the Orientals. In 1962 St. Thomas Christians began their missionary work in the North, and now the recent decision of Pope John Paul II (May 28, 1987) has opened the way for the Thomas Christians to establish their mission throughout India.

CONTRIBUTIONS OF THE ORIENTAL CHURCHES

In the remaining part of the chapter I would like to trace the contributions of the Oriental churches with regard to the process of dialogue with Hindus and the emerging theological consciousness of this community. Dr. A. M. Mundadan gives a provisional classification of the trends and approaches of the Christians in India to non-Christians as 1) spiritual-contemplative, 2) intellectual-theological, and 3) social.[27] This classification refers to the trends among Christians in India in general, and the same framework can be used to assess the contributions made by the St. Thomas Christians.

The Spiritual-Contemplative Approach: The early Christian community in India had a monastic tradition, though we are not sure whether it was of an Indian ashram style. At present there are a few ashrams to promote the monastic vocation within the Indian framework. Kurishimala Ashram in Kottayam district is an example of such a venture. The monks are members of the Syro-Malankara rite. The liturgy is of an experimental nature to include the riches of different traditions. This ashram has its influence through members who have started similar centers in other parts of Kerala, for instance, Father Sylvester Kozhimannil in Dhyana Ashram, Wynad; Father Philipose Nadamala in Chayalpadi Ashram, Angamoozhi; and so on. The Christu Dasa Ashram is part of the Mar Thoma Church's mission field program in Palghat.[28]

The Carmelite Fathers (CMI) also have started a number of centers during the last decade to promote dialogue with the Hindus through common prayer meetings, get-togethers and discussion. These include Upāsana Centre at Thodupuzha; Viswadarsana at Trichur; Sangamam at Mattupetty; Divyodaya at Coimbatore; and so on. They are not ashrams in the strict sense but centers where an openness to other religious traditions is created among the ordinary people.

The specialty of the Eastern Churches lies in its liturgy and the contemplative approach in its spirituality.[29] Its distinguishing mark is said to be witnessing to the kingdom as a praying community. That is in keeping with the Indian tradition, they claim; hence evangelization has to be seen in this light, making the kingdom visible in its worshipping communities, emphasizing the Syrian liturgical spiritual heritage. Though four churches (the Church of Edessa, the Church of Seleucia-Ctesiphon, the Church of Persia and the Church of India) claim apostolic origin through St. Thomas, which explains the intimate fellowship in liturgy and hierarchical communion along with the linguistic, cultural and commercial affinities, the Church of India has certain elements not found in the other three churches. These elements are partly due to the contact with Hindu culture. They are seen in social life, sacramentals, ceremonies and celebration of the sacraments. Hence a rediscovery of St. Thomas Christian tradition in the line of spirituality has brought a new theological awakening, and the role of Hinduism in challenging Christians to come to this stage of thinking cannot be minimized.

The Intellectual-Theological Approach: Among the Orientals there is an attempt to study the implications of the social customs among the St. Thomas Christians before the sixteenth century. With the help of the recent development in Christian theology, they would like to make thematic what was unthematic in the lifestyle of the early Christians in India. At times one wonders whether they are not reading into the early Christian thinking the theological insights of the post-Vatican II era. To speak of an incarnational theology in the early Christian community or to read a theology of inculturation in their thinking reveals over-enthusiasm on the part of some of the writers at the expense of historical perspective. This, however, has its positive elements insofar as an attempt is made to articulate the emerging theological consciousness among the Orientals today and to unlock the wisdom of such a lived approach of the early Christians in terms of dialogue today.

The prolonged struggle to maintain a separate identity chiefly through their liturgical form (Malabar or Malankara) as against the Latin rite has brought different reactions. One group wants to go back to the ancient rite, and the Syrian garb or the Chaldean elements in the liturgy do not strike them as incongruous. They perceive similarities — linguistic and cultural — as belonging to Eastern tradition. The other group admits that the present Malabar rite itself needs to be transcended in favor of a new Indian rite since "in the past too much dependence on the East-Syrian Church was detrimental to the development of the Indian church."[30] This trend is evident among the Orientals who have moved out of Kerala and have been exposed to other changing factors in the country. This process itself is a creative awareness that enables them to sift the helpful Chaldean elements in the hitherto liturgical form in order to work out a theological vision. This stage of awakening is partly due to the openness toward other religions, especially Hinduism, through an existential dialogue that is taking place at home.

Establishment of a Center for the Study of World Religions in Bangalore (1971) and the Center for Indian and Interreligious Studies, sponsored by the Bangalore Center, in Rome (1977) is an interfaith dialogue venture. The *Journal of Dharma* from Dharmaram College is fully devoted to inter-faith studies. These are some of the initiatives of the CMI fathers in India. J. B. Chethimattam, Thomas Manickam, A. M. Mundadan, Albert Nambiaparambil and Mathew Vellanickal, among the Catholics, and M. M. Thomas, C. P. Mathew, Paul Varghese, T. V. Philip and Paulose Mar Gregorios, among the non-Catholic Syrians, are some of the writers who are promoting dialogue at different levels through their writings.

One of the theological problems that has to be tackled is the Christian understanding of evangelization and conversion, especially in the context of dialogue. There is a wide spectrum in the thinking process of the Christian community in India with regard to the question of dialogue. There are still church leaders among the Orientals (also among the others) who proclaim that the fullness of Christ is found only in the Catholic Church; they would like to convert everybody to this one church and obviously *extra ecclesiasm nulla salus* is still the norm of their thinking. But there are others who say that our mission is to discover the spirit of God at work in different religions and cultures. "If the incarnation is to the whole human history, it is at home in every culture which is groaning for the appearance of the son of God. . . . The genuine osmosis between the authentic life experience of a people and the living faith received through history is the exciting and dynamic aspect of evangelization."[31]

In this context some Orientals would underline the Oriental approach to conversion itself. The conversion movement as it was initiated in India by the Portuguese and others is an attitude of conquering colonizers. That is not the Oriental approach. Hence any imposition on others or aggressive attitude has to be dissociated from the mission. The Oriental tradition is more of bearing witness to God through praying communities. Hence a new missionary style is to be evolved in line with the Oriental tradition and the Indian tradition. This realization is already a major step toward dialogue.

The Social Approach: The advocates of this approach hold the view that the gospel transcends all cultures and can transform all cultures. They emphasize the common humanity of humankind and the common mission of all to work for the genuine humanization of life in the modern world. M. M. Thomas (b. 1916, in Trivancore), a lay member of the Mar Thoma Syrian Church, has made significant contributions to this approach. He advocates a theology related to modern secular India. His chief concerns are dialogue with religions and secularism, the Renaissance of Hinduism and the development of an Indian theology. He wants the Syrian churches, along with the other churches, to look afresh at the whole meaning of confession of faith in Christ in the setting of India's needs through the demands of political democracy, industrial development and the socialist pattern of society.

This collaboration or dialogue is Christian. As he puts it: Whatever affirms humanization of nature, human creativity, liberation from social bondage and realization of love in human liberation is integral to the faith and hope of the Christian gospel. "One thing is absolutely clear," he writes. "Participation in the struggle of Asian peoples for a fuller human life in state, society and culture in a real partnership with men of other faiths and no faith, is the only real context for realizing the true being of the Church and exercising the Church's ministry and mission. . . . And it is a theological truth of first importance that only those who participate in the struggle of a people for fuller life receive the call to exercise the prophetic ministry of criticism. Only participants can be prophets."[32]

According to Thomas, interfaith dialogue is a process of mutual understanding among men and women at the level where they seek to know the mystery of human existence.[33] Hence Christian mission is no longer a clash among religions, so that one is constrained to prove the superiority of his or her religion, but it is rather to participate in dialogue in the common search of all religions after the mystery of existence.[34]

This sort of "dialogue" approach at the level of humanization and transformation of society is shared by many other thinkers like Paul Devanandan, R. Panikkar, Samuel Rayan, S. Kappan and others. But here the focus is on the contribution of St. Thomas Christians alone. J. B. Chethimattam shares similar views, namely that secular problems affecting human existence should become central in our dialogue ventures. "The missionary should not pretend that he is a dispenser only of spiritual goods and that he cannot get involved in the social, economic and political struggles of the human community. In situations of hunger, poverty and misery and of institutionalized injustice it is not enough to pray with the people and even to suffer with them but also to fight with them for justice."[35]

CONCLUSIONS

Given the fact that their tradition dates back to the time of the Apostle St. Thomas, one would expect from the St. Thomas Christians a theological vision about dialogue and an independent liturgical form. Unfortunately this did not take place, because of their dependence on the East Syrian churches and later on the Roman jurisdiction. Even today fresh initiatives from the Indian Christians in this direction are few. It is striking when one contrasts the accommodating trend in Hinduism toward other religious neighbors and the fact that Christians did not make any creative contribution in this line. Even the dialogue initiative did not originate from the Indian Christian community, though in India more religious groups meet and mingle in day-to-day life.

It is interesting to note that at present dialogue is carried on by and large by the clergy; the laity in the Catholic church is not fully involved in this process.[36] This is explained by the church structure, where it is taken for granted that the initiative comes from the top or needs the approval of the structure if it originates elsewhere, and the laity does not play any major role in the church structure. All the same, one has to qualify the statement about the "passivity" of the laity when one considers the dialogue that is going on at the existential level among the ordinary people. The laity at all times has been making a life-contribution (not conceptualized) to the process through what appears in the history of Christianity in India as religious syncretism. We have a long list of banned socio-religious practices among the Christians in Goa by the Inquisition as late as the middle of the eighteenth century. These practices were banned because they contained too many Hindu elements. In this process the role of clergy versus laity gives us a different picture.[37]

Further, church training is not oriented toward collaboration and dialogue but toward obedience and respect for authority. Lack of adequate training of the clergy is more and more felt now when the South Indians go to North India as missionaries. The traditional training of the clergy is geared toward maintaining the Christian communities where sacraments are administered and church services are conducted. But in the North the majority are Hindus, and in some parishes there are only a handful of Christian families to be looked after; and so the clergy find themselves unemployed unless they start English medium schools or social work projects, which are in themselves of great value. But the fact is that they are not trained to deal with people of other religions; neither are they equipped with a theological vision, nor are they sufficiently informed about other religious communities.

Also, the economic situation forces the majority of Christians to be preoccupied with their security, leaving the clergy to be busy with the church affairs. Here one has to keep in mind that dialogue can take place only among people who are mature and strong in faith and in society. Theological maturity and social security are important factors in this venture. When my security is threatened, I do not propose a theology of pluralism; and if I do, it is taken to be a survival tactic by the majority community, especially when the initiative comes from the minority group. It is true that my faith conviction should be the motivating force to enter into dialogue, but such a theological thinking should not be seen isolated from the sociological factors of the believing communities.

Even after two decades (since Vatican II) and in spite of many dialogue centers and publications, Christians, both clergy and laity, have as yet no clear idea of dialogue itself. For many it seems to be another name for a new method of converting people to Christianity. The dialogue language is used, but the basic thinking remains as of old because there is not sufficient scope within the Christian community itself for dialogue, an intrareligious dialogue. First of all, the dialogical principles have to be learned within a believing community—to respect the other, to share and to be at home with others in freedom and without fear, to discover the working of the Spirit among the members of the believing community. Secondly, through this process the Christians are called upon to recognize, to respect and to respond to the workings of the Spirit among different people, in different ways and at different periods of history. Hence intrareligious dialogue trains people to enter into other believing communities so that they are ready to give themselves as they are to the other and seeks also to know the other as he or she is. Nonetheless, a theological awakening is evident today among the Christian community in India in general and among St. Thomas Christians in particular. Apart from the theological maturity and growing self-confidence that one perceives among Indian Christians, one can also notice that the social situation of India in the form of poverty and communal violence challenges Christians more and more to join hands with other religious communities as collaborators and to make the concept of dialogue a living reality. The process has begun in a modest way, and we hope that this thinking becomes more and more articulate in the entire community.

NOTES

1. R. L. Howe, *The Miracle of Dialogue,* Indian ed. (Bangalore: MBW Publications, 1963), p. 49.

2. A. M. Mundadan, *History of Christianity in India,* vol. 1 (Bangalore: Theological Publications in India [TPI], 1984), pp. 21, 29.

3. Joseph Thekkedath, *History of Christianity in India,* vol. 2 (Bangalore: TPI, 1982), pp. 24-25.

4. See Leslie Brown, *The Indian Christians of St. Thomas: An Account of the Ancient Syrian Church of Malabar,* rev. ed. (London: Cambridge University Press, 1982), chap. 13, "The Identity of the St. Thomas Christians," pp. 297-307; Paul Varghese, ed., *The Syrian Churches in India* (Stuttgart: Evangelical Publications, 1974).

5. Different dates are given for the formation of the Mar Thoma Church. Though the origin could be traced back to 1837, when Abraham Malpan made some liturgical changes, or to 1843, when Deacon Mathews was consecrated as Metropolitan and returned to Malabar, the final court verdict came in 1889.

6. A. M. Mundadan, "Emergence of Catholic Theological Consciousness in India," *St. Thomas Academy for Research Documentation (STAR),* no. 7, Bangalore, 1985: 2-10.

7. Anthony Mookenthottam, *Indian Theological Tendencies* (Berne: Peter Lang Verlag, 1978), p. 24.

8. Paul Thenayan, *The Missionary Consciousness of the St. Thomas Christians* (Cochin: Viani Publications, 1982), p. 34.

9. Placid Podipara, *The Malabar Christians* (Allepey: 1972), p. 27ff. This description of Podipara is criticized by J. Kottukapally as theologically unsound, "as though faith could remain floating over a culture capped by a liturgy created in some other cultures." "The Rite Controversy: Should the Stalemate Continue," *Indian Missiological Review* 9 (1987): 79ff.

10. Thekkedath, p. 136.

11. Ibid. pp. 139-40.

12. Mundadan, p. 27.

13. E. R. Hambye, "The Syrian Christians in India," *Clergy Monthly* vol. 16, no. 10 (1952): 386.

14. Thenayan, pp. 100-3.

15. Ibid. 79-92.

16. See Asoka's Rock Edict XII. "The faiths of others all deserve to be honoured for one reason or another. By honouring them, one exalts one's own faith and at the same time performs a service to the faith of others. By acting otherwise, one injures one's own faith and also does a disservice to that of others." N. A. Nickam and Richard McKeon, *The Edicts of Asoka* (Chicago Press, 1959), pp. 51-52.

17. Paul Hacker, *Inklusivismus, Eine indische Denkform.* Ed. Gerhard Oberhammer (Vienna: Publications of the De Nobili Research Library, 1983).

18. See "Hindu Christian Dialogue in India," *Pro Mundi Vita Bulletin* 88 (January, 1982): 23.

19. Duncan B. Forrester, *Caste and Christianity: Attitudes and Policies on Caste of Anglo-Saxon Protestant Missions in India* (London: Curzon Press, 1979). In this section I am following the sources and conclusions of Forrester.

20. Ibid. p. 16.

21. Ibid. pp. 100-1.

22. Brown, p. 173.

23. Thekkedath, p. 22.

24. Forrester, p. 112.

25. Ibid. pp. 104, 114.

26. Forrester comes to this conclusion as opposed to C. J. Fuller, who argues that "the egalitarian aspects of Christianity, as of Islam and Buddhism, have had negligible effect on the Hindu way of life." "Kerala Christians and the Caste System," *Man* (N.S.) 2, p. 65 (1981). Quoted by Forrester, p. 103.

27. A. M. Mundadan, "Hindu-Christian Dialogue: Past Twenty-Five Years," *Jeevadhara* vol. 11, no. 65 (1981): 379-94.

28. Michael O'Toole, *Christian Ashrams in India* (Pune: Ishvanikendra, 1983).

29. See James Aerthayil, *The Spiritual Heritage of the St. Thomas Christians* (Bangalore: Dharmaram Publications, 1982).

30. A. M. Mundadan, "Emergence of Catholic Theological Consciousness in India," p. 34.

31. J. B. Chethimattam, "The Eastern Theological Heritage and the Task of Building an Indian Theology." Paper presented in a seminar held in Dharmaram College, Bangalore (August 4-7, 1987).

32. M. M. Thomas, *Christian Response to the Asian Revolution,* Indian ed. (Lucknow Publishing House, 1967), pp. 104, 108.

33. M. M. Thomas, "Understanding Neighbours in Faith," in *Religion and Society* (1965): 3.

34. Sunand Sumithra, *Revolution As Revelation* (Tübingen: International Christian Network and New Delhi: Theological Research and Communication Institute, 1984), pp. 109-10.

35. Chethimattam.

36. *Pro Mundi Vita Bulletin* 88 (January, 1982): 16.

37. I am grateful to Dr. Teotonio R. de Souza, Director, Xavier Center of Historical Research, Goa, for drawing my attention to this fact while commenting on this paper.

2

The Response of the Hindu Renaissance to Christianity

RONALD NEUFELDT

While time and effort have been put into Buddhist-Christian dialogue in recent years, little has gone on in the way of Hindu-Christian dialogue except in the form of isolated publications and a few institutions. For the most part the interest that is shown in dialogue comes from Christian theologians trying to come to grips with "Hinduism." This should not be surprising, given the relatively exclusive claims that have characterized Christian theology through the centuries. In the case of Hindus, little attention is currently paid to dialogue, at least as this is generally understood, possibly because of the exasperating tendency of the educated spokespersons to claim a kind of all-inclusiveness for Hinduism. Given this all-inclusiveness there is very little need to respond, except to say that in essence all religions are the same or lead to the same goal.

In the nineteenth century, however, there was a fair bit of interaction between Hindu spokespersons on the one hand, and Western scholars and missionaries on the other. Many of the thinkers of the Renaissance engaged the claims of Christianity, incorporating some aspects of what they heard and saw and rejecting other aspects.

My concern here is to deal with the nature of the responses of the Hindu Renaissance to Christianity. The treatment will be restricted largely to the nineteenth century with some reference to the early part of the twentieth century. This is admittedly somewhat arbitrary, since one can argue that the Renaissance is still going on. Traditionally, however, a distinction is made between the Hindu Renaissance and Hinduism in the twentieth century. In dealing with the Renaissance I will not attempt to be exhaustive, describing in detail individual thinkers and movements. That story is widely known. Rather, I will attempt to deal in general terms with the context to which the Renaissance figures were responding, as well as the responses, in an attempt to highlight significant parallels between the two. This will serve as a basis for the discussion of dialogue with respect to the Hindu Renaissance.

In order to begin to speak about the responses of the Hindu Renaissance, a number of clarifications are in order. First, it is important to emphasize the plural in the word *responses*. The responses vary from movement to movement and from thinker to thinker. This is not simply because all movements are not the same, but also because movements and thinkers operate in different time periods. As times change, movements and thinkers respond to different situations.

Secondly, the groups to which Renaissance figures respond also vary. The Christian missionaries, for example, are not all of one piece. Their theological perceptions and their views of missions shift from group to group and from time period to time period. Nor are missionaries the only type of Christian spokesperson to which the figures of the Hindu Renaissance respond. There is also the presence of indologists, particularly British indologists, who as teachers in India made known their views on Hinduism in talks, writings and discussions. Furthermore, prominent British indologists were also confessing Christians of a sort and therefore responded to India not only from their perspective as indologists but also from their perspective as Christians. This means that when one speaks of the Hindu Renaissance responses to Christianity one must take into account a rather fluid situation. And this fluidity has two aspects. The Hindu Renaissance itself is not a monolithic entity but is made up of different movements and spokespersons. Secondly, the situation to which Renaissance movements and thinkers are responding is not monolithic either, but is made up of a variety of views and groups.

THE CHRISTIAN CONTEXT

Two recent books have dealt with missionary activity in India in the nineteenth century. Eric Sharpe's treatment in *Faith Meets Faith* is a more general treatment, which not only deals with the nineteenth but also includes the twentieth century. John Webster's volume, *The Christian Community and Change in Nineteenth Century North India*, is confined to the efforts of Presbyterians in North India in the nineteenth century. Both treatments agree that there is a significant shift in at least some missionary attitudes to India in the latter part of the nineteenth century. Both also agree that the shift characterizes the minority rather than the majority of the missionaries.

Sharpe points out that much early missionary activity was fostered by a view that tended to see all of humankind as fallen from grace and therefore condemned. The world itself was seen as an enemy and therefore something from which all people must be saved. Given this general view, Hinduism had to be seen as false and as falling far short of the enlightened views of Christianity. Hinduism simply did not measure up to proper standards of decency, plainness and morality. Salvation, if it was to be had, was to be had through Christ only.[1] The opposition to Hinduism therefore had to be unequivocal. This can be seen clearly in the conflict between Rāmmohun Roy and the Serampore Baptists over the teaching of Jesus. For Roy the essence of those teachings and therefore of Christianity was their ethical or moral quality, not any dogmatic or doctrinal assertions about the divinity of Jesus. For the Baptists the essence was the issue of salvation from guilt and the power of sin, and this could be had only through the saving power of Jesus as the Christ and the Son of God. This essence was simply missing from the texts and practices of Hinduism.

Sharpe's description is clearly supported by the research of Webster on Presbyterian missionaries in Northern India, particularly the Punjab. The point of Presbyterian efforts was evangelism informed by the view that the sensibleness of the gospel would be obvious against the nonsense of Hinduism. The dominant position was a high view of the inerrancy of scripture combined with an appeal to the primacy of reason. The reasonableness of the gospel was seen as so self-evident that failure to accept it was seen as the result of a low moral state rather than a deficiency in the evidence.[2] The interaction was therefore one-way—the missionary bearing truth to the Hindu. The missionary had little or nothing to learn from the Hindu or from the Hindu's religion. If attention was paid to Hindu practices and texts, it was primarily to point out the problems and falsehoods of what was being studied. Salvation was to be had only through Christianity. That it could not be had through Hinduism was amply shown by Hindu practices, which were seen as corrupt and as proof that the texts and history must be corrupt as well.

Examples of this vision are not difficult to find, even in the twentieth century, nor is it difficult to flesh out the details of such a vision. A case in point is the book *Reformers in India*, in which Kenneth Ingham attempts to depict the missionary movement in India between 1793–1833. The views he enunciates are clearly views he also shares. The image of India that emerges is not a flattering one. Hindu religion is pictured as incapable of reform, the social system as changeless and incapable of remedy, and the Indian spirit of inquiry as stagnant. If reform is to be achieved it will be achieved only through the infusion of new ideas from without, principally through the development of a Western system of education. India is seen as backward, ignorant and a slave to superstition. Such a picture is clearly implied in Ingham's depiction of the educational work of the missionaries.

The promotion of Christianity called for the extension of education to assist in the attack upon the superstition and mental slavery fostered by ignorance. For education to flourish it required in turn a literature capable of conveying and inspiring new ideas, and a lan-

guage sufficiently rich and flexible to express them. At the beginning
of the nineteenth century the majority of the languages and dialectics
of India possessed neither of these features.[3]

This image is very much the same as the image one gets in reading a
work like that of William Ward, an early Serampore missionary, on the
history, literature and mythology of the Hindus. That is, everything with
respect to India can be described in terms of a single word, *paganism*, or
the synonymous expression, *heathenism.* While the author expresses some
admiration for the philosophical, devotional aspects of Hinduism and the
tremendous exertions of yogis and devotees to attain a state of abstraction,
he sees these aspects and exertions as devoid of any moral and spiritual
qualities whatsoever. The yogi is seen to be devoid of any feeling or desire
for either God or creatures, and the devotee's devotion is seen to lead him
or her to the abnormal activity of self-annihilation. Both are judged highly
deficient in that the yogis one sees are a very poor copy of the ideal and
the devotion one sees is ineffective in that it does not seem to lead any
Hindus to abstraction.[4]

Whatever merit might exist in the philosophical and devotional expression is nullified by the fact that the large majority of the population
expresses its religion in the form of popular ceremonies that have no re-
deeming qualities whatsoever. They are, in Ward's eyes, nothing but rank
superstition and ignorance.[5] Indeed the system, according to Ward, is essentially a vicious one condemning the Hindus to an existence of ignorance,
cruelty, hopelessness and the unrestrained exercise of pride, deceit, avarice,
falsehood and sexual license, and this under the influence of their sacred
writings, yogis, priests and brahmins.[6] Little wonder that Ward sees in Britain's coming to India the work of Providence to bring intellectual and moral
improvement to India and from India to the rest of Asia.[7]

The important point here is that Ward is typical of that emphasis which
understands India in terms of what was practiced rather than the expressed
ideals of the traditions of India. In other words, the Hinduism being judged
is the Hinduism that missionaries saw practiced around them and not the
Hinduism of the rich, textual traditions of the *darśanas.* Although one finds
reference to the textual traditions and even *darśanas*, very little attention
is paid to this. And that attention is not given in order to point out the
wealth and sophistication of these traditions, but to show that the observed
corruption has a basis in the historical and textual traditions of India. If a
society is registered as pagan then little good can be admitted even about
the past of that society.

It should be pointed out that one must, of course, allow for the shock
of seeing and experiencing things that were simply different and new and,
in terms of what one was used to seeing, must have seemed at least a little
odd. But there is clearly an *a priori* flavor in this vision of India. What is
seen can be neither moral nor good if one is, after all, bringing the light of

culture, truth and civilization to a benighted nation. There may be an admission that Hindu law, though partial, contains some excellent principles, but the observed system that emerges is "essentially vicious and intolerable."[8] One may even find the grudging admiration of an Alexander Duff for the Brāhmo Samāj, but it is an admiration expressed for the strength of an enemy who must nevertheless be challenged and overcome.[9]

While this vision of India may have been the dominant one, it was not the only one. There were those who admitted to some truth in Hinduism and insisted that Hinduism should be studied with integrity to a depth approaching that of the indologists. While salvation was still very much the central issue, it was not to be achieved through Christianity, but through the simple gospel of Jesus, and this gospel was to be understood as the goal or *fulfillment* of the aspirations of all religions. Toward the end of the nineteenth century such a position found clear expression in the writing of J. N. Farquhar, who argued that in the figure of the historical Jesus we have a purely spiritual and ethical religion, an object of worship surpassing anything that might be found in Vedanta.[10] Scriptures were to be put on a continuum, and the argument was not to be about the inerrancy of scripture but about the adequacy of scriptures in fulfilling human needs. The Christian scriptures, of course, were seen as fulfilling those needs better than others. This point is clearly demonstrated in Farquhar's comparison of Hindu reform movements with the noble aspirations of the New Testament.[11] The non-Christian scriptures and traditions are worth studying not for salvation but for what they reveal about human nature and the evolutionary process toward higher truth. While truth may be admitted in texts other than the Bible, this truth is only of a preliminary or preparatory nature, pointing to its fulfillment in the revelation of God in the Bible.

The sources of this more sympathetic approach to Hinduism are various. In part it is seen in the work of certain missionaries like T. H. Burns, James Long and C. H. A. Dall, who through their interest in reform came to see something of worth in reform movements like the Brāhmo Samāj and consequently befriended and supported Hindu reformers.[12] There were also those like Farquhar, who became fine indologists in their own right, concerned about the understanding and description of the ideals of the classical texts of Hinduism.[13]

The work of indologists themselves must be seen as an aid in making this more sympathetic view possible. Not only did they make the original texts available, but through their work in these texts helped to shift attention from what was seen practiced in Hinduism to the high ideals expressed in these texts. Certainly they were willing to think that there was truth to be found in these texts.[14]

Finally, there were influential theological currents forcing a reassessment of the relationship of Christianity to non-Christian traditions. In general terms one can point to a new liberalism, which accepted scientific and historical scholarship and an evolutionary view of history and culture. Certainly the evolutionary view meant that revelation must be sought in more than one book or one culture.[15] More specifically, the fulfillment notion can be found as early as 1845 in F. D. Maurice's influential Boyle Lectures entitled *The Religions of the World and Their Relation to Christianity*. The religions, he maintained, are more than priestcraft and falsehood. They reveal something of the relationship of people to God, the desire for the unseen world. Their aspirations, however, are incomplete and answered fully only in Christianity.[16] Webster, in his treatment of the background of the foreign missionaries, makes the distinction between the theology emanating from Princeton with its emphasis on scriptural infallibility and the resulting image of India as a land of darkness, and the theology emanating from Union with its emphasis on Christianity's adequacy in meeting human needs and its application of the notions of evolution and progress to explain the relationship between Christianity and other religions. This latter theology was admittedly a minority position and made itself felt relatively late in the nineteenth century.[17]

A general description of the Christian context would be incomplete without some attention to the views of indologists, particularly those who spent some time teaching and studying in India. Of particular importance are those who were confessing Christians as well as indologists; in their writings they tended to see and interpret India from the standpoint of their convictions. In one important respect, however, indologists were different from the vast majority of missionaries. Their primary concern and resource was the reservoir of ancient texts inundating the West. Their vision of India, or at least what was best about India, was confined to the world of the texts. In some instances they could not help but take note of religious practices, particularly if they were stationed in India for a time, but their primary concern was with deciphering texts, commenting on the ideals expressed in these texts, and, from time to time, making relatively favorable comparisons to their understanding of the ideals of Christianity. A case in point is the tradition of British indology in the nineteenth century.

Perhaps it is easiest to begin at the end with F. Max Müller, given his enormous influence on the development and popularization of indology and his role in the beginning stages of the science of religion or the comparative study of religion. He is a strange case in that he never visited India. Nonetheless, his views are the culmination of British indology in the nineteenth century and are quoted frequently in the writings of Hindu Renaissance figures. He saw the Sanskrit texts of India, particularly the *Rig Veda*, as central not only for understanding the history and religious sensitivities of the Hindus but also for understanding the religious and intellectual developments of humankind. Given his commitment to an evolutionary understanding of the development of human civilization, and the notion that in the Sanskrit texts we come close to the dawn of human civilization, it is not surprising that in the *Rig Veda* and the Upaniṣads he should see the clearest examples of the evolution of religion from the simple to the complex and sublime, and the true or essential representation of what Hinduism is all about and where it is headed.[18]

In India Max Müller believed he could find the origin, growth, decay and regeneration of religion, and the development of thought from the beginnings of language to the highest stages of rational thought. He applauded the people of ancient India for their concepts, mythologies, laws, philosophy and ideas of godhead, which he maintained were purer and higher than those of the Greeks, Romans and Jews. India, he felt, had much to teach the West about the true identity of the self with respect to the meditative and philosophical sides of the human being since India is essentially a nation of philosophers and mystics.

This narrow and romantic vision of India was largely controlled by Max Müller's interest in Sanskrit and Sanskrit texts, particularly the *Rig Veda*, the Upaniṣads and Vedanta.[19] The thought of the latter two he felt, was quite compatible with Alexandrian Christianity, which he viewed as the culmination point of all religious thought. This literature was full of human interest for him but the human interest he had in mind was the answers he supposed he could derive from this literature concerning the development of the human mind in general and the development of religion in particular. The true history of India was to be found in the poets of the *Rig Veda*, the writers of the Upaniṣads and the founders of Vedanta and Sāṃkhya, not in the millions of villagers who die every day steeped in the drowsy life of their ritual and devotional practices, essentially ignorant of the higher thoughts of India's ancient texts. Later developments like the Purāṇas were for Max Müller intellectually bankrupt, a kind of rubbish that had over the centuries overlaid the great intellectual monuments of India.

Many of Müller's ideas echo ideas enunciated elsewhere in the world of British indology. One can, in fact, find aspects of these ideas handed down, so to speak, from H. T. Colebrooke to H. H. Wilson to Monier-Williams and E. S. Cowell. Each of these writers confesses dependence for his understanding of Hinduism on his predecessor. If we begin with Colebrooke, he maintains that "the real doctrine of the whole of the Indian scripture is the unity of the deity" and that while the Vedas do mention three principal manifestations of this divinity, the business of deified heroes and incarnations of deities is not Vedic but is introduced at a later time.[20] The implication of this is that these later developments are not Hinduism or at least real Hinduism, and if one wants to refer to them as Hinduism one should see them basically as corruptions of the real thing. Hindu theology as enunciated in the Veda and even in the Purāṇas, contrary to the view of modern Hindus, is thought to declare the unity of the godhead and therefore to be consistent with monotheism, although admittedly it does contain the seeds of polytheism and idolatry.[21] Thus real Hinduism has decidedly monotheistic leanings, although these leanings are not altogether clear. This judgment applies as well to the so-called orthodox systems of philosophy.

H. H. Wilson quotes Colebrooke with obvious favor, emphasizing the notion that the real teaching of the whole of the Indian scripture is the unity of the godhead.[22] As does Colebrooke, he sees the earliest form of Hinduism in the Vedas and sees this as superseded by image worship and idolatry, the apex of which is the Purāṇas.[23] His opinion of the Puranic developments is not good in that he sees them as contradictory and as assigning reality to that which was meant to be essentially metaphorical and mystical.[24] He sees an early division taking place in Hinduism, which separated practical and popular beliefs from the speculative or philosophical aspects. The former receives a rather negative response while the latter receives at least some favorable support inasmuch as it is theology or philosophy.[25]

Monier-Williams, who confesses a dependence on the work of H. H. Wilson, goes beyond much of what we see in his predecessors in that he takes pains to pay elaborate attention to the religious life of Indian people outside of the niceties of the traditional *darśanas*. Indeed, he takes indologists to task for dogmatizing about India beyond their "book-learning" and missionaries for perpetuating false notions because they do not know Sanskrit. In a lengthy appeal to undermine common derogatory notions he states:

> I am deeply convinced that the more we learn about the ideas, feelings, drift of thought, religious development, eccentricities, and even errors and superstitions of the natives of India, the less ready shall we be to judge them by our own conventional European standards; the less disposed to regard ourselves as the sole depositories of all true knowledge, learning, virtue, and refinement existing on the earth; the less prone to despise, as an inferior race, the men who compiled the Laws of Manu, one of the most remarkable literary productions of the world; who thought out systems of ethics worthy of Christianity; who composed the *Rāmāyaṇa* and *Mahābhārata*, poems in some respects outrivalling the *Iliad* and the *Odyssey*; who invented for themselves the science of grammar, arithmetic, astronomy, logic, and who elaborated independently six most suitable systems of philosophy. Above all, the less inclined shall we be to stigmatize as "benighted heathen" the authors of two religions, which—however lamentably antagonistic to Christianity—are at this moment professed by about half the human race.[26]

It is interesting to note the emphasis in the appeal. For the most part it has to do with what others would call the high points of Indian civilization, and this despite Monier-Williams' concern to describe the everyday life of Indian religiosity and despite his mention of eccentricities, errors and superstitions. In one sense one might call this fair game, in the sense that the usual measuring stick for Western civilizations is the high points of these civilizations, not the low points, or what one might call common culture. To his credit Monier-Williams does recognize aspects of great value and beauty in Indian religious traditions and rejects the sweeping negative judgments and the notion that India's religions were destined for eradication under the onslaught of Western education and Christianity. However, his view is based on a threefold distinction in India's religious development. The earliest phase is the worship of deified forces or natural phenomena. This is followed by Brahmanism, the merging of all natural forces under a universal spirit. Hinduism is Brahmanism run to seed under a confused tangle of divine personalities, divinities and superstitions.[27] According to Monier-Williams what we have in India are rather lofty systems developing from a previous, more infantile stage, and then degenerating into gross superstitions and objectionable practices.[28] Of particular delight is philosophical Brahmanism, which he sees as based on the Upaniṣads, the hidden spiritual doctrine of the Vedas. It is here that he finds the most similarity to Christianity,[29] and the belief and expressions of thoughtful orthodox Brahmins.[30] Hinduism, on the other hand, is directly opposed to this teaching and is made up of Śaivism, Vaiṣṇavism, Saktism, worship of tutelary deities, demon worship, ancestor worship, animal worship, plant and tree worship, and worship of natural objects.[31]

He sees some laudable attempts to rise above this nonsense in figures like Roy, Sen and Dayānanda. However, these figures are not to be seen as inculcating a reformed Hinduism. Rather they are to be seen as returning to the Indian theism of the Vedas and Vedanta. Nevertheless this return cannot succeed in rising above the panetheism built into Vedanta and the corrupt influence of the Vaiṣṇava teaching of repeated incarnations.[32]

For the most part the ideas enunciated by the nineteenth-century indologists are not new but are perhaps more sophisticated repetitions of the ideas put forward by civil servants and indologists in the latter part of the eighteenth century. The most significant idea was the distinction between popular Hinduism and philosophical Hinduism, an idea that predated the eighteenth century and was to live long after the nineteenth century.[33] Indeed, anyone with knowledge of the present state of indology will recognize the distinction as a current one. For this study its significance lies in its currency among the reformers of the Hindu Renaissance. Popular Hinduism was condemned as idolatry, error and superstition while philosophical Hinduism was seen as containing ideas on a level with Western philosophical and religious concepts. Such notions were clearly enunciated already in the eighteenth century by Holwell and Dow, who found in Hinduism basic notions such as monotheism, immortality and an acceptable moral code.[34] The well-known William Jones asserted that Hinduism contains fundamental religious concepts and an acceptable moral code, principally because, as taught by Genesis, humankind originated in one place. Therefore one should find similarities among the great religious traditions.[35]

HINDU RENAISSANCE

If one analyzes the usual figures associated with the Hindu Renaissance, one is immediately struck by an overarching concern, that is, the concern to reform, refine and define Hinduism. The concern for reform is, of course, not new, but runs through Indian history as far back as the Upaniṣads. What is new is the focus on Hinduism. This is largely a concept forced onto India from the outside, at least in its use to define religion. And, once it became current, the spokespersons for the Renaissance began to argue and think in terms of Hinduism.

There are two important points that must be made about the attempts to reform and define Hinduism. The first is that there is little agreement on what constitutes the essentials of Hinduism. In another context I make the point that the figures of the Renaissance simply do not agree, and this to the extent that each sees aspects of another's vision as coming close to irreligion or, put more mildly, as incomplete or misleading. In other words, one reformer's Hinduism differs significantly from another's.[36]

Secondly, in the interests of simplification, one can point to two broad categories of disagreement, or two trends in attempts to define Hinduism. On the one hand, there are those who self-consciously move in the direction of theism. This camp would include Samaj figures like Rāmmohun Roy, Keshub Chunder Sen, Dayānanda Sarasvatī, M. G. Ranade, and Chandavarkar. On the other hand, there are those who see theistic notions, or God as personal, to be lower levels of truth. They will define Hinduism in terms of a non-dualistic experience in which there is ultimately no distinction between the individual and the impersonal absolute. This differs radically from the creator/creature language of the theists. To this camp belongs Ramakrishna (although some would argue that he is hopelessly eclectic); his disciple Vivekananda; and more recently Aurobindo and Radhakrishnan. Some writers have in fact credited Vivekananda with being the father of this particular perspective, and hence of much of English-speaking Hinduism.[37] It should be pointed out that spokespersons for both of those perspectives were quite aware of religious pluralism, the attacks of Christian missionaries and the work of indologists, and were responding to this milieu, at least in part.[38]

If this is so, then one should find parallels between the language and preoccupations of the reformers and the language and preoccupations of missionaries and indologists. The starting point for speaking of such parallels must be the use of the term *Hinduism*. The basic idea involved — that there is an essence that can be found in spite of the incredible historical growth in beliefs and practices — shows a clear indebtedness to missionaries and indologists; to the missionaries for their notion that there is a system of Hinduism that is open to attack, and to the indologists for speaking in terms of a single philosophically consistent core and by implication treating everything else as not really Hinduism. What ties the Renaissance figures together is this talk of an essential core for Hinduism, whatever the content that is attributed to this central core. In part, at least, this language is a response to Westerners who think in terms of Hinduism. This comes through clearly in Rāmmohun Roy's somewhat bitter response to the missionaries for not comprehending the depth and sublime mystery of Hindu thought.[39]

The language of essentialism moves in two directions. In the case of the Samajes, one sees obvious parallels with the language of the missionaries. That is, true Hinduism or *Sanātana Dharma* is theism; it is the worship of a personal, just and merciful god and the performance of ethical actions in keeping with the belief in a creator God who rules the universe with justice and compassion. The reformers, with perhaps the exception of Dayānanda, are careful to point out how close some of their perceptions are to Christianity. Even Dayānanda, it can be argued, will find something of truth in Christianity and other religions.[40] This language accounts for at least some of the missionaries' sympathetic response to the work of the reformers.

The prime example of this, and one often overlooked in the study of the Renaissance figures, is Justice M. G. Ranade, a central figure in the early years of the Prarthana Samāj and the National Social Conference. In him we find language reminiscent of the rationalism that characterizes much of nineteenth-century theology. Civilized faith, he maintained, is the belief that there is a mind that plans and governs the universe by way of an eternal law of justice, equality, pity and compassion, and the suggestion of conscience in the human being. This belief allowed him to see the coming of the British as providential in that it was to remind the Hindus of the essential theism of their own tradition. This reminder, in turn, would serve to purify India for the sake of the fulfillment of her mission, which was to present the world with purified Hinduism, the universal faith that will bring the golden age to the world. This purified Hinduism is superior theism in that it is non-historical or not bound to a particular prophet or saint, but has an open-ended revelation, emphasizes direct communication with the Absolute, and teaches karma, toleration for all, self-sacrifice and love for all animated beings. Interestingly enough, Ranade sees this to be in line with the Protestant reformation of the sixteenth century.[41]

Aspects of these ideas are to be found in other reformers such as Roy, Tagore, Sen and Dayānanda. So is the basic premise on which these ideas rest—that it is rational to believe in a God who rules the universe and that he rules the universe with just and compassionate laws. Roy, in his attacks on the idolatry of his fellow Hindus, argues that the true teaching of the Upaniṣads is theism. This has two aspects: the worship of the one true God by whom everything is created, and a treatment of all humankind in line with such a belief. This is supportable through common sense and the dictates of reason.[42] Even in the case of Dayānanda, whose relationships with Christians tended to be polemical, one finds an emphasis on a personal

God who rules in terms of justice, compassion and orderliness and the assertion that these beliefs are in accord with the dictates of conscience and reason.[43] Clearly there is much here that parallels the language of missionaries and indologists alike, and in some cases at least there is the admission of indebtedness to the teachings of the Bible and the missionaries.

In the case of the Ramakrishna Mission, the language of essentialism moved in another direction, that of Advaita. One finds in the literature of the mission an abundance of God-talk, but this is used not to substantiate theism but to move the audience, whether Western or Eastern, beyond that level to an understanding that God is entirely within. The non-dual experience, in other words, is ultimate. While one can argue that for Ramakrishna there does not seem to be a concerted effort to subsume the experience of a personal god, or *bhakti*, to the non-dual experience, it is different for Vivekananda. He accepts for a time the importance of the *bhakti* experience during the period of his discipleship under Ramakrishna. Later, however, the Advaita experience comes to define religion for him and the religions, including *bhakti*, become the "little loves" one must at some point transcend on the way to the non-dual experience. He becomes highly critical of those who stay within the confines of "lower" ceremonial and institutional religion. The church, for example, is all right as a starting point, but one dare not stay there.[44] The essence of Hinduism, then, becomes the experience of non-dualism.

This position is reinforced by later neo-Vedantins like Radhakrishnan and Aurobindo. Radhakrishnan for example, argues for Vedanta as the ultimate expression of Hinduism, relegating other forms of experience to a lower but still valid level. The worship of God as personal and the worship of incarnations rank below the non-dual experience. In Aurobindo, the experience of brahman as both being and becoming relegates everything else to an inferior position. Most religions are seen as a source of discord and retardation given their tendency to degenerate to ceremonial ritual and fixed dogma. The emphasis on dogma is seen as a problem particularly for Western traditions. To progress one must renounce religions, including Christianity and Hinduism.[45] The notion of fulfillment is obvious here, except that the non-dual experience, not Christianity, fulfills the aspirations of the religions.

There is clearly an affinity between the emphasis on the philosophical in the indologists and the emphasis on the philosophical in the neo-Vedantins. It is not at all far-fetched to assume that exposure, not just to Western forms of education, but also to the arguments of missionaries and indologists in defense of religion had an influence on Renaissance figures like Roy, Vivekananda, Aurobindo and Radhakrishnan. The sometimes enunciated statement that the Bengal Renaissance begins with the Orientalists is particularly pertinent here. Radhakrishnan, in particular, is influenced by his teachers, particularly A. G. Hogg, in eventually coming to the position that Vedanta is the ultimate expression of Hinduism. He moves from a position that is not critical of Hindu village religion to a position that relegates village religion to a lower position.[46]

The parallels do not, of course, stop at the level of language. One can see them, for example, in the emphasis on written scripture, a book by which one judges whether things are true or false. In other words, there is a trend in the Renaissance to make Hinduism into a religion of the book and Hindus a people of the book. This reaches its height in Dayānanda, who comes to regard the four Vedas alone as inerrant scripture. The arguments for inerrancy sound suspiciously familiar. The Vedas are reasonable, they are internally consistent, they accord with the qualities of God, and so forth. To a point one can see the same trend in the neo-Vedantins in their emphasis on Vedanta, particularly the Upaniṣads as the sum and substance of true religiosity.

Perhaps most significant in the arena of parallels is the development of institutions, both educational institutions and institutions devoted more directly to the business of social uplift — orphanages, widows' homes, hospitals, schools for women, and so on. The missionaries' emphasis on education and social reform and institutions to effect reform has long been known. But this is also an outstanding characteristic of the Hindu reformers. In many instances what has survived of the Samajes is precisely their schools and philanthropic endeavors.

The real significance of this development lies in the motivation for these institutions. In rough terms one can call it the development of a social conscience, which parallels the emphasis of the missionaries on the reform of the societies in which they work. In more accurate terms it is the extension, or broadening, of the idea of liberation beyond the sphere of the individual to society itself. The reformers argue that a liberation directed only to oneself is not really liberation, that true liberation looks for the liberation of all of society as well as oneself. For the Samaj figures this is based on the belief that all are the children of God, while for the neo-Vedantins it is based on the notion that all are essentially and potentially divine. Out of this kind of consciousness comes language very familiar in the world of the missionaries — the notion of the kingdom of God on earth to be achieved through the reform of the whole society. This language is applicable not just to the reformers who insist on monotheism as true Hinduism, but also to the neo-Vedantins who emphasize involvement in life to further the evolutionary march of all of society to higher levels of being.[47]

While the parallels do exist and point to considerable interaction between missionaries and indologists on the one hand and the Renaissance figures on the other, there are limits to the parallels. It is clear that on the level of language some of the formulations of the Renaissance figures are welcomed by missionaries, but others are not. In the case of the key figures of the Samajes, while the language of monotheism is welcomed to the point that missionaries were tempted to see types like Roy and Sen as close to

Christianity, the rejection of the notion of incarnation was simply unpalatable. Further, the penchant of the neo-Vedantins to relegate the worship of a personal deity to a lower form of religion was simply not acceptable, nor was their tendency toward what was regarded as pantheism. Conversely, some formulations of the missionaries were not acceptable to the Renaissance figures either. The most graphic illustration of this is found in the lengthy polemic of Dayānanda against notions of forgiveness and original sin.[48] But he is not the only example of polemic against Christian doctrinal formulations. Roy ridicules trinitarian formulations and clearly implies that the dogma of the divinity of Jesus was a huge mistake perpetrated by the apostles and early church fathers.[49]

Arguments concerning belief in doctrinal formulation inevitably involve views of scripture or truth. In the case of the missionaries the Bible is authoritative whether one opts for radical exclusivism or the notion of fulfillment, even though the idea of fulfillment does make it possible to see some truth in scriptures other than the Bible. The British indologists were willing to accord some value to the philosophical systems, particularly to Vedanta, but value is accorded to the extent that Hinduism approximates Christian views and/or Western philosophical perceptions. While the Renaissance figures tend to see their views as universal and therefore enunciated in other scriptures as well, the measure for truth everywhere becomes the Vedas, or the Upaniṣads, or Vedanta. This is true even for Vivekananda and Ramakrishna, who have traditionally been regarded as eminently tolerant. The real teaching of all scriptures, Vivekananda claims, is Vedanta, if only we have the eyes to see this. This is underlined by the ordering of religious experiences, which occurs in both Ramakrishna and Vivekananda. The religions are preparatory to religion that just happens to be described in terms of Advaita.[50] We see other versions of this hierarchy in Aurobindo, who states that religions have to be renounced, and in Radhakrishnan who relegates the religion of village India to a lower but still valid level.[51]

It might be supposed that at least on the institutional level, that is, the level of social and educational reform, there is room for much agreement and cooperative effort. To a certain extent this is the case. Clearly the Hindu reformers welcomed and applauded the efforts of the foreigners at reform, at least in theory. And certainly the missionaries and indologists saw the Hindu reform efforts as true signs of vitality. However, there is also a competitive note. On the one hand, institutions such as schools, orphanages, widows' homes, printing presses and ashrams were designed to develop and change society. On the other hand, these institutions also had a protective purpose, in this case the protection of Hinduism. Debendranath Tagore, for example, established schools to educate children in the Hindu tradition. Dayānanda instituted Shuddhi (a purification ritual to enable one to again practice Hinduism) to reclaim converts to Christianity and other traditions. The Mission set up publishing houses and ashrams in order to preserve and perpetuate Vedanta.

CONCLUSION

If it is correct to see parallels on a number of levels between the Hindu Renaissance figures on the one hand, and missionaries and indologists on the other, and to see the development of these parallels at least in part as a result of the influence of missionaries and indologists, what does one make of this for a Hindu-Christian dialogue? What one makes of it depends very much on what is meant by dialogue.

I do not accept the all-too-frequent understanding of dialogue, that is, discussion for the sake of finding points of agreement under the assumption that it is the points of agreement that tell us what the various religions are really about. Such an assumption makes a mockery of religious discourse and is not necessary for dialogue to take place. Indeed, in dialogue there should be the possibility for a fair bit of disagreement as well as agreement. The issue in dialogue is not agreement or disagreement, but an attitude of openness and seeing the other as significant in the exchange of ideas and the argumentation that is aimed at understanding and allows for the possibility of both education and change. The goal of dialogue is understanding, whether one agrees with the opposing position or not. The understanding may lead to a recognition of basic agreement, but it may also lead to the recognition of fundamental disagreement. This separates dialogue from polemic, the goal of which is denunciation of the opposing position, and apologetic, the goal of which is defense of one's own position.

Understood this way, dialogue is a less frequent factor than are polemics and apologetics in Hindu Renaissance responses to Christianity. Clearly the interaction resulted in change and, in some cases, a new appreciation for traditions that were not one's own. This happened on both sides. Missionaries who spoke in terms of fulfillment saw genuine spiritual aspirations in Hinduism. Indologists saw parallels between the philosophical aspirations of the West and those of educated Hindus. Figures like Roy, Ranade, Sen and Vivekananda saw clear parallels between the best in Christianity and the best in their versions of Hinduism. Indeed, indebtedness to Christianity, whether in the form of texts or teachers, was admitted openly by Roy and Radhakrishnan. One might even make the case that Roy began with genuine attempts to enter into dialogue with Christian missionaries, but was so surprised by the reaction of missionaries to his depiction of Jesus that he soon resorted to apologetics and, in some cases, polemics.

The changes that occur, then, must be viewed with care lest one see them as moving the Hindus and Christians involved closer together, making them more like each other. In a sense they become more like each other, but on the level of tactics and argument, not on the level of agreement on how it is that the human being finds true meaning and fulfillment. That is, the changes that did occur in the Hindu Renaissance occurred to protect

Hindus from the appeals of Christians. The appeal to an essence, whether in the form of monotheism or non-dualism, must be understood at least in part as a protectionist move. The arguments for an essence or for the primacy of the Vedas or Upaniṣads, are in some respects borrowed arguments, but used to support a particular perception of Hinduism against the incursions of Christianity. Certainly many of the institutional developments have a protectionist aspect to them. It is this protectionist aspect that limits further dialogue in that it is essentially a debate in which both sides become satisfied with emphasizing certain similarities but asserting at the same time that it is their respective traditions to which all other traditions point and which therefore should be used to interpret the true meaning of all traditions. At times the apologetics are replaced by outright polemics, as in the case of Dayānanda's *magnum opus*. And the arguments involved are in many cases familiar in that they appear in missionary denunciations of Hinduism.

The influence of Christianity on Hinduism, then, was not exactly what missionaries and indologists might have expected or might have had in mind. Ideas and institutions were borrowed, not necessarily to make Hinduism like Christianity but to assert the validity and perhaps superiority of Hindusim over Christianity. One could say that the Renaissance figures learned their lessons well, but the lessons were not exactly those that their self-proclaimed educators had in mind.[52] This is a point made powerfully by recent research on the Śaiva response to Protestants in Jaffna in the nineteenth century. The point made is that the Śaivites imitated their Protestant teachers on a number of counts, not with the intent of becoming Christian, but with the intent of strengthening Śaivism against the attractions of Christianity.[53]

NOTES

1. Eric J. Sharpe, *Faith Meets Faith. Some Christian Attitudes to Hinduism in the Nineteenth and Twentieth Centuries* (London: SCM Press, 1977), pp. 5-9.

2. See the description of the missionaries in John C. Webster, *The Christian Community and Change in Nineteenth Century North India* (Delhi: Macmillan of India, 1976), pp. 1-45.

3. Kenneth Ingham, *Reformers in India, 1793-1833* (New York: Octagon Books, 1956), p. 96.

4. William Ward, *A View of the History, Literature, and Mythology of the Hindus: Including a Minute Description of Their Manners and Customs, and Translations from Their Principal Works* (Port Washington, NY: 1970), pp. xxi-xxiii. The original work was published in three volumes in 1822.

5. Ibid. pp. xxxiii-xxxiv.

6. Ibid. pp. xxxiv-xxxvi.

7. Ibid. p. liv.

8. Ibid. pp. vii-viii.

9. Meredith Borthwick, *Keshub Chunder Sen, A Search for Cultural Synthesis* (Columbia, MO: South Asia Books, 1978), pp. 34-35.

10. See J. N. Farquhar, *The Crown of Hinduism* (New Delhi: Oriental Books, 1971 reprint of the 1913 ed.), particularly the chapter entitled "The Religious Organism," pp. 445-58.

11. See J. N. Farquhar, *Modern Religious Movements in India* (Delhi: Munshiram Manoharlal, 1967) in which the Hindu reform movements are not only described but also compared to Christianity in order to point out the shortcomings of the Hindu movements.

12. Meredith Borthwick, p. 9. A good example of the interaction between missionaries and Hindu reformers is the account of Long's campaign against indigo planters in G. A. Oddie, *Social Protest in India: British Protestant Missionaries and Social Reform, 1850-1900* (Columbia, MO: South Asia Books, 1978), pp. 173-92.

13. See, for example, J. N. Farquhar, *An Outline of the Religious Literature of India* (Delhi: Motilal Banarsidass, 1984 reprint of the 1920 Oxford ed.). See also his description of Hindu reform in *Modern Religious Movements in India*.

14. Sharpe, p. 16.

15. Ibid. p. 21.

16. Ibid. pp. 13-14.

17. Webster, pp. 30-40.

18. For a summary of Max Müller's views, see the concluding chapter in Ronald W. Neufeldt, *F. Max Müller and the Rg-Veda* (Calcutta: Minerva Associates Publications, 1980).

19. For a fuller discussion of this vision see Ronald W. Neufeldt, "Western Perceptions of Asia: The Romantic Vision of Max Müller," in *Traditions in Contact and Change*, ed. Peter Slater and Donald Wiebe (Waterloo, Wilfrid Laurier University Press, 1983), pp. 593-606.

20. H. T. Colebrooke, *Essays on History, Literature and Religions of Ancient India* (New Delhi: Cosmos Publications, 1977), pp. 110-11.

21. Ibid. p. 196.

22. H. H. Wilson, *Purāṇas, An Account of Their Contents and Nature* (Chandigar: Arun Publications, 1983, first pub. in 1897), p. 2.

23. Ibid. p. 3.

24. Ibid. p. 6.

25. H. H. Wilson, *Essays and Lectures Chiefly on the Religion of the Hindus*, vol. 1 (London: Tribner & Co., 1962), p. 1.

26. Monier-Williams, *Religious Thought and Life in India* (Calcutta: K. P. Bagchi and Company, 1978, reprint of 1883 edition), pp. v-vii.

27. Ibid. pp. 2-3.

28. Ibid. pp. 18-51.

29. Ibid. p. 34.

30. Ibid. p. 57. See also E. B. Cowell's distinction between the Pundits and the mass of the uneducated in George Cowell, *Life and Letters of Edward Byles Cowell* (London: Macmillan & Co. Ltd., 1904), p. 152.

31. Ibid. p. 71.

32. Ibid. pp. 476-520.

33. See P. J. Marshall, ed., *The British Discovery of Hinduism in the Eighteenth Century* (Cambridge: University Press, 1970), for a discussion of the eighteenth century and the preceding era.

34. Ibid. pp. 27-28.

35. Ibid. pp. 35-40.

36. See Ronald Neufeldt, "Religion and Irreligion: A Historian's Perspective," in H. A. Meynell, ed., *Religion and Irreligion* (Calgary: The University of Calgary Press, 1985), pp. 25-44.

37. See the discussion by George Williams, "Swami Vivekananda's Conception of Karma and Rebirth," in R. W. Neufeldt, ed., *Karma and Rebirth: Post Classical Developments* (Albany: State University of New York Press, 1986), p. 41.

38. I have heard it claimed, for example, that the Bengal Renaissance begins not with Roy, but with the indologists like William Jones and H. T. Colebrooke. This was stated by historian Professor Haridass Mukherjee in a lecture in Calcutta on 14 August 1987. The point here is the Hindu Renaissance figures were not working in a vacuum but were feeding off and responding to a milieu, some of which preceded them.

That there was interaction between Hindu Renaissance figures and Christians, whether missionaries or indologists, is well-known. The interaction begins already with Roy in his celebrated disputes with the Serampore missionaries over his depiction of Jews. It continues in Debendranath Tagore's educational ventures to combat missionary activity. Sen got some of his education from liberal missionaries like Burns, Long and Dall, and was criticized by others for his free use of biblical phrases. M. G. Ranade was noted for his willingness to cooperate with missionary reform efforts.

Education too plays a role in this interaction. Figures like Vivekananda, Ranade, Aurobindo and Radhakrishnan received a Western education in colleges sponsored by the British raj or by missionaries. British indologists themselves, like Wilson and Monier-Williams, were teachers at some of these institutions and report in their writings knowledge of and acquaintance with some of the Renaissance figures. The influence of the Orientalists in the Bengal Renaissance has been well documented by David Kopf in *British Orientalism and the Bengal Renaissance* (Berkeley: University of California Press, 1969). See particularly the chapter "Transmission of Orientalist Ideals," pp. 178-213, and the chart detailing contacts with Orientalists, pp. 210-11.

39. Excerpts of Roy's attack on Christian missionaries are continued in William Theodore De Bary, ed., *Sources of Indian Tradition*, vol. 2 (Princeton: Princeton University Press, 1968), pp. 26-28.

40. This is clearly implied in Dayānanda's statement of his beliefs in *Satyarth Prakash* (New Delhi: Sarvadeshik Arya Pratinidhi Sabha, 1975), p. 723.

41. See Ronald Neufeldt, "Hindu Protestantism: The Case of Justice M. G. Ranade," in *Journal of Religious Studies*, vol. 10 (Fall 1982): 1-14.

42. See the excerpt from Roy's "Abridgement of Vedanta" in De Bary, ed., *Sources of Indian Tradition*, vol. 2, pp. 21-23.

43. See Dayānanda's statement of beliefs and also his attack on the Bible in *Satyarth Prakash*, pp. 589-648. For a thorough treatment of Dayānanda's views on religious pluralism see H. G. Coward's paper in *Modern Indian Responses to Religious Pluralism*, edited by Harold Coward (Albany: SUNY Press, 1987) pp. 39-64.

44. See Ronald Neufeldt, "The Response of the Ramakrishna Mission," in Coward, pp. 65-84.

45. For a thorough treatment of Aurobindo and Radhakrishnan on religious pluralism, see R. N. Minor, "The Response of Sri Aurobindo and the Mother" in H. G. Coward, pp. 85-104; and R. N. Minor, "The Christian Education of Sarvapelli Radhakrishnan," an unpublished paper delivered in Atlanta at the AAR, 1986.

46. Minor, "The Christian Education of Sarvapelli Radhakrishnan."

47. See, for example, R. N. Minor's treatment of Aurobindo and Radhakrishnan, "In Defence of Karma and Rebirth: Evolutionary Karma," in R. W. Neufeldt, *Karma and Rebirth,* pp. 15-40.

48. See Dayānanda, *Satyarth Prakash*, chap. 13, which examines the doctrines of Christianity.

49. See the excerpt from *The Precepts of Jesus* in De Bary, pp. 23-25.

50. See Ronald Neufeldt, "The Response of the Ramakrishna Mission," in Coward.

51. See R. N. Minor, "The Response of Sri Aurobindo and the Mother" in Coward, pp. 85-104, and "The Christian Education of Sarvapelli Radhakrishnan."

52. See Paul B. Courtright, "When East Meets West: Cross-Cultural Encounters in the Indian Context," an unpublished paper presented in Atlanta in 1986 at the annual meeting of the AAR. It is a response to five case studies.

53. D. Hudson, "A Śaiva Response to the Protestants: Arumuga Navalar of Jaffna (1822–1879)," unpublished paper presented in Atlanta in 1986 at the annual meeting of the AAR.

3

Trialogue: The Context of Hindu-Christian Dialogue in Kerala

ROLAND E. MILLER

There are many persuasive arguments supporting the concept of dialogue. There are also some good arguments that speak for a concept of *trialogue.* Trialogue, understood as *meaningful engagement among three religious communities,* presents some interesting and promising prospects. It has the potential to soften the encounter aspects of dialogue, compel attention to universal elements, and in some areas bring the discussion closer to existential reality. It may be argued that as a practical goal trialogue is complex and unworkable, and further that it fundamentally alters the goals and dynamics that make dialogue such an enriching process. Trialogue, it may be suggested, represents another genre of interaction rather than a simple extension of dialogue.

Without debating that issue, I would suggest that there are instances where, at the least, *trialogical awareness* becomes essential to the conduct of dialogue. The social and religious milieu of India, especially in certain regions such as Kerala, may be viewed as an example. Even if Hindu-Christian dialogue in these areas does not run the danger of representing a truncated version of reality, at a minimal level it cannot be carried on without an awareness and sensitivity to the living interaction of three religious communities—Hindu, Muslim and Christian.[1] This is certainly a requirement if dialogue of any kind is to go beyond the confines of mere theoretical discussion and doctrinal concern and reflect real life.

This chapter will therefore attempt to look at the long-term interaction among Christians, Hindus and Muslims within the general region of Kerala in southwest India in order to provide the trialogical context for Hindu-

Christian dialogue in that area. While the exact place of dialogue within the academic study of religion is a debated issue, the objective description of what has happened in interreligious relations clearly belongs to the scope of the discipline. Such description, however, must include more than the bare recital of events; it also involves the question of the foundation on which those relationships appear to have been based. The following treatment of the Kerala experience, accordingly, will also attempt to analyze the nature of the relationships and the attitudes on which they were based. We will conclude with a final reflection. In the light of this long experience, is it possible to suggest an answer to the frequently-raised question: What is a sound and enduring basis for viable interreligious living in a pluralistic world?

KERALA

The state of Kerala provides a unique history of trialogical relationships, a kind of laboratory even within multireligious India.[2] A union of former Travancore, Cochin and Malabar, Kerala is located on the southwest coast of India. Only about three hundred sixty miles long and fifty to seventy miles wide, a total of 15,002 square miles, it contains within its bounds 25,453,680 people (1981 census; present estimate is twenty-seven million). This makes it perhaps the most densely populated geopolitical area in the world (1,697 per square mile in 1981; ca. 1,830 per square mile today), and much can be said about the impact and implications of this demographic situation. The area has a culture and a language called Malayalam, and its citizens are named Malayalis.

Kerala's western openness to the sea and the attractiveness of its spices have made it a crossroads of trade from ancient times, opening its people to a host of influences over the years. In modern time the state has been marked by a combination of progressiveness and turbulence, and has often been called the barometer of the nation. Its people are alert in mind and sensitive in emotion; on the one hand, individualistic and divided, on the other hand, marked by group loyalties; in general well-educated, yet economically poor, bearing in microcosm almost all the problems of India; restless and prophetic. It is here, in this complex milieu, that an unusual religious situation prevails.[3]

Kerala is the only place in the world where Hindus, Muslims and Christians live together in such numerical equilibrium (although Assam may be compared). Hindus comprise 58 percent, Christians 21 percent, and Muslims 21 percent of the population (1981: Hindus 14,801,347; Christians 5,233,865; Muslims 5,409,687). There is only a tiny sprinkling of other religious adherents, including the remnant of a once-flourishing Jewish community. The bare statement of official membership statistics, of course, does not do justice to the inner complexity of the religions; within Christianity, for example, there are more than sixty distinct groups. Furthermore, the erosive effect of secular and materialist philosophies on traditional religious allegiance blurs the distinctions. (Modern Kerala has freely elected three Marxist governments since 1956.) Nevertheless, the reality that three major world religions co-exist in extremely close quarters and in relatively similar proportions creates a unique situation and makes the question of interreligious relations a highly existential one.

RELIGIOUS INTERACTION IN THE PAST

The need for the different religions to find a viable way of interacting has been a fact of life throughout the history of Kerala. Early Dravidian religion, Aryanizing Brahmanism, Jainism, Buddhism, monism, *bhakti*, Judaism, Christianity and Islam each fed the broad stream of Malayali religiosity. Sreedhara Menon summarizes the development in these words:[4]

The story of the confluence of religions in Kerala is an exhilarating subject for study. Even in the ancient period Kerala became a meeting ground of all the Indian religions and philosophic systems, as well as the most important world religions.

In the light of this development, the early period of Kerala must be considered a remarkable one. Seldom in world history has there been such a "successful" era of positive interreligious living as that which existed in this region from the eighth to the fifteenth centuries. That conclusion is not an unreasonable one, even though the evidence is somewhat circumstantial in nature and its interpretation is conditioned by nostalgia. Kerala Hindus, sharers of a faith noted for its spaciousness, were at their most hospitable stage. Jews came, possibly after the destruction of Jerusalem, and were given a welcome and special privileges. Christians arrived, perhaps first as West Syrian traders in the fourth century, although Malayali Christians firmly hold that St. Thomas founded the church.[5] They settled in the southern area of the region, were received with kindness, intermarried with high-caste Hindus and founded the Syrian Church of Kerala (Syrian Christians, interspersed among several denominations, comprise about sixty-five percent of Christians in Kerala today).[6]

The Syrian Christians of Kerala maintained a strong link with Medieval Christians in the Middle East. During the early period of the church's existence that link was forged not only by the strong St. Thomas tradition itself, nor through the retention of Syriac in the liturgy, but also through continued immigration, occasional personal contact and the provision of episcopal leadership. While in everyday matters Syrian Christians in Kerala absorbed indigenous Malayalam culture patterns, in ecclesiastical matters they looked to the Middle East, especially for the supply of clergy.[7] At an early stage they established a working relation with the Seleucia-Ctesiphon Church of Persia, expressing allegiance through the see of Rewardashir.

Thus the Nestorian orientation of Syrian Christianity, which lasted for centuries, was established. Later, when the advance of Islam made it more difficult to maintain the Persian connection, Kerala Christians gradually began to turn to West Syria for clerical help, thus bringing the influence of Antioch and the Jacobite tradition into Malayali Christian life. With the coming of the Portuguese, Syrian Christianity in Kerala formally divided into Romo-Syrian and Orthodox Jacobite streams. Despite these affiliations and influences, however, there is no evidence that Malayali Christians themselves became involved in the Christological controversies that underlay these divisions; indeed, since the New Testament was not translated into Malayalam until 1830, the basis for such involvement was absent.

It was not only Christians from the Middle East who entered Kerala at an early stage. Arabs also came, both before and after the advent of Islam, in connection with their control of the Indian Ocean trade. They too intermarried and interacted with Hindus, and the large Mappila Muslim community of Kerala developed. The word *Mappila,* applied to both Muslims and Christians (but now more and more limited in use to the Muslims of Malabar), was an honorific term designating respected and welcomed visitors from abroad.[8] Granted that our sources of information are scanty, through this development we do not discern any sign of the intrusion of religious militance or even any overt indication of unhappy relationships. As far as can be known, the four communities co-existed in a positive and friendly manner, and even K. M. Pankikkar's strong conclusion may be valid:[9] "Malabar was leading a comparatively happy, though politically isolated life. . . . Trade flourished, different communities lived together without friction, and absolute religious toleration existed." We cannot rule out the possible existence of some tensions and, of course, it must be remembered that the numbers of Jews, Christians and Muslims at this stage were relatively small.

It is possible that the phrase "friendly and practical working accommodation" might effectively capture the mood of this unusual period. It was more than a form of co-existence. There was a kind of unabashed mutual acceptance that resulted in intermarriage, and there was cooperation in affairs of common advantage. Underlying the mood was an apparently implicit assumption that interreligious harmony is good. We do not, however, gain any sense that theoretical positions on the relationship among the religions were articulated, nor do we have the impression that formal methods for achieving such harmony were adopted. The latter appears to have been a by-product of other considerations. Trialogical awareness was surely there. Trialogical life was an obvious reality. Trialogue as meaningful engagement is not in evidence.

What was the real paste or dynamic that held things together in this "golden age" of toleration? It appears to have been primarily *mutual commercial advantage.* The Syrian Christians and Arab Muslims were predominantly traders, and they collaborated with the Hindu rajas and merchants to establish a flourishing trade with China, the Middle East and Europe. The interrelationships in Kerala originally started in a friendly way for this reason, and it was to the advantage of all concerned that they continue. There are also some indications that the positions of the religions themselves were less hardened than they were to become at a later stage.

This history raises a question appropriate for our time; namely, Is mutual commercial advantage a sufficiently enduring basis for interreligious harmony? The Kerala experience informs us that commercial interaction is indeed an important binding factor in human relations, but what happened next also indicates that interrelationships based on economic self-interest alone are built on an inadequate foundation. Something more than utilitarianism is needed.

With the coming of the fifteenth century, the age of harmony based on commerce moved to an age of rivalry based on economic and political domination; the period was also characterized by a militant religious flavor. The people who ushered in the new age were the Portuguese, agents of manifest destiny, and the partly unwitting destroyers of a precious interreligious harmony. They made this impact, largely, by taking over the trade between Kerala and the rest of the world, blocking out the Arabs and the Muslims, and to some extent the Syrian Christians, thus removing the primary basis for the existing relationship. That harmony had not become a deep life principle and so could not resist the new influences. The Portuguese further disturbed matters by making religion itself a part of the fabric of domination, uniting religion, politics and economics into one imperialistic whole. Within a century the patterns of interreligious living were radically altered, and up to the twentieth century we have a history of rivalry, deteriorating relations—especially between Hindus and Mulisms—and a great deal of tragic violence.

THE IMPACT OF PORTUGUESE CHRISTIANITY

The story of the Portuguese incursion into Kerala, and its subsequent impact, has yet to be fully told.[10] There is no doubt, however, that the crusading spirit of the Portuguese, born in the Medieval matrix of Christian-Muslim encounter, introduced a major new element into the religious scene of southwest India and contributed significantly to a dramatic reversal in relationships.

We will not attempt to trace the history of Portugal's rise to a dominant maritime power. It *is* important to recognize, in the expressions of that power, an extension of the same spirit that drove the Moors from southern Portugal.[11] Prince Henry the Navigator (1394-1460) led the way. The intrepid and brilliant Master of the Order of Christ—which had replaced the Knights Templar in Portugal—he probed the western coast of Africa, seeking a river connection with the believed-in Christian kingdom of Prester John. He hoped this linkage would result in the defeat of the Muslims and the regaining of the Holy Land. "It is certain," comments Jayne, "that the master motive which animated the Navigator was neither scientific, commercial nor political. . . . It was essentially religious. Before all else, Prince Henry was a crusader."[12]

It is somewhat difficult, however, to assess the actual primacy among the various motivations for the Portuguese expansion. Clearly there were intertwined factors of commerce, imperial power, national energy and religious zeal. The specific goal of the daring enterprise was the search for a sea route to India. Arabs in conjunction with Egyptians and Venetians controlled the rich India trade, and there was an old and fervent desire to break that strangle-hold. As Panikkar suggests: "It was the desire to reach Indian waters and share in the spice trade without going across Egypt that provided motive for the high adventure."[13]

What turned this dream into a nightmare for Kerala was its marriage with a militant religious vision and method. Papal bulls (1493 and 1506) had been promulgated, blandly dividing the New World into Portuguese and Spanish hemispheres in the interests of religious conquest, as well as imperial power and commercial advantage. That purpose was clearly evident in the *padroado,* the papal charter granted to the Portuguese.[14] When Vasco da Gama finally landed in Calicut in Malabar (North Kerala) in 1498 in his small but heavily-armed vessel, the *San Gabriel,* he ushered in the era of European dominance in Asia. This was not only a portent for the future of trade, but it was also a religious sign to the nations. It was not long before the sign was fulfilled. There was a brief, almost humorous moment of rapprochement immediately after landing on the shore when da Gama and his followers prayed in a temple, believing they were in a Christian church.[15] But when the Hindu ruler of Calicut, the Zamorin, hesitated to make a trading agreement with the newcomers, and was persuaded by his allies, the Muslim merchants, to oppose their initiatives, da Gama and the Portuguese struck back with a series of sea attacks marked by frequent cruelty. This resulted in the consolidation of Portuguese power in key centers along the Malabar coast.

The religious theory and policy very quickly became explicit. When Pedro Cabral followed da Gama in the second voyage to Malabar (1502), King Manuel of Portugal gave the following instructions (as reported by João de Barros):

In order to persuade these people to accept the truths, the priests and friars were to put before them all natural and legal arguments, and employ ceremonies prescribed by Canon Law. And if these people were stubborn in their errors, and would in no wise accept the tenets of the true faith, denying the law of peace which should unite mankind for the preservation of the human race, and raising difficulties and obstacles to the exercise of trade and commerce, the means by which peace and love among men are established and maintained – for trade is the basis of all human policy—they should in this case be taught by fire and sword and all the horrors of war.[16]

In interpreting the pope's right as reflected in the papal bulls, de Barros further affirms:

The Moors and Gentiles are outside the law of Jesus Christ, which is the true law that everyone has to keep under pain of damnation to eternal fire. If then the soul be so condemned, what right has the body to the privilege of our laws? It is true ... they are reasoning beings and might if they lived be converted to the true faith, but inasmuch as they have not shown any desire as yet to accept this, we Christians have no duties toward them.[17]

It was the redoubtable Alfonso Albuquerque (1453-1515), with his deep hatred for Muslims, who became the living exemplar of that approach. When he captured Goa in 1510, thereby establishing Portuguese power on a strong footing, he sent the following letter to the king of Portugal:

I burnt the city and put all to the sword. . . . Whenever we could find them, no Moor was spared, and they filled the mosques with them and set them on fire. I ordered the farmers and Brahmins to be spared. We counted and found the 6,000 souls of Moorish men and women had been slain. . . . This is the first time that vengeance has been taken in India for the treachery and villainy the Moors have done to your Highness and your people. . . . I am not leaving a single Moorish tomb or building standing, and the men taken alive I have roasted. . . . We took here some Moorish women . . . and some poor fellows wished to marry them and remain in the country. . . . I am handing over the property and lands of the Mosque to the church of St. Catherine, on whose day the Lord gave us the victory on account of her merits, and I am building this Church in the large enclosure of the fortress.[18]

This was the same Albuquerque who conceived a plan to invade Medina, seize the bones of the Prophet Muhammad and hold them in ransom in exchange for the Holy Land!

It seems as though the Crusades were being reborn in southwest India, and the Portuguese did not greatly differentiate in applying their sanctions against those who opposed their will, whether Christian, Muslim or Hindu. This became clear at the Synod of Diamper in 1599 when Archbishop Menzies compelled the Syrian Christians to make public profession and written adherence to the Catholic faith, in the process extirpating their relation with the patriarch of Babylon, burning valuable Syrian manuscripts and books, and placing Malayali Christians under subjection to the Goa

Inquisition. It is perhaps too strong to say, as Dorsey does, that "Christian persuasion was quite the exception in the Portuguese system of conversion, and persecution the almost universal rule."[19] There were some thoughtful attempts at communication, while persuasion through the giving of gifts was a normal procedure,[20] but an atmosphere of antagonism prevailed.

The impact of the Portuguese period, followed by the Dutch, British and French incursions, was far-reaching. Hindu raged against Hindu, the Zamorin of Calicut cooperated with Muslims against Portuguese, while the Raja of Cochin opposed his neighbor. Christians turned against Christians, as the Syrian and Latin traditions struggled and divided.[21] Indigenous Christians, tending to align with the Christian foreigners, became alienated from those who opposed them. Hindus became suspicious of Christians, and the entente between Hindus and Muslims was shattered. Muslims particularly were in a state of distress, as represented by the tragic cries of the famed historian Zein-ud-Dīn in his *Tuḥfat al-Mujahidīn.*[22] There was confusion and trauma; violence was not uncommon. It was only the vital, everyday relations of ordinary Hindus, Muslims and Christians in the towns and villages of Kerala that preserved society from permanent alienation. While not all of the weaknesses in community relations could be laid at the door of the Portuguese, there can be no doubt of the dramatic and deleterious effects of this period, which continued to modern times.

In the course of time the Hindus and foreign Christians achieved a kind of cautious *modus vivendi,* and in the end it was the Muslims who remained in a state of alienation. They were oppressed by the formidable Hindu-Christian combination, now apparently turned against them, and were burdened with economic grievances. These emotions were fired by the intrusion of the *jihād* spirit into their active philosophy, partially as the result of a temporary period of Muslim rule from nearby Mysore. This militant spirit from the north, channelled through the Tipu sultan, now penetrated Mappila psychology. Deeply aggrieved and almost hopeless, the Mappila Muslims reacted in a way that is common to oppressed and despairing people anywhere — severely and often violently. The flame that was kindled in Portuguese days burned furiously throughout the subsequent British period, and Malabar especially became notorious for its communal unrest. Interreligious living in Kerala had become interreligious struggle, and the golden age of harmony was now only a fading memory.

The period from 1500-1921 roughly encompasses this history of deterioration in human relationships, and its lessons are transparent. The most obvious one is that violence in religious interrelationships never solves anything and leaves a heritage of bitterness for generations to come. A second lesson is that interreligious living characterized by the active dominance of one religion is doomed to difficulty. If Kerala is any example, such a situation inevitably produces reactions, usually resulting in abrasive conflicts.

A third, less obvious lesson is that mere co-existence, possibly enforced by some external schoolmaster, such as the British came to be in Malabar, is also not a viable pattern for successful interreligious living. The British took effective control of Malabar for over one hundred fifty years (1792-1947) and enforced an uneasy peace. Hindus and Muslims cautiously co-existed under that hegemony. Yet despite the many fine exceptions that could be noted, it cannot be said that the religious communities were really living *together*. They were co-existing; mere co-existence, however, is essentially a vacuum, which at first opportunity gets filled up with "seven other devils." The century 1821-1921 alone produced a total of fifty-one major Mappila outbreaks.

One final lesson from the experience of this period may be pointed out, namely, the futility of basing relationships on common enmity. This is illustrated by a series of startling events that took place in Malabar from 1919 to 1921. In India as a whole the Hindu-dominated Non-Cooperation Movement, dedicated to the liberating of the nation from foreign rule, and the Muslim-dominated *Khilāfat* Movement, dedicated to the defense of the historic Caliphate in Turkey, were drawn together by their opposition to a common foe—the British. During this period amazing demonstrations of religious amity took place in Malabar. It was only a marriage of convenience, however, with no enduring strength. A variety of unfortunate circumstances soon led to the notorious Mappila Rebellion of 1921, which wound up with Muslims violently attacking and at times forcibly converting Hindus, and Hindus joining with the hated British Christian imperialists to suppress the Muslims. The wheel of history had now fully turned.

So Kerala entered the modern period, the heir of both positive and negative experiences in interreligious living. Individually the people of the area were living together in all sorts of ordinary, pragmatic and healthy day-to-day relationships. Intuitively they also knew that as religious communities they had to find more positive ways of living together than those of the past four centuries, whose memories cast a pervasive pall over societal life. The answer, however, was not clear. Apart from a common sense of humaneness and pragmatic neighborliness, in part drawn from the insights and nourished by the spirit of the religions themselves, nothing had clearly emerged to replace the unifying bonds of commerce that had snapped under pressure. There was no sustained intellectual and emotional effort to isolate and promote a formal principle of action that could be applied to the area of interreligious living. Is the search for such a formal principle arbitrary, artificial and illusory? On the other hand, if it is not possible to identify something stronger than is evident in the long history of Kerala relations, are we then doomed to ongoing forms of conflict? Questions such as these faced Malayalis of Kerala as they began their life in free, post-partition India.

INTERRELIGIOUS LIVING IN KERALA TODAY

An answer to such questions was suggested by the new India.

On the wider Indian scene the great new event since 1947 is nation-building, and this has introduced to the people of India a new and conscious policy related to interreligious living. The nation must be unified and developed, and religious interaction must be seen in that light. While the freedom movement tended to make things less advantageous for Indian Christians, and the partition resulted in serious disadvantages for Indian Muslims, the great leaders of India's independence movement stood for religious respect, a special form of secularism that was value-laden, and the affirmation of minorities as key principles for the new nation. Mahatma Gandhi in effect gave his life for those principles, while Pandit Nehru on his part resisted any suggestions that India should revert to some form of a Hindu raj. With the help of colleagues he succeeded in fashioning it as a secular state, marked by respect for religion in general and equality for all religious expressions.[23]

At the same time, however, India embarked on a determined scheme of national integration, the intention of which was to diminish all social, religious and other differences in the interest of a "larger" principle, namely, the good of the nation. Individual religions were not thereby downgraded; in fact, considerable efforts were taken to ensure their legal protection. But hard edges were to be softened, historical differences brought forward from the Classical and Medieval periods were to be dispelled, and people were to see each other as co-workers in a common cause. Gandhian philosophy was the model for a basic education scheme that expressed in curricular terms the idea that all children were to experience some form of common prayer and praise as part of their individual development and growing together.

Kerala did not remain unaffected by this national impulse. The process of integration in the state was further accelerated by the Aikya Kerala Movement ("United Malayalis in one state!"), which in 1957 resulted in the formation of the present state of Kerala with its linguistic and cultural homogeneity. This development introduced fresh dynamics that supported the principle of integration. The democratic system of government threw together adherents of all religions in a give-and-take legislative process. The state government, the chief Kerala employer, transferred its huge staff every three years, without particular regard for religious affiliation. Development programs of various kinds involved members of one religious persuasion in the service of members of other religious communities. Leaders of all religious communities began throwing their influence into support of the new directions. The revered father of modern Kerala, K. P. Kesava Menon, proposed love of country as the common and binding factor that would overcome communalism. Religious and cultural differences, he said, would remain, but "the consciousness that they are Indians must grow, and in that they should take pride."[24]

The spirit of love for country, encouraged by pragmatic governmental pressures toward national integration—is this the looked for, needed and adequate dynamic for viable interreligious living? Like the economic factor it certainly represents a healthy, powerful influence. There is evidence to suggest, however, that it is not strong enough to prevail when the going gets difficult. Not only has some of the initial excitement and impetus toward integrative programs diminished but, more seriously, in both India as a whole and in the state of Kerala there have been many communal incidents that have seriously disturbed relationships.[25] The development of the crisis in Punjab is perhaps the greatest single indicator that the search for the ultimate dynamic must still go on, even as the proponents of an integrating patriotism continue their efforts.

There are three other factors in contemporary Kerala life that influence developments in interreligious relations. They are secularization, the search for self-esteem, and growing mutual respect.

Secularization or secularism in Kerala has many forms. In general it is characterized by an emphasis on the practical, tangible, material side of life in this world, with lesser value placed on spiritual concerns. As traditional religious allegiance correspondingly declines in importance, the very problem of interreligious living is set aside as a non-issue. One form of this approach is communism, a long-time force in the state, which holds that religion is a private matter and not worthy of struggling about as a formal issue. In Kerala it seeks to solve the "problem" of religion by privatizing it and by lowering the common estimation of its importance in society, if not actually denigrating the subject. While this point of view has brought a new perspective to the question of religious interaction and has helped to soften communal emotions, it fails as a principle for interreligious living because it does not take seriously the subject of religion itself.

The strong desire for community self-esteem is an aspect of the growing sophistication of the population of Kerala, which in turn may be traced to the influence of modernism and education. There is a growing feeling among ordinary people that they do not want to engage any further in the old forms of religious struggle. They believe that the old style militancy and the contentious relationships of the past reflect invidiously on the public image of the particular religion and religious community. In the interest of self-respect, it is felt, such reactions are henceforth to be avoided. This dynamic is felt particularly by the Muslim community in Kerala, a society trying to escape from its inherited reputation for fanaticism, and within the Mappila community it is especially the younger and progressive elements that maintain this view. Christians and Hindus also participate in the thrust for community pride, and community uplift has become a kind of slogan for everyone. What will be the impact of this search for self-esteem on interreligious relations? While the element of community pride has significantly helped, and can further help, to create a peaceful context for religious interaction, it is doubtful whether such an *inner-directed* concern can be considered as the final and effective power for viable interreligious living.

There is something further in Kerala that seems to come closer to that goal. Within the contemporary experience there is clearly visible a fundamental attitudinal change that is perhaps best described as growing mutual respect. The word *respect* may seem prosaic. In Kerala, given its history, the term represents a powerful force that affects a broad range of relationships. There are many overt and documentable signals of this new feeling:

— Muslims picking out universals in the Qur'an and emphasizing them in their literature.
— Muslims speaking words such as these: "In our community living, we have to set aside many misunderstandings, and then we can develop close and affectionate relations with others."
   Or saying this: "Because there will soon be a division between those believing in God on one side and those not on the other, the religions must subdue their differences and stand together."[26]
— Muslims in a Malabar village (Kodur) co-sponsoring a program of Christian songs, together with Christians and Hindus.
— Christians donating funds for the construction of Muslim mosques and orphanages.
— Christians giving employment to Hindus and Muslims in their charitable institutions.
— Hindus describing Muslims as "serious about their faith" instead of the pejorative language of the past.
— Hindus working together with the Muslim League, a Muslim communal organization, in state politics.
— A Hindu (Krishnan) giving his life in a flaming hut to save the children of his Muslim neighbor, in the village of Mannarghat, Palghat District.

The growing respect includes the area of interreligious communication. The élan and sense of mission of the three religions is still vital, and energies and resources continue to be expended on the intentional promotion of the respective faith. The expressions of mission, however, now generally reflect a more sensitive and thoughtful approach, and aggressive militance is uncommon. Change in religious affiliation, though seldom appreciated, is generally condoned when spiritual concerns and conscience are clearly involved. Informal religious communication takes place at an increasingly friendly level, and here and there intellectual leaders of the religious communities have engaged in formal dialogue.

The signals are everywhere, and mutual respect is a powerful force. Is it strong enough? Is this the principle upon which positive interreligious living can be built?

A REFLECTION

Mutual Respect

The element of mutual respect by itself, it may be surmised, is likely to be inadequate to bear the structure of religious harmony. Standing alone, it may be as fragile as other principles. It is also possible to surmise, however, that combined with three other elements, it may achieve the strength given by four pillars. Those elements are the substrate of mutual knowledge, the inlet of motivation, and the outlet of cooperative action.

Mutual Knowledge

Mutual respect must be founded on an educated awareness of other religions. Within Kerala there is a considerable quotient of interreligious knowledge in terms of the practices of the religious traditions, rituals, festivals and the like. But there is little mutual knowledge of the intellectual expressions of the respective religions, and still less of the noble aspects of their artistic and literary heritage. Wherever efforts have been made to set forth these elements with accuracy, fairness and common sympathy, the results have been a tangible increase in respect and understanding.

Motivation

Mutual respect does not grow without an inflow of motivational force. There must be a kind of "I want to" instilled into the process; that is, I want to respect you and therefore I will, even though we may not agree. The possible source of that inflow is known. It is within the power—and regarded by many as an obligation—of the religious leaders of each of the three major religions, within their own terms of reference, to plant an "I want to" seed in the heart of their tradition's adherents. That obligation of the religious leadership is thus far only sporadically accepted and lightly proclaimed in Kerala.

Cooperative Action

Mutual respect must be given an outlet for cooperative action for the general good. Wherever interreligious living is both a necessity and a goal, nothing exceeds the value of bringing people together in common action for the common good.[27] A notable example of such progress in Kerala is its Mahila Samajum organizations, gatherings of women from every segment of society, which are dedicated to practical efforts in life improvement and social uplift.[28]

Is mutual respect, founded on objective knowledge, fed by motivational inspiration and released in cooperative action, the possible principle for positive interreligious living in Kerala? Will it succeed in modifying the heritage of the past and introducing something better? Will it be a force that moves trialogical living and trialogical awareness to a higher plane of steady, meaningful and positive engagement?

A Fifth Pillar

There are those who think that the issue is more profound than anything that has been stated in the above, that in fact there must be a kind of fifth pillar in the midst of the four, and that the ultimate principle to be espoused is *self-giving and for-giving* love. No one in Kerala has made this point better than Khan Bahadur K. Muhammad in his book, *Māppilamār Engottu (Whither the Mappilas?)*. He declares: "When two communities live together, they must forgive much and forget much,"[29] and he calls on his fellow Mappilas to cast out all religious hostility, to cooperate wholeheartedly and trustfully with Hindus, to change the attitude of others by their own behavior, and "to give honor to all." Although he does not use the terms, this distinguished Muslim educator is evidently talking about the principles of self-giving and for-giving love. This is the force that can really throw bridges across the chasms of misunderstanding and alienation, and, K. B. Muhammad might suggest, those who believe that have a lot of bridge-building and bridge-living to do.

Nevertheless, since this widely commended and recognizably salient principle of love may not become an actually operative one in human society, is it perhaps wiser to settle for a penultimate principle that is also worthwhile struggling for and that can be practically advanced? Is that principle mutual respect, joined with educated awareness, motivated understanding and cooperative action? Or is it something else? If it is not the above, what, then, is a sound, sufficiently dynamic and enduring basis for viable interreligious living in Kerala and in a pluralistic world?

The long search must close in on the answer. It seems appropriate to conclude with a line from Sanjayan (d. 1942), a Malayali poet:

നേരമാകുന്നു, നേരമാകുന്നു
നീയെവിടെയെൻ സ്വപ്നമേ?[30]

> It's getting late, it's getting late.
>   Where are you,
>   My dream?

NOTES

1. An example of the opposite of trialogical awareness is represented by Balraj Madhok, *Indianisation* (Delhi: Hind Pocketbook (P) Ltd., 1970). A leader in the Jana Sangh party, he affirms that "there is no such thing as Muslim culture or Christian culture in India. There is only one culture which is common to all India" (pp. 27f.), and he commends Indian Muslims who "continued to follow the Hindu way of life" (p. 53).

2. Hindus make up 82.64 percent of the Indian religious tapestry; Muslims 11.43 percent; and Christians 2.43 percent. These and following statistics are taken

from the *Census of India, 1981*, especially Paper 4 of 1984: "Household Population by Religion of Household," which corresponds to Series C-VII of 1961 and 1971 Census (Delhi: Registrar General, Government of India, 1984).

3. For the treatment of Kerala I have made extensive use of Roland E. Miller, *The Mappila Muslims of Kerala—A Study in Islamic Trends* (Madras: Orient Longman, 1976).

4. Sreedhara Menon, *A Survey of Kerala History* (Kottayam: National Book Stall, 1967), p. 87. Cf. his chapter, "The Confluence of Religions," pp. 87-112.

5. The traditional date cited for the coming of the Jerusalem merchant, Thomas of Cana, is A.D. 345. G. Moraes, *A History of Christianity in India* (Bombay: P. C. Manantala & Sons, 1964), chap. 2, argues strongly for the St. Thomas tradition and provides a convenient summary of the data. L. W. Brown, *The Indian Christians of St. Thomas* (Cambridge: Cambridge University Press, 1956), pp. 43-65, holds that the evidence is inconclusive. For the Nestorian background to the Syrian church of Kerala, see E. Tisserant, *Eastern Christianity in India* (Westminster, MD: Newman Press, 1957), pp. 181ff.

6. Manfred Turlach, *Kerala, Politische-Soziale Strukture und Entwicklung eines Indischen Bundeslades* (Wiesbaden: Otto Harrassowitz, 1970) has an excellent statistical analysis. In 1961, 59 percent of Kerala Christians were Roman Catholic (22 percent Latin Catholic, 36 percent Syrian Catholic); 20 percent were Orthodox Jacobite Syrian; 8 percent were Mar Thoma; 5.5 percent were Church of South India; and 7.5 percent were others.

7. Brown affirms: "They were Christians of Mesopotamia in faith and worship and ethics; they were Indians in all else (p. 2)." Menon observes of Syrian Christians today that they "have completely assimilated themselves in the community in which they live by adopting the language, dress and habits of their Hindu brethren. Though Christians in faith, they are Keralites in all other respects (p. 102)."

8. Cf. Miller, pp. 39-51, for the origin of Muslims in Kerala, and pp. 30-32 for the significance of the name Mappila.

9. K. M. Panikkar, *Malabar and the Portuguese* (Bombay: D. B. Taraporevala Sons, 1929), p. 24.

10. Edgar Prestage, *Alfonso de Albuquerque* (Watford: no. pub., 1929), p. 13; pp. 7-13 provide an excellent evaluation of the extensive Portuguese sources. For the general background to the Portuguese advance, see Charles E. Nowell, *A History of Portugal* (New York: D. Van Nostrandt Co., 1952). Discussions of the Portuguese entry into Kerala include: Alex J. D. Dorsey, *Portuguese Discoveries, Dependencies and Missions in Asia and Africa* (London: Allen & Co., 1893); K. G. Jayne, *Vasco da Gama and His Successors, 1460-1580* (London: Methuen & Co., 1910); F. C. Danvers, *The Portuguese in India*, 2 vols. (London: W. H. Allen & Co., 1894); K. M. Panikkar, op. cit.; R. S. Whiteway, *The Rise of Portuguese Power in India, 1497-1550* (Westminster: Constable & Co., 1899). For Albuquerque see also *The Commentaries of the Great Alfonso Daboquerque* (by his son), trans. W. de Gray Birch from the Portuguese ed. of 1774, vol. 4 (Hakluyt Society, 1884); and H. Morse Stephens, *Albuquerque* (Oxford: Clarendon Press, 1897). Many of the voluminous and often imaginative reports of the Portuguese explorers and administrators are as yet untranslated into English. To be noted are *The Three Voyages of Vasco da Gama*, trans. H. E. J. Stanley from Gaspar Correa's *Lendas da India* (London: Hakluyt Society, 1869). To be preferred is E. G. Ravenstein's translation of Roteico, the only manuscript by one who actually accompanied the voyage, *A Journal of the*

First Voyage of Vasco da Gama (London: Hakluyt Society, 1898). See also Duarte Barbosa, *The Book of Duarte Barbosa,* trans. M. W. Dames, 2 vols. (London: Hakluyt Society, 1918). For Portuguese methodology in religious work see Moraes, op. cit., pp. 121ff.; and for the role of the factory-fortress in extension of commercial, missionary and political influence, see Marcel Caetano, *Colonizing Traditions, Principles and Methods of the Portuguese* (Lisbon: Agencia Geral do Ultramar, 1951), pp. 20ff. For the well-documented decline of Portuguese life and influence, see K. P. P. Menon, *A History of Kerala,* ed. T. K. Krishna Menon, vol. 1 (Ernakulam: Cochin Government Press, 1934-37), pp. 184ff. For Muslim feeling and opposition, cf. Shaykh Zaynu'd-Din, *Tohfut-al-Mujahidin,* trans. S. Muhammad Nainar (Madras: Madras University Press, 1942); and O. K. Nambiar, *The Kunjalis, Admirals of Calicut* (Bombay: Asia Pub. House, 1963). For the Hindu opposition see K. V. Krishna Ayyar, *The Zamorins of Calicut* (Calicut: Norman Publishing Bureau, 1938).

11. Jayne, p. 4. Moraes affirms that "the Portuguese enterprise was thus a crusade against Islam. It was an act of defense against the Muslim menace" (p. 21); he makes the astonishing statement that "the Portuguese dealt a staggering blow to aggressive Islam in India and saved South India for the Hindu religion and culture" (p. 119).

12. Jayne, p. 11.

13. K. M. Panikkar, *India's Contact with the World in the Pre-British Period* (Nagpur: Nagpur University, 1964), p. 67.

14. Danvers, p. xxxvi. Cf. also pp. 21, 39f.

15. Roteico was an eyewitness of this peculiar event. King Manuel's triumphant letter to Ferdinand and Isabella of Spain "concerning the Christian people whom these explorers reached" is also recorded (App. A, p. 114). He declares that "when they have been fortified in the faith, there will be opportunity for destroying the Moors of those parts."

16. Gaspar Correa in R'emy, *Goa, Rome of the Orient,* trans. L. C. Sheppard (London: Arthur Baker, 1957), p. 34; for another translation, cf. H. E. J. Stanley's version in *Three Voyages* (1869), p. 186, fn. 1.

17. Whiteway, p. 21.

18. *Cartas,* I, 26, quoted in Prestage, p. 43.

19. Dorsey, p. 180.

20. Portuguese records frankly reveal the variety of means employed to carry out the mandate of the *padroado.* Moraes, p. 137, reports that after some time outright grants of money in Goa were discontinued in favor of giving rice at the close of the church service. Writing to the king, a Portuguese official suggests (*Documentacão* 1, pp. 212f.): "If your Highness desires that many people should turn Christian, order the same gifts to be given to some of the chief men, because when they are converted, the lower people will emulate their example. This can be negotiated with little trouble, as each one has his price."

21. From 1599 the Syrian Christians were loosely united under the Catholic archbishop. In 1653 a section of the Syrian church broke away from the Portuguese and papal jurisdiction, resumed its independence, established relations with the patriarch of Antioch and became the Jacobite Church, the forerunner of today's Syrian Orthodox Church of Kerala.

22. Shaikh Ahmad Zein-ud-Dīn, *Offering to Jihád Warriors.* Zein-ud-Dīn (1498-1581) belonged to a noted family of Mappila divines, who wrote chiefly in Arabic.

23. Prime Minister Rajiv Gandhi, speaking in the Lok Sabha, 27 February 1986,

summarized the Indian view of secularism: "We are a secular country. But how do we define secularism? Do we define it as 'no religion'? We define it as the right of every religion to co-exist with other religions. We acknowledge that right of co-existence by allowing religions to have their own Personal Laws. It does not reduce our secularism. It is, in fact, a strong constituent of our secularism. It is the basic strength of India that every religion has its own freedom of functioning within our framework and we do not try to suppress or change any religion" (*Muslim India*, no. 39, March 1986, p. 133).

24. K. P. Kesava Menon, "Communal Sound and Fury in Our Land," in *Mathrubhūmi Annual* (Calicut: Mathrubhūmi Pub. Co., 1973), p. 132.

25. Within Kerala, notably Tellicherry in 1971, Trivandrum in 1982 and Nilakkal in 1983. Discussion of communalism and the analysis of communal incidents is an ongoing preoccupation in post-partition India, and the published literature is extensive. There is a current tendency for Christians and Muslims to recognize their mutual interests as minorities. For a convenient survey of the issues, see A. Asghar Engineer, ed., *Communal Riots in Post-Independence India* (Bombay: Sangam Books, 1984).

26. These are paraphrases of oral comments made by Muslims; the other examples cited in this section are drawn from the personal experience of the author.

27. The writer found it somewhat ironic in this connection to have recently discovered notes of an address that he gave in Lebanon in 1972, the final remark being: "My most deeply-felt advice to you is: somehow get interaction between Christians and Muslims in neutral social concerns."

28. An excellent demonstration of the effectiveness of the Mahila Samajum program took place in recent years at Malappuram, a town noted in Malabar history for its division. Christian, Hindu and Muslim women drew together in a determined and united effort toward community uplift that bore remarkable fruits. It should be noted that various Bala Samajums (youth groups) in the state have had a similar effect.

29. Khan Bahadur K. Muhammad, *Māppilamār Engoṭṭu* (Trichur: Mangalodayam [Pvt.], 1956).

30. K. C. Chaitanya, *A History of Malayalam Literature* (New Delhi: Orient Longman Ltd., 1971), pp. 256, 558.

4

Francis Xavier in the Perspective of the Śaivite Brahmins of Tiruchendur Temple

RICHARD F. YOUNG

In the view of M. Dhavamony, a thoughtful Tamilian Roman Catholic, "Śaiva Siddhānta stands closer to Christianity than any other Hindu religious system."[1] Considering how highly this indologically-trained theologian esteems Śaiva Siddhānta, and in recognition of the contribution he has made to a deeper reflection upon it, it seems appropriate to supplement his textual and philological approach with another dimension of understanding the Śaivite-Christian interface. This can be attained by analyzing instances of interaction, at the level of faith and belief, between Śaivites and Christians. One of the earliest surviving records of Śaivite-Christian "dialogue" is that of the Jesuit Francis Xavier with the brahmins of Tiruchendur Temple in the mid-sixteenth century.[2]

How did Francis Xavier and the Hindu brahmins, who had no preconceptions about what interreligious dialogue should be, handle the problems that arose when the Hindu and Christian religions met? The encounter of Xavier with the Tiruchendur brahmins was, as far as we know, a brief one; his letters refer to only one meeting occupying less than a day out of the one year (October 1542–September 1543) that he spent on the Fishery Coast (the eastern tip of Cape Comorin to Vēmbār), where his principal ministry was to the Paravas (or Bharathas). They were a downtrodden people caught in the vortex of vicious competition over the annual Pearl Fishery for which they had traditionally provided skilled manpower in return for a meager share of the proceeds. They had converted to Christianity before Xavier's arrival in exchange for Portuguese protection from their victimizers. During this year Xavier was preoccupied with creating meaningful ecclesiastical life in the twenty or so Parava villages dotting a coastline about a hundred miles long. In the course of pastoral visits he passed by all three major Śaivite temples on the coast—Sucindram in the south, Ramesvaram in the north, and Tiruchendur in the center. There were several occasions when brahmins approached Xavier and voiced complaints. Evidently they were apprehensive about the overall socio-economic implications of his work amongst the Paravas. Only once did he converse with brahmins—who happened to be Śaivites—on matters more pertinent to faith and religion. Xavier's 15 January 1544 account of the Fishery Coast includes a summary of this discussion,[3] which occurred between April and September 1543 at a certain temple, which may be identified as Tiruchendur in the present-day Tinnevely District, Tamil Nadu. What happened is that Xavier, who was in the temple grounds, put several questions to the brahmins he met there. Unsatisfied, he proclaimed the gospel and was "applauded." They then proceeded to question him. Lastly, when exhorted to become Christians, they declined. Each phase in the encounter is more than merely the constituent part of a relatively unimportant episode in the life of an outstanding Jesuit missionary. Unfolded, they reveal features that are symptomatic of Hindu-Christian dialogue.

In reconstructing this encounter our approach will necessarily be largely conjectural. In the first place, Xavier may have been subject to the unconscious distortion called devout partiality—a problem that imposes limitations on using early Jesuit documents as historical sources. There are no contemporary Śaivite accounts of the meeting, as far as we know. S. Neill has written that Christianity in India has hardly ever been more than a ripple upon its placid surface,[4] and of no other era was that more apt than of these years when Christianity was not yet widely recognized as a religion. The absence of any Śaivite reference to this encounter thus comes as no surprise. As for the letter itself, it has an element of authenticity when Xavier reports what the Tiruchendur brahmins said. It is entirely lacking in the standard Westernized summations of Hinduism, such as one finds in the letters of Robert de Nobili (1577–1656), whose knowledge of Hinduism was infinitely greater. The very originality of what Xavier attributes to the Śaivites in some sense validifies itself. According to Schurhammer-Wicki, the questions addressed to Xavier were: 1) Does the soul die with the body as it does in the case of brute beasts? 2) Where does the soul of man go after death? 3) When a person sleeps and dreams, is he in the same place with his friends and relatives, or does the soul go there and cease to inform the body? 4) Is God black or white? Doubtless these were not exact translations of what Xavier heard—he had no capacity to understand Tamil of more than elementary difficulty—and yet one can detect therein elements reflective of *Pati* (Master or Lord), *Paśu* (Soul) and *Pāśa* (Bond), the three core categories of Śaiva Siddhānta devotion.

ON THE FISHERY COAST

"These brahmins have barely a tincture of learning," Xavier wrote, "but they make up for their poverty of learning by cunning and malice."[5] If the

Fishery Coast brahmins deserved such censure—the disreputable brahmin is a not uncommon theme in Indian literature—Xavier was hardly in a position to judge. It was, of course, partly the fault of the brahmins that the Paravas turned to Christianity, just as neglect had compelled under-privileged castes elsewhere in India to embrace Islam. But putting aside his moral indictment of them, how just was it of Xavier to depict them as unlearned in view of the fact that he neither understood Tamil nor had a better-than-superficial acquaintance with Hinduism? Xavier appears never to have grasped the importance of learning Tamil himself—though he encouraged other Jesuits to do so—and virtually everything he said had to be mediated through assistants who may have been Tamil-speaking Malayalis.

Toward Hinduism he evinced a "relentless hostility" acquired in Goa, where he tacitly approved of the "Rigor of Mercy," as the Portuguese policy of Christianizing the Goan islands was known.[6] It was during the voyage to the coast that he first came into contact with Hinduism in the mixed Luso-Indian port town of Calicut and Cochin in Malabar. He had more time to become acquainted with Hinduism in Tuticorin where he spent four months. Although it was here that he and his assistants busied themselves with rendering into Tamil the catechism of which more will be said below, Hinduism cannot have escaped his attention. If one can infer from the letters of his Jesuit companions, it was the gods depicted in animal form that fixed in Xavier's mind an image of Hinduism: Nandin the reclining bull, Hanumān the ape-god and fat-bellied Puleyār with his elephant trunk.[7] During the 1540s missionaries paid little attention to Hinduism beyond that which offended them. But, as in language acquisition, so in the study of religion, this was to change, though not before Xavier's encounter with the brahmins of Tiruchendur.[8]

TEMPLE AND CATHEDRAL

Situated on a sandstone bluff overlooking the sea, Tiruchendur is dedicated to Skandha, second son of Śiva, called Murukan in Tamil, or, within the temple precincts, Subrahamanya. Iconographically his principal image is the six-faced Ārumuga Perumāl. In the inner sanctum he sits astride his peacock mount, brandishing in his twelve hands the sword, discus, noose and other symbols of divinity. Had Xavier been able to enter the sanctum, he would have been struck by the absence of tranquility in the sense to which he was accustomed in Europe; he would have experienced the buzz of conversation between adults, the chatter of children, the cacophony of cymbals, bells, drums and chanting when the deity is awakened, washed and fed. The sensual impact of camphor, incense and flowers would have been potent. The excited emotionality exhibited by devotees of Subrahamanya would have heightened the effect.[9] But that Xavier, who had been visiting a Christian Parava village on the outskirts of Tiruchendur, could have entered the sanctum even if he had wanted is doubtful. The brahmins who came to meet him would understandably have been concerned about why he had come even as far as the outer precincts. They must have heard that the Paravas were smashing, trampling and spitting upon their "idols" with Xavier's benign, if not active, encouragement. It is possible, therefore, that they intended to intercept him before he reached the zone where his presence would have threatened the purity of the sanctum. Had he gone that far, the image and its surroundings would have been defiled. Such an act would not only have been sacrilegious but would also have necessitated expensive and time-consuming purificatory rituals. If the sanctum had been closed to pilgrims for cleansing, the loss of revenue would have been damaging. In order to obviate such an eventuality, there had traditionally been (until the Temple Entry Act of 1939) "differential limits on permitted proximity to the central sancta" of Hindu temples.[10] Individuals were permitted only as close as their purity allowed, brahmins the closest while untouchables, such as the Paravas, were not allowed in at all. Enforced with rigor in the Tamil region, such rules reflected the brahmin–non-brahmin distinction that has always been an irritant in Tamil society. By extension, the same restrictions would have applied to Xavier, a barbarian *(mleccha),* who as such was debarred by the classical religio-legal texts from entering temples.[11]

Simply by being in the vicinity of the sanctum, Xavier, without realizing it, was endangering a complex of ideas centered on the Tamil concept of the temple, "a refuge from reality," its perimeters demarcating "a zone of total purity. . . outside the corrupt dimension of time."[12] This was the Kali Yuga, the age when barbarians propagating false and delusory doctrines were believed to be infiltrating temples such as Tiruchendur. It would be no surprise if Xavier's presence had aroused alarm; he might be an agent of yugic corruption. Just being there was derogatory to the brahmins whose preeminence was unchallenged and disruptive to Hindus engaged in devotional activities. More will be said of this notional complex later. Here we simply note that Xavier had no eligibility to be there at all, having not been born a Hindu. For, although it is generally not a principle of the Christian religion to exclude non-Christians from churches, it is a principle of Hinduism — recognized under the "secular" constitution of India — to exclude non-Hindus from temple sancta.[13] No matter how well the subsequent dialogue might have gone, Xavier would nonetheless have been denied the prerogatives in the sanctum to which Hindus are entitled: *darśana,* a "view" of the deity as manifested in the image, to receive its grace *(prasāda),* and to pass his hand through the camphor flame after it had been waved before Subrahmaṇya. In view of this, he would have had no grounds to complain, supposing he had been aware that the sanctum was out of bounds to one like himself.

THE BRAHMINS

Symptomatic of Xavier's ignorance was his application of the undifferentiated category "brahmin" to all such individuals whom he knew. One therefore cannot be sure precisely whom he met at Tiruchendur. The pilgrims probably included Aiyyars and other brahmins of non-priestly subcastes. But the delegation that greeted — or confronted — him is more likely to have consisted of male priests *(arcakas)* and servants *(paricārakas)* of the Ādiśaiva brahmins who are consecrated to serve Śiva. The Ādiśaivas ("first Śaivas") are internally differentiated and ranked depending on whether the pilgrims they engage as clients are brahmins and if they perform funerary rites. The status of the Ādiśaivas vis-à-vis other brahmins is a complex issue. Here it need only be noted that priestly brahmins are generally considered inferior by other brahmins — though usually not by other castes — due to the pollution derived from contact with non-brahmins and also perhaps to the notoriety they have of being ritualists ignorant of the traditions entrusted to them. Although it is often assumed that brahmins, whoever they are, can take their preeminence in South India for granted, the Ādiśaivas were — according to anthropologists, still are — uneasy about their status and prerogatives. They claim they are descended from a line of five sages who emerged from the five-faced *Sadāśiva* (Eternal Śiva), but this is not taken seriously by other brahmins, and the Hindu legal tradition generally confirms that temple priests belong to a degraded rank of brahmins.[14] It is nonetheless true, according to the same tradition, that, like other brahmins, the Ādiśaivas are imbued with the highest divinity even if ignorant and must not be despised (Manu 9:317-19). Even before he stepped into the temple precincts, Xavier had made it clear that he would not defer to their preeminence — whether *de jure* or *de facto* — about which they may already have been defensive.

The pious but simpleminded brahmin who is more dear to God than those who take pride in being learned, is a familiar motif in Śaivite devotional literature. It is particularly evident in the local legend-book, the *Tiruccĕntūrppurāṇam,* written by one Vĕnṟimālaikkavirāyar, who composed it some fifty years after Xavier's visit (presumably on the basis of a Sanskrit original then existing) to celebrate the divine theophany at Tiruchendur. Explaining why the temple occupies a significant place in the sacred topography of India, the purāna says that Tiruchendur's greatness stems from the characteristic Ādiśaiva brahmin (known as *Tirucutantirar*) who dwells there, exemplified by the poet himself, who had been a mere servant, although one whose devotion had melted the heart of the deity he adored. Vĕnṟimālaikkavirāyar was a cook in the temple kitchens because he had no aptitude for remembering the Sanskrit prayers and formulas that had to be memorized if an Ādiśaiva were to be entrusted with prestigious functions within the temple or with the conduct of worship on behalf of pilgrims inside the sanctum. One day he became so rapt in meditation that he neglected to prepare the symbolic meal presented daily to Subrahmaṇya. Dismissed from his humble office by the other more learned but heartless brahmins, he threw himself into the ocean but was carried back to shore where Murukaṇ now stood. Told that his time to die had not come because he alone was able to compose in Tamil the praise of Tiruchendur, he protested that he was insufficiently learned for such a task. But when he assented, he was "overcome by a flood of poetry," in consequence of which he was granted the title King of Poets Having a Garland of Victory (Vĕṉṟimālaikkavirāyar), proving that the kitchen-attendant could not be such a simpleton as everyone had supposed.[15]

Xavier committed a similar mistake in underestimating the Tiruchendur brahmins, for the questions they put to him indicate that they were more learned than he thought. Indeed, what they asked of him was intended to determine how learned *he* was. Brahminical religion in South India was accustomed to interreligious challenges like this. The Śaivites had in turn struggled with Materialists, who denied the existence of God and soul; Buddhists, who rejected caste distinctions; and the Jains, who disputed the efficacy of sacrifice. In consequence, a militant, sectarian and apologetically sophisticated ideology became dominant in the Śaivite tradition. Shulman observes, "In the hagiographies of the poet-saints . . . one sees the *bhakti*-hero intervening again and again against the politically or socially powerful heretics in order to save the threatened Hindu community and its precarious ideas."[16] Xavier was, as noted, not yet well understood to be something called Christian, but it was obvious that he was a politically and socially powerful individual committed to a different social — and *ipso facto* religious — *dharma* (truth or teaching) that was inimical to their own, as that of the Materialists, Buddhists and Jains had been. In wanting to determine where he stood in relation to these heresies, the Tiruchendur brahmins acted in conformity with the claim of Śaiva Siddhānta to be "the final authority, the terminus of religio-philosophical thought,"[17] which presupposes that other religions, sects or schools can be classified into the outermost, outer, inner and innermost, insofar as they approximate Śaiva Siddhānta. In this gradualist scheme of subordination, Materialism, Buddhism and Jainism are in the lowest category because they reject the Vedas and Śaiva Ágamas as authoritative. This model of orthodoxy was utilized before Xavier, but the sixteenth century was a period when it was being more highly refined by the systematist Śivāgrayogin. The Tiruchendur brahmins would have been familiar with it, and what they asked Xavier was formulated with precision in terms of the Śaiva Siddhānta test of doctrinal orthodoxy.

LA GLORIA

Unsurprisingly, the Tiruchendur dialogue did not get off to a good start. The brahmins were ill-prepared for the question that Xavier abruptly posed, and he was unable to comprehend their response to his question: "In order to gain eternal life (*la gloria*), what have your gods and idols told you to do?" To this they reacted with consternation, and after a dispute over who should reply, an aged brahmin was pushed forward, saying that

Xavier ought first to answer his own question. This might have been evasive, as Xavier supposed. It could just as well have been a refusal to dispute theological points with an intruder until it had become clear whether he denied the authority (*pramāṇatva*) of the Veda — a reluctance to debate on other grounds would be consistent with the stance taken by Hindu traditionalists in contemporary India.[18] But Xavier pressed the man, and this, in effect, is what he said: The Gods have given two commands to be observed by those who wish to enter their abode: 1) they should not kill cows, for they are worshipped; and 2) they should give alms to the brahmins who serve in temples. Here, indeed is a classic instance of the priority of orthopraxy over orthodoxy in Hinduism.

Xavier, who detested the images of divinities in the shape of animals that he had seen during the journey south and in Tuticorin, reacted strongly when the brahmin referred to the sanctity of the cow. But why had the subject been raised in the first place? It is unlikely that Xavier had entered the temple wearing leather. He did possess a leather mantle for protection from the sun, but seems not to have used it on the coast, and indications are that he went barefoot there as he did in Travancore. Neither did his spartan diet include beef. The Portuguese living along the coastline did, however, eat beef, and the constantly recurring instances of cow slaughter must have horrified the Hindu community just as it did across the continent in the Maratha homelands where Śivājī (1627-80) would inculcate cow protection as a cardinal virtue along with the veneration of brahmins. This point was probably raised to express repugnance at the ritually defiling conduct of the Europeans and to protest an act that was offensive to Hindu sentiment. Xavier's *dharma*, in short, was being judged by its attitude toward the cow. Mistreatment of cows was to the Tiruchendur brahmins no less an abomination than idolatry was to Xavier. Tension over this matter continued, and in 1590 the sanctum of their temple was desecrated by the butchering of a cow by Portuguese in retaliation for an attack on the village of Christian Paravas to whom Xavier had been ministering when this dialogue took place.[19]

In raising the topic of donations — the Ādiśaivas of Tiruchendur being the implied recipients — the brahmin reinforced the bias Xavier already had, that they were deficient in theological knowledge, crafty, malicious and intent on bilking their credulous clients of all their worth. But the Paravas, who had suspended their pearl-offerings to Tiruchendur when they became Christians, must have precipitated a financial crisis for the temple treasury, and resentment over this was then directed at Xavier.[20] More than petty economic jealousy must have been involved, however, because in theory brahmins have no source of income other than the gifts of the faithful. They might well have thought, therefore, that Xavier was denying their residual right to property owned by other castes, a legal principle tradition affirmed (Manu 1:100-01) in light of the fact that it was thanks to their benevolence that others prospered.

Xavier was probably displeased with this beginning to their dialogue because, instead of a definitive doctrinal statement on the subject of salvation according to Hinduism that he could then have tried to refute, the brahmin answered in terms of what Hindus *do* rather than what they *believe*, as if the content of faith did not matter. That is, to be a Hindu Xavier assumed one must believe in certain propositions, and he was disappointed to find that there was no such theological component in what the brahmin said. From their perspective Xavier's approach must have been equally baffling. Having suddenly gotten into discussion with an individual whose presence in the temple was proof that proper conduct meant little to him, but that doctrinal matters did, the brahmins could well have been reminded that the Materialist, Buddhist and Jain heresies likewise made light of normative social behavior and quarreled with Hinduism on theoretical grounds instead.

WARMING UP

What next happened violates every *sine qua non* of interreligious dialogue as contemporarily understood and yet may have been precisely what had to happen before the Tiruchendur brahmins could acknowledge that Xavier was a deeply religious individual. Had he not been impatient, the discussion that had just begun could have become profoundly enlightening as to the kind of religion Hinduism is. But, imperiously signalling the brahmins to seat themselves, he began to recite in Tamil the Apostles' Creed, Decalogue and a sermon translated by his Tuticorin collaborators. In view of the difficulty he must have had in approximating correct Tamil pronunciation on the basis of the romanized text he had memorized, we may suppose that a Tamil-speaking assistant repeated what he said for the sake of clarity. The original has not survived, but we know it retained Portuguese words for Christ, Holy Spirit, grace, heaven and perhaps even for God, soul, and spirit.[21] The Tamil itself was hopelessly vitiated, and of this Xavier became aware only after the Tiruchendur episode. Of Xavier's homily there is no information, except that it concerned what being a Catholic means. Probably it was a pastiche of hortatory prayers he had used in Goa, such as the following: "You, my God, have made me to your likeness, and not the *pagodas* idols, which are the gods of the heathen in the form of irrational cattle and beasts of the devil. I renounce all *pagodas*, magicians, and soothsayers because they are the slaves and friends of the devil."[22] We find here, in short, all that would make a specialist in dialogue cringe.

Despite mispronunciation and mistranslation, what, if anything, did Xavier convey to the Tiruchendur brahmins? Nothing, if doctrinal criteria matter—and they did to him—as will become evident. He might as well have not spoken at all in view of how his audience began to question him as if he denied the very beliefs he had publicly professed. It was evident, however, that he believed in something fervently and was ardently trying to tell them what it was. This underlines the importance of the "human nexus" in dialogue, which is not between religions as such, but rather between persons who are religious. One cannot, therefore, ignore the way Xavier's personality loomed over the relationships in which he became involved. His passion for whatever he was saying may then be the key to the startling response that the Tiruchendur brahmins made, for Xavier says that when he finished they applauded him (*"Y me dieron grandes abrazos"*). This may be overstated, but the dynamics of the situation would be misconstrued if one were to doubt that some gesture of approbation or encouragement was proffered. Somehow Xavier's ardor *did* stir them. Here, then, is a breakthrough: fervor was a quality they could appreciate. They sensed that the *dharma* about which he was excited could not have been as radically pessimistic or inimical to the emotional life of Hindusim as were the austere ideals of the Jains and Buddhists.[23] It would be too much, however, to say that the Tiruchendur brahmins recognized Xavier as a *bhakta* (devotee) of some unknown deity. First they had to establish that he was not something as "bad" as a Jain or Buddhist—a Materialist masquerading as a theist.

NOT BY HUMAN ARGUMENTS

Being disputatious, Xavier left the Tiruchendur brahmins no other alternative than to view him as an opponent or, in his own terms, a "pagan" or "heathen." However fervently held, his beliefs had to be tested and, if necessary, refuted so that godlessness and heresy, which abounded in the Kali Age, would not infiltrate the shrine where the *siddhānta*, the final truth, finds refuge. Unknown to him, he was about to be interrogated to ascertain how closely his beliefs approximated that of the *bête noire* of Hinduism, the sect of the *Cārvaka,* or Materialists. Incredible as this suspicion might seem, it was standard procedure in Śaiva Siddhānta—and in the Indian apologetical tradition as a whole—to work inward from the outermost perimeter of orthodoxy to the center. It would, moreover, have been surprising if the Tiruchendur brahmins had not noticed a disturbing parallel between Xavier's criticisms of Hinduism and the polemic traditionally associated with Materialism: "The Veda is tainted by the three faults of untruth, self-contradiction, and tautology . . . and the Vedas themselves are simply the means of livelihood for those devoid of wit and virility."[24] Xavier's anti-brahminical bias has already been noted. As for being anti-Vedic, it would be anachronistic to say that he was, in light of the fact that the European discovery of the Veda had not yet occurred. There nonetheless was, in the argument based on natural reason that he utilized—"Even though," as he wrote in retrospect, still underestimating the intellectual capacity of the Tiruchendur brahmins, "the rational grounds which must be used with the uneducated cannot be as subtle as those found in the writings of the teachers in universities"[25]—a speculative *(tārkika)* tendency suggestive to his audience of another characteristic of the *Cārvaka* sect, indeed synonymous with it, *yuktimadvacana,* "words of [human or speculative] reason," devoid of *pramāṇatva,* the authoritativeness of revelation.[26]

With their initial question, "Does the soul die with the body as it does in the case of brute beasts?" the Tiruchendur brahmins were asking whether Xavier was like the *dehātmavādin,* the *Cārvaka* who denied the existence of a soul (*ātman*) independent of the body (*deha*)—the first of two classical varieties of Materialism demolished in the opening chapter of Aruḷnanti's *Śivañāna Cittiyār* (ca. A.D. 1253). According to the *Cārvaka* caricatured in this widely-known commentary on Tamil Śaivism, perception (*pratyakṣa*), the one source of valid knowledge acknowledged by him, can affirm only that the four elements (earth, water, fire, air) and their respective qualities (smell, taste, form, touch) interact in such a manner that from their union arises consciousness, like the reddish saliva in the mouth of someone chewing betel leaf, areca nut and lime. If one element is separated from the rest, consciousness vanishes.[27] The next question, "Where does the soul of man go after death?" was one that Xavier enthusiastically addressed, but in so doing missed the point, which had less to do with heaven and hell than with the contention of the Materialists that a transmigrating, auto-luminous soul can be postulated only on the basis of an invalid analogy, or, as the saying went, "Can the light still shine when the wick burns out?" Not yet off the hook, but having evidently passed the initial test, Xavier had now to answer whether he might not like the *sūkṣmadehātmavādin,* the second variety of Materialists mentioned in the *Cittiyār,* quite different from the first in that they acknowledged the existence of a soul separate from the corporeal body (*sthūlaśarīra*) but confused with the subtle (*sūkṣma*) body. This entity cannot be the *ātman,* according to Aruḷnanti, because it consists of the five vital breaths (*prāṇa*), the organs of thought (*manas*), knowledge (*jñānendriyas*) and action (*karmendriyas*), which the soul inhabits during dreams (*svapna*) and transmigration when experiencing the repercussions of its karma. Without this context one could only wonder how Xavier responded to the third question: "When a person sleeps and dreams is he in a place with his friends and relatives, or does the soul go there and cease to inform the body?" Compounding its difficulty, this question appears to presuppose not only that dreams are morally cathartic but epistemologically real instead of illusory, as would generally be assumed.[28] In any event, to satisfy the Tiruchendur brahmins, he would have had to say that something other than the subtle body must account for the fact that upon waking one is able to say, "I saw a dream" or "I did not dream," that is, the soul. Again, Xavier missed the point.

The anti-*Cārvaka* apologetic of the Śaivite tradition cannot so easily account for the fourth and last question, "Is your God black or white?" which was, as it were, a priestly way of raising the issue of whether God has form (*uruvam* [Skt. *rūpa*], a multivalent term that means either shape or color, would have been appropriate in such a context). Materialism was a concern not only of philosophers but also of servants in temples—the

Tiruchendur brahmins were—which the *Cārvaka* dishonored by ridiculing the nature of God as understood in Tamil Śaivism: "If you say God is *arūpī* (formless), then he is unknowable like the open space (*ākāśa*). If He is *rūpī* (form), then he is one of the five elements of the world. If He is *rūpārūpī* (formless form) . . . can you suspend a stone in the sky?"[29] The *Cārvaka* diatribe did influence Śaivite theology in that to counteract it the *Cittiyār* clarifies that God's manifestations are immaterial, the product of *śakti* (power), not *māyā* (appearance), the material evolute. If this was what the Tiruchendur brahmins were driving at, the point was lost on Xavier, who commented in the strongest possible terms on the "frightful stench" of their ghee-smeared "idols."[30]

Before Xavier killed their interest in what he was saying by criticizing the sanctity of the temple—in consequence of which they predictably declined his invitation to become Christians—the brahmins may have realized that Xavier was not indifferent to religion, unlike the archetypal *Cārvaka*, who says, "The only liberation is the dissolution of the body." His impressive zeal should again be taken into account; it may have cleared away doubts his "words of human wisdom" had raised. If so, they may actually have been asking how he thought God leads the fettered soul to liberation. Given the unknowability of the divine nature, as Aruḷnanti taught, God must reveal himself to his *bhakti* in bodily form.[31] They had in mind not an impersonal Upaniṣadic Absolute, but a deity who, though transcending the universe, is immanent in a particular place, Tiruchendur, where the localization of the divine presence guaranteed rewards for the pilgrims who worshiped there.[32] Being themselves dedicated to the service (*cārya*) of God, they have perhaps heard in what Xavier was saying a resonance of *bhakti* and wondered in which *rūpa*-form the deity to whom he ministered had been manifested: a green like the *mūrti* (image) of Mīnākṣī at Madurai, dark, white or, as at other Tamil shrines, in other hues.[33] A colorless God, so to speak, would not do at Tiruchendur, just as a philosophical abstraction would not do in Christian faith. But the doctors of theology in Europe had not equipped Xavier—to whom, against all expectation, an opportunity to enter the sanctum of Śaivite faith had gradually unfolded—to think of Hindu "Gentiles" except as simpletons, on whom even natural reason was ineffective. It was on the basis of this misunderstanding of the Tiruchendur experience that the Abbé Dubois (1765-1848), missionary in the carnatic and later director of the Missions Étrangères in Paris, wrote discouragingly of India: "The disappointment and want of success of Xavier ought to have been sufficient to damp the most fervent zeal of persons disposed to enter the same career. When a man of his temper, talents and virtue had been baffled in all his endeavours to introduce Christianity into India, his successors could scarcely flatter themselves with the hope of being more fortunate."[34]

GOD AND *THE* GOD

If Xavier did not genuinely care what the brahmins believed, how had the Śaivite *mahāchārya* (great teacher) Aruḷnanti predisposed them toward him as the devotee of a different God? An Indocentric, sectarian attitude toward non-Śaivites can be inferred from the *Cittiyār*: The soul "wends its way through numberless transmigrations until it is born in the land where the Vedas and Śaivāgamas are taught. The path then leads from the outermost religions through the outer, from the inner to the innermost, until the soul is finally born within the Siddhānta fold itself."[35] Restricting salvific potentiality to one variety of Hinduism, into which individuals are born after acquiring a karmic eligibility in lesser sects and religions of Indian origin, was a common apologetic motif that was later extended to explicitly include Christianity.[36] Karmic anomalies occur, but presumption was against the possibility that Xavier was entitled or competent to teach them anything; nor were his interpreters, who were an affront to Hindu sentiment, which tolerates non-traditional ideas if the source is unequivocally brahmin.[37] The *Cittiyār* also claims to comprehensively include, rectify, and supplement the conflicting and partial truths of other teachings.[38] The brahmins would therefore not have reacted well had they known the *rūpa*-form of Xavier's God was similar to the avatars of Vishnu that the Siddhānta had already rejected: "It is sheer blasphemy even to suggest that (Śiva) can be . . . subject to births and deaths that whirl round and round . . . in the ocean of saṃsāra till they attain beatitude."[39] Despite this, the *Cittiyār* offers a basis for conditionally affirming Xavier's faith in Jesus Christ, an *a fortiori* karmic and samsaric deity: "Creator of heaven and earth" (Śiva survives the dissolution of the cosmos when Brahma, Vishnu and Rudra, its creator, preserver and destroyer, are reabsorbed into *māyā*) of whom the Tamil catechism said: "conceived," "born," "suffered," "crucified," "died," "descended into hell," "ascended into heaven":[40] *bhakti* directed to other deities is upgrading to man *but* downgrading to God; Xavier's faith is functionally equivalent to theirs, but the highest, most efficacious worship is offered to Śiva.[41]

PRAEPARATIO DIABOLICA

Indicative of profound changes in religion since Xavier strode into the shrine of Subrahmaṇya is that Christians are reconsidering whether salvation is Christocentric or theocentric. The eternal (*sanātana*) religion, Hinduism, also faces the problem of continuity. Neo-Hinduism has arisen, abandoning the *extra Vedos nulla salus* dogma, as did the Vatican its teaching on salvation outside the Church. A loss of confidence in argumentative approaches to existential matters of faith lying beneath consciousness and rational thought has generated an ambience different from what prevailed then. Tiruchendur is not, however, discontinuous with the present. There is a legacy in "the human nexus" — as evidenced by unending quarrels over the conversion of underprivileged castes — and a lingering uncertainty as to whether Christianity might not be a variant of Materialism — a suspicion not as clearly voiced but as persistent as the parallel notion that Hindus become Christians only if offered material inducements. Occasionally in the folk milieu, no more plausible explanation of the supposed decline of Hinduism has suggested itself than a resurgence of the *Cārvaka* who have corrupted morality and made the population karmically vulnerable to Christianity.[42] Of more philosophical concern is why Christians neglect to discriminate—like the *sūkṣmadehātmavādin*—between the *ātman* and *jīvātman*, the psycho-physical apparatus it ensouls.[43] Also symptomatic of the image of Christianity is a forensic medium of religious discourse reminiscent of *yuktimadvacana*, the Materialist's love of argument for its own sake. No doubt the discovery that Christian faith might be more than this—indeed that Christianity *is* a religion—was made more difficult than it had to be by Xavier and other generations of missionaries who disregarded the Abbé Dubois' advice and repeated the mistakes of Tiruchendur all over India. The other side of the coin is that one should not idealize a pristine equanimity among religions that were in perfect harmony until Xavier came to Tiruchendur. The local purāṇa cites a victory over the Jains, less celebrated but as triumphant as that of the Śaiva saint Tiruñāṇacampantar at Madurai.[44] The Tamils were accustomed to this kind of ferment; diatribe, polemics, apologetics and dialogue contributed profoundly to Śaiva Siddhānta's understanding of itself. On a larger scale, one can say the *Sanātana Dharma* is still with us, despite Materialists, Jains, Buddhists and Christians, whose arrival is but as yesterday. It was in this same dynamic and complex process of survival and self-transcendence that Christianity won recognition as a religion in its own right—a phase, as it were, of religious accreditation that had to occur before dialogue could be conceived—and in which Hinduism acknowledged as religious those individuals from whom it expected the least evidence of faith.

NOTES

1. Mariasusai Dhavamony, *Love of God According to Śaiva Siddhānta: A Study in the Mysticism and Theology of Śaivism* (Oxford: Oxford University Press, 1971), p. 378.

2. See Nicholapillai Maria Saverimuttu, "Relations Between Roman Catholics and Hindus in Jaffna, Ceylon, 1900-1926" (Ph.D. diss., University of London, 1978). The present writer is researching the period preceding 1900 in Jaffna.

3. Georg Schurhammer and Josef Wicki, ed., *Epistolae S. Francisci Xaverii* 1 (Rome: 1944-45), pp. 171-73.

4. Stephen Neill, *A History of Christianity in India* 1 (Cambridge: Cambridge University Press, 1984), p. 63.

5. Henry James Coleridge, trans., *The Life and Letters of St. Francis Xavier* (London: Burns and Oates, 1881), p. 158.

6. Neill, p. 143.

7. Georg Schurhammer, *Francis Xavier: His Life and Times* 1 (Rome: The Jesuit Historical Institute, 1977), pp. 304-6.

8. Jarl Charpentier, ed., *The Livro de Seita dos Indios Orientais* (Uppsala: Almqvist and Wiksell, 1933), pp. xxxviii, xliii.

9. This description, actually based on observations of the Mīnākṣī Temple in Madurai, is from C. J. Fuller, *Servants of the Goddess: The Priests of a South Indian Temple* (Cambridge: Cambridge University Press, 1984), p. 5.

10. Ibid. p. 42.

11. Ibid. p. 190.

12. David Shulman, "The Enemy Within: Idealism and Dissent in South Indian Hinduism," in *Orthodoxy and Dissent in India,* ed. by S. N. Eisenstadt et al. (Berlin: Mouton, 1984), pp. 12-13.

13. J. D. D. Derrett, "Examples of Freedom of Religion in Modern India," *Contributions to Asian Studies* 10 (1977): 42-51.

14. Fuller, pp. 49ff.

15. David Shulman, *Tamil Temple Myths: Sacrifice and Divine Marriage in the South Indian Śaiva Tradition* (Princeton: Princeton University Press, 1980), pp. 34-37.

16. Shulman, "The Enemy Within," p. 12.

17. John Piet, *A Logical Presentation of the Śaiva Siddhānta Philosophy* (Madras: Christian Literature Society, 1952), p. 2.

18. Agehananda Bharati, *Hindu Views and Ways and the Hindu-Muslim Interface* (Santa Barbara: Ross-Erikson, 1981), p. 74.

19. Schurhammer, p. 296.

20. In 1557 a drought in the vicinity of Tiruchendur was blamed on the Parava Christians, who no longer contributed to the financial upkeep of the temple. Ibid. p. 321.

21. Ibid. p. 308.

22. Ibid. p. 221.

23. Cf. Shulman, "The Enemy Within," p. 35.

24. Wendy Doniger O'Flaherty, "The Origin of Heresy in Hindu Mythology," *History of Religions* 10 (1977): 275.

25. Schurhammer, p. 357.

26. Natural reason, from the standpoint of Indian logic, would be categorized as *anumāna* (inference), the validity of which Materialism denied. Presumption was against Xavier, not on grounds of inference as such but on its independence from the Veda and Śaivite Āgamas.

27. J. M. Nallaswami Pillai, *Śiva Jñāna Siddhiyār of Arulnandi Śivāchārya* (Madras: Meykandan Press, 1913), pp. 10-11.

28. A scriptural basis for the realist view of dreams was found in the *Bṛhadāraṇyaka Upaniṣad* (4.3.10: "There no chariots exist. . . . Then he produces chariots.") How common this position was in Śaiva Siddhānta cannot be confirmed. Cf. the interpretation of Rāmānuja: "When someone lying in his (bed-)chamber dreams that he goes off in the body to another place, there to be crowned king or have his head chopped off, these experiences, which are the fruits of merit or demerit, are made possible by the (Lord's) production of another (i.e., dream) body similar in configuration to the recumbent one." See Julius Lipner, *The Face of Truth: A Study of Meaning and Metaphysics in the Vedāntic Theology of Rāmānuja* (Albany: State University of New York Press, 1986), pp. 56-62.

29. Nallaswamy, *Śiva Jñāna Siddhiyār,* p. 12.

30. I am grateful to Professor Paul Younger of McMaster University for the suggestion that the question, "Is your God black or white?" may refer to deities grouped under the Tamil word *māl* (black), revered mainly by Vaiṣṇavas, and to

deities designated *tāl* (white or red), venerated mostly by Śaivas. If so, the purport of the question would be, "Are you a Vaiṣṇava or a Śaiva?" This intriguing solution cannot be discounted, but in view of how the discussion has developed along the lines of the anti-*Cārvaka* apologetic of Śaiva Siddhānta up to this point, it would be more consistent if the brahmins were here probing Xavier on the more general issue of whether, like the *Cārvaka*, he denied on logical grounds that God could be *rūpī*, *arūpī* or *rūpārūpī*. Younger may well be right, however, that the form in which the question was put reflects one of the ways in which Tamils were accustomed to ask one another about their religious affiliations.

31. Dhavamony, pp. 226-27.

32. Shulman, *Tamil Temple Myths,* pp. 82, 352.

33. Ibid. pp. 139, 291.

34. J. A. Dubois, *Letters on the State of Christianity in India* (New Delhi: Associated Publishing House, 1977 [1823]), p. 3. De Nobili, a more seasoned missionary than Xavier, rarely reported *in extenso* on his dialogues with Hindus, despite his voluminous studies of Hinduism. An exception connected with the question of God's *rūpa*-form, in which he employed scholastic arguments typical of his age, is found in a letter to Fr. Mascarenhas, dated 27 November 1627, from Tiruchirappali. The following extract—heretofore unpublished in English—is from the Shembaganur ms. of A. Sauliere, S.J. It merits attention, being indicative of how prevalent the topic was: "Rumor spread in the town that I was preaching a new doctrine. Pandarams [priests who perform rituals either for vellalas or pariahs, but not both] and many other followers of the sect of Rudra came to me as I was saying mass. Since I claimed to teach who the true God is, they desired me to tell them what shape he had. 'We all believe,' said a pandaram, 'that there is only one God, but we should like to know what is the shape or form of that God.' 'It is true,' I replied, 'that you confess there is only one God but you act as if there were many. Regarding God's form, if you mean he has five faces, four arms, etc., I answer that God cannot be such, for if he were he would be composed of parts, which must be joined together to make a whole. We must, therefore, give God another form which is necessarily uncreated by another and possesses in itself the necessity to exist. For such is the meaning of "infinite." So that to be God is to be infinite wisdom, power, etc., in one indivisible substance.' One of those who accompanied the pandarams asked: 'What is the form of that infinite wisdom, power, etc.?' 'You are mistaken,' I answered, 'if you think that God is distinct from his infinite wisdom, etc. This is the uncreated form of the true God; there can be no other. You dishonor him when you say that God has five faces, a moon on the head, a serpent round his neck, and a wife by his side.' They answered, 'If God has not the form we ascribe to him, he can have no other, for the one you ascribe to him is unintelligible.' 'The very admission,' I said, 'that outside the things we perceive there are infinitely more which we neither perceive nor understand with our weak intelligence is in itself some knowledge and understanding of God.' 'But,' asked a pandaram, 'If God has no figure, how is it that he makes things with such a variety of figures? No one gives what he has not.' [According to the *Cittiyār*, Śiva assumes a manifest form (*uru mēni*) when engaged in causing the cycle of the world's evolution and dissolution.] I explained to him that when wise men say God is everything, they do not mean that God is a camel, an elephant or a man, but that he has in himself the ideas of all that is possible and the power of making it. Such was the conference we had." (Abr. mine.) August Sauliere, "The Life of Fr. Robert de Nobili, S.J., 1577-1656,"

(Shembaganur, Tamil Nadu: Undated ms., Archives of the Jesuit Province of Madurai), pp. 472-78.

35. Piet, p. 123; cf. Nallaswamy, pp. 191, 227.

36. Richard Fox Young, *Resistant Hinduism: Sanskrit Sources on Anti-Christian Apologetics in Early Nineteenth-Century India* (Vienna: Indological Institute of the University of Vienna, 1981), pp. 161-65.

37. Derrett, p. 45.

38. Nallaswamy, p. 229.

39. S. Sabaratna Mudaliyar, quoted in Piet, p. 133.

40. "Manifestation" and "incarnation" were sharply differentiated by the Śaivite apologist, Ārumuka Nāvalar (1822-79), in an 1854 treatise addressed to Protestant missionaries in Jaffna: "You hold that the Hindu sacred texts say that Lord Śiva has form. You argue that he who has form cannot be God. Now wait! He did not get his form because of his past karma like your God. Your God attained a form with bones, skin, etc., and passed through his mother's vagina. He underwent great tribulations and died. So don't compare the form of our God with the form of your Jesus. The various forms of Śiva are manifestations of his *śakti*" (trans. S. Jebanesan, Jaffna). Ārumuka Nāvalar, *Caiva tūṣana parikāram (Rejoinder to Calumny Against Śaivism)* (Madras: N. pub., 1956 [1854]).

41. Nallaswamy, pp. 170-71.

42. A preface to *Ñānakkumi*, a Jaffna Śaivite parody of Christianity reprinted frequently since the 1840s, says: "The Materialists placed a high value on worldly pleasures and propagated false teachings which hid the reality of Śiva. At such times, eminent Śaiva saints, who had experienced the reality of Śiva, appeared. Even then, in the latter days, owing to karma, few could know that Śiva was real. Some people, under the influence of Materialism, therefore embraced Christianity, got the worst of it and suffered grievously" (trans. C. S. Sathyanarayanan, Kodaidanal). Muttukkumārak Kavirāyar, *Ñānakkumi (Wise Song)* (Chunnakam, Ceylon: N. Pub., 1926 [ca. 1845]), p. 2.

43. Nīlakaṇṭha (Nehemiah) Goreh (1825-85), a Benares brahmin raised as a Vedantin, who became a Christian in the 1840s and spent the next four decades trying to explain to other Vedantins why, was often told that what he called *ātman* was what they considered to be the *jīva*; e.g., "Even what the Sāṃkhyas say about the *puruṣa* is more perceptive than what such crude thinkers as you Christians and the Naiyāyikas say about the *ātman*" (trans. mine). Nīlakaṇṭha Goreh, *Saḍḍarśanadarpaṇa (Mirror of the Six Hindu Philosophies)* (Calcutta: Bishop's College Press, 1860), p. 210.

44. Shulman, pp. 37, 362.

5

Gandhi and the Christians: Dialogue in the Nationalist Era

JOHN C. B. WEBSTER

Mohandas Karamchand Gandhi was both a Hindu *mahatma* and an eminent Indian nationalist leader. It was as such that, during the 1920s and 1930s, he entered into an ongoing dialogue with Christians in India through personal interviews, addresses to Christian audiences, and especially through the press. Theirs was, as a result, a very public dialogue, which was to have a lasting impact upon Hindu-Christian relations in India. This essay examines that historic dialogue as it appeared in Gandhi's two newspapers, *Young India* and *Harijan,* as well as in a sampling of the Christian press with whom articles and editorial comments were exchanged. Since Gandhi carried on his dialogue almost exclusively with Protestants, even though all Christians were implicated in it,[1] four Protestant newspapers published in India have been selected for examination: *The Guardian,* an Indian Christian nationalist weekly; and representing primarily missionary views, *The Indian Standard;* its successor, *The United Church Review;* and *The Indian Witness.* Because the dialogue was, despite its significance, a priority on neither the Gandhian nor the Christian agenda for India, it is set here within the context of the broader concerns of both parties and treated chronologically, each of the three stages between 1919 and 1939 being opened by a new Gandhian initiative, which gave fresh substance to the dialogue. The first such initiative was the political events of 1919–22.

1919–29

At the beginning of the 1920s Gandhi was leading a nation-wide rebellion against the British raj. The Rowlatt *satyagraha* in 1919 as well as the *Khilāfat* Movement and Non-Cooperation movements in 1920–22 were, to

Gandhi, not simply protests against specific government actions but expressions of a deep disillusionment with modern civilization in general and British rule in particular. *Hind Swaraj* (1909), which he brought out in a new edition and had distributed at the time, was the manifesto of the Gandhian revolution. Indian Home Rule was not to be "English rule without Englishmen" but a reassertion of Indian civilization. Moreover, it was to be achieved not by British parliamentary methods but by, on the one hand, a widespread, non-violent refusal to use or participate in those institutions of modern civilization (schools, hospitals, modern industry) and British government (the legislatures and the courts) that held India in the British grip and, on the other hand, a constructive program of developing, revitalizing and introducing Indian alternatives. During 1919–22 Gandhi sought to use the widespread sense of grievance over the passage of the Rowlatt Bills into law, the "Punjab Wrongs," and the Treaty of Sevres to motivate, to mobilize and to unify the loose constellation of classes, communities and religious groups of which Indian society was comprised for a national campaign.[2]

The Christians, both Indians and foreign missionaries, were one such religious group. Gandhi shared a social stereotype of Christianity as an aggressive, alien and alienating presence, and of Indian Christians as an inconsequential aberration on the Indian social scene. This stereotype, rooted in boyhood experience in his native Kathiawad,[3] had not really been changed by his subsequent work with Indian Christians in South Africa where many of the initial members of the Natal Indian Congress and volunteers in his first campaign for racial equality had been Christians. So too were some of the volunteers in his ambulance unit during the Boer War as well as some of his associates and inmates in his ashrams during his major campaign against the Asiatic Registration Bill.[4] Yet side by side with this social stereotype went considerable reading in Christian literature as well as a genuine appreciation both of the New Testament, the Sermon on the Mount in particular,[5] and of several Christian friends of broad sympathies such as Joseph Doke in South Africa, C. F. Andrews and S. K. Rudra in India, who presented a pleasing contrast to the narrower European Christians who had tried so hard to convert him in South Africa.[6]

In India Christians were a small minority, according to the 1921 census a mere one and one-half percent of the population, concentrated in the South.[7] While most of them were villagers from untouchable castes who had converted in large numbers in the late nineteenth century, there were at the end of World War I a significant number of well-educated urban Christians as well. What organization they had was religious rather than political in nature. These were still dominated by foreign missionaries, although that was being challenged increasingly.[8] Equally important, the Protestant missionary enterprise was heavily committed to such institutions of modern civilization as schools, colleges, hospitals and dispensaries as important means of evangelizing India either directly or indirectly through cultural influence. Through these, Christians believed they had contributed significantly to the Indian Renaissance. The major Christian political organization was the All India Conference of Indian Christians (AICIC), which was both in style and in structure modelled on the Indian National Congress. Its political program was definitely moderate rather than extremist when Gandhi came to the political forefront in 1919.

The missionary response to Gandhi's appeal to the Indian people to join the Rowlatt *satyagraha* and then the Non-Cooperation and *Khilāfat* Movements was not positive. While *The Indian Standard* remained scrupulously silent on the subject until early 1922, *The Indian Witness* took a consistently hostile stand. Clearly its editors and contributors were disillusioned neither with modern (Western) civilization nor with the British raj! They were willing to support the Rowlatt Bills,[9] the constitutional reforms of 1919,[10] and the treaty of Sevres.[11] In general they favored a lawful, evolutionary approach to change;[12] were very critical of, even sarcastic about, *satyagraha;*[13] and displayed a mistrust of the masses and mass action that Gandhi obviously did not share.[14] The issue between Gandhi and the missionaries at this stage is beautifully summed up in a letter from a missionary who had been set upon by non-cooperators in Madras. Gandhi published and commented upon this letter in February 1922 just before he called off non-cooperation. The missionary, G. M. Macfarlane, professed belief in the good intentions both of the British government and of Gandhi; upheld the principle of evolutionary change as divinely ordained; and accused Gandhi of stirring up violence and disorder, of refusing to cooperate with the forces of constructive change, and of offering no practical ideas for the attainment of *swaraj* (independence) beyond "the puerile and impracticable ones of *khaddar* (homespun cloth) and *charkha* (spinning wheel), mere childish notions of what is to benefit the whole of a great nation." In reply, Gandhi condemned hooliganism in a campaign based on non-violence as un-Indian and dishonest, yet understandable; upheld the principle of revolutionary alongside evolutionary change; indicated that the sum total of the government's activity had been "moral, material and political injury to India"; and claimed that his movement had "brought about a tremendous awakening among the people."[15]

Indian Christian opinion was somewhat more mixed, and it was clear that it was the Indian Christians rather than the foreign missionaries Gandhi was concerned about.[16] The AICIC at its annual meeting in 1919 suspended judgment on the "Punjab Wrongs" and pressed for a greater degree of self-government than the government had granted.[17] In 1920 it debated non-cooperation at great length and, after noting that "there are some causes for the present discontent in the country," ended by strongly condemning it as "impracticable, unwise and unnecessary and is suicidal to the best interest of the country."[18] In 1921 it urged conciliation upon the government, withdrawal of non-cooperation by its leaders, and a Round Table Conference to work out a compromise. At the same time it also passed a *swadeshi* (self-sufficiency) resolution urging that the *swadeshi* spirit dominate all aspects of Indian Christian life, that Christians wear clothes of Indian manufacture, and

> that in view of the fact that the Indian Christian Community has been very frequently and severely accused of lacking the Swadeshi spirit, this Conference recommends that all its Provincial Leagues make strenuous efforts to find ways and means of inculcating the Swadeshi spirit among Indian Christians through the local Leagues and lose no time in putting such a programme into effect.[19]

Gandhi described the tone of the conference as a whole and of the *swadeshi* resolution in particular as "very encouraging" in *Young India*. He also expressed the hope that it would be followed up with appropriate action and that Hindus and Muslims would cherish the friendliest relations with their Christian fellow countrymen.[20] However, Professor S. C. Mukerjee, president and leading spirit of that AICIC session, came in for quite a bit of criticism from fellow Christians for being out of touch with Indian Christian opinion, which was more loyalist.[21]

Gandhi called off non-cooperation on 24 February 1922 and on 18 March was sentenced to six years imprisonment. However, he was released two years later and devoted the remainder of his sentence to his constructive program: Hindu-Muslim unity, hand-spinning and the removal of untouchability. The Christian press showed much greater appreciation for this work than for non-cooperation, and there were signs of growing Christian support for Gandhi and his program.[22] From 1924 to the end of the decade Gandhi's dialogue with the Christians shifted away from the political to the religio-cultural part of the nationalist agenda. Not only did Gandhi address a number of Christian gatherings at which he raised religio-cultural issues, but between 1925 and 1927 he also wrote his autobiography in serial form for *Young India*. In this he shared those earlier experiences that had shaped his views of Christians and Christianity.

The dialogue during this period focused upon Gandhi's agenda, albeit often at Christian invitation. Three interrelated themes, in which the influence of *Hind Swaraj* remains apparent, dominated the conversations. The first of these was the missionary attitude toward India, which was the subject of an address to a missionary conference in Calcutta on 28 July 1925. After describing his long acquaintance with Christianity and the conclusions his own religious quest had led him to, that is, that Hinduism satisfied his own soul as well as that all religions are both right and imperfect, Gandhi called upon the missionaries to change their negative views of India. What he had in mind specifically were their notions that India is "a land of heathens, of idolators, of men who do not know the true meaning of religion" on the one hand, and, on the other, their desire to give to India but not to learn or receive from her. In the end he urged the missionaries to identify with the masses of India. When asked how, he gave them two answers: Ask C. F. Andrews (whom Gandhi considered a model Christian) and use the spinning wheel.[23] In commenting upon Gandhi's speech both the presiding officer at the meeting and the editor of *The Guardian* noted that Gandhi's views on missionary attitudes were dated; these had in recent years become much more appreciative.[24]

Gandhi picked this theme up again in mid-1927 when addressing first the students of United Theological College and then a missionary gathering in Bangalore. He urged the students to identify with the masses by using Hindi instead of English, and by giving the spinning wheel priority over literacy in uplift work among the masses. He also tried, as in Calcutta two years earlier, to get the missionaries to change their attitudes toward the Indian people whose faith they should not seek to undermine and from whom they had much to receive.[25] He had stated this view most succinctly in a conversation with two Danish missionary visitors earlier that year: "Let them [the missionaries] go to the people not as patrons, but as one of them, not to oblige them but to serve them and to work among them."[26]

This theme also found an early place in Gandhi's autobiography. As a schoolboy in Rajkot he heard a missionary street preacher "pouring abuse on the Hindus and their gods" and resented it. After a well-known local Hindu was baptized, the talk of the town was that he had to eat beef, drink liquor and wear European clothes.[27] The Rev. H. R. Scott, the only missionary posted in Rajkot at that time, wrote Gandhi denying most emphatically that he ever preached near the school, "poured abuse on the Hindus and their gods," or required converts to change their eating, drinking or clothing habits. He suggested that these were rumors spread to deter earnest young inquirers after truth, like Gandhi himself, from considering Christianity. In reply Gandhi said he remembered the incident and the talk, but accepted Scott's repudiation. He also said that subsequent experience with missionaries and Indian converts confirmed the general truth to which the incident pointed. He ended by noting the growth of a more liberal spirit among missionaries and his own conviction that "much remains to be done in that direction."[28]

This leads to the second theme dominating Gandhi's dialogue with the Christians during the mid and late 1920s, namely the Europeanization of Indian converts to Christianity. He referred to it in his replies to the Bangalore missionaries[29] and especially in an address to the Trichinopoly YMCA later that year. Gandhi not only pointed out that Christianity often gets mixed with Europeanism and becomes restricted in the process, but also offered the opinion that "it is not at all ... necessary for a single Indian to cease to be an Indian because he calls himself a Christian." The editor of *The Guardian,* in commenting upon these remarks, stated that "Mahatmaji touched here on one of the weaknesses of the Indian Christian community," which he attributed to the influence of European missionaries, to the fact that many converts knew only the lowest form of Indian civilization, and to the fact that some things in European civilization were help-ful and convenient. The best course, in his view, was "preserving all in Indian life and custom that is good and taking only those things from our European friends which are really beneficial to us and in keeping with our needs and resources."[30]

The third theme concerned religious change. Gandhi was of the view, as indicated above, that all religions are right but imperfect, that people should remain within the religion into which they were born, and that therefore religious change should consist of making Hindus better Hindus, Muslims better Muslims, and Christians better Christians.[31] Change should thus come from within rather than without and should consist of improve-ments within one's inherited religious tradition. Gandhi, therefore, was a persistent advocate of religious toleration and opponent of conversion. Moreover, in evaluating religion, Gandhi gave behavior patterns primacy over belief systems; behavior was more important than and affected beliefs, not the other way around as the proponents of conversion held. Hence Gandhi urged the Bangalore missionaries both to let their lives rather than their words speak for them and to get untouchables to change their habits and then their belief "rights itself."[32]

The most thoughtful response to Gandhi on the matter of conversion during this period was that of R. C. Das, a North Indian convert from Hinduism. Das noted a widespread apprehension, suspicion and hostility to conversion. Despite Christian sympathy for national aspirations and Christian contributions to nation-building, other Indians "freely assert that the evangelistic work—the process of conversion—is an essential part of the conquest of India by the West." He pointed out that conversion gen-erally occurs at the initiative not of the missionary but of the inquirer who, because "the Hindu possesses an instinct for initiation by which a definite step is taken for the rest of his life," desires baptism. Converts become alienated from their Hindu kinfolk not because they want to be but because they are forced to be, through excommunication, ostracism, or by not being permitted to live among relatives according to their own Christian princi-ples. Das saw Gandhi's opposition to conversion in this context. He felt that Christians had no choice but to endure it and hope that "as the political status of India improves the attitude will change towards appreciation or at least to honest toleration." However, on that point Das was not very optimistic.[33]

Gandhi's Hindu nationalism shaped both his attitude toward and his dialogue with Christians in India during the 1920s. He was very blunt in his advice to missionaries, his comments on converts, and his statements about conversion and about the fact that the missionary movement was still infected with attitudes of Western superiority and aggressive imperialism. In making such criticisms he clearly placed educated Indian Christians in particular on the defensive. They acknowledged that his criticisms were not without foundation and felt very uneasy about them. They considered themselves nationalists also, but were committed to a different path of religio-cultural as well as political change for India. They also held a different view of religious toleration, as would soon become quite apparent.

1930–32

The years 1930–32 witnessed Gandhi's second nation-wide campaign against British rule. Civil disobedience, authorized by the Indian National Congress on 31 December 1929, went through several stages. The first began on 12 March 1930 with Gandhi's "March to the Sea" to make salt from sea water. This action gave the signal for the non-violent disobedience of the salt law and other similar laws. The government met this first with firmness and then with increasingly violent repression. Gandhi was arrested on May 5, but civil disobedience spread. On 25 January 1931 he and other Congress leaders were released unconditionally. This led to a period of conciliation culminating in a pact with the viceroy, Lord Irwin, on March 4 and Gandhi's departure on August 29 for London as the Congress' sole representative at the Round Table Conference, which was working on a new constitution for India. The talks there were inconclusive, Gandhi arrived back in India on December 28, and a week later was back in jail. Then a new period of civil disobedience and government repression began.

The civil disobedience movement proved to be a turning point in the Indian Christian community's relationship both to the national movement and to Gandhi. While cautious at the beginning of civil disobedience, Christian opinion swung around during the first stage of the movement. *The Guardian* indicated in its 29 May 1930 issue that while many young Christians had joined the movement, the leadership of the community had not.[34] When the Rev. B. A. Nag, president of the AICIC, sent a telegram to the viceroy supporting the government's repressive measures, there was widespread repudiation of this action from within the Christian community[35] and the AICIC Executive Committee reversed Nag's decision.[36] By July 1930 the Christian leadership was, according to *The Guardian*, pretty well behind Gandhi.[37] After the Gandhi-Irwin Pact even the previously critical *Indian Witness* was effusive in praising Gandhi.[38]

Perhaps the most instructive dialogue on civil disobedience during this period took place right at the outset in April 1930 between Joseph Cornelius Kumarappa, a Christian Gandhian and frequent contributor to *Young India* before the government closed it down, and Foss Westcott, Bishop of Calcutta and Metropolitan in India of the Anglican Church. On April 17 Kumarappa sent "An Appeal to Christian Workers and Missionaries," in which he made the point that while Christians may disagree about civil disobedience, they could not disagree about non-violence as that was not a policy but a Christian principle. He therefore called upon these Christians "to impress upon government the duty of using non-violent methods" in maintaining law and order and, in a covering letter to Westcott, asked that he use his influence to that end. Westcott took this as a request to support Gandhi and so argued by an appeal to natural law that civil disobedience was not God's way of ordering the world. He also quoted both Jesus and Paul on obedience to law and government as well as protested against using the example or teaching of Christ as a warrant for civil disobedience. In reply Kumarappa pointed out that Westcott had misunderstood the intention of his appeal, which was not to solicit support for Gandhi but to ask that Westcott and others "urge government to use non-violent methods." Kumarappa then went on to condemn as callous Westcott's aloofness in the face of government brutality and to remark:

> You will forgive me if I say that most of our missionaries and other leaders of the Christian Church seem to be Britishers first and Christians afterwards if convenient. You remember how during the World War practically every pulpit was turned into a recruiting sergeant's platform and every Church service ended with that morbidly narrow nationalistic song, "God Save the King" which embodies the 'tribal God' idea of King David. Christ's teachings are torn from context and twisted passages are partially quoted to meet their national needs and the flocks committed to their charge are being misled. This is a grave charge which seems to apply even to you as I shall proceed to show presently.

And so he did at quite some length.[39] S. K. George, another Christian Gandhian, writing in *The Guardian,* saw in the *satyagrahis'* willingness to suffer at the hands of the government for the sake of the poor of India something profoundly Christian. "Gandhiji," he said, "did not create the disaffection against the government. He has only given it a non-violent turn."

> Unmerited suffering in resisting evil is calculated to convert the evil doer. Nothing less than that is the grand hope of Mahatma Gandhi. It is the way of the Cross and the Cross rightly endured inevitably leads to victory. We have the proof and the assurance of it in the Cross and Resurrection of Christ. And shall we stand aside when the soul of India is travailing? Not if we have caught anything of the Spirit of our Master. Not if we have his hope in the regeneration of humanity, in a Kingdom of God on Earth.[40]

The dialogue between Gandhi himself and the Christians took an important turn in April 1931 when he was quoted in the press as making the following statement about foreign missionaries.

> If instead of confining themselves purely to humanitarian work and material service to the poor they limit their activities, as at present,

to proselytising by means of medical aid, education, etc. then I would certainly ask them to withdraw. Every nation's religion is as good as any other's. Certainly India's religions are adequate for her people. We need no converting spirituality.[41]

This produced a strong reaction. What was at stake was nothing less than the future of foreign missionaries under a *swaraj*, which was obviously on its way. The editor of *The Guardian* could not believe that Gandhi had actually said these words.[42] Taken aback, even stung, by the response, Gandhi wrote in *Young India* that the quotation was "a travesty of what I have always said and held." He then offered a revised statement as a corrective.

If instead of confining themselves purely to humanitarian work such as education, medical services to the poor and the like, they would use these activities of theirs for the purpose of proselytising, I would certainly like them to withdraw. Every nation considers its own faith to be as good as that of any other. Certainly the great faiths held by the people of India are adequate for her people. India stands in no need of conversion from one faith to another.[43]

In early May, in responding to a Ceylonese Christian, he added,

In India under Swaraj I have no doubt that foreign missionaries will be at liberty to do their proselytising, as I would say, in the wrong way; but they would be expected to bear with those who like me, may point out that in their opinion the way is wrong.[44]

As if to justify his disapproval, a month later he published an unflattering, quotation-laden description of how missionaries proselytize by a retired government official, with the suggestion that missionaries might want to do some soul-searching on this matter.[45]

Christian reaction to Gandhi's corrected statement was mixed. The editor of the *United Church Review* condemned, with Gandhi, the use of humanitarian work as a " 'cat's paw' by which proselytes might be dragged into the Christian fold," but upheld its use as in accordance with the example of Jesus Christ, whose first concern was not simply imparting instruction or healing bodies but "with a man's soul."[46] *The Indian Witness* printed excerpts from an interview Gandhi gave E. Stanley Jones in which he indicated that even if missionaries proselytized, "they would have the legal liberty to do so."[47] An Indian Christian, writing to *The Statesman*, said "Mr. Gandhi's 'Swaraj' means the end of religious and other liberties."[48] The editor of *The Guardian* found the correction acceptable, felt "quite sure that no future Swaraj government is likely to hamper the efforts of Christian bodies in India," and urged foreign missions to hand over control to Indian church bodies as quickly as possible.[49] The Indian Christians of Tinnevelly passed a resolution asking Gandhi to withdraw his statement and to work for "such safeguards in the new constitution as would guarantee to all religionists their right to practice and preach their religions"[50] and there was similar concern reported in Madras.[51]

Clearly Gandhi, without intending to do so, had posed a threat to the future religious liberty of Indian Christians and foreign missionaries. Speculations on the subject varied,[52] but both Indian Christians and foreign missionaries found assurance in the resolutions of the Unity Conference of 1924 and of the Karachi meeting of the Indian National Congress following the Gandhi-Irwin Pact, both of which guaranteed religious liberty.[53] A memorial of support presented by some Indian Christians to Gandhi on his departure for London to attend the Round Table Conference included this important statement on religious liberty.

> We are in general agreement with the Fundamental Rights drawn up by the National Congress. We welcome in them especially the right of religious liberty. We believe it implies the right to share with others our religious convictions and experience. We can think of no effective Freedom of Conscience without the right to preach our faith openly and freely. To us, as to you, the use of corrupt and unfair methods of conversion is distasteful. We condemn them wholeheartedly. But we may not be denied the right to preach the Gospel. That is a sacred duty which our Lord Himself has especially enjoined on us, and in the discharge of that duty have our Saints and Martyrs laid down their lives. We believe that Truth transcends all racial and geographical barriers and it will be therefore not at all in conformity with India's age-long traditions to close her doors against the religious ideas and experience that come from outside. We hold that the permeation of Christian ideals of life and society will but enrich the culture and civilization of our country. Good Christians are ever good citizens and we believe that India will never have cause to regret the growth of the Christian Church.[54]

As this statement indicates, Gandhi had also succeeded in provoking some serious soul-searching among Christians with regard to their missionary methods. Stanley Jones, writing on the difference between proselytism, which involved a change of religious affiliation without an inner moral and spiritual change, and conversion, which involved both, acknowledged and condemned the former but upheld the latter. He expressed the hope that Gandhi's statements would remove the spirit of proselytism from the church.[55] Several Indian Christians, while agreeing with Jones, went much farther than he. Cyril Modak saw the need for a cultural and national conversion of the Christian community as well as for an Indian interpretation of Christianity.[56] A. A. Paul urged upon his fellow Christians a greater degree of effort in friendly and cooperative actions with people of other faiths.[57] The editor of *The Guardian* pointed once again to the urgency of a transfer of power within the church from foreign missionaries to Indian Christians.[58]

Gandhi's final dialogue with Christians before returning to jail at the beginning of 1932 took place on 8 October 1931 in London where he met with leaders of British missionary societies while attending the Round Table Conference. Gandhi began by explaining the controversial misquotation and then laid the audience's mind to rest on the issue involved by saying, "Any suggestion that I should want legislation to prohibit missionary enterprise or to interfere with the beliefs of other people is unthinkable." He also declared that he stood by the resolution of the Unity Conference, which explicitly granted the right to convert.[59] The conversation then centered on Gandhi's personal views on conversion, which, as William Paton, Secretary of the International Missionary Council, indicated in his closing remarks, revealed that Gandhi "was not desirous only that missionaries should be courteous and self-effacing, and should identify themselves with the people of the country, but was opposed to something which was fundamental to Christianity."[60] In a Christmas talk on shipboard, Gandhi said that Christianity, the life of which the Sermon on the Mount speaks, has yet to be lived. When the hungry are fed and peace comes to our individual and collective life, then Christ is born. Both his miraculous birth and his crucifixion were thus less historical than eternal events, to which life lived not words spoken bore witness.[61]

1932-39

On 17 August 1932, while Gandhi was still in prison, the British prime minister announced the government's decision to make separate electorates for, among others, the untouchables, part of the new constitution. Gandhi took such strong exception to what he considered to be a division within Hinduism and perpetuation of the "bar sinister" between caste Hindus and untouchables that he threatened to fast unto death unless it was removed. His fast, begun in prison on 20 September 1932, marked the beginning of both his most serious effort to end untouchability and of a new stage in his ongoing dialogue with the Christians.[62]

Gandhi took an essentially religious view of both untouchability and its removal. Untouchability was a sin, he believed, rooted in the hearts and minds of caste Hindus. Only if they repented of and atoned for that sin through acts of love and service for the untouchables, would they be purified and would Hinduism deserve to live. Since repentance and atonement were voluntary acts, they could not be coerced through legislation but only evoked through persuasion. Moreover, repentance meant attitudinal and not necessarily structural change. The centerpiece of Gandhi's campaign was not the destruction of the caste system but temple entry, which symbolized religious equality and solidarity. The body through which this total program was carried out was the Harijan Sevak Sangh, a service organization of "repentant caste Hindus" rather than a more inclusive body.

The Christians, who had spent more than half a century working among untouchables in almost every part of India, took great interest in Gandhi's anti-untouchability campaign. *The Guardian* was very supportive of Gandhi's reasons for the fast and its initial positive results.[63] So too was *The Indian Witness*.[64] However, as the campaign progressed and encountered the inevitable obstacles, Christians raised questions about basic assumptions, about priorities and about methods.[65] There were two issues on which they were in fundamental disagreement with Gandhi. The first of these was their conviction that attitudinal change was not enough; the caste system also had to be changed. A lead article in *The Indian Witness* put the matter this way:

> The present campaign against untouchability is being carried on together with an attempt to preserve the four main castes of Hinduism. Just where the untouchables are to find themselves placed in the scheme of caste is not made clear, but if the caste system remains we may rest assured there can be no place for the untouchables. None of the present castes are going to offer to include the untouchables and no present caste will consent to a new social alignment that will place the untouchables on social equality with them. The whole caste system must go, then it will be possible to have a social order that is based on our common humanity, otherwise untouchability is certain to remain for it was produced by the caste system.[66]

A case study of Allahabad pointed to the same conclusions. Fred Perrill showed that the real resistance to the work of the Harijan Sevak Sangh was coming from those castes just about the untouchables group as the former "are determined to retain their superior position in the social scale."[67] In an interview with Stanley Jones, Gandhi defended his focus upon attitudinal change. Castes, he argues, are a social institution; they have served useful purposes as trade guilds. However, the four *varnas* (castes) are sanctioned by the Hindu scriptures and are inherently equalitarian rather than hierarchical in nature. The real problem is thus one of wrong attitudes, specifically about superiority and inferiority.[68]

The other issue of fundamental disagreement was the perennial one of conversion, which now took on new dimensions. As indicated earlier, the removal of untouchability was in Gandhi's view a purely Hindu affair aimed at the purification of Hinduism. As he explained to Dr. John R. Mott in 1936:

> So far as I am concerned with the untouchability question, it is one of life and death for Hinduism. As I have said repeatedly, if untouchability lives, Hinduism perishes, and even India perishes; but if un-

touchability is eradicated from the Hindu heart root and branch, then Hinduism has a definite message for the world. . . . If untouchability is an integral part of Hinduism, the latter is a spent bullet. But untouchability is a hideous untruth. My motive in launching the untouchability campaign is clear. What I am aiming at is not every Hindu touching an "untouchable," but every touchable Hindu driving untouchability from his heart, going through a complete change of heart.[69]

He therefore asked the Christians to adopt essentially a hands-off policy with regard to the untouchables, or Harijans (children of God) as he called them,[70] while he himself would not become involved with untouchable converts to Christianity.[71]

This, however, could not be. For one thing, the untouchables themselves weren't simply going to wait around indefinitely for appropriate signs of repentance and acts of atonement from caste Hindus. This was demonstrated most dramatically on 13 October 1935 when Dr. Ambedkar, the untouchable leader at the Round Table Conference who had signed the Poona Pact ending Gandhi's fast three years earlier, announced to a large public gathering, "I had the misfortune to be born with the stigma of 'untouchable.' But it is not my fault, but I will not die a Hindu for this is within my power." The conference he was addressing then passed a resolution stating they would leave the Hindu religion and join any other religion that promised them equal treatment with others.[72] This resolution did not receive the approval of all untouchable leaders.[73] Gandhi considered it unfortunate for three reasons: untouchability was, in his view, on its last legs; one cannot change one's religion so easily; and it wouldn't help the untouchables anyway because their lives were still intertwined with those of caste Hindus.[74] The Christian response was, it should be noted, remarkably cautious; they did not rush right in to court Ambedkar as other religious leaders did.[75] *The Guardian* saw the declaration as basically a protest,[76] while *The Indian Witness* considered such a massive exodus from Hinduism quite unrealistic.[77]

It was also too much to expect the Christians simply to step aside. They believed, on the basis of their lengthy experience, that Christianity had something special to offer that the untouchables were responding to. This view was reinforced in 1933 by the publication of J. W. Pickett's *Christian Mass Movements in India*, a survey of movements in five different parts of India. Pickett concluded that more than half of the converts surveyed had done so for spiritual and just over ten percent for secular or worldly reasons. Moreover, a number of improvements had followed conversion, especially among those who had regular worship and pastoral care; for example, less drinking and fear of evil spirits, better health and housing, greater interest in education, and a better public image locally.[78] These findings gave Christians fresh confidence in the efficacy of their work among the untouchables and became part of their apologetic.

In his criticism of Christian efforts at converting untouchables, which became more frequent and more bitter in the years following Ambedkar's declaration, Gandhi took issue with both of Pickett's findings. On the one hand, he considered untouchables incapable of understanding the Christian message or of evaluating it in relation to the alternatives. He asked John R. Mott, "Would you preach the Gospel to a cow? Well, some of the untouchables are worse than cows in understanding. I mean they can no more distinguish between the relative merits of Islam and Hinduism and Christianity than a cow."[79] He also denied the Christian assertion that spiritual hunger led untouchables to become Christians.

Presentation, with a view to conversion, of a faith other than one's own, can only necessarily be through appeal to the intellect or the stomach or both. I do maintain ... that the vast mass of Harijans, and for that matter Indian humanity, cannot understand the presentation of Christianity, and that generally speaking their conversion wherever it had taken place has not been a spiritual act in any sense of the term. They are conversions of convenience. And I have had overwhelming corroboration of the truth during my frequent and extensive wanderings.[80]

On the other hand, Gandhi reported and commented upon cases of unfair means and exaggerated claims brought to his attention by the Harijan Sevak Sangh.[81] He also took note of instances of caste and untouchability continuing in the churches.[82]

Disagreements with Gandhi on this issue went beyond differences concerning specific facts about the motives for and consequences of conversion. Whereas Gandhi considered all religions on a par, if not similar, in that they were both true and flawed, the Christians saw religions as basically distinct, each with differing gifts to offer. Moreover, whereas Gandhi sought to remove untouchability and the disabilities from which untouchables suffered without destroying the existing socio-religious order, the Christians, like Ambedkar, considered social conflict the inevitable price of meaningful change. This comes out clearly in many Christian statements, including the one on "Christian Attitude to Harijan Revolt" issued by the Bangalore Conference Continuation in June 1936. This statement, unlike a later one "Christian Evangelism in India" prepared by the National Christian Council,[83] was sensitive to reformist Hindu concerns and fearful of aggravating communal rivalries. It therefore urged Christians to continue their work among untouchables with great care and even to exercise "a ministry of reconciliation between caste Hindus and Harijans."[84]

Perhaps the most thoughtful and sensitive Christian response to Gandhi's concerns came from a group of fourteen nationalist Christians who wrote a careful statement entitled, "Our Duty to the Depressed and Back-ward Classes: An Indian Christian Statement," in March 1937. On one hand, it recognized the fact that untouchables were seeking the fellowship of the church and that it was the duty of the Christian church to receive such seekers as well as to awaken spiritual hunger. On the other, it urged restraint, so as not "to alienate the sympathy and spoil the open-minded-ness of the Hindu to the Gospel by any ill-considered attempts at external results of a questionable value."[85] Gandhi called this an "unfortunate doc-ument" as its main purpose, in his reading, was "not to condemn unequivo-cally the method of converting the illiterate and the ignorant but to assert the Right of preaching the Gospel to the millions of Harijans."[86] The editor of *The Guardian*, one of the fourteen co-signers, took issue with Gandhi's remarks at several points and concluded that Gandhi's criticism does not allay Muslim and Christian suspicions that "Mahatma Gandhi is a down-right communalist and cannot but fight as a Hindu in spite of his nation-alism."[87]

Yet this period also witnessed the emergence of what might be called Gandhian Christianity. Gandhi's close friend, C. F. Andrews, anticipated this development and perhaps contributed to it by shaping some of Gandhi's ideas about Christianity.[88] Close as they were, Gandhi and Andrews still disagreed in principle about conversion, as a conversation published in 1936 indicated.[89] Following Andrews, whose *Mahatma Gandhi's Ideas* appeared in 1929, Frederick B. Fisher, a Methodist missionary bishop, and Jaswant Rao Chitamber, soon to become the first Indian Methodist bishop, pub-lished very appreciative (although not always very accurate) biographies of Gandhi in the United States in which they argued that Gandhi was putting Christian ideals into practice.[90] Rajkumari Amrit Kaur and especially S. K. George reveal a greater internalization of Gandhi's religious outlook in their writings during this period.[91]

CONCLUSION

It is important to recognize that Gandhi's dialogue with the Christians took place within a colonial context that tended to pit religions against one another. While British rule gave freedom of religion to India, it also pro-vided, from 1909 onward, powerful political inducements to religious com-petitiveness in the form of separate electorates for different religious communities, a decision opposed by Gandhi, the Indian National Congress and the All India Conference of Indian Christians. Since the proportional representation of the various religious communities in the central and state legislatures was determined in part by the census figures, mass conversions from one religion to another had serious political implications. This was most apparent during the 1931 census, which was taken when a new con-stitution granting more self-government to Indians was in the offing. Com-munal competition for the allegiance of the untouchables in particular was unusually intense, while the untouchables themselves, under Dr. Ambedkar's leadership, sought recognition as a separate political entity in order to gain a measure of political power.

The dialogue between Gandhi and the Christians from 1919 to 1939 was thus no esoteric philosophical exercise. It focused upon issues vital to both parties as well as to India as a whole. Gandhi held the initiative and kept the Christians on the defensive throughout. One can see, as a result, during the course of this period a greater degree of movement emanating from this dialogue among Christians than on Gandhi's part. His positions remained, for all intents and purposes, unchanged, while Christians reexamined and redefined their positions in ways that drew them closer to him. By the end of the 1930s the dialogue had become very intense because the untouchability issue proved vital to the integrity of Hinduism as Gandhi saw it and of Christianity as Christians saw it. It was, moreover, an issue on which they differed profoundly on matters of principle, on which they therefore had to oppose each other, and on which they could do each other considerable harm.

The political context of Hindu-Christian dialogue in India has changed dramatically since Independence. The British are gone; Hindus are clearly dominant; Christian churches are under Indian leadership; there are no separate electorates. Yet even though the particular circumstances that influenced Gandhi's dialogue with the Christians no longer prevail, the stereotypes of Christians and Christianity, the major subject of the dialogue throughout, the very public nature of which helped to popularize and give credence, have affected the position of the Christian minority in independent India. Moreover, Gandhian images, perceptions and arguments, which were products of that historic dialogue, have helped shape recent official decisions concerning public issues vital to Christians, such as how the constitutional provision for religious liberty is to be interpreted, how Christian evangelistic activities are to be viewed, and whether Christians from untouchable backgrounds are eligible for Scheduled Caste benefits. The Christian community in India today has thus been encapsulated by its historic dialogue with Gandhi. Whether either Gandhian Christianity or even Hindu-Christian dialogue itself can prove to be a useful resource in breaking out of that bondage to the past remains to be seen.

NOTES

1. This weightage in the dialogue is apparent from the editorials and conversations Gandhi published in his own newspapers. For a good selection of the most significant of these see M. K. Gandhi, *Christian Missions: Their Place in India* (Ahmedabad: Navajivan Press, 1941).

2. This analysis follows that of Ravinder Kumar in *Essays in Gandhian Politics: The Rowlatt Satyagraha of 1919* (Oxford: Clarendon Press, 1971), pp. 1-16 and *Essays in the Social History of Modern India* (Calcutta: Oxford University Press, 1983), pp. 47-56.

3. M. K. Gandhi, *An Autobiography or The Story of My Experiments with Truth*, 2d ed. (Ahmedabad: Navajivan Publishing House, 1959), pp. 24-25. A lengthy discussion of this is provided in Chandran D. S. Devanesen, *The Making of a Mahatma* (Madras: Orient Longmans, 1969), pp. 46-64.

4. See Mohandas Karamchand Gandhi, *Satyagraha in South Africa: The Selected Works on Mahatma Gandhi*, vol. 3, ed. Shriman Narayan (Ahmedabad: Navajivan Press, 1968), pp. 62, 114, 298, 321-22, 384, 391-92.

5. Gandhi, *Autobiography*, p. 49.

6. For Doke see Gandhi, *Satyagraha in South Africa*, pp. 234-35, and on Rudra see M. K. Gandhi, "The Late Principal S. K. Rudra," *The Guardian* (July 16, 1925): 343. (Hereafter referred to as *G.*) His views on Andrews are spread throughout his works.

7. Of these eight percent were Orthodox and the rest were about evenly divided between Protestants and Roman Catholics. W. S. Hunt, "Christianity in India," *Church Missionary Review* 75 (September 1924): 202, 206, 207.

8. See Daniel Johnson Fleming, *Devolution in Mission Administration* (New Jersey: Fleming H. Revell, 1916) and John C. B. Webster, *The Christian Community and Change in Nineteenth Century North India* (Delhi: Macmillan, 1976), pp. 208-226, 234-39.

9. *The Indian Witness* (March 12, 1919), p. 162. (Hereafter referred to as *IW.*)

10. C. A. R. Janvier, "The Missionary Situation Created by the Reforms," *IW* (June 29, 1921), pp. 481-83 and "A Message from the Viceroy," *IW* (October 12, 1921), p. 779.

11. *IW* (March 31, 1920), p. 243; *IW* (June 2, 1920), p. 410.

12. *IW* (March 12, 1919), pp. 162-63; *IW* (April 9, 1919), pp. 225-26; "Anti-Non-Cooperation," *IW* (May 11, 1921), pp. 363-64; "The Present Situation," *IW* (January 4, 1922), pp. 3-4.

13. *IW* (March 12, 1919), p. 162; *IW* (May 14, 1919), p. 306; Brenton T. Badley, "The Folly of Non-Cooperation," *IW* (August 18, 1920), p. 624; "Non-Cooperation: The Sequel," *IW* (September 28, 1921), p. 740.

14. *IW* (April 16, 1919), p. 242; *IW* (April 30, 1919), p. 1; "Anti-Non-Cooperation," *IW* (May 11, 1921), pp. 363-64; Ganga Nath Shukul, "Cooperation," *IW* (June 1, 1921), p. 412.

15. "A Christian Missionary's Generalisations," *Young India* (February 2, 1922), pp. 78-79. (Hereafter referred to as *YI.*) My earlier study of missionary response to Gandhi during these years, based more on private correspondence than on public statements, reveals a somewhat less negative attitude, especially during Non-Cooperation. John C. B. Webster, "Presbyterian Missionaries and Gandhian Politics, 1919-1922," *Journal of Presbyterian History* 62 (1984): 246-57.

16. See *YI* (September 22, 1921), in Mahatma Gandhi, *Young India 1919-1922: With a Brief Sketch of the Non-Cooperation Movement by Babu Rajendra Prasad*, 2d ed. (Madras: S. Ganesan, 1924), pp. 439-40 and "Notes," *YI* (January 12, 1922), p. 14. He also complained that Sadhu Sundar Singh's views were being misrepresented to "wean Indian Christians from the movement," "Notes," *YI* (February 9, 1922), pp. 85-86.

17. *The Report of the Sixth All India Conference of Indian Christians Held at Cuttack on December 29th, 30th & 31st, 1919* (Ranchi, 1920): 12-20, xxii-xxv. (Hereafter *AICIC Report.*)

18. *AICIC Report, 1920*: 26-36.

19. "The All India Christian Conference, Lahore, 1921," *The Indian Standard* (March 1922), pp. 72-75. (Hereafter referred to as *IS*.)

20. "Note," *YI* (January 12, 1922), p. 14.

21. "Indian Christians and Non-Cooperation," *IS* (May 1922), pp. 148-51.

22. *IW* (October 1, 1924), p. 630; Fred M. Perrill, "When Mahatma Gandhi Came," *IW* (October 28, 1925), p. 671-72; M. D., "Weekly Letter," *YI* (March 31, 1927), p. 102; "Our Western India Letter," *G* (April 14, 1927), pp. 171-72.

23. "Mahatma Gandhi's Address," *G* (August 6, 1925), pp. 376-79.

24. Ibid. pp. 373-79.

25. Gandhi, *Christian Missions*, pp. 156-62.

26. Ibid. p. 155.

27. Gandhi, *Autobiography*, pp. 24-25.

28. Gandhi, *Christian Missions*, pp. 12-14. Gandhi did not report this incident to his first biographer, Joseph Doke (written in 1908), but gave a very different account of Scott and Christianity in Rajkot.

In Rajkot rumors of Christianity found their way into the school, and so into the home. But they were vague and by no means attractive. The Presbyterians had a Mission in Rajkot and at one time our school was deeply stirred by the authentic report that a well-known Hindu had become a Christian. The idea among us of what becoming a Christian meant was not complimentary to Christianity. The School boys had the firm conviction that conversion meant eating meat and drinking wine.

"Had they no idea of the doctrines taught?" "None whatever. These acts, which are both abhorrent to Hindus, were for them the symbols of Christianity, beyond this they knew nothing. Sometimes, on our way to school, we could see a crowd near the school gate, catch a glimpse of Mr. Scott preaching, or hear his voice in the distance. Occasionally we heard rumors of his ill-treatment by the people, but I, at least, never went near him then. Later I got to know him and admire him."

This much earlier report and then Gandhi's subsequent reference to this incident after its authenticity had been called into serious question, are indicative of stereotyping bordering on prejudice. See Joseph J. Doke, *M. K. Gandhi: An Indian Patriot in South Africa* (Madras: G. A. Natesan, 1919) and Gandhi, *Christian Missions*, pp. 160-70.

29. Ibid. p. 160.

30. *G* (October 13, 1927), p. 466.

31. This is best stated in Mahadev Desai's description of the International Fellowship Convention in Gandhi, *Christian Missions*, pp. 188-94.

32. Ibid. p. 162.

33. R. C. Das, "Proselytism vs. Evangelism," *G* (September 20, 1928), pp. 448-50.

34. *G* (May 29, 1934), p. 254.

35. *G* (June 19, 1930), p. 290.

36. *G* (July 17, 1930), p. 338.

37. Ibid.

38. "The Congress Meets," *IW* (March 26, 1931), p. 194; "Mr. Gandhi and America," *IW* (May 28, 1931), p. 1.

39. J. C. Kumarappa, "When Angels Are Accursed," *YI* (June 26, 1930), pp. 275-79.

40. S. K. George, "An Indian Christian Attitude," *G* (June 19, 1930), pp. 293-94.

41. *G* (April 9, 1931), p. 158.

42. Ibid.

43. M. K. Gandhi, "Foreign Missionaries," *YI* (April 23, 1931), p. 83.

44. M. K. G., "Foreign Missionaries Again," *YI* (May 7, 1931), p. 102.

45. M. K. G., "Missionary Methods in India," *YI* (June 4, 1931), pp. 134-35.

46. "Editorial Comment," *United Church Review* (June 1931), pp. 169-70. Elsewhere in the same issue R. H. Ewing simply clarified the meaning of Gandhi's revised statement. See "Things New and Old," ibid., p. 186.

47. "Dr. E. Stanley Jones Interviews Mahatma Gandhi," *IW* (June 18, 1931), p. 1.

48. Quoted in "The Missionaries and Mr. Gandhi," *Women's Missionary Magazine* (August 1931), pp. 34-35.

49. "Notes," *G* (April 30, 1931), pp. 193-94.

50. *G* (May 14, 1931), p. 218.

51. "Madras Letter," ibid., p. 226.

52. See William Paton, "Mr. Gandhi and Christian Missions," *G* (May 28, 1931), p. 246; A. A. Paul, "The Future of Religion in Swaraj India," *G* (June 4, 1931), pp. 256-61; "X," "The Missionary Message," *G* (June 18, 1931), pp. 281-83; "Religion Under Swaraj," *G* (July 2, 1931), pp. 303-4; "Notes," *G* (August 6, 1931), p. 363.

53. See e.g., Paton, and "Notes," *G* (August 6, 1931), p. 363.

54. "Indian Christians and the National Demand," *G* (September 10, 1931), p. 423.

55. E. Stanley Jones, "To Proselytize or to Convert Which?" *IW* (June 18, 1931), p. 387.

56. Cyril Modak, "The Christian Indian Attitude," *G* (May 28, 1931), pp. 244-45.

57. Paul, op. cit.

58. "Notes," *G* (August 6, 1931), p. 363.

59. "Mahatma Gandhi and Missions," *G* (December 10, 1931), pp. 571-72.

60. "Mahatma Gandhi and Missions," *G* (December 17, 1931), pp. 584-85.

61. "The Jesus I Love," *YI* (December 31, 1931), pp. 429-30.

62. Much of the analysis in this section is based on my earlier work; "Christians and the Depressed Classes in the 1930s," in *Economy, Society and Politics in Modern India*, ed. D. N. Panigrahi (New Delhi: Vikas Publishing House, 1985), pp. 313-44.

63. "Notes," *G* (September 15, 1932), p. 377; *G* (September 22, 1932), p. 389; "The Fast and After," *G* (September 29, 1932), p. 403; C. E. Abraham, "The Significance of Mahatmaji's Fast," *G* (September 30, 1932), pp. 405-6; "Notes," *G* (October 20, 1932), p. 437-38.

64. "Gandhiji's Threat," *IW* (September 15, 1932), pp. 577-78; "Untouchability Repudiated," *IW* (September 29, 1932), p. 610.

65. Two excellent articles of this type are "The Anti-Untouchability Movement—I," and "The Anti-Untouchability Movement—II," in *G* (November 17, 1932), pp. 487-88 and *G* (November 24, 1932), p. 499.

66. "Why Untouchable," *IW* (July 13, 1933), pp. 433-34.

67. F. P., "Where Untouchability Reigns," *IW* (August 10, 1933), p. 505.

68. M. K. Gandhi, "Dr. E. Stanley Jones Visits Yeravda," *IW* (March 2, 1933), pp. 134-35. Quoted from *Harijan*.

69. Gandhi, *Christian Missions*, p. 236.

70. The other alternative was to work under the Hindu banner. Gandhi, *Christian Missions*, pp. 72-73.

71. "Notes," *G* (March 23, 1933), pp. 133-34; and *Christian Missions*, p. 301.

72. "Bombay Harijans' Resolution," *G* (October 17, 1935), p. 670.

73. John C. B. Webster, "Christians and the Depressed Classes," pp. 325-26.

74. "Unfortunate," *Harijan* (October 19, 1935), p. 288.

75. John C. B. Webster, "Christians and the Depressed Classes," p. 326.

76. "Notes," *G* (October 24, 1935), pp. 673-74; *G* (November 14, 1935), p. 721.

77. "The Depressed Classes' New Day," *IW* (October 31, 1935), p. 690; and "Caste and Untouchability," *IW* (November 14, 1935), p. 1.

78. J. W. Pickett, *Christian Mass Movements in India* (New York: The Abingdon Press, 1933), *passim*.

79. M. K. Gandhi, *Christian Missions*, p. 98.

80. Ibid. p. 105.

81. Ibid. pp. 92-97, 106-12.

82. Ibid. p. 301.

83. "Christian Evangelism in India," *G* (January 28, 1937), p. 60.

84. "Christian Attitude to Harijan Revolt," *G* (June 11, 1936), p. 372. Some of the background discussion leading to this statement is given in "Bangalore Conference Continuation," *G* (June 18, 1936), pp. 389-90.

85. *G* (March 11, 1937), pp. 150-51.

86. Gandhi, *Christian Missions*, p. 129.

87. *G* (June 3, 1937), p. 338.

88. Andrews anticipated Gandhi's critique of Christianity's foreignness in India in *North India* (London, 1908) and *The Renaissance in India: Its Missionary Aspect* (London 1912).

89. From *Harijan* (November 28, 1936) quoted in M. K. Gandhi, *The Message of Jesus Christ*, ed. Anand T. Hingorani (Bombay: Bharatiya Vidya Bhavan, 1963), pp. 89-92.

90. Frederick B. Fisher, *That Strange Little Brown Man Gandhi* (New York: Ray Long and Richard B. Smith Inc., 1932); Jaswant Rao Chitamber, *Mahatma Gandhi: His Life and Influence*, Foreword by John R. Mott (Chicago: The John C. Winston Company, 1933).

91. G. Borkar, ed., *Selected Speeches and Writings of Rajkumari Amrit Kaur* (New Delhi: Archer Publications, n.d.), pp. 55-77; S. K. George, *Gandhi's Challenge to Christianity* (London: George Allen and Unwin Ltd., 1939) is thoroughly Gandhian.

6

Hindu-Christian Dialogue in Europe

ERIC J. SHARPE

"Dialogue," wrote Carl Fredrik Hallencreutz in 1977, "has become a permanent Christian obligation."[1] He was of course not speaking only of the actualities of dialogue between Christians and Hindus, whether in Europe or anywhere else in the world, but rather of an ideal stance many liberal Christians over the past quarter-century or so have come to accept as normative in their relations with those who live by other disciplines, laws and insights than those supported by any of the many branches of the Christian tradition. I say that this is a *liberal* Christian stance quite deliberately; we all know perfectly well that there are great blocks in the Christian world that do not share it. It is also in large measure a modern stance — a modern application of a set of modern ideas to the intricacies of a modern situation. Were we to restrict the term *dialogue* to its simple dictionary meaning of "conversation," that is, without the theological and other overtones it has acquired since the 1960s, then of course there have been Hindu-Christian conversations on various levels in many parts of the world for many centuries. Few of them, I suspect, would have corresponded very closely to what the present-day dialogical stance is assumed to be; all, on the other hand, may perhaps be seen as themes in a long and intricate prologue leading up to the situation in which we now find ourselves. It is largely that prologue which I shall be discussing in what follows.[2]

The geographical definition "in Europe" is slightly problematical. If we were to interpret it absolutely literally, we should have to exclude every encounter that did not actually take place in person-to-person terms on European soil. But there is a form of dialogue in the reading of a book or in an exchange of correspondence. Also, in a period in which there has been vigorous travel between Europe and India, first mainly by Christians and subsequently by growing numbers of Hindus, it may be arbitrary to judge encounters by where on the earth's surface they have happened to take place. Attitudes formed in one place are carried over to another—in both directions. This I trust goes without saying, and although in this chapter I shall remain *in* Europe as far as possible, the Hindu contribution to the dialogue there mostly has to be seen against the background of events in India. Had there been sizable Hindu communities in Europe since the 1850s—which of course there have not, a significant Hindu influx having taken place only since the 1950s—then the terms of the "preparation for dialogue" with which I shall be concerned would have been different. We must remember the relative size of the parties, the range of interests each represented, the socio-political backdrop against which the drama was played out, and the long-term and short-term goals that each had in mind in opening communications with the other.

If dialogue, properly so called, requires a face-to-face encounter, then Hindu-Christian dialogue in Europe began only in the 1830s, at the point at which individual Hindus first dared to brave the "dark waters." The pioneer in this regard was of course Rāmmohun Roy, who was sent to Europe in connection with the 1833 revision of the Charter of the East India Company, and died in Bristol, England, on 27 September 1833. Eleven years later, in 1844, there followed Dvarkanath Tagore, grandfather of the Nobel Prize-winner Rabindranath. In 1870 Keshab Chunder Sen visited Europe. These three encounters between individual Hindus and individual Christians—for there was no real institutional contact involved in either direction—may be taken as typifying the first phase of Hindu-Christian dialogue in Europe, a phase over which we may set the word "reform."[3]

In each case the Hindu visitor was received warmly and indeed enthusiastically by the majority of those with whom he came in contact, not least because each was seen as a realization in human terms of what previously had only existed, for Europe's part, mainly on the level of the romantic imagination. Or, alternatively, they were seen as emerging out of an undifferentiated region of "heathen darkness" upon which the light of the Christian gospel was shining only locally and fitfully. Between the romantic and the missionary images of India there was little in common, since the two groups, though looking at the same India, were seeking and finding there different things. By the 1870s the romantics had an extensive and growing collection of material with which to flesh out their images, as had the scholars (not a few of whom were themselves great romantics); the missionaries and their supporters were also well-supplied with the stuff out of which heroics could be constructed. A third European (in this case British) group was made up of those whose interest in India was pragmatic, mercantile and political, and who remained ostentatiously noncommittal where religion was concerned. This is not to say that none of the servants of the raj were Christians: obviously many were. But their Christianity leaned mostly in an evangelical direction, as did the Christianity of a few Orientalists—Cowell in Cambridge and Monier-Williams in Oxford, for instance.

The second of the trio of representative Hindu visitors to Europe need not detain us for long. Tagore was a conspicuously rich man and was received by Paris and London "society" as such, staying in the best hotels, meeting the best people and distributing lavish gifts. When he met Friedrich Max Müller, at that time slaving away at his Vedic texts in Paris, part of their time was spent with Max Müller at the piano and the visitor singing Italian songs! Otherwise Tagore was more the potentate than the mystic. He had a hearty dislike of "priestcraft," whether Hindu or Christian, and is said to have kept a private scrapbook of anti-clerical press cuttings—alas, a somewhat ominous foretaste of later Hindu attitudes to institutional Christianity.[4]

I have used the word *reform* to characterize the first phase of Hindu-Christian dialogue in Europe. Arguably, the two major motives leading to interreligious dialogue have been apologetical on the one hand, and reformist on the other. One may enter into conversation with a "partner" in order to attempt to persuade that person that one's own tradition as it stands is worthy of his or her serious consideration—to commend and bear witness to that which one has oneself found in it. That the partner should be doing precisely the same thing in reverse is normal and natural. Reformist dialogue is harder to characterize, but it begins with the conviction that there is that in *one's own* tradition which is in need of reform, and that the partner may perchance be engaged in a similar quest. Therefore let there be a pooling of insights and a sharing of convictions already held, in the hope of deepening them jointly. There are of course hidden pitfalls in every attempt to compartmentalize anything as erratic as human discourse on religion. In this case, the reformist belonging to one tradition may be trying to persuade a partner belonging to another (who may or may not be a reformist) that the reformist position is preferable to any other, in which case there is a sizeable element of apologetics involved in the exercise (apologetics remain apologetics, even when there is no recognizable orthodoxy involved).

Rāmmohun Roy has been called a Unitarian. In Christian terms, obviously he was not. He was, on the other hand, a theist, and was anxious (especially in later life) to relate creatively to theists belonging to other traditions. In 1820 he published his own "theistic New Testament," *The Precepts of Jesus* (made up of New Testament passages, but excluding metaphysics, Pauline forensic theology and apocalyptic),[5] and in later years related happily to a minute company of Christian Unitarians (theists) in Calcutta. In one sense his concerns were similar to those of the Unitarian movement in Europe; in another, they were quite different. They were similar in that they were monotheistic, socio-ethical and universalist; they were different in that they had different points of departure and were reacting against different "abuses" (Christian theists were doing battle not with idolatry, widow-burning and infant marriage but with pietism, evangelicalism and post-Reformation Protestant scholasticism). Still, there was a common theistic theme, which ensured Rāmmohun a warm reception in Europe among the heirs of the Enlightenment, though scarcely among those whose Christian heritage was more that of Luther and Calvin, Wesley and Whitefield.

However, in the 1830s it was still too early for Europe and India to react other than superficially to one another. The substructure simply was not in place. Translations from the one group of languages to the other were as yet few and rudimentary, and although a minority on each side was beginning to lay foundations, there remained a gulf of mutual incomprehension to be bridged, and the bridges were being built only very slowly. Hindus viewed Christianity mainly in its evangelical image, with all the moralistic intransigence that implied. Christians saw Hindus as latterday survivals from a bygone age of myth and ritual, mystery and metaphysics, comparable with ancient Greece and Rome, but hardly with anything belonging to the age of steam and telegraphic communication.[6]

An early sign of a new attitude to Hindus from a Christian direction came in 1845, with Frederick Denison Maurice's Boyle Lectures on *The Religions of the World*, which in a manner of speaking provided the Christian side of the encounter with a new and more generous theological framework within which to operate.[7] When Keshab Chunder Sen came to London in 1870, Maurice was one of the Christians he met. Another thing that happened was that four of Keshab's most important Calcutta lectures delivered over the past four years were reprinted in a London cheap edition under the title *The Brahmo Samaj*.[8] The most celebrated of those lectures, "Jesus Christ: Europe and Asia," had spoken so warmly of Jesus that Keshab seemed already to be a Christian in all but name; added to which, Keshab had said that he had come to England "to study the spirit of Christian philanthropy, of Christian charity, and honourable Christian self-denial"[9] — precisely those virtues to which in his earlier lectures he had given most attention. The point here was the Keshab desired, not to exchange his Hindu heritage for any existing form of Christianity, but to enter into dialogue with Christians in the interests of joint reform and regeneration. His 1868 Calcutta lecture, "Regenerating Faith," republished in London in 1870, concluded with the exhortation to seek first the (ethical) kingdom of God:

Fall beneath the feet of the great God, the Father and Saviour of us all. Put your entire faith and trust in that ever-living and ever-present Reality, the Personal God of righteousness and mercy who encompasseth you. . . . His holy spirit working through such faith will effect individual and national regeneration, and establish the kingdom of heaven in all hearts, in all families, and amongst all the nations of the earth.[10]

That all true theists would find common ground and common faith, Keshab had no doubt; nor had the Christian theists of the time. And twenty years later the Chicago World's Parliament of Religions was to be set up, chiefly by Swedenborgians, whose theism was very similar in many ways to that of the Unitarians, as a reformist forum under the theistic motto, "Have we not all one father? Hath not one God created us?' (Mal. 2:10).[11]

Ironically, it was at this point that the reformist stream of Hindu-Christian dialogue came to be overlaid by another, in which the nationalist element was more in evidence. It was one thing to say that developed religious traditions, Hindu and Christian alike, had superimposed harmful accretions on pure theism; that was the classical Brahmo-Unitarian position. But it was another to claim that Hindus, as theists, have a "truer" view of Jesus Christ than that held by most Christians in the West. The "East-West" divide may have been first opened up by Keshab; but it was considerably widened by a Keshab disciple, Pratap Chandra Mozoomdar, in his book *The Oriental Christ* (1883), with its claim that Christ "belonged" to the East, and that the West therefore was bound systematically to distort him.[12] There followed wild speculations about Jesus' "basic training" in the East; and about his death and burial in Kashmir.[13] By this time, too, the Theosophical Society was beginning to assume its extraordinary role of brokerage between Euro-Americans and Indians, though on tenuous intellectual foundations; they had a role in the "dialogue" story, but not one into which we can enter further here.[14]

The beginnings of the modern Hindu "mission" to the West are commonly, and quite rightly, traced back to Swami Vivekananda's four years in Europe and America between 1893 and 1897. In fact, the Swami visited Europe four times between 1895 and 1900. On his own admission, he at first disliked the British,[15] but soon he made European friends — among them the indologists Max Müller and Paul Dessen[16] — and found devotees. Vivekananda, like the Brāhmo tradition from Roy to Sen and Mozoomdar, drew a sharp distinction in his estimate of Christianity between Jesus of Nazareth and the churches created in his name. Of his sincere reverence for Jesus there could be no doubt; but his Jesus and that of the European Christians were hardly the same Jesus. In terms practically identical to those stated in *The Oriental Christ*, Vivekananda pointed out:

My view of the great Prophet of Nazareth would be from the standpoint of the Orient. Many times you forget that the Nazarene was an oriental of orientals. With all your attempts to paint him with blue eyes and yellow hair, the Nazarene was still an oriental.[17]

Although Jesus is a "great Messenger of light," "a marvellous manifestation of spiritual power," and to be worshipped "as God and nothing else," the West, despite "text-torturing" had never been able to make up its mind what he was.[18] Let the East therefore teach the West the meaning and power of its own Prophet, not as unique in the world of the spirit, but as one Teacher among many:

> Let us, therefore, find God not only in Jesus of Nazareth but in all the great Ones who preceded him, in all who have come after him, and all who are yet to come. Our worship is unbounded and free. They are all manifestations of the same infinite God.[19]

The first and most militant phase of the Indian national movement began in 1883, when a minor adjustment in the Indian legal system (the Ilbert Bill) created the first major outburst of racial feeling in India since the Rebellion, and went on with only short intermissions until the outbreak of war in 1914. During those three decades Hindus and Christians were hardly able to consort on terms of equality. Those Hindus who came to Europe did so in order to qualify themselves for positions in the law, the Indian Civil Service or the Indian universities. One of them was Gandhi, who studied law in London from 1888–91, that is, from five years after the Ilbert Bill to two years before Vivekananda's visit to Chicago. Although it is on record that Gandhi once visited Cardinal Manning, and on various occasions listened to Nonconformist Christian preachers,[20] among them Spurgeon and Parker, one can speak of his having participated in a dialogue of religions only with reservations. But those reservations having been made, something important remains. As the celebrated episode with the Theosophists and the reading of the *Bhagavadgita* shows, in these years Gandhi was hardly in a position to serve as an informant.[21] He was, on the other hand, anxious to learn, and part of what he learned would seem to have been a more conscious mode of being Hindu. His reading was never extensive, but what he read, he read with intensity. He had no very high opinion of missionary Christianity and was familiar with only fragments of the Bible (notably, of course, the Sermon on the Mount). In time many Christians were to think of him, Hindu as he was, as an exemplary Christian and even as a saint, but not in his student years. It has been said that of all the Indians who visited Europe at that time, he was the only one who emerged unconverted.[22] But this is hardly the case. He *was* converted, in part, from being Hindu by birth to being Hindu by conviction. And that too is a legitimate outcome of dialogue — not the submissive reshaping of one's convictions in response to what one's partner(s) might seem to require, but a fresh appreciation and appropriation of what one's *own* tradition contains.

As the Victorian age drew to its close, there were two opposite impulses complicating the emergent dialogue. From the British side, a fully conscious imperialism, of which Rudyard Kipling was the popular spokesman; and from the Indian, an intensifying national movement, which was coming to express itself more and more in Hindu terms. Hindus in Europe, still for the most part students, were more likely to form themselves into semi-secret revolutionary societies than to engage in dialogue with the Christian majority surrounding them.[23] The Christian communities of Europe, looked at as a whole, were much less interested in either India or mission than we sometimes tend to suppose and had very little real understanding of the complexities of either. However, knowledge of India and Hindu belief and practice had become steadily more available as the bibliographies of the time show. The trouble was that the words *Christian* and *Hindu* had wide ranges of meaning; in each there were historical, traditional, popular, sectarian and reformist secularizing tendencies, and the textbooks were seldom able to relate these to one another. Europe's knowledge of the Hindu world was partly text-based and partly phenomenological, Orientalists answering for the former and anthropologists and missionaries for the latter. And when Hindus came to Europe, they came with images of Christianity derived from one or other of Christianity's two major modes of operation in India, higher education on the one hand, and what we might perhaps call "bazaar preaching" on the other. One provided ideals; the other actualities. Across the whole there was stretched the canopy of East-West, Indian-European, Hindu-Christian relations as experienced first in India and subsequently in Europe. The terms had become to all intents and purposes interchangeable: East equalled Indian equalled Hindu, West equalled European equalled Christian, with the former politically and economically subservient to the latter.

After World War I, and still more after the tragedy of Amritsar (1919), it became virtually impossible for the Hindu-Christian dialogue anywhere in the world to proceed calmly and dispassionately without the political factor intruding. The war had had a devastating effect, both on the East's image of the West, and on the West's self-confidence. Shattered by the grotesque outcome of a century of unbroken progress, Christian Europe collapsed into a morass of self-recrimination and was only too prepared to allow Hindu nationalism to assume the upper hand in matters of tolerance, pacifism and spirituality. Gandhi and Tagore taught the West ethics and aesthetics, respectively. Sarvapelli Radhakrishnan taught religion and philosophy. Hindu subservience was a thing of the past. Keshab Chunder Sen had come to Europe to learn; Gandhi and Aurobindo Ghosh and Nehru to acquire an education; Radhakrishnan, like Vivekananda before him, came to teach.

Throughout his career Radhakrishnan waged tireless war against religious exclusivism and the attitudes it bred, and although in theory this was a matter concerning all traditions equally, generally speaking it was the exclusivism of Christians he had in mind. On his first visit to Europe in 1926 he devoted one of his Upton Lectures to the Hindu attitude toward the conflict of religions.[24] Again it is necessary to remember that he was on this occasion lecturing not to orthodox Protestants or Catholics, but in the Unitarian headquarters, Manchester College, Oxford. Of course, in speaking of "the Hindu attitude" he was doing in his way what many Christians had been doing for many years, contrasting the ideals of one tradition with the actualities of another. But by this time the Ramakrishna-Vivekananda version of Hinduism had laid firm hold on the mind of the Western-educated Hindu, and it was this interpretation Radhakrishnan was expounding. Between that and the run-of-the-mill evangelical statement of Christianity there was a considerable gap and an abrupt contrast: on the Hindu side, "an attitude of comprehensive charity," and on the Christian, "a fanatic faith in an inflexible creed."[25] This being so—and leaving aside the troublesome question of the actual extent of that ideal Hindu attitude—Radhakrishnan was able to envisage a dialogue between a Hindu guru and a Christian disciple:

> Suppose a Christian approaches a Hindu teacher for spiritual guidance, he would not ask his Christian pupil to discard his allegiance to Christ but would tell him that his idea of Christ was not adequate, and would lead him to a knowledge of the real Christ, the incorporate Supreme.[26]

Again and again Radhakrishnan returned to the theme of tolerance and intolerance in religion, the former being characteristic of Hinduism, the latter of all "narrow monotheism" bent on enforcing "mechanical uniformity of belief and worship" by obliterating the opposition.

> To obliterate every other religion than one's own is a sort of bolshevism in religion which we must try to prevent. We can do so only if we accept something like the Hindu solution, which seeks the unity of religion not in a common creed but in a common quest.[27]

Always Radhakrishnan had a low view of actual, empirical Christianity, especially in its Western forms. The West, he firmly believed, had systematically falsified the "Eastern" message of Jesus, substituting regimentation for growth and freedom, unnecessary complexity for spiritual simplicity, and nationalist pride for universal humility. Against Western "critical intelligence" he juxtaposed Eastern "creative intuition." But East and West in religion may meet nonetheless, and

> pave the way for a firm spiritual unity, if mutual appreciation takes the place of cold criticism and patronizing judgment.[28]

But let us remember that Radhakrishnan was writing during a critical period in India's history. In India, Britain, and hence Christianity, was still in a position of power and authority. The Indian national movement had entered a fresh phase under Gandhian leadership, a phase in which to be Indian was to be Hindu (India's Muslims were being pushed more and more to the sidelines of the political process) — not *smarta* (orthodox) Hindu, but reformed Hindu according to the precept and example of the Roy-Ramakrishna-Vivekananda tradition (a tradition to which Gandhi hardly conformed, but to which Radhakrishnan most certainly belonged). The connection between Christianity and the British presence in India was well-established as an image of compulsion and oppression. So too was the "great reversal," which had begun with Vivekananda's mission to the West in the 1890s. In May 1927, a few months after Radhakrishnan's Upton Lectures in Oxford, Katherine Mayo's celebrated (or notorious) book *Mother India* appeared. Whatever its intentions, which still remain obscure, it told the world that India was hardly fit for self-government due to the unhealthy hold of Hindu tradition on the country.[29] Katherine Mayo was an American and not a European. But she would seem to have had contacts in high places in London, and if her book was designed to be non-political, it must have been incredibly naive. Be that as it may, it had the effect of reminding the West that the Hindu world was occupied by others than Gandhis and Radhakrishnans, and of providing a scandalous counter-image to those supplied from his Oxford lectern by Radhakrishnan, or for that matter to those coming from the brilliant pen of Romain Rolland in France.[30]

After India's independence in 1947, the Hindu-Christian dialogue was bound to move into a fresh phase. However, it is impossible here to attempt to sketch all that took place over a long stretch of time to place the dialogue on a new footing. Let me mention, however, some of the most important elements. The first was the status of India as a secular state, by now separated from Muslim Pakistan. The second was the post-war reshaping of Christian theology on the Protestant side, and the belated entry into the discussion of Roman Catholics in the wake of the Second Vatican Council. The third was the Hindu mission to the West from the mid-1960s on, and the considerable extent of its appeal to (chiefly) middle-class young people from Christian and Jewish backgrounds. With uncanny timing the communications revolution virtually annihilated the factor of distance in determining the locus of the dialogue. A final element to be remembered concerns patterns of post-war migration, chiefly to Britain; however, the Hindu element in this population movement was smaller than the Muslim and Sikh.

In a period of self-questioning and self-recrimination, in which post-colonialist guilt was widely and deeply felt among liberals in the West, calm and sober analysis was a relative rarity. That interreligious dialogue was now mandatory no liberal questioned and practically no evangelical accepted. An immense impetus was added to the worldwide dialogue movement by some of the statements of the Second Vatican Council, notably those in *Ad Gentes* and *Nostra Aetate*, which urged the faithful to follow the way of dialogue and collaboration in their relations with those of other faiths and ideologies.[31] In 1964 the Roman Catholic Church set up a Secretariat for non-Christians, and four years later the World Council of Churches in Geneva appointed an Indian Christian, S. J. Samartha, head of a section on "Dialogue with Men of Living Faiths and Ideologies." Rome and Geneva were in Europe, certainly; so too (from time to time) were Maharishi Mahesh Yogi, whose Swiss headquarters were uncomfortably close to those of the World Council, and numerous other jet-age gurus. But there was a certain gap between the two types of movement. Each was a mission in its own way, but while Christian mission had by the late 1960s become notably sociologized, the Hindu counter-mission was aimed at individuals first and societies only incidentally.

In recent years the dialogical stance has indeed become, as Hallencreutz said, "a permanent Christian obligation" to liberal Christians in Europe.[32] Various results have flowed from this, some theoretical and some practical.

To begin, briefly, on the educational front. In those European countries in which the teaching of religion occupies a significant place on various rungs of the educational ladder, recent developments have meant the virtual elimination of the apologetical element from the teaching of Hinduism, and its replacement by a sympathetically factual approach to the Hindu sources.[33] Common enough at the university level since before the turn of the century, this approach has since the 1960s filtered down to the secondary, and even in some cases to the primary schools. Apologetically-slanted textbooks are now largely a thing of the past. Mention may also be made of the BBC TV and radio series, *The Long Search* and *The Long Search Continues,* as examples of media support tending in the same direction.

A slight word of caution may however be necessary, since although the Hindu material has since the late 1960s certainly been better presented than previously, there remain great problems in the matter of Christian attitudes. A more sympathetic attitude to the Hindu point of view has been known to be a reverse image of a rejection of Christianity, acutely so on the non-evangelical wing of student opinion. This however is far too intricate a question to examine further here. Suffice it perhaps to say that however valuable the dissemination of information may be, of itself it guarantees nothing where the more comprehensive dialogue is concerned.

Also on the "practical" side of the ledger may be counted the many instances in which Christians and Hindus, individually and in groups, have met either to discuss issues of common concern or to share spiritual insights and practices. I do not propose to attempt to catalogue these. Writing from Australia, I am simply not well enough informed on the subject to do it justice; more seriously, it is at least doubtful whether any outside observer or report-reader could capture the atmosphere or estimate the value of such gatherings.

Moving on to the Christian sense of obligation with respect to the dialogical approach—a sense perhaps felt rather more strongly by post-Conciliar Catholics than by the majority of Protestants—the theoretical dialogue literature of the period since the late 1960s had been vast. Much of it has been generated in Europe. In 1968 the Report of the Uppsala Assembly of the World Council of Churches had stated that dialogue had now become a single undifferentiated Christian stance *vis-à-vis* the world as a whole, secular as well as religious:

> The meeting with men of other faiths or of no faith must lead to dialogue. A Christian's dialogue with another implies neither a denial of the uniqueness of Christ, nor any loss of his own commitment to Christ, but rather that a genuinely Christian approach to others must be human, personal, relevant and humble. In dialogue we share our common humanity, its dignity and fallenness, and express our common concern for that humanity.[34]

This ideal led to the setting up of the World Council's subdepartment, Dialogue with People of Living Faiths and Ideologies, based in Europe, but prepared to meet and work anywhere in the world. However, the Hindu-Christian dialogue was not high on its list of priorities. To judge from its later activities and publications, for instance, its journal *Current Dialogue* (since 1980), the dialogue with the Jewish and Muslim worlds has overtaken that with Hindus, both quantitatively and (one must add) qualitatively.[35] Political and economic considerations aside, Christian scholars and church leaders have always been better equipped to approach the Jewish and Muslim worlds with a measure of understanding than they have Hinduism. In the past the equipment was often not well-used, but it is there for all that.[36] South and East Asian languages, histories and traditions are known imperfectly, or not at all. In the past many Christians spent a lifetime of active work in India, were linguistically proficient, and generally aware of the dangers of providing ready-made Christian answers to Hindu questions.[37] Western Orientalists were similarly well-equipped, on the linguistic level. In recent years, on the other hand, and with certain outstanding exceptions, the Hindu-Christian dialogue has sometimes been written about by Christians having a deep commitment to theology but relatively little interest in religion.

The Hindu-based "new religious movements" of the 1960s and 1970s might have provided a corrective, but generally did not, perhaps because the majority of those Europeans attracted by TM, ISKCON, Divine Light, Yoga of various kinds and Ananda Marga, to name but a few, were so far alienated from Christianity as to have neither the desire nor the ability to sustain a dialogue. So while these movements were combed over by sociologists and psychologists for every shred of evidence they might provide about the state of Western religion in crisis, no dialogue of any consequence emerged. The phenomenon as such was in any case surrounded by an atmosphere of proselytism and counter-proselytism.

A periodical such as *New Religious Movement Update* initially produced in Aarhus, Denmark, by the Dialogue Centre directed by Johannes Aagaard, later allied with the ill-fated "Spiritual Counterfeits Project" in the United States, and most recently transferred to Hong Kong, has always been basically evangelical-Christian in its stance. Since the late 1970s it has interpreted *dialogue* chiefly in the sense of employing accurate first-hand research to establish the methods and intentions of new religious movements (including of course those of Hindu origin). In June 1984 an *Update* issue was devoted to "New Religions in Europe," and in September 1985 there was a short item on "Hindus Abroad," in which was reproduced the startling claim from a New Delhi paper that "Europe was a non-Christian, Hindu, Vedic region until just 1,600 years ago."[38] Dialogue in the *Update* sense has therefore been a Christian stance in response to what is seen as being a deliberate and powerful Hindu counter-mission to the West. A similar position has been occupied by the *Arbeitsgemeinschaft fur Religions-und Weltanschauungsfragen*, led by Friedrich-Wilhelm Haack and based in Munich. It differs from the anti-cultism of the Christian right in that it has been able to draw on greater scholarly expertise as a basis for its analysis, and in not indulging in polemics of the cruder sort; not however in its refusal to compromise the Christian message as it understands it.

In Leonard Swidler's definition of dialogue as

a conversation on a common subject between two or more partners with differing views, the primary purpose of which is for each participant to learn from the other so that he or she can change and grow[39]

the "so that" clause would seem to be more important that the actual conversation. One must not debate; one must be "at least minimally self-critical," while remaining at the same time "within a religious tradition with integrity and conviction."[40] Another statement emerging from Geneva in 1984 made a similar point: that each of the world's religions must be understood as "a valuable discrete [separate and distinct] reality," that Christian dialogue with Judaism, Hinduism, Islam and Buddhism will bring about different "changes in Christian theology," and that each confrontation "requires a separate re-evaluation of Christian faith."[41]

In the nineteenth century theists on the fringes of the Christian and Hindu "great traditions" met in Europe, as well as in India, in order to affirm common ground; earlier this century the encounter was so far politicized as to push much of the emergent dialogue in the direction of an affirmation of the rightness of the neo-Hindu and the wrongness of the traditional Christian position (a judgment with which liberal Christians were often prepared to concur); in the 1980s, as the statements just quoted show, the element of self-criticism on the Christian side has become even more insistent. But each "great tradition" is made up of innumerable "little traditions;"[42] there are, one might say, neo-Christians as well as neo-Hindus, and in any case it is simply irresponsible to assume that a Christian dialogue with Hinduism, initiated by Christians belonging to only one branch of the Christian tree, must result in a single "re-evaluation of Christian faith," different from that provoked by an encounter with, say, Judaism. But what *kind* of Hinduism does Geneva have in mind? And what *kind* of Christian is fitted to champion the Christian cause? There is an evangelical Christianity of Lausanne as well as a liberal, ecumenical Christianity of Geneva, just as there are Hindus of the villages and tight little European migrant enclaves as well as Hindus of the universities, medical schools, hospitals, embassies and consulates. And let us not forget, there are the Western devotees, disciples and Western-sannyasis.

A phenomenologist might perhaps be able to sort out the confusion. The historian of religions might have something to contribute, alongside the sociologist. Until the dialogical enthusiast learns to take seriously the possibility that there might be more than one explanation of temporarily acceptable forms of words, the actual encounters of actual Hindus and actual Christians, in whatever part of the world, may well remain subordinate to speculation about the ultimate meaning of those encounters.

It has been said that interreligious dialogue takes place "*in communities* where people of different religions live as neighbors in a common context."[43] But as between Hindus and Christians in Europe, this has seldom happened. Christian individuals and Hindu communities? Hindu individuals and Christian communities? No doubt, in a few cases either way. Christian and Hindu individuals in the mode of "secular dialogue" in schools, colleges and workplaces? Certainly, in innumerable instances. But for every such instance there has been a corresponding denunciation from some conservative quarter.

It is now more than fifteen years since John R. Hinnells and I produced a textbook on Hinduism for use in British schools.[44] It was written by eight academics from primary school to university level, and totally avoided the dialogue question (the word was not even mentioned in its pages). But our introduction contained the words:

> [Hinduism] contains within itself so many paradoxes, anomalies and apparent contradictions that the unwary student may, by studying only one "Hindu" tradition, construct for himself an entirely false picture of the nature of Indian religion.[45]

I would be disposed to say precisely the same of Christianity. What, then, of the dialogue between the two great traditions? As between individual Hindus and individual Christians there may well be—indeed there are—conversations, arguments, disagreements, tempers kept and tempers lost, dominations and submissions. But in no case has the tradition *as a whole* been involved. Between two contemplatives there may be a wide measure of agreement on the nature of the *theologia negativa*, but between conservatives little could be expected save bitter disputation. Verbal disputation is, however, a form of dialogue, provided that there is a measure of listening as well as talking. To put the matter slightly differently, there is no conceivable reason to limit, on *a priori* grounds, Hindu-Christian dialogue only to that form of verbal (or other) communication that results in agreement or eliminates witness and affirmation, in either direction, on principle. To do so would be neither Hindu nor Christian, though it might suit the modern semi-secular cast of mind very well.

The Hindu-Christian dialogue in Europe has always been small-scale when compared with India. But it is not therefore unimportant, either theologically or sociologically. In Europe Hindus have always been a tiny minority, as Christians have been in India. When a majority in one part of the world becomes a minority in another, shifts of emphasis and attitude are inevitable, and these are compounded by adjustments in patterns of world power and influence, and in the self-understanding of the individuals and communities concerned. Here I have been able only to hint at some of the complexities that need to be taken into account in looking into that most intricate of all subjects — the meeting of person with person, tradition with tradition, faith with faith.

NOTES

1. Carl Fredrik Hallencreutz, *Dialogue and Community: Ecumenical Issues in Inter-religious Relationships* (Uppsala: Swedish Institute of Missionary Research, and Geneva: World Council of Churches, 1977), p. 34.

2. Elsewhere I have written on dialogue issues in, for example, "Dialogue and Faith," in *Religion* 3/2 (1973): 89–105; "The Goals of Inter-Religious Dialogue," in *Truth and Dialogue in World Religions*, ed. Hick (Philadelphia: The Westminster Press, 1974), pp. 77-95; *Faith Meets Faith* (London: SCM Press, 1977), *passim*; and "Dialogue of Religions," in *Encyclopedia of Religion* 4, ed. Eliade (New York: Macmillan, 1987), pp. 344-48.

3. Friedrich Max Müller, *Biographical Essays* (London: Longmans, Green, 1884), p. 33: "He [Rāmmohun Roy] wished to reform his religion, not to reject it."

4. Frederich Max Müller, *Auld Lang Syne* 2 (New York: Scribner's, 1899), p. 13.

5. My copy of what is now an extremely rare work was produced in Boston by the (Unitarian) Christian Register Office in 1828. It is worth noting that it is fewer than one hundred pages in length and is made up almost entirely of passages from the synoptic gospels, arranged in the order in which they appear in the New Testament. It contains only four and a half pages from the gospel of John. In the 1880s Max Müller recorded: "This book has become very scarce, and I doubt whether it ever influenced even its own followers" (*Auld Lang Syne,* 111).

6. Cf. Sharpe, *The Universal Gita* (London: Duckworth, 1985) pp. 3ff.

7. Cf. Sharpe, *Faith Meets Faith*, pp. 13ff.

8. Keshab Chunder Sen, *The Brāhmo Samāj: Four Lectures* (London: W. H. Allen).

9. Müller, *Biographical Essays*, p. 74.

10. Sen, p. 97.

11. For more details on the Swedenborgian involvement in Chicago 1893, which

has gone almost unnoticed by later writers on the Parliament, see Sharpe, "Nathan Söderblom, Sadhu Sundar Singh and Emanuel Swedenborg," in Sharpe and Hultgård (eds.), *Nathan Söderblom and His Contribution to the Study of Religion* (Uppsala: Söderblom Society and Leiden: Brill, 1984), pp. 70f.

12. This stereotype, fortunately more or less forgotten today, for many years confused the incipient dialogue. It was still very much in evidence in the work of Radhakrishnan.

13. The only recent account of these speculations known to me is in Swedish: Beskow, *Fynd och fush i Bibeins varld* (Discoveries and Deceptions in the World of the Bible) (Stockholm: Proprius, 1979), pp. 78-86. It is important to state that neither the story of Jesus having visited India before his ministry nor that of his death in Kashmir has any basis whatsoever in history. Cf. J. N. Farquhar, *Modern Religious Movements in India* (1915 reprint, Delhi: Munshiram Manoharlal 1967), pp. 137ff; Walter, *The Ahmadiya Movement* (Calcutta: Association Press and London: Oxford University Press, 1918), pp. 93f.

14. The role of the Theosophical Society in Indian religion and politics between the 1880s and the death of Annie Besant in 1933 is still in need of investigation, most accounts hitherto having been too partisan to be of much value to the historian.

15. Quoted by Marlowe, "Vivekananda in Europe," in *Swami Vivekananda in East and West,* ed. Gharararda and Parrinder (London: Ramakrishna Vedanta Centre, 1968), p. 107.

16. Ibid. pp. 116, 124.

17. Yale, ed., *What Religion Is in the Works of Swami Vivekananda* (London: Phoenix House, 1962), p. 206.

18. Ibid. pp. 207-9.

19. Ibid. p. 212.

20. *Mehta, Mahatma Gandhi and His Apostles* (New York: Viking Press, 1977) pp. 92f. According to H.S.L. Polak, Gandhi once received Cardinal Newman's blessing. Polak et al., *Mahatma Gandhi* (London: Odhams, 1949), p. 19.

21. Cf. Sharpe, *The Universal Gita,* pp. 113ff.

22. Woodcock, *Gandhi* (London: Collins/Fontana, 1972), p. 15.

23. Cf. Karan Singh, *Prophet of Indian Nationalism* (Bombay: Bharatiya Vidya Bhavan, 1970), p. 38.

24. Radhakrishnan, *The Hindu View of Life* (London: Allen and Unwin, 1965, originally 1927), chapter 2.

25. Ibid. p. 28.

26. Ibid. p. 34.

27. Ibid. p. 43.

28. Radhakrishnan, *East and West in Religion* (London: Allen and Unwin, 1949, originally 1933), p. 69.

29. Katherine Mayo, *Mother India* (New York: Harcourt, Brace, 1927) was called by a writer in the *New Statesman* "one of the most powerful defenses of the British *raj* that has ever been written" (July 16, 1927). For this reference I am indebted to William W. Emilsen's paper, "Gandhi and Mayo's 'Mother India,' " presented to the Asian Studies Association of Australia in May 1986. In the late 1920s Mayo's book generated an enormous literature.

30. Romain Rolland (1866-1944): historian, art historian, musicologist, winner in 1915 of the Nobel Literature Prize. In the 1920s he published books about Gandhi and about Ramakrishna and his disciples. For his personal *apologia,* see *Life of*

Ramakrishna (Almora: Advaita Ashtrama 1944), pp. 1-15.

31. Cf. Sharpe, *Faith Meets Faith*, pp. 124ff.

32. For the institutional aspect, see (for the period pre-1968) Vallée, *Mouvement oecuménique et religions non chrétiennes* (Tournai: Desclée and Montreal: Bellarmin, 1975), and (for the later period) Hallencreutz. The 1977-87 period does not seem to have been chronicled.

33. Cf. Sharpe, "Eastern Religions in the Western Classroom," in *South Asian Review* 8/3 (April 1975): 225-37.

34. Goodall, ed., *The Uppsala Report 1968* (Geneva: World Council of Churches, 1968), p. 29.

35. Very few articles in this semi-official journal refer to Hindu-Christian dialogue. It is both interesting and a little depressing to note that one which does, Rambachan, "A Hindu Model for Interreligious Dialogue," in *Current Dialogue* 12 (June 1987): 7-12, simply follows the Vivekananda-Ramakrishnan line and is innocent of anything classified as contemporary analysis of a contemporary problem.

36. L. Said, *Orientalism* (London: Routledge & Kegan Paul, 1978) is a widely read but unsympathetic account of the shortcomings of Western scholars attempting to interpret Islam. But at least those scholars knew Arabic, and it is a barren exercise to criticize them for their failure to measure up to the standards of a later age. In this present case Christians approaching Hinduism in the 1920s and 1930s were generally far better equipped to read texts and reach conclusions than their counterparts in the 1970s and 1980s. That, though, is an educational rather than a theological matter.

37. This point was first made by A. G. Hogg in his criticism of Farquhar's *The Crown of Hinduism* (1913). It is still relevant. Cf. Sharpe, *The Theology of A. G. Hogg* (Bangalore: CISRS, 1971), pp. 50ff., 110ff.

38. *Update* 9/3 (Sept. 1985): 52.

39. L. Swidler, "The Dialogue Decalogue: Ground Rules for Interreligious Dialogue," *Current Dialogue* 5 (Summer 1983): 6.

40. Ibid., p. 8.

41. Brockway, "Notes on Inter-Religious Dialogue," in *CD* 7 (Autumn 1984): 14.

42. I am using the terms "great tradition" and "little tradition" here in the sense intended by M. Singer, *When a Great Tradition Modernizes* (London: Paul Mall, 1972).

43. A World Council document, quoted in *CD 11* (December 1986): 20.

44. Hinnells and Sharpe, ed., *World Religions in Education: Hinduism* (Newcastle upon Tyne: Oriel Press, 1972).

45. Ibid. p. x.

PART TWO

Current Perspectives
on Hindu-Christian Dialogue

7

Current Hindu-Christian Dialogue in India

RICHARD W. TAYLOR

From my seat in New Delhi and Bangalore, Hindu-Christian dialogue does not seem very popular. Nor does it seem very common. There are few who promote it, a number who oppose it, and many who avoid it. And, there seem few opportunities for those kinds of dialogue that come spontaneously. I will try to describe some of what is going on—or not going on, trying to include all types of Hindu-Christian dialogue.[1]

Several years ago there appeared in Delhi a Protestant ecumenical organization based in Aachus. Led by a senior missiologist with decades of experience in the programs of the World Council of Churches, it was intent upon founding a Christian Center for the Study of Hinduism with the purpose of exposing all that the organization members felt was false and lewd in modern Hindu sectarianism. Their motivation seemed to be to protect European young people from being lured into following Hindu groups. They did this by leading tours to Hindu centers in North India, lecturing and publishing widely—constantly distorting the best in Hinduism to make it look bad, evil and silly. My colleagues and I saw this as a massive exercise in anti-dialogue. It was largely backed by the Lutheran World Federation, and executives of several other important denominations supported it. Its initial focus was to be on Hinduism in Rishikesh, where Hindu-Christian dialogue had had positive moments since the 1930s (usually between South Indian Hindus of high caste and Western Christians).[2] We saw this anti-dialogue venture as a threat to the very existence of a small Christian ashram then beginning in Rishikesh, as well as a threat to all future possibilities for Hindu-Christian dialogue in that uniquely open place. While this proposed Center in Rishikesh has not found ecumenical backing, it has been started in a small way in Delhi. Even there it is con-

sidered a great threat by Christians concerned for Hindu-Christian relations, because they knew that this group, from its European base, has widely
distributed a video on Hinduism filled with great distortions that show
Hinduism as quite awful. Nevertheless, some Christians in Delhi, including
one bishop, have continued to support the program of this Center.

Another Christian position toward Hinduism that has considerable following in India is also negative toward Hindu-Christian dialogue. This is
the position of John R. W. Stott and others. On a continuum from dialogue
through encounter to confrontation, they sometimes speak of dialogue in
a not wholly negative way, but nevertheless take a position somewhat to
the right of the center of this continuum.[3] Foreign proponents of this view
are very influential in powerful agencies that fund many Christian projects
in India. This may contribute to the popularity of this view in many Indian
churches. It certainly is popular; and it certainly does not encourage dialogue.

Since the 1960s, within the circle of the Christian Institute for the Study
of Religion and Society (CISRS) there has been a substantial decrease of
leaders in the study of Hinduism and in the doing of Hindu-Christian dialogue. A significant number of such persons have moved to jobs abroad—
as have some Hindu scholars from the same circle.[4] This was a time when
almost any Indian with solid credentials in the academic study of Hinduism
could get a teaching job in North America. At about the same time the
program of the World Council of Churches (WCC) in interfaith dialogue
expanded and began to make use of the very same Hindus who had been
involved in CISRS programs. Thereafter some able Hindu dialogists spent
more time on the international dialogues circuit than on the domestic circuit. So did a few India-rooted Christian dialogists. At about the same time
the Catholic involvement in the Hindu-Christian dialogue business began
to enlarge, both domestically and internationally. Many of the same individual dialogists were drawn into Catholic ventures; in part, perhaps, because of the "pizza effect"[5] of their reputations in CISRS and WCC
dialogue efforts. This sort of "brain drain" has certainly slowed down the
development of Hindu-Christian dialogue in India, although it may have
speeded it up elsewhere, particularly in North America, Geneva and Rome.
It has also brought into play a kind of market mechanism with regard to
dialogists, both Hindu and Christian, with some of the ablest and some of
the "slickest" (these are not always the same) getting the most invitations
and invitations to the most desirable places.

Still, there is much positive to observe. In our National Study of Theological Education[6] we asked large samples of residential theological students, pastors, theological school teachers, external theological students,
theologically-trained women and heads of churches in India questions
about themselves and about their judgments concerning theological education. One of the questions we asked of members of all of these groups,
1603 carefully selected respondents in all, was whether they agreed or dis-

agreed with this statement: "A strong emphasis should be given to training persons to engage in dialogue with other faiths." Over ninety percent of the external theological students agreed with this statement. Between 72.9 percent and 77.7 percent of all of the other groups also agreed with it. This seems to suggest that a majority of theologically-trained Protestants and others in India are reasonably positive toward Hindu-Christian dialogue.

Still, while 77.7 percent of a very carefully selected and distributed sample of over four hundred pastors agreed with the above statement, nevertheless, in a series of somewhat similar statements about the importance of training in other areas, much larger percentages of the pastors felt that these were either very important or somewhat important.

Area of training described	Percentage of pastors thinking it important
Training in preaching	99.6
Training in planning and administering church programs	98.6
Training in pastoral visiting of members	98.4
Training to administer sacraments	96.5
Training to provide a teaching ministry	96.2
Training to lead worship	95.4
Training to write and publish Christian literature	95.4
Training to counsel troubled persons	92.9
Training to promote reconciliation	92.0
Training to promote concern for social problems	89.6
Training to undertake social service	85.5
Training to engage in community action	77.7
Training to use radio and TV	75.0
Training to engage in political education	43.1

These questions and the one about training in interfaith dialogue were presented in different ways and in different settings, so the responses to them cannot be compared with great accuracy. Still, it does seem that the pastors, at least, in their 77.7 percent positive response on interfaith dialogue were indeed being positive, but not nearly to the extent that they were about the importance of training in ministerial basics like preaching, teaching, worship, sacraments and pastoral care.

It interests me that the Lutheran response to our basic question about a strong emphasis to training persons to engage in dialogue with other faiths seems consistently more positive than that of the total sample for residential theological students (Lutherans 84.6 percent, total sample 76.4 percent), external students (Lutherans 97.8 percent, total 91.1 percent) and theologically-trained women (Lutherans 90.9 percent, total 72.9 percent). No other denomination differs so markedly. I suppose that this positive Lutheran response is at least in part a function of the seminaries that most Lutherans attend. Residential students from most of the Lutheran seminaries and from most of the interdenominational seminaries that Lutherans attend tend to be more positive on this interfaith dialogue question than the total sample of residential students. And students from some of the more evangelical interdenominational seminaries that Lutherans tend not to attend tended to be considerably less positive. For instance, while 76.4 percent of the residential students were positive on this question, the Allahabad Seminary students were only 33.4 percent positive, the Southern Asia Bible College students 42.8 percent positive, and the United Biblical Seminary (Poona) students 51.7 percent positive. Since the total size of the sample of residential students was over seven hundred and exhaustive of several specific classes in the seminaries, these percentages are certainly suggestive, although the classes in some of the seminaries are so small that what we have here is not statistically conclusive. That the students of conservative seminaries are less than wholly positive may come as no surprise. But I venture that this empirical confirmation of this tendency does underline the cultural-cum-theological drag on Hindu-Christian dialogue from some parts of the Indian church.

Yet not all of those who are positive about Hindu-Christian dialogue actually give it much priority in practice. And not all those who are positive about Hindu-Christian dialogue are very good at it. Several years ago one of the Catholic church congregations, which concentrates on Hindu-Christian dialogue and has garnered some reputation and power in the process, sent one of its promising priests to study for his doctorate in Hindu religious studies in one of the most well-known departments in India—that of Banares Hindu University. He was invited to live in the home of a professor who was active in dialogue activities. The priest was thought to be moving ahead wonderfully in dialogue. Then, the professor reports,[7] the priest tried to convert the professor's daughter. That was the end of Hindu-Christian dialogue in that house and, to some extent, on that campus. As described to me, it was another kind of anti-dialogue!

It appears that a good share of Christians who give Hindu-Christian dialogue high priority spend most of their time in preparation for that dialogue and in enculturation and liturgics. Even the remarkable group of the Cuttat Circle,[8] which undertook a program intended to lead to Hindu-Christian dialogue, which they called external dialogue, actually got little farther than what they called internal dialogue—by which they meant a Christian understanding of Hindu spirituality and participation in Hindu spirituality as Christians. Such dialogists seem to engage in dialogue with *Hinduism*. They testify to how much they as Christians have learned from Hinduism,[9] and about how this has enriched their Christianity. But they all too often spend very little time in dialogue with Hindus.

Perhaps things are not much different on the Hindu side. Only recently an Anglican missionary—involved in preparation for dialogue for decades, a member of the Cuttat Circle, an editor of key material about dialogue and the involvement of Christians in Hindu spirituality, speaker of excellent Hindustani—told me, regarding Hindu-Christian dialogue, that there are very few Hindus really interested in dialogue, although many are prepared to lecture Christians on Hinduism. He could think of only two Hindus whom he felt were really interested in Hindu-Christian dialogue—Swami Chidananda of Rishikesh, who is abroad most of the time, and an autonomous Ramakrishna Mission monk from around Almora. He attributes this in part to the fact that he finds *no* Hindus interested in taking Jesus and/or Christianity really seriously, as some Muslims do and as a good few early Brāhmos did.[10]

Recent research by Anthapurusha seems to confirm this lack of interest in dialogue from the Hindu side.[11] In his empirical survey he selected about a dozen Christians active in Hindu-Christian dialogue. In reply to a question about the Hindus' overall reaction to Christian attempts at dialogue, Bede Griffiths, a Catholic missionary long involved in a Christian appreciation of Hinduism and in using Hindu scriptures as an aid to Christian spirituality and within Christian worship, responded that "Hindus as a whole are not much interested in dialogue. They tend to think that all differences in religions are unimportant."[12] Here, it seems to me, Father Bede echoes from the South the pessimistic feeling about dialogue reported by the Anglican missionary from the North.

Anthapurusha also selected twelve representative Hindus who were given a questionnaire and interviewed. His difficulty with arranging the interviews suggested that most of his selected informants were not much interested. Some had been selected because they or their organizations were thought to have participated in organized dialogue in the past, others because of their importance in the Calcutta area.

Professor Y. D. Tiwari, a leading Christian participant in Hindu-Christian dialogues, told Anthapurusha: "It is a common notion among Hindus that dialogue seems to be a cover under which the Christians want to convert Hindus and increase their numbers."[13] Tiwari suggests that the initiative for dialogue has not come from Hindus because of the "fear of proselytization and conversion."[14]

Even rather open Hindus who are otherwise friendly to Christian dialogists frequently denounce dialogue. R. K. Guru Dutt does this sharply and at some length, accusing P. D. Devanandan and M. M. Thomas of being tempted to use dialogue to promote Christian purposes and ends.[15] P. Sankaranarayanan questions the utility of interfaith dialogue.[16] And Sivendra Prakash, so ably presented by Murray Rogers, questions the very basis of formal and academic Hindu-Christian dialogue.[17] Little wonder that the very few intellectually or spiritually respectable Hindus who are really interested in interreligious dialogue seem so precious to us.

It seems to me that negative stereotypes, some deeply and almost unconsciously held, haunt both sides of most well-intentioned attempts at Hindu-Christian dialogue. Christians seem to assume that Hindus need conversion. And Christians also seem to assume that Hinduism and certain cultural ways completely overlap. One day, some years ago, I called at the home of one of my Christian colleagues, a leader in Christian studies of Hinduism and a leader in Christian ventures in interfaith dialogue. He was a member of a very Westernized regional Indian Christian community. He was not at home. His son came to the door, and I explained who I was and where I was staying. Later my colleague came to find me and told me that his son had told him that a white Hindu had been looking for him. I had been wearing white kurta-pajama, which most men of certain social classes wore in that part of North India without differentiation among religious communities. And, of course, Gandhians and certain politicians dressed this way—nation-wide. But the dialogist's son thought that only Hindus dressed so—and Christians otherwise. A small thing, but very basic. Further, racism, casteism and communalism are very common on both sides, even among some pastors of elite English congregations and some theological professors. But then, there are professors of Hindu philosophy who delight in describing some Christian professors of Hinduism by saying, "He (or she) knows everything there is to know about Hinduism; he (or she) just doesn't understand it." This has been used of a past-president of the Indian Philosophical Society by a professor of Banaras Hindu University, and it has been used of a professor in a renowned Western university who is a profound student of religious Banaras by a known pandit there. Both of these Christian professors have been very active in the interfaith dialogue business. Of course, none of us is perfect as a dialogue partner. And not all stereotypes are totally baseless. Those who intend to engage in dialogue must avoid these small but misleading things.

Of late barriers between religious communities in many parts of India seem to be going up, and tensions increasing. This does affect efforts at dialogue. Often Hindus perceive threats from Muslims, as in the Uttar Pradesh, or from Christians, as in Kerala. Rath Yatras move across the land to rally Hindus, often to preserve the birthplace of Lord Rama from the encroachments of Islam. While they represent a sort of Hindu fundamentalism opposed to a sort of Muslim fundamentalism, they include an anti-Christian mentality as well. Kalyan Ashrams[18] to reconvert the Christian tribals and to protect the other tribals by incorporating them into Hinduism spread and multiply and become more activist, so much so that the tribal Bishop Nirmal Minz, who did such fine work on Mahatma Gandhi and interreligious dialogue,[19] is far too engaged in defending his church and his people to have time for dialogue at present. And in North America, conservative Hindus of the same strain attack those two most creative Catholic centers of dialogue concern in India: the Shantivanam Ashram of Fr.

Bede Griffiths and the Jeevandara Ashram of Sr. Vandana and Sr. Ishapriya. They allege that these ashram leaders are misappropriating Hindu style and content in order to mislead Hindus and to engage in illicit religious conversions to the detriment of the Hindu society. While this attack is nonsense or worse, it certainly clouds any setting for dialogue.[20] And the attacks tend to restrain those Hindus who might otherwise be more interested in or more cooperative toward dialogue. Many in already liberal Hindu organizations dare not be seen cooperating too much with Christians in times like these.

Christian ashrams have been a focus for Christian concern for Hindu-Christian dialogue in India.[21] They have also been an important locus for such dialogue. The late Fr. Matthew Lederle took a major part in the Catholic ashram movement precisely because he recognized its importance for dialogue with Hindus.[22] He did this in addition to founding and running a remarkable dialogue center in Poona, based on a Jesuit pattern also followed in Calcutta and in Madras. C. Murray Rogers' Jyotiniketan Ashram was the center and base for his interest in dialogue when he was in India. Shantivanam Ashram was the basis for Abhishiktananda's formation in dialogue. When he left Bede Griffiths moved there and continued to grow in dialogue. Christavashram in Manganam became systematically involved in dialogue as its inspiration, Sadhu Mathai, seems to have been from the beginning. Sr. Vandana, after refounding the historic Christa Prema Sangha Ashram in Poona with some concern for dialogue then moved north to Sivanandaji's Ashram in Rishikesh before founding Jeevandara Ashram, where spirituality and dialogue are her focus. Sara Grant stayed on in Poona and was the obvious person to deal with Hindu-Christian dialogue in an ashram context in a CISRS consultation on the Praxis of Inter-Faith Dialogue a few years ago.[23] My colleagues in the CISRS chose to put my own first article on Christian ashrams in a number of our quarterly that had the theme "Theology—From Dialogue and for Dialogue."[24]

Who engages in Hindu-Christian dialogue in India? From the Christian side, at the intellectual level at least, it is overwhelmingly outsiders, that is, people outside the mainstream of the Indian Christian community. It is, with very few exceptions, Westerners, recent converts from high-caste origins, and Syrian Christians who rank with or near brahmins in their home state of Kerala. Those mentioned so far in this paper are Swiss, English, a Brahmin convert, a Parsi convert, German, French, and Syrian Christian.

Of all those mentioned by name so far as Christian dialogists only P. D. Devanandan and Nirmal Minz are not such outsiders. Two of the three major Jesuit dialogue centers in India were founded by foreigners. Even the director of the new anti-dialogue center in Delhi is a brahmin convert. This involvement mostly of Christian outsiders seems very strange, and stranger when we remember that a large majority of Christians in India come from untouchable origins. Many of these prefer to call themselves Christian *dalits* (untouchables) now.

Because the Christian dialogists are outsiders and are largely Western-ers, what I have called the Ramakrishna Mission Fallacy tends to get con-firmed frequently. This is the practice in interreligious meetings in India of having the Christian speaker/participant always be a Westerner while the Hindu is always an Indian. This fallacy is used to assert that in India Christianity is really foreign—both now and forever. It is not true. In the dialogue business we should try to avoid it.

Is it possible to have Hindu-Christian dialogue of the usual type involving more mainstream Indian Christians? Most Hindu participants in such dia-logue are upper-caste. How can such Hindus dialogue with untouchable Christian *dalits*? This is related to a larger problem. When most Christian historians of religion turn to India they study higher Hinduism, which hap-pens to be the Hinduism of the higher castes. Socially this might be seen as the treason of the academic historians of religions. Then these historians of religions and their theologian colleagues tend to become the majority of Christian dialogists and dialogue with high-caste Hindus about the Hin-duism of the higher castes. Theologically this would be the treason of the dialogists. Now, when the plight of the oppressed is so high on most agen-das, it might be well to look more closely at the religion of the *dalits*.[25] Be that as it may, perhaps a Hindu-Christian dialogue between *dalits* and Christian *dalits* would be appropriate (remembering that some activist *dalits* deny that they are Hindus or have ever been Hindus).

In India most Hindu-Christian dialogue has continued to be in a context and content largely set by the Westerners who pioneered such dialogue. And there is, as I have indicated above, considerable bad news about such dialogue, although it must be added that there are younger Christian men and women in many places around India who have gathered Christians and Hindus for interreligious dialogue, sometimes in religious settings and sometimes in weekend live-together settings. Most of these younger Chris-tian dialogue leaders are Catholic religious or are somehow related to the CISRS. Still, perhaps it is time to take the position of M. M. Thomas in his classic debate with Klaus Klostermaier at the historic Bombay confer-ence on dialogue more seriously.[26] He suggests that the locus of Hindu-Christian dialogue need not be entirely religion and spirituality but should be in areas of common human social concern. The professional persons and groups supported by the CISRS in Bangalore, Madras and Madurai were an effort in that direction. Recently the Joint Women's Programme had a major conference on the position of women in family and society according to the religious scriptures and practices of the different religious communities.[27] It has also had several meetings on marriage, divorce and inheritance rules and laws in the different communities. All of these meet-ings have involved serious Hindu-Christian dialogue. This dialogue was fruitful but might have been even more fruitful if dialogue had been more of a recognized part of such meetings. I also know of political meetings and of conferences on the arts where such dialogue might have taken place more fully if it had been recognized as a likely place for it. Many Christians in India have surprisingly little scope in their regular lives for such dialogue, or at least so we found in our study of the parish of St. Mark's Cathedral, Bangalore.[28] Perhaps creating situations enlarging such scope would be helpful.

NOTES

1. For more on typology of dialogue see Richard W. Taylor, "The Meaning of Dialogue" in *Inter-Religious Dialogue*, ed. Herbert Jai Singh (Bangalore: The Christian Institute for the Study of Religion and Society, 1967), pp. 55-64.

2. Over the years Leonard Schiff, Mary Weston, E. Stanley Jones, Denys Routledge, P. D. Devanandan, Francis Acharya, Abhishiktananda, Vandana Mataji, Roger Hooker and other Christians interested in dialogue have had very positive experiences in Rishikesh. Some of these are described in Richard W. Taylor, *Modern Indian Ashrams* (Bangalore: CISRS, forthcoming).

3. John R. W. Stott, "Dialogue, Encounter, Even Confrontation" in *Mission Trends No. 5: Faith Meets Faith*, ed. Gerald R. Anderson and Thomas F. Stransky (Ramsey: Paulist Press, and Grand Rapids: Wm. B. Eerdman's Publishing Company, 1981). For more on this see Richard W. Taylor's review of Anderson and Stransky, *Mission Trends No. 5* in *Religion and Society*, vol. 28, no. 3 (Sept. 1981).

4. See Richard W. Taylor, "Still Cutting: Ruminations over the CISRS after Twenty-Five Years" in *Essays in Celebration of the CISRS Silver Jubilee*, ed. Saral K. Chatterji (Madras: CLS for CISRS, 1983), p. 254.

5. The "pizza effect" is a suggestive concept crafted by Agehananda Bharati.

6. The National Study of Theological Education was directed by Hunter P. Mabry, T. K. Oommen, Richard W. Taylor and John S. Augustine. It was sponsored by the Board of Theological Education of the Senate of Serampore College and conducted under the general oversight of its Commission on Priorities in Theological Education. More than a dozen preliminary reports were made to the Board of Theological Education. Reports of parts of the Study have appeared in *Religion and Society*, vol. 28, no. 4 (December 1981); vol. 31, no. 3 (September 1984); vol. 32, no. 3 (September 1985); and vol. 33, no. 4 (December 1986). More will appear.

7. The professor, a collaborator of the CISRS, told me this story in considerable detail some years ago.

8. Formed by Dr. J. A. Cuttat and Swami Abhishiktananda in about 1963, this largely Catholic group included at least two Anglicans and one Orthodox. Later several Presbyterians and Methodists were included. Dr. Cuttat, author of *The Encounter of Religions*, was then Swiss ambassador to India.

9. This trend continues. The chair of the WCC concern on Interfaith Dialogue, Professor Diana Eck, only recently wrote at length of her learnings from Hinduism in the *Harvard Divinity School News*, ca. 1985.

10. Any list of such Brāhmos would have to be headed by Rāmmohan Roy, K. C. Sen and P. C. Mujumdar among others.

11. Anthapurusha, *The Hindu Response in Dialogue Initiated by Christians*, typescript, Serampore B.D. thesis, Calcutta Bishops College, 1987.

12. Ibid. p. 67.

13. Ibid. p. 67.

14. Ibid. p. 66.

15. R. K. Guru Dutt, "Is Inter-Religious Dialogue Possible?" in *Religion and Society*, vol. 23, no. 3 (Sept. 1976).

16. P. Sankaranarayanan, "Hinduism and Its Attitude to Christianity" in *Religion and Society*, vol. 6, no. 1 (Feb. 1959).

17. C. Murray Rogers, "Hindu-Christian Dialogue Postponed" in *Dialogue Between Men of Living Faiths,* ed. S. J. Samartha (Geneva: World Council of Churches, 1971), pp. 22-25.

18. See Taylor, *Modern Indian Ashrams*, chap. 2.

19. Nirmal Minz, *Mahatma Gandhi and Hindu-Christian Dialogue* (Madras: Published for the Christian Institute for the Study of Religion and Society by the Christian Literature Society, 1970).

20. The last three sentences are based on my "Editorial" in *Religion and Society*, vol. 33, no. 3 (Sept. 1986) and refer to *Hinduism Today* ("An International Bi-Monthly Fostering Hindu Solidarity Among 650 Million Members of a Global Religion"), vol. 8, no. 6 (Nov./Dec. 1986), pp. 1, 23, 25, 26.

21. See Taylor, *Modern Indian Ashrams*, chaps. 4 and 5.

22. See Jyoti Sahi, "Foreword," in Matthew Lederle, *Christian Painting in India Through the Centuries* (Bombay: Heras Institute of Indian History and Culture, 1987), p. 17.

23. Sara Grant, "Reflections on Hindu-Christian Dialogue in an Ashram Context," *Religion and Society*, vol. 26, no. 1 (March 1979), pp. 42-58.

24. *Religion and Society*, vol. 24, no. 4 (December 1977).

25. Following the lead of A. M. Abraham Ayrookuzhiel—a scholar at the Christian Institute for the Study of Religion and Society, Bangalore, India.

26. *Religion and Society*, vol. 16, no. 2 (June 1969). The findings incorporate Thomas's concerns, among others, but his point is best made in the "Editorial," which he drafted.

27. Most of the papers from this conference on "Authority of the Religions and the Status of Women" are in *Religion and Society*, vol. 32, no. 2 (June 1985).

28. Partially reported in Richard W. Taylor, *A Remembered Parish* (Delhi: published for the CISRS by the Indian Society for the Promotion of Christian Knowledge, 1986).

8

Hindu-Christian Dialogue in Canada

DAVID J. GOA

The history of the relationship between the Asian community (and this of course includes Hindus) and Canadian society has yet to be written.[1] It is important to note, however, that a racist thread exists in Canada and has been reflected in law, particularly immigration law. A brief outline of this relationship is useful as background to the significance of the Hindu/Christian dialogue.

The demographic shape of Canada has changed rather markedly in recent years. Over ninety percent of the people entering Canada in 1945–54 were of European birth, while for the current period (1981 census) this figure has dropped to 36.2 percent, with Asia, South and Central America, the Caribbean Islands and Africa accounting for 24 percent.

Statistics Canada reports 69,500 Hindus in Canada.[2] They are spread throughout the country with the highest concentration in the major industrial cities in Quebec, Ontario, Alberta and British Columbia. The vast majority of these people have entered Canada since 1972.

The Asian community wishing to live in Canada has had to cope with a shifting immigration law and policy, a movement that reflects the racial prejudice of Canadian society. It began shortly after 1902 when the first South Asian ethnic group came to Canada. They were Sikhs and part of the Hong Kong military contingent travelling to the coronation of Edward VII. Some returned and settled in British Columbia and by 1908, when Asian immigration was banned, about five thousand had settled. Their population was reduced to about two thousand as a result of the ban. The shape of the Asian community began to change slowly in the 1950s as immigration resumed. With the substantial change in the quota of Asians allowed to immigrate to Canada in the 1970s it has been possible for the community to grow to its current size.

There has yet to be an adequate study of the relationship between the Asian community and the rest of Canadian society. Prejudice and discrimination are commonly discussed within the Hindu community, and there has been a spate of incidents brought before the courts. In general, Hindus have worked hard to help other Canadians understand their faith and cultural values. Certainly their contribution to Canadian society has been beyond reproach.

This paper is based on an initial survey of the conversation between Hindu and Christian faiths in Canada. I developed a questionnaire and sent it to twenty-five people[3] involved in the dialogue across Canada, talked with some of them and attended several meetings.

The data gathered includes printed programs related to the dialogue, papers presented by both Hindu and Christian participants, and journal articles that resulted from the conversation. I have restricted my research to the conversation at the local level; the contribution of Canadian scholars to the international conversation was deemed beyond the purview of this paper.

In the questionnaire I asked each informant to identify the sponsoring organization, the participants and their faith, and the date of the dialogue. Many provided printed materials that advertised the program and some publications which resulted from the encounter. In addition I asked them to address the following questions:

(a) How did the sessions contribute to the dialogue between the faiths?

(b) How did the sessions contribute to the self-definition of the devotees?

(c) Comment on the contribution made by the sessions to understanding between the faiths (of tradition, religious practice, theology/philosophy).

(d) The Hindu-Christian dialogue is taking place in Canada. Does this conversation have a specific character due to the Canadian cultural context? Are there particular issues that need to be addressed? Can each faith make specific contributions to the other faith because of their current historical and cultural situations?

I received a generous response from the informants. In general, the dialogue is at the "stroking" stage characterized by attentive listening, a striving to speak of one's own faith in terms often drawn from the other's faith. I will elaborate on this shortly. There are, however, several examples where the dialogue has moved in a substantive way. I will briefly discuss the responses to the initial enquiry, then develop my analysis of three case histories. These three examples illustrate directions the dialogue has taken.

The chapter will conclude with a discussion of future perspectives, drawing on various comments made by the informants.

The bulk of the programs, addresses and discussions throughout Canada have taken place in Hindu temples or related institutions. They occurred because several people thought it would be valuable, a way of living out the principles of Vedanta. The only Christian churches that formally support the dialogue — and this through the provision of space and some commitment on the part of pastors and lay people — are the United Church of Canada and the Anglican Church. The founders and directors of the Monchanin Cross-Cultural Center, Montreal, are priests in the Roman Catholic Church, and this may signal some tacit support. I am unaware of any formal support. On one occasion a Baptist minister has been involved. Another organization that would appear to be a promoter of the dialogue is the Ahmadiya Muslim Association of Canada, which periodically sponsors Religious Founder's Day symposiums in which Christians and Hindus exchange talks on the person and meaning of Christ and Krishna or some other comparative theme.

A review of the various programs presented across Canada and of the published materials, including lectures, suggests a remarkable homogeneity of both theme and sensibility. On the Christian side there is a noticeable embarrassment over the identification of Christianity with the colonial period in the history of British India. The traditional emphasis of Christianity on Jesus as the "only begotten Son of God," and the path to salvation, is hardly discernible below the layers of universal values acclaimed by "all religious people." One is inclined to think that a Vedanta version of the Savior from Nazareth is being promulgated. The Hindu side is dominated by the Vedanta perspective filtered through the writings of the Sri Ramakrishna and Vivekananda. They are quoted continually. They are also used as models of the dialogue. They are the constant touchstone for the summing up of the nature of the dialogue.

Mishra N. Deo, president of the Vedanta Society of Calgary, noted that promoting the philosophy of Vedanta is the aim of the meetings he has so vigorously contributed to. He suggests that Vedanta is "religiously neutral" even though it is perceived, because of its historical origins, as Hindu. He remarked that the universalism of Vedanta is "assisted by the pluralism" of Canadian society.[4]

Dr. Batukeshwar Dutt and Mrs. Rani Dutt, along with Dr. Satyendra Nath Banerjee have contributed to the dialogue in the Vancouver area. Numerous multifaith sessions have been held with an emphasis on the "unity aspects of the great faiths." Some specific theological ideas and religious images have been discussed — incense, tabernacle, trinity — and I am assured in the correspondence that they have a common religious source. There has been a concern to deepen the understanding between neighbors, to participate in the concerns for world peace through the Conference on Religion and Peace, and to join forces with various Christian groups to lobby for the rights of Japanese Canadians deprived of their livelihood during the Second World War. Dr. Banerjee has suggested that "the similarities between most of the three faiths brought home the universality of all religions. The differences between the Western and Eastern religions became very clear during the sessions and these differences (were) appreciated." A concern was raised that Christianity still defines much of Canadian life and that participants became convinced "that no one religion is the chosen one. There are other great ones which also lead to God."

In Edmonton, under the leadership of Mr. Sushil Kalia, the lay priest of the Hindu Temple, a very active program engaging other faiths and speaking about the Hindu faith has gone on for six years. Mr. Kalia regularly invites Christians, both scholars and clergy, to speak following a *puja* (worship service). They have been asked to address the theme "Our Lord Jesus Christ" and the Christian understanding of salvation. For several years now this has been planned for one of the Christian feast days, Christmas or Easter. Mr. Kalia participates regularly in the Religious Founder's Day sponsored by the Ahmadiya Muslim Association, addressing the question of salvation in Hindu theology and discussing Lord Krishna. He is also a founding member of the Edmonton Interfaith Council and Canadians for Interfaith Awareness and Harmony.

The general pattern reflected in this review follows throughout the country. The three case histories I will now discuss illustrate directions that are at work in Canadian society and may be hallmarks of the dialogue.

MONCHANIN CROSS-CULTURAL CENTER

This center was started in 1963 and named for "a pioneer in intercultural experiences between radically different traditions: Jules Monchanin (1895-1957)."[5] Father Monchanin was a French priest and indologist who travelled in 1939 to study with the spiritual masters of India. He founded a simple Christian ashram at Kulittalai, South India. A good deal has been written about him. Roger Vachon, director of the Montreal center for a number of years, told me that Monchanin remains a symbol for the center, but its work is really informed by the thought and writings of Raimundo Panikkar. The center's work is quite wide-ranging, and it publishes the journal *Interculture* (originally called *Monchanin Journal*) in English and French editions.

The Monchanin Cross-Cultural Center engaged in an intensive four years of work on Hindu-Christian dialogue from 1967 to 1971. A number of themes were addressed during this rich period. There were presentations bringing Christian and Hindu traditions to bear on international development issues. The study of pertinent texts from scripture, meditation and prayer, and the eating of a symbolic meal with the poor focused the participant's attention. A number of sessions on the saints of both traditions were held. Ramakrishna, Nanak, Vivekananda and Gandhi were considered alongside Francis of Assisi, Teresa of Avila, the Virgin Mary, Martin Luther King and Jules Monchanin. These sessions included silent meditation and a Christian meal. In 1970 and 1971 the sessions focused on a variety of ritual acts and forms of prayer and meditation. There were sessions on Christian initiation, silent prayer, yoga, conversations in which Christians and Hindus asked questions about each other's faith and responded to them. More formal presentations were made on the essentials of Hinduism, *gita*, duty, *dharma*, truth, and personal reflections voiced on important aspects of the faith by individuals. One session in July 1971 dealt with the "heart and gentleness of the East *vs.* the aggressiveness of the West: what to do?" The dialogue concluded with a weekend seminar on Swami Vivekananda. A discussion of his life and work was conducted in rhythm with the practice of spiritual discipline and eating together.

What is clearly noticeable in the work of the center is its concern for bringing people of the two faiths together to learn about each other's faith, to be touched by the spiritual power of its texts, spiritual exercises and masters. Its method bridges the potential gap between contemplation and action. This dynamic approach is reflected in the journal, *Interculture*, as well.

The work of the center has led to an understanding of the nature of dialogue that is worth noting. Kalpana Das, the current director, highlights these in, "Hindu Perspective: 'Dialogue' Between Cultures and Religions."[6] In the conclusion of this article Das draws out the implications of the Hindu view. She argues that "dialogue is a spiritual duty, a divine act aiming at experiencing the oneness with all which is the highest peak of spiritual consciousness." It also means the "discovery of the unity or the relatedness (*samanvayata*) between cultures and religions, not just by finding similarities, but by transcending differences. In the process, however, the differences do not need to be dissolved into mere 'standardization' or uniformity."[7] What is needed is a praxis of dialogue rather than a reflection on the doctrines of the faiths. Institutions for dialogue are considered secondary to "the presence of personages who are living witnesses to and actual embodiments of the unity and harmony."[8] From the Hindu side she sounds a warning that no culture and religion can claim the totality of the mystery of existence. The Hindu view of life is no exception. She cites three areas of vulnerability. The Hindu tradition puts

—such an emphasis on the universal as being Reality itself, that it deflects attention from the particular and the unique;

—the Eternal or the Infinite is sought after while the temporal is neglected and is considered to be unable to bring about human salvation;

—an uncritical tolerance encourages a certain passivity and indifference toward the events of life.[9]

A similar consideration of the Christian tradition would be useful and perhaps has been done by the center. I am unaware of it at this writing.

Robert Vachon, director of research for the center, is currently engaged in developing a theory (and praxis) drawing on the experience of the last twenty-five years. His initial consideration is contained in the article, "The Main Orientations of Our Institute," published in the journal *Interculture*[10] (April 1986). It hinges on what the center claims is "the discovery of a new field of research in the socio-cultural area: interculturality."[11]

The center continues to address the existential need for dialogue between people. It is also working vigorously at developing a methodology for this work.

CHRISTIAN FAITH AND OTHER FAITHS

The series of studies, dialogues and visits to various religious communities called *Christian Faith and Other Faiths* occurred early in 1987. It was sponsored by the Division of Church in Society of the Calgary Presbytery of the United Church of Canada, planned by Fritz Voll, director of the Canadian Council of Christians and Jews, Calgary, and held at the Foothills United Church. One session in the twelve-part series was devoted to "The Hindu Guru and the Christian Pastor." This was in the context of a program of study for participating Christians shaped by Fritz Voll through a series of pamphlets. The first introduced the theme of interfaith dialogue, suggesting that its deepest motivation was in the love of God and one's neighbor. It goes on to suggest that since "God was in Christ, reconciling the world to himself ... and placing in us the word of reconciliation" (2 Cor. 5:19), the Christian had both the responsibility and opportunity of finding the Christ in conversation with the faithful of other religions. It argues that there is no place for a "missionizing" stance, a patronizing attitude or the exercise of power in dialogue. Dialogue is not compromise. It may involve tensions, but they will reflect the struggle to understand between human beings. Ultimately dialogue is successful only to the degree that it promotes peace and justice.

The pamphlet, "What Christians Should Know About Hinduism," very briefly describes *anadi* (beginninglessness), *karma* (moral law), *samsara* (rebirth), *moksha* (release), Brahman and the Vedas. A questionnaire is used to help the study group focus on the meaning of pastor in Hebrew scripture, the model of Jesus, examples of ministry in the early church and contemporary needs in this area. Suggested questions to ask Hindu dialogue partners are also provided. They include the usual concerns for the meaning of reincarnation, the nature of worship and a focus on the nature and role of the guru in the life of Hindus in India and Canada. The final question, the one I think sets the tone of the dialogues, is: "What do Hindus expect of us Christians?"

This program of study and dialogue has set out to inform the participants and give them a foothold for beginning a discussion between the faiths. It assumes that the Christians will deepen their own faith in the conversation with Hindus and learn to appreciate the genius of this tradition. It would be useful to explore with both Christian and Hindu participants the meaning of the program for them and how it deepened their faith. The use of a particular idea, in this case the guru and pastor, goes a long way toward rooting the conversation in the tradition, theology, scripture and the living faith of the people one is talking with.

IN THE STILLNESS DANCING

The third development I would like to discuss is the contribution of Dom John Main, who, from his monastery in Montreal, has exercised a modest influence in Roman Catholic circles (and beyond) on the recovery and development of prayer in the life of human beings.

As a young lawyer with the British Colonial Service in Malaya, John Main was initiated into meditation by a Hindu monk. He describes this encounter in *Christian Meditation: The Gethsemani Talks:*

I was first introduced to meditation long before I became a monk, when I was serving in the British Colonial Service in Malaya. My teacher was an Indian swami who had a temple just outside Kuala Lumpur. When I first met him on some official business or other I was deeply impressed by his peacefulness and calm wisdom. I was pleased to see that he seemed willing to talk on a personal level. . . . He then asked me if I was a religious man. I told him I was a Catholic. He then asked if I meditated. I told him I tried to and, at his bidding, described briefly what we have come to know as the Ignatian method of meditation. He was silent for a short time and then gently remarked that his own tradition of meditation was quite different. For the swami, the aim of meditation was the coming to awareness of the Spirit of the universe who dwells in our hearts.[12]

Main began to meditate using a mantra under the guidance of Swami Satyananda. Thus began a process that led Main to experience what the Swami taught: "The mantra is like a harmonic. And as we sound this harmonic within ourselves we begin to build up a resonance. That resonance then leads us forward to our own wholeness. . . . We begin to experience the deep unity we all possess in our own being."[13] It also led Main back through his Christian tradition to the work of Cassian and particularly to chapter 10 of the *Conferences.* Here the early Christian master describes the use of the mantra. Main describes how it was "with wonderful astonishment that I read of the practice of using a single short phrase to achieve the stillness necessary for prayer."[14] He is referring to Cassian's comment, "The mind thus casts out and represses the rich and ample matter of all thoughts and restricts itself to the poverty of a single verse."

Main eventually entered the Benedictine order and after an arduous struggle founded what was to become the Benedictine Priory and Meditation Center of Montreal in the autumn of 1977. Here he worked, building a new kind of community centered on meditation, till his death in 1982. The community passed to its current Prior, Father Laurence Freeman, and has flowered under his steady hand.

The contribution of the Benedictine Priory is clearly in its teaching numerous Christians how to pray. Here we have a vivid example of a Hindu master touching the life of a Christian and opening him through a spiritual exercise to the gift of meditation and the richness of his own tradition. In turn this has been passed on through John Main to a generation of people seeking a deeper spiritual experience.

CONCLUSION

The Hindu-Christian dialogue in Canada is very young and only beginning to take form. Only in a few cases do we see an encounter between these two great faiths in which each is taken on its own terms. The few examples we have examined do suggest an emerging direction.

1. The dialogue between Hindus and Christians has led some Christians to a deep renewal (often discovery) of their spiritual disciplines. The understanding of prayer and a method of contemplation using the mantra have enriched the practice of Christians and contributed to the recovery of dormant practices in the faith.

Similarly, in the Calgary dialogues the Christian participant engages the Hindu tradition with a view to how it informs the Christian faith. This is not to say there is no concern for the structure and content of Hinduism. Indeed, that is an issue as well. The thrust of the program, however, is directed toward what Hindu tradition and experience can teach Christians about their own faith.

2. Hindus in Canada have been reaching out to the Christian community for support on a range of social and cultural issues. This is evident in the work of the Monchanin Cross-Cultural Center and in the work of the Vishva Hindu Parishad (Dutts and Banerjee) in Vancouver. Further, John Berthrong, Interfaith Dialogue Secretary for the United Church of Canada, noted in his response to my questionnaire that in the fall of 1986 the Canadian Council of Hindus in Toronto invited a number of Christians from the ecumenical community to speak to them about the religious roots of Christian social action. He speculates that this concern will accelerate as the Canadian policy on immigration and refugees comes under closer scrutiny.[15] In discussion with John the Hindus wondered why they were not included in the "broader conversation about the nature of Canadian life. They are always happy to talk about their special customs and festivals, but they also feel that they have something to contribute when talk turns to

refugees, immigration, capital punishment, the environment, etc."

It seems rather simplistic to suggest that the Christians may have an opportunity to contribute to the social well-being of Hindus in Canada and Hindus to the spiritual well-being of Christians in creation. But it seems to be shaping up that way.

NOTES

1. See Norman Buchignani, "Research on South Asians in Canada: Retrospect and Prospect," *The South Asian Diaspora in Canada: Six Essays,* ed. Milton Israel (Toronto: The Multicultural History Society of Ontario, 1987).

2. All census details are drawn from *1981 Census of Canada,* Canada Update (April 26, 1983) Ottawa: Statistics Canada.

3. I would like to thank the following people who so generously responded to the questionnaire that forms the basis of this study: Prof. K. Silvaraman, Religious Studies, McMaster University; Prof. Joe O'Connell, Religious Studies, University of Toronto; Prof. R. Ravindra, Religious Studies, Dalhousie University; Prof. Helen Ralsten, Religious Studies, Saint Mary's University; Prof. John Sahadat, Religious Studies, Laurentian University; Prof. Frank Thompson, Religious Studies, University of Waterloo; Prof. Clifford Hospital, Religious Studies, Queen's University; Prof. Klaus Klostermaier, Religious Studies, University of Manitoba; Prof. Roland Millar, Religious Studies, University of Regina; Mr. Fritz Voll, Canadian Council of Christians and Jews, Calgary; Mr. Dwiveda, President, Hindu Society of Calgary; Dr. David Appavoo, Concordia College, Edmonton; Dr. Robinson Koilpillai, Edmonton; Mr. Gian Chandra Shastri, Vedic Shastri Foundation, Vancouver; Dr. D. P. Goel, Vancouver; Dr. Satyen Bannerjee, Richmond, British Columbia; Dr. N. N. Backhashi, Saskatoon; Mr. Ramesh C. Airi, Regina; Dr. K. N. Jha, Regina; Dr. S. Banerjee, Dr. Batukeshwar and Dr. Patubatukeshwar and Mrs. Rani Dutt, North Vancouver; Mr. N. D. Mishra, Calgary; Dr. Udayan P. Rege, Saskatoon; Fr. Thomas Ryan, Canadian Center for Ecumenism, Montreal; Dr. John Berthrong, Interfaith Dialogue Secretary, United Church of Canada, Toronto; Mr. Sushil Kalia, Edmonton; Prof. R. L. Kushwaha, Saskatoon; Lawrence Freeman, Abbot, The Benedictine Priory, Montreal; Dr. Charles Paris, Canadian Council of Christians and Jews, Vancouver; Robert Vachon, Centre Interculturel Monchanin, Montreal.

4. Correspondence, 15 May 1987.

5. *Interculture* 90 (January 1986): 4.

6. Kalpana Das, "Hindu Perspective: 'Dialogue' Between Cultures and Religions," *Monchanin Journal* 57, vol. 10, no. 4 (October-December 1977): 11-16.

7. Ibid. p. 13.

8. Ibid. p. 14.

9. Ibid.

10. Robert Vachon, "The Main Orientations of Our Institute," *Interculture* 91 (April 1986).

11. Ibid. p. 1.

12. John Main, *Christian Meditation: The Gethsemani Talks* (Montreal: The Benedictine Priory of Montreal, 1977).

13. Ibid. p. 4.

14. Ibid. p. 5.

15. Correspondence with John Berthrong, 16 April 1987, p. 2.

9

Krishna and Christ: ISKCON's Encounter with Christianity in America

STEVEN J. GELBERG

INTRODUCTION: UNIQUE ENCOUNTER

Hindus and Hindu thought have had a measurable and documentable presence in North America at least since Swami Vivekānanda brought down the house at the World Parliament of Religions in Chicago in 1893, and forty years earlier when Thoreau glorified the *Bhagavad Gītā* ("... in comparison with which our modern world and its literature seem puny and trivial") in *Walden*.[1] Although North America has had emigré Hindus and expatriate swamis with small coteries of followers for well over a century, until fairly recently contacts between Hindus and Christians in this part of the world have been somewhat limited, haphazard, and restrained. Emigré Indians have tended to value social assimilation over cultural self-affirmation, and thus have not been terribly interested in establishing a public "Hindu presence." Visiting and expatriate Hindu religious teachers have, for their part, tended to present somewhat intellectualized, ritually sanitized, and culturally streamlined versions of Hinduism that appear to have provoked relatively little organized Christian response.

The situation changed dramatically when, beginning in the late 1960s, Hindu teachers in North America began to attract significant numbers of Westerners to more intensive missionary forms of Hinduism. Though the Krishna consciousness movement is not the first Hindu missionary organization to have made its presence felt in the West, among all such groups it appears to have evoked the most sustained and strongly-felt response from its predominantly Christian host society. One might suggest, provocatively perhaps, that it is precisely in Christians' reactions to the presence of a vital missionary Hinduism in their midst that we might more clearly discern their attitudes toward Hindu tradition than in any measured response, on their part, to a remote textbook Hinduism, or to the tame and muffled Hinduism of the urbane, Westernized Indian, or to the modest preachings of a streamlined, intellectualized Hinduism.

Reaction is one thing, dialogue another. At first glance it might appear that there is little to report concerning dialogue between Christians and members of the Krishna consciousness movement—a worldwide Hindu pietistic movement with roots in the Caitanya-Vaiṣṇava tradition of India,[2] founded in the United States in 1966 by A. C. Bhaktivedanta Swami Prabhupāda.[3] To date there has been little formal dialogue between the two in terms of officially-sponsored interfaith conferences and symposia. No book-length study by either party compares the two. There have been no official exchanges of monastic personnel, no cooperative humanitarian ventures, no joint declaration on the moral and political issues of the day.

To say that there has been little formal dialogue is not, however, to suggest that the Krishna consciousness movement has not engaged the attention of its largely Christian host society and elicited a reaction. That it certainly has. Historically, religions generally have met and interacted not in polite and rarefied academic atmospheres, but in the "streets," as it were. For the last two decades, an ongoing, organic, grassroots interaction has been taking place between American Christians of various denominations and these American converts to a foreign and seemingly exotic religion from India. Members of ISKCON (the International Society for Krishna Consciousness)[4] have, since the mid-1960s, been the most highly visible (one could say flamboyant) form of Hinduism in America and the West generally. Few Christians have not gazed in some wonderment upon shaven-headed, berobed, drum- and cymbal-playing devotees dancing and chanting the sacred Sanskrit names of Krishna in the streets of numerous Western cities and towns. Not many have managed to escape the long arm of persistent ISKCON fundraisers. Some tens of millions have returned home carrying a copy of *Back to Godhead* magazine or an English translation of the *Bhagavadgītā* or some other Hindu scripture. ISKCON summer festivals in the streets and parks of major cities have provoked the ire of evangelical and fundamentalist Christians, who have come out to heckle from the sidelines with imposing banners proclaiming "Get Smart, Get Saved!" and "Turn or Burn!"

Away from the streets, Krishna devotees have frequently been invited to address Catholic seminarians, Protestant missionaries-in-training and students in denominational schools, colleges and universities. ISKCON centers regularly host visits by students in all these categories. Though ISKCON itself has no formally-constituted department or office of interfaith affairs, individual members have on their own initiative entered into conversation with priests, ministers, theologians, monks, bishops and cardinals.

The Krishna consciousness movement presents an interesting and somewhat unique test case for Hindu-Christian encounter for a number of reasons. First, in the encounter with ISKCON devotees, the arena of dialogue has shifted from a foreign missionary field—the traditional setting for Christians' encounters with Hindus—to the home front, where the partners in dialogue may be viewed as having made an incursion into Christian territory. Second, the Hindus thus encountered are not Hindus by birth and enculturation, but by choice and conviction, most being Western converts from Protestantism and Catholicism. Third, being converts, these Western Hindus tend to take their newly-embraced faith very seriously, are willing to sacrifice much for the attainment of spiritual goals, and like many of the Christians who confront them, have their own missionary agenda.

Fourth, unlike most Hindu participants in formal dialogue, the Western Krishna devotee has been schooled and formed in the distinctly theistic tradition of Krishna-*bhakti*, the worship of Lord Krishna—a richly devotional and salvation-oriented tradition that bears remarkable theological resemblance to Christianity. The Hinduism of ISKCON is markedly different from the monistic "Thou art That," "We are all God" Hinduism promulgated by visiting swamis and promoted by most popularized versions of Indian spiritual teaching available in the West.[5] ISKCON texts deal in depth and at length with theological categories many Christians traditionally have believed to be exclusively biblical: the personal God, soul, sin, faith, grace, heaven and hell, salvation.

A Christian encountering a Western Krishna devotee is, then, facing a theological cousin who, for that very reason, is simultaneously a theological "competitor," that is, one who speaks a similar theological language but with a different ultimate referent, and one who is, further, out to win souls for his or her Lord. More than any other Hindu organization that has been operative in the West, the Krishna consciousness movement has provoked a strong response from some Christians precisely because it challenges, by its mere existence, the normative Christian claim to exclusivity of grace and salvation.

There are other intriguing aspects of the encounter between Christians and Krishna devotees. One concerns the matter of inclusivism and exclusivism in approaches to religious pluralism. Hinduism (if one could speak of it in any sense as an integrated, definable tradition) is usually presented by its adherents as having a benignly tolerant, liberally inclusivistic attitude toward other religions. Whether or not this is a fair claim—and Christian scholars and others have disputed it—most forms of Hinduism that Westerners have encountered have indeed assumed a fairly inclusivistic attitudinal posture and rhetoric. Though, as we will see later, ISKCON's theology of religions is deeply informed by that attitude, its inclusivism is modified by a strong dose of what at least appears like exclusivism. For example, though Christianity may be seen as theoretically "true," one is hard-put to find Prabhupāda acknowledging that it is effective in contemporary practice. Furthermore, as Christ is viewed as the loving son of Krishna, Christ consciousness is completed by Krishna consciousness. Thus, though ISKCON's own rhetoric sometimes lapses into what sounds like bland inclusivism, its theological position is somewhat more exclusivistic than Christians usually expect from Hindus.

Another unique feature of the Christian encounter with ISKCON is that the Krishna consciousness movement, being in many ways a melding of East and West, itself embodies a kind of organic intercultural encounter as well as, to borrow Raimundo Panikkar's term, an individual *intrareligious* dialogue. Its institutional existence having originated in America, and its members emerging mainly from Western societies, it has been observed that ISKCON has, to some degree, assumed a Western, Christian attitudinal ambiance. Klaus Klostermaier, for instance, suggests that ISKCON "resembles a nineteenth-century British puritanical pietistic movement," and that its members "have inherited from their own culture something of the Christian drive to save the world."[6]

The intrareligious dialogue feature of ISKCON derives from the fact that many of its members are individuals for whom, at one time or another during their pre-ISKCON lives, Christianity made a deep personal impression. There may be ways in which for these devotees the experience of Vaiṣṇavism has been filtered through Christian beliefs, attitudes and expectations. This might suggest that some devotees are, in some sense, simultaneously Hindu and Christian — themselves interior arenas for Hindu-Christian encounter. Examination of Prabhupāda's letters to disciples reveals that some of them brought into their new faith long-standing attachments to the person of Jesus Christ and felt the need to reconcile Krishna consciousness with their former Christian beliefs and sentiments. Larry Shinn, for instance, in his book on ISKCON, relates the case of one young convert who, before moving into an ISKCON temple, first went to her Catholic church, knelt before the altar, assured Jesus that she was not rejecting him and prayerfully sought his permission to join the movement. As she relates, "I was not turning my back on my faith, nor was I rejecting Catholicism. . . . I saw my joining ISKCON as a natural extension of my Catholic spirituality."[7]

It would appear, then, that there exists within some Occidental Krishnaites, at least subtly or subconsciously, an ongoing, interior interreligious conversation, one that is not unnatural for those who have delved deeply — sequentially — into two distinct religious traditions. A Christian in dialogue with a Krishna devotee consequently may, if he or she digs deeply enough and is sufficiently perceptive, also be in dialogue with a self-contained, ongoing Hindu-Christian dialogue.

A final point worthy of note is that the ISKCON-Christian encounter is an encounter not only between two distinct traditions, but also between two phases in the historical development of religious traditions; that is, between a long-standing tradition and a still young religious movement. The ISKCON critique of Christianity is, in large part, the critique of a self-assured, high-intensity, world-renouncing and world-transcending movement of a tradition it perceives as compromised and accommodated. Though that kind of aggressive critique might often seem shallow and arrogant, and irritate not a few, a number of Christian commentators have, as we'll see, nevertheless viewed ISKCON as a potential, indirect contributor toward Christian renewal through its very example of anti-materialism and intense spiritual commitment.

These, then, are some factors that suggest a certain degree of uniqueness, as well as historical, cultural and theological significance, in the encounter between Christians and Krishna's Western devotees. In the following section I will survey—vignette-like and with minimal comment— the range of Catholic, Protestant and Evangelical responses to Krishna consciousness. As we shall see, the forceful presence of a Hindu revitalization movement on Western soil has provoked not a small amount of published Christian commentary, some off-handed and some deeply considered; some denunciatory, some laudatory; some provocative, some conciliatory. There are commentators who have viewed ISKCON as a fearful omen of the collapse of Christian civilization, and others who view it as a God-sent stimulant to Christian renewal. Devotees have been judged both as blest and as damned, anonymous Christians and unabashed pagans.

Next I will survey ISKCON's founder's views on Christian tradition, views that are both appreciative and conciliatory and also highly critical. Christians have, I think, rarely been the objects of such a frankly critical assessment by a Hindu teacher speaking from a theological and ethical standpoint. Prabhupāda's views on Christianity (more so of Christians, as such), elaborately systematized here for the first time, are bound to provoke discussion. In the concluding section I will offer some reflections on the problems and prospects for dialogue between the two traditions. Though this chapter focuses on ISKCON-Christian encounter in the United States, I have included a few Christian responses to ISKCON from abroad, inasmuch as they are relevant to that encounter.

CHRISTIAN RESPONSES TO KRISHNA CONSCIOUSNESS

Catholic

Perhaps the first published Catholic response to Krishna consciousness is contained within Thomas Merton's foreword to the first edition of Prabhupāda's translation and commentary on the *Bhagavadgītā*.[8] While mostly offering his own reflections on the significance of the *Gītā*, Merton writes:

> The present translation and commentary is another manifestation of the permanent living importance of the *Gītā*. Swami Bhaktivedanta

brings to the West a salutary reminder that our highly activistic and one-sided culture is faced with a crisis that may end in self-destruction because it lacks the inner depth of an authentic metaphysical consciousness. Without such depth, our moral and political protestations are just so much verbiage.[9]

Fr. Edward McCorkell, O.C.S.O., formerly Abbot of Holy Cross (Cistercian) Abbey in Berryville, Virginia, and currently Executive Secretary of the North American Board for East-West Dialogue, reports on a "monastic encounter" with the author.[10] He describes "a personal encounter with a rich spiritual tradition different from my own and yet, as I discovered to my delight, one in which I have felt 'at home.' " He continues,

As a disciple of Bhaktivedanta Swami Prabhupāda Subhānanda had entered into a rich tradition ... firmly rooted in Hindu spirituality and culture and representing the theistic side of the Indian religious tradition. ... In comparing my own Benedictine-Cistercian monastic tradition with his, I can see much in common: commitment to a discipline, tutelage under a spiritual master, poverty, simplicity, sacred reading and prayer, as well as celibacy.[11]

He exhorts his readers to "approach a rich tradition like this with open minds and hearts, asking the Holy Spirit of truth and charity to enlighten them and reveal to them the abundant spiritual riches to be found in that tradition. Both justice and charity call for a breaking down of the walls of prejudice in our interreligious encounters and dialogues.[12]

In an article that asks, "Will India's Past Be America's Future?"[13] Klaus Klostermaier, an important voice in Hindu-Christian dialogue, discusses the attractiveness of ISKCON to some Western seekers partly in terms of its "revolutionary conservatism." Its anti-scientism, anti-intellectualism, scriptural literalism and asceticism appeal to many who are disenchanted with various aspects of modernity. Though its origins are clearly Indian, ISKCON's conservatism has been formed, in part, within its present Western cultural matrix: "The Western Hare Krishna people have inherited from their own culture something of the Christian drive to save the world. ... They feel an urge to establish what they consider to be the true *sanātana dharma*, the Vedic tradition, in the whole world."[14] In fact (perhaps this is just a bit overstated), in some ways ISKCON "resembles a nineteenth-century British puritanical pietistic movement much more than a typical Hindu religious movement. Its ideas of orderliness, cleanliness, efficient work and literal following of the commands of the master have hardly any parallel in Indian traditional religious history."[15] Though "overzealous neophytes" in ISKCON may sometimes project an image of the movement as bizarre and outlandish, ISKCON is an authentic movement within the Caitanya-Vaiṣṇava tradition, deserving of the respect of Christians: "If Western Christians consider their Indian converts to be members of a 'Church' (and not a 'cult'), then Western adherents of an Indian *sampradāya* (the Indian equivalent to 'Church') also have a right to be taken seriously as a religious body."[16]

In the concluding sections of a broad survey of Christian and Jewish responses to ISKCON, Fr. John A. Saliba, S.J.[17] offers suggestions of his own for the implementation of ISKCON-Christian dialogue. Christians need not view ISKCON as a competitor for converts and an enemy to be defended against ("There are reasons to believe that most Hare Krishna devotees should be judged not as apostates from the religion of their up-bringing but rather as young adults who are embarking on a religious journey for the first time").[18] The challenge of the Hare Krishna movement "can be seen positively as an opportunity for self-growth and self-under-standing which would lead one to rediscover and build upon the richness of one's own tradition."[19]

For their part, Krishna devotees should avoid a too-facile condemnation of Christianity as compromised and effete: They "should judge Christianity not by the behavior of those Christians who perhaps have not lived up to their outwardly acknowledged commitment but rather by the saintly lives and high aspirations which have been characteristic of many Christians throughout the ages."[20] The most serious obstacle to ISKCON-Christian dialogue is "the mutual perception of sectarian proselytization." Attempts at conversion by one or the other "are always bound to be seen as a challenge, an affront which demands rebuttal."[21] Referring to contributions by ISKCON intellectuals toward constructing a foundation for ISKCON-Christian dialogue, Saliba judges dialogue to be a realistic possibility.[22]

Mainline Protestant

Philip Lochhaas, spokesman for the Lutheran Church—Missouri Synod on cults and non-Christian religions, takes a rather dim view of ISKCON and Eastern religions in general. While advising that "argument that belit-tles the religious conviction of another should be avoided,"[23] he describes Eastern religions in general as man-made, devoid of divine scripture, Sav-ior-less, grace-less and salvation-less.[24] ISKCON devotees in particular pur-sue a futile path to an illusory salvation:

The tragic aspect of the Hare Krishna movement is that the devotees pursue an elusive merger with divinity in which none of them can be certain where he stands at any given moment. While the "mercies" of Krishna may be sung by the devotees, they know nothing of the pure mercy—grace, undeserved kindness—of God in Jesus Christ. . . . The Krishna devotee can only drive himself into more ritual and hope that in his last moment of consciousness before death he is filled with thoughts worthy enough to elevate him to a higher existence than he had before.[25]

Christians wishing to proselytize Krishna devotees "should be prepared to face repeated frustration" because "some Krishnaites may have a low regard for the sincerity of Christians."[26] Parents wishing to extricate their adult offspring from the "anti-Christian context" of an organization like ISKCON can—if they've first exhausted all legal options, considered the risks and consulted with their pastor—perform Christian "civil disobedience": disregard whatever laws (for example, kidnapping, false imprisonment, assault and battery) stand in the way, and rescue their son or daughter from the clutches of such a false, non-scriptural religion.[27]

Gary Leazer, associate director of the Interfaith Witness Department of the Home Mission Board of the Southern Baptist Convention (Atlanta, Georgia), attempts to describe ISKCON in a one-page article in an HMB periodical.[28] He provides a description of ISKCON beliefs and practices that, though not intentionally or overtly malicious, is flawed by frequent exaggeration and error. In particular, ascetical attitudes and practices are exaggerated (for example, "the physical body is an object of enmity") and beliefs are inaccurately depicted (for example, "a person can save his own soul," and "all life is divine"). Young Baptists should be prepared to meet the challenge of Hare Krishna by exposing them to Christianity as "a personal experience expressed in every facet of life," and by instructing them in proper Christian doctrines.

A more accurate and respectful account of Krishna consciousness is found in another Home Mission Board publication, *Beliefs of Other Kinds*.[29] Though "radical" theological differences are cited, devotees are credited with demonstrating "a high level of commitment" and with "not looking for cheap grace." Though Christians may have little success in proselytizing Krishna followers, "a consistent demonstration of the Christian lifestyle of sacrifice and servanthood may be effective in creating an atmosphere in which a Christian can explain how Jesus meets personal needs and offers release from the Krishna devotee's constant search for peace and purpose."

In response to a request by the ISKCON community in Melbourne, Australia—then facing the possibility of repressive "anti-cult" legislation—the Rev. Robin H. S. Boyd, a local Uniting Church minister, author of several important books on Indian Christian theology and subsequently director of the Irish School of Ecumenics in Dublin, prepared a statement for publication and distribution in which he analogized the missionary efforts of ISKCON in the West to his own experience as a missionary in India and questioned the wisdom of the proposed legislation:

The followers of the Hare Krishna movement should be regarded as genuine missionaries of a genuine and well-authenticated Hindu tradition. I myself spent twenty years as a Christian missionary in India.

I know what it is like to witness to one's faith in a different cultural environment. India is predominantly a Hindu country, yet its constitution ensures that every citizen is free not only to practice but also to propagate his faith, whatever that faith may be. ... As one who enjoyed religious freedom in India, I feel it is essential that we in Australia should ensure similar freedom to people of all faiths. ... The success of the Hare Krishna movement in the Western world is a challenge to Christians to listen, to understand, to learn, and then to re-examine their own faith. To react by encouraging repressive legislation would be a denial of the liberty which we claim for ourselves, and which we must share with others.[30]

Perhaps the most thoughtful and sympathetic Protestant response to ISKCON has been that from Baptist theologian Harvey Cox. To Cox, ISKCON is "a fascinating and challenging spiritual and theological movement,"[31] embodying certain attitudes and practices very similar to elements within Christian tradition: "Here you have the idea of a personal God who becomes incarnate in a particular figure revealing what God is about and eliciting a form of participation in the life of God."[32] In particular, Cox finds Krishna consciousness structurally analogous to conservative, pietistic Christianity: both emphasize religious feeling (the "devotion of the heart"), the joy of praising God, puritanical and ascetical virtues, scriptural fundamentalism and a de-emphasis on religious transformation of the present world in favor of concern for "a future life or another world."[33]

Cox's chief interest in Krishna consciousness involves what he views as the movement's potential for stimulating the religious life of the West, Christianity in particular. He described this potential contribution, placing it within a Christian theological context, in a talk at Harvard's Center for the Study of World Religions in 1976:

Could it be that we have allowed Christianity itself and perhaps Judaism to be so identified with the values of accumulation, profit, performance, success, and material gain—which are, after all, the main values of our society—that it takes something as apparently esoteric and exotic as a movement coming from India to remind us that there is, in fact, another way of life, that there is a way of life that is not built on accumulating profit, property, success, and degrees, but has at its core a certain kind of simplicity and plainness of living, if you will? Isn't it strange that that message can now be presented to us by movements coming from so far away, when the prophets of our own tradition—the ones that we officially celebrate but often ignore—have a message so similar? Jesus of Nazareth; St. Francis of Assisi, who certainly worried *his* parents when he made his strange decision to put on a new kind of clothing, to go out to sing and dance in the streets and to talk to the birds ...

Why is it that we can't hear the voices of these prophets from our own tradition, and yet somehow people from as far away as India can bring a message that in some ways sounds so similar? Maybe this is a way that we are being called back to something more essential in our own tradition—a way that God has of reminding us of what we've left behind and forgotten and ignored. . . .

Maybe one of the results of this Hare Krishna movement will be to stimulate us to rediscover some things that we've ignored and suppressed in our own religious heritage. I think it may happen. And if it does, then I'm very grateful for the kind of gift that they bring.[34]

Conservative/Evangelical Protestant

Not surprisingly, the most unfriendly and vociferous Christian response to ISKCON has come from evangelical Protestants, many of whom judge Krishna consciousness not only as spiritually errant, but as Satanic. A pamphlet published by "Jesus People U.S.A." opens with a testimonial by a "saved" ex-devotee describing how a miraculous vision had revealed to him that Krishna was, in truth, the devil—horns and all—and closes with the declaration that "the Bible does not agree with the Krsna scriptures on any points. . . . No matter how sincerely a devotee follows the Krsna teachings and calls on the name of Krsna, it is in vain."[35]

A voluminous anti-ISKCON polemical literature—appearing in Christian anti-cult books, religious periodicals and pamphlets, and exhibiting frequent cross-quoting and conceptual inbreeding—has attacked Krishna consciousness (and often Hinduism in general) as unbiblical and unchristian. Though devotees are sometimes conceded points for worshipping a personal god and for sincerity, they are generally condemned for worshipping idols, exalting a mere man (the guru), "vain repetition" (Mt. 6:7) of the Hare Krishna mantra, allegedly emphasizing works over faith and devaluing the material world. Testimonies by ISKCON apostates who have found Jesus are featured (such as "Escape from 'Godhead,'" "From Krishna to Christ," "Hare Krishna Starved My Soul") and instruction is provided on witnessing to and converting devotees.

In a guide to cults published by the Committee for Christian Education and Publications of the Presbyterian Church in America (headquartered in Decatur, Georgia),[36] ISKCON's Vaiṣṇava theology is systematically misrepresented and ridiculed in a lighthearted and off-handed manner. ISKCON was started by a "strangely dressed man" who was "an instant hit with certain [Greenwich] Village residents who had otherwise struck out in life."[37] Devotees worship dolls (temple icons), shrubs (the sacred *tulasi* plant) and a God who is "no match for the majesty of Jesus Christ."[38] "For some reason Krishna could take on 16,000 women and conduct a super-super affair with his girl Radha, while his followers are all but totally denied even one legitimate relationship."[39] ISKCON is, nonetheless, attractive to some, mainly due to a lack of real moral and religious standards in society ("When we abandon God, as he is revealed in the Bible, then anything goes. Even Hare Krishna"[40]) and also due to the fact that "the movement does faintly resemble Christianity," though it is a "poor imitation."[41] The deep personal commitment of Krishna devotees is, however, "embarrassing to us," and a cause of Christian defections to ISKCON.

ISKCON fares little better in an article prepared for a Reformed Presbyterian seminary course on cults and later published in a church periodical.[42] A reasonably accurate review of ISKCON teachings is followed by an enumeration of its theological errors (ignorance of God, scripture, Jesus, etc.) and a warning that ISKCON "is not harmless" because it teaches that any person, including a Christian, can benefit from chanting Hare Krishna and reading *Bhagavadgītā*.[43] "The Christian community needs to take steps to quench the group as a whole," suggests the author, and in an unusual expression of Christian agape, he advises, "To properly love them we should seek to pull the rug out from under them."[44]

In the minds of most conservative evangelicals, there is little room for serious, mutually-respectful dialogue with Krishna devotees, because their religion is totally false:

> Since ISKCON has a different God, a different [understanding of] Jesus, and a different way of salvation from what the Bible reveals, it is impossible for there to be any compatibility between the two. They differ on all crucial issues. A person must choose between Krishna and Jesus; no harmony can exist between the sect of Hare Krishna and Christianity.[45]

PRABHUPĀDA ON CHRISTIANITY BACKGROUND

Background

Emerging from a conservative religious milieu, when Prabhupāda arrived in America he knew little of Christianity and subsequently made little effort to acquaint himself with that tradition in any systematic way. He had come to America fired with a strong sense of mission: to teach the absolute and revealed message of the *Bhagavadgītā* and *Śrīmad-Bhāgavatam* (*Bhāgavata-Purāṇa*) and free Americans from ignorance and suffering. That most of those Americans professed allegiance to some form of Christianity was incidental, as Prabhupāda saw it, since they too were essentially materialists, absorbed in *māyā* (worldly illusion), and thus in need of enlightenment as much as anyone else. If in their religious tradition there was truth, they certainly were not living it, and it was his job to give them the liberating message of the Vedas.

Though an author of learned commentaries on the texts of his tradition, Prabhupāda's interest in religion was not intellectual and scholastic, but personal, mystical and evangelistic. Consequently he did not consider it important or necessary to write treatises on comparative religion, to offer any sustained, systematic critique of Christianity, or to cultivate dialogical relationships with church leaders or thinkers (though quite a number of informal meetings did occur). What Prabhupāda did say and write about Christ and Christianity most often was in response to questions and comments by others, and has a somewhat *ad hoc* quality. Nonetheless, a close scrutiny of these statements, scattered throughout his writings, does reveal a somewhat consistent position, and it is that to which I now turn.[46]

The Meaning and End of Religion

True religion, according to Prabhupāda, its truths and its codes for human conduct, is a direct creation of God.[47] As religion, by nature, is of divine origin, it "cannot be manufactured even by great saintly persons."[48] The essential purpose of religion is to restore the soul to its original and eternal nature (*sanātana dharma*), which is to be a loving servant of the Supreme Lord. "Anything which does not lead to the devotional service of the Lord is irreligion," writes Prabhupāda, "and anything which leads to the devotional service of the Lord is called religion."[49] Religion may take different forms in different historical and cultural contexts, but it is this *bhakti*, love for service to God, which is the basic principle.[50]

The God of religion, the supreme object of love and worship, is one, though "He is appreciated according to different angles of vision."[51] The eternal, universal, transcendental principles of religion become refracted through conditioned human nature, and thus a variety of religious systems exist "according to place, the disciples, and the people's capacity to understand" those transcendent truths.[52] The Lord periodically incarnates within the world, within different cultures and societies, revealing as much Truth as can be understood according to time and circumstance:

It is not a fact that the Lord appears only on Indian soil. He can manifest Himself anywhere and everywhere, and whenever He desires to appear. In each and every incarnation, He speaks as much about religion as can be understood by the particular people under their particular circumstances. But the mission is the same — to lead people to God consciousness and obedience to the principles of religion. Sometimes He descends personally, and sometimes He sends His bona fide representative in the form of His son, or servant, or Himself in some disguised form.[53]

Christ and His Path

Whatever his sources of information about Jesus Christ might have been, Prabhupāda accepted Christ as an authentic representative of God, and he expressed genuine, heartfelt appreciation, even affection, for the person of Christ:

> Jesus Christ was such a great personality—the son of God, the representative of God. He had no fault. Still, he was crucified. He wanted to deliver God consciousness, but in return they crucified him—they were so thankless. They could not appreciate his preaching. But we appreciate him and give him all honor as the representative of God. ... [W]e adore Lord Jesus Christ and offer our obeisances to him.[54]

To one disciple he wrote, "Perhaps you have marked it in my preaching work that I love Lord Jesus Christ as good as Krishna, because He rendered the greatest service to Krishna according to time, circumstances and society in which He appeared."[55] Any such selfless servant of the Lord is to be considered a guru—an infallible preceptor worthy of submission:

> Once, in Melbourne, a group of Christian ministers came to visit me. They asked, "What is your idea of Jesus Christ?" I told them, "He is our *guru*. He is preaching God consciousness, so he is our spiritual master." The ministers very much appreciated that.
> Actually, anyone who is preaching God's glories must be accepted as a *guru*. Jesus Christ is one such great personality. We should not think of him as an ordinary human being. ... If Jesus Christ were an ordinary man, then he could not have delivered God consciousness.[56]

It is precisely the extraordinary ultimate success of Jesus' mission to spread "God consciousness" that led Prabhupāda to assign to Christ the technical Vaiṣṇava theological category *śaktyāveśa-avatāra*,[57] referring to an individual directly empowered by God to do his work in the world (although, notably, he rejected the Christian claim of exclusive avatarhood for Jesus).[58]

Christ's authenticity as a representative of God acknowledged, Prabhupāda seems also to acknowledge that there is genuine spiritual efficacy in following his path—that Christianity can "work." Discipleship to Christ can, at least theoretically or potentially, even liberate one from karma-*saṃsāra*, sin and its reactions, and the cycle of transmigration. Acknowledging the salvific power of the crucifixion, Prabhupāda states, "A Vaiṣṇava is unhappy to see the sufferings of others. Therefore, Lord Jesus Christ agreed to be crucified—to free others from their suffering. ... Christ can take the sufferings for the previous sins of his devotees."[59] And, "one who is guided by Jesus Christ will certainly get liberation."[60]

One element within some Christian traditions that Prabhupāda viewed as particularly spiritually efficacious is the invocation of the name of Christ ("Everyone who calls upon the name of the Lord will be saved" [Rom. 10:13]). According to his own Vaiṣṇava beliefs, the names of God are spiritually co-equal with God, and the devotional recitation or singing of those holy names is the supreme form of religious worship in the current age, the Kali Yuga.[61] He viewed this principle as operative within all religious traditions that recognize God and the power of his name. Thus, according to Prabhupāda, if one is reluctant to use the Hare Krishna mantra (consisting of Sanskrit names of God), viewing it as a sectarian Hindu practice, one can use other divine names: "We say that if you have a name which is actually referring to God, that will also do. . . . We are not asking that you chant 'Kṛṣṇa.' "[62] A Christian can "attend the Christian church and sing there. There is no difference between this process and that process."[63] Speaking with a Benedictine monk, Prabhupāda suggested that he "chant the holy name 'Christ.' . . . The Bible demands this of you. . . . [I]f you simply chant the name of God found in your own scriptures, you will attain the spiritual platform."[64]

Christianity and Sanātana Dharma

In spite of these affirmations of Christianity's legitimacy as a religious path, Prabhupāda's theology of comparative religion clearly assigns a subordinate ontological status to Christianity in relation to Krishna consciousness. He makes a distinction between transcendental (*para*) and material (*apara*) religion. Transcendental religion is *Sanātana Dharma*, Eternal Religion: the primordial, essential nature and function of the soul when in its pristine, liberated state, free from the effects of the *guṇas*, illusioning powers of material nature (*prakṛti*). That essential spiritual nature is *bhakti*, love of God. Material religion, on the other hand, is a product of, and caters to, the variety of mental and bodily conditions of still-illusioned souls who have motives ulterior to selfless surrender to God. Whereas *Sanātana Dharma*, being of the essence of the soul, is eternal and unchangeable, mundane religion, being contingent upon the vicissitudes of historical, cultural, and psychological relativity, can and does change. Thus the variety of religions in the world are reflections of the varieties of human conditioning.[65] On the "absolute" platform of transcendence, however, religion is one:

> The Absolute Truth is one, and when one is situated in the Absolute Truth, there is no disagreement. . . . On the absolute platform, the worship is also one. That process is *bhakti*. . . . As confirmed in the *Bhagavad-gītā* (18.66): *sarva-dharmān parityajya mām ekaṁ śaraṇaṁ vraja* ["Abandon all varieties of religion and just surrender unto Me."] The word *ekaṁ* means "one," Kṛṣṇa.[66]

Thus, transcendental religion is defined as surrender and selfless, loving service (*bhakti*) to Krishna. When Christians worship Jesus Christ, who is none other than the son of Krishna, they are practicing *bhakti-yoga* (the path of *bhakti*), and their Christianity is a form of Vaiṣṇavism.[67] As all souls are, by spiritual constitution, eternal servants of Krishna, sincere Christians are, to turn the tables on Karl Rahner, anonymous Vaiṣṇavas. Though their understanding may be limited and their motives mixed, through sincere worship of God they "will one day become pure Vaiṣṇavas."[68] Prabhupāda implies that they will attain the highest state of religion only when they develop explicit knowledge of Krishna: "Real *dharma* is attained when we come to the conclusion that Śrī Kṛṣṇa is everything . . . [I]n the words of Śrī Kṛṣṇa in *Bhagavad-gītā* (7.19): 'After many births and deaths, he who is actually in knowledge surrenders unto Me, knowing Me to be the cause of all causes and all that is. Such a great soul is very rare.' "[69]

As Krishna is revealed in (indeed, is the supreme revelation of) the Vedas,[70] one must ultimately learn *dharma* from that sacred source: "*Dharma*, religion, refers to that which is ordered in the Vedas, and *adharma*, irreligion, refers to that which is not supported in the Vedas."[71] Other scriptures have, at best, a vague notion of God.[72] Though Christianity may teach that God is great, "the actual greatness of God can be understood from the *Bhagavad-gītā* and Śrīmad-Bhāgavatam,"[73] because the Vedic literatures are "older and disseminated by many, many superior *ācāryas* [religious preceptors]."[74] Krishna consciousness transcends all sectarian views and is "the post-graduate study of all religious conceptions of the world."[75] Krishna devotees cannot accept the Bible as authoritative because "sometimes it is learned that the words are not actually spoken by Christ, but they are so set up by the devotees."[76] Even if the Bible does contain the words of God, such teachings "are not always applicable to us" since they were delivered to "a different [less spiritually advanced] class of men."[77]

Further, because in this age Krishna, the Lord, has incarnated as his holy name,[78] one "should chant the holy names of Hari and Krishna, the *mahā-mantra*. That is the sum and substance of eternal religion, known as *sanātana-dharma*. . . . Those who want to attain life's ultimate goal must follow this principle."[79] Indeed, one must do so "if one actually wants to become religious."[80]

As Krishna is God, and as he himself incarnated in this age as the sixteenth-century Bengali saint Śrī Caitanya specifically to teach the pure path of Krishna-*bhakti*, Caitanya's tradition "is richer than any other . . . the living religion of the day with the potency for spreading as *viśva-dharma*, or universal religion."[81]

Mundane Christianity

Up to this point Prabhupāda's pronouncements on Christianity have dealt with that tradition in terms of its innate spiritual status (in relation to *Sanātana Dharma*), and its intrinsic capacity and potential for granting enlightenment and salvation. In this and the next section, I will look at

Prabhupāda's informal critique of Christianity as actually practiced, especially as he had come to observe it in the West.

For Prabhupāda, genuine religion is never compromised with and accommodated to "the world"; it must, indeed, instill a sense of *vairāgya*, detachment from the world. The genuine religionist must choose God over mammon: "The aim of any scripture of any country . . . is simply to get us back to Godhead. . . . [T]ake any great representative of the Lord—none of them will tell you to make your best plans to live peacefully in this material world."[82] Christians' addiction to fleeting, illusory pleasures (*māyā-sukha*), and to security and success, diverts them from their own spiritual path: "As far as the Christian religion is concerned, ample opportunity is given to understand God, but no one is taking it."[83] "Because at present people do not follow the rules and regulations of Christianity— the commandments of Jesus Christ—they do not come to the standard of God consciousness."[84] Whatever their religious affiliation, most people "don't care for God. They simply take an official stand, but actually, from the depth of their heart they have no idea what is God."[85]

Though Prabhupāda seemed to accept that Jesus Christ, through his crucifixion, could free his followers from sin and suffering, he felt that this genuine act of mercy was rendered meaningless and non-operative by Christians who do not, in response to this divine dispensation, renounce sin. Rather than "Go, and sin no more" (Jn. 8:11), such followers callously abuse Christ's salvific mercy by willfully continuing to sin, and thus "crucify the Son of God afresh" (Heb. 6:6):

> Lord Jesus Christ agreed to be crucified—to free others from their suffering. But his followers are so unfaithful that they have decided, "Let Christ suffer for us, and we'll go on committing sin." They love Christ so much that they think, "My dear Christ, we are weak. We cannot give up our sinful activities. So you please suffer for us." . . .
>
> Christ can take the sufferings for the previous sins of his devotees. But first they have to be sane: "Why should I put Jesus Christ into suffering for my sins? Let me stop my sinful activities.[86]

That they do not abandon a life of materialistic self-indulgence (sin), Prabhupāda interpreted as proof of spiritual insincerity.

As Prabhupāda saw it, whereas in contemporary practice Christianity doesn't "work," Krishna consciousness does. To a journalist who asked why so many young people leave Western religions for those of the East, Prabhupāda replied: "Because Judaism and Christianity are not teaching them *practically*. I am teaching them *practically*. . . . Love of Godhead is being taught both in the Bible and in the *Bhagavad-gītā*. But today's religionists are not actually teaching how to love God. I am teaching people how to love God—that is the difference."[87] Prabhupāda believed that the evidence for the effectiveness of Krishna consciousness lay in his disciples' demonstrated disinterest in worldliness and materialism, and their positive attachment for self-sacrificing service to Lord Krishna: "[T]heir only desire is to serve Kṛṣṇa's service. This is called *kevalayā*, pure; for them there is no other business."[88]

Carnivorous Christians

Prabhupāda's most strongly-felt criticism of Christians concerned the eating of animal flesh. For Prabhupāda, this was not a matter of arbitrary dietary preference, but an ethical imperative: A person who loves God cannot kill his creatures. The matter is basic and fundamental: The unnecessary taking of innocent animal life is barbarism, pure and simple. The consumption of dead animal bodies is an act not fit for a civilized, especially a religiously-sensitive, human being. The eating of animal flesh implicates one in an act of wanton violence against life made no less barbaric by one's detachment from the original act of slaughter. It is violence that is inconsistent with the essential spiritual attribute of compassion. Compassion for other living beings derives, Prabhupāda felt, from spiritual empathy—the viewing of all life forms as creatures created by a common Father. Without this charitable vision, one becomes callous to suffering. "The Christians . . . think the animals have no soul, and therefore they think they can freely kill billions of innocent animals in the slaughterhouses."[89] For Prabhupāda, the vegetarian imperative does not rest merely upon the belief that animals have souls, but upon the dual principles of compassion and non-violence:

> Everyone should be unhappy to see others in distress and happy to see others happy. *Ātmavat sarva-bhūteṣu*: one should feel the happiness and distress of others as his own. . . . We feel pain when someone disturbs us, and therefore we should not inflict pain upon other living beings. . . . One cannot continue killing animals and at the same time be a religious man. That is the greatest hypocrisy.[90]

Prabhupāda chides "superficially religious" persons who "adhere to their religious principles very nicely but are not equal to all living entities." Their religiosity "has no meaning" because a genuine devotee of the Lord "is a friend to everyone (*suhṛdaṁ sarva-bhūtānām*)" and thus cannot kill innocent animals.[91] To think that animal killing does not detract from spiritual realization, is "nonsensical."[92]

Prabhupāda rarely discussed Christianity or conversed with Christian clergy without bluntly and insistently raising the meat-eating issue. To him, the biblical commandment (of both Testaments) "Thou shalt not kill" self-evidently applied both to the human and the non-human. Christians' interpretation of this moral axiom as applying only to human life was nothing more than a willful misinterpretation in order to justify gratuitous killing of animals for the satisfaction of the tongue. "Jesus Christ said, 'Do not kill,' but hypocrites nevertheless maintain thousands of slaughterhouses while posing as Christians."[93] Theological niceties were rendered irrelevant when simple murder was the issue. Like a judge refusing to engage in disputation on fine points of jurisprudence with a convicted murderer, Prabhupāda rarely allowed theological dialogue to get beyond what for him was an elemental issue of life and death. A disciple who served as Prabhupāda's secretary writes:

> He talked often with the Christians about why they disobey God by killing other living entities. Finally, one of them complained that we were just talking the whole time about meat-eating. "Why can't we talk of higher principles?" they asked. Śrīla Prabhupāda said, "So long as one is sinful, there is no question of understanding higher principles."[94]

As far as Prabhupāda was concerned, "although there are many persons who profess to be Christians, it would be very difficult to find one who strictly follows the instructions of Lord Jesus Christ."[95] "One who is guided by Jesus Christ will certainly get liberation. But it is very hard to find a man who is actually being guided by Jesus Christ."[96]

PROBLEMS AND PROSPECTS FOR DIALOGUE

Though an encounter has occurred, it would appear that thus far there has been little real dialogue between Christians and members of the Krishna consciousness movement. There have been, to be sure, critiques, assessments, constructive and non-constructive criticisms, judgments, reactions, condemnations and testimonials, but little serious, patient, sustained, face-to-face, soul-to-soul dialogue. How many Christians, for instance, have allowed themselves, through an openness to and patient hearing of the message of Krishna consciousness, to be "called back to something more essential" in their own religious heritage, as Harvey Cox wrote — "to discover some things that we've ignored and suppressed"? How many Krishna devotees have sought the fellowship of a Christian contemplative in order to gain insight into the sublime person of Lord Jesus Christ, the *śaktyāveśa-avatāra* and loving son and servant of Lord Krishna, and to seek the "unknown Krishna of Christianity"?

There have certainly been obstacles to true dialogue. From the Christian side there has been a good deal of religious narrowmindedness, ignorance, and missionary triumphalism. Perhaps there has also been a feeling among many Christians that ISKCON devotees, being Westerners by birth, do not really "count" as authentic Hindus — faddists, enthusiasts, counterfeits perhaps, but not real emissaries of an ancient and venerable religious tradition — and thus are not worthy of being taken seriously. By such logic, however, one would be forced to discount the Christian conversions of

Asian Indians. Such an attitude mistakenly reduces spirituality to ethnicity, and implicity and arbitrarily denies to Vaiṣṇava-Hindu tradition that which Christianity claims for itself: that it is a truly universal movement of the Spirit that transcends geographical and cultural relativity.

From the ISKCON side (and here I am speaking not only of Prabhupāda but of his movement), there have also been obstacles to real dialogue. Devotees' reluctance to actively pursue dialogue with Christians has, in part, been a function of the movement's youth: its preoccupation with the fundamental tasks of building a stable institution, defending itself from external harassment, surviving internal upheaval (following Prabhupāda's death in 1977) and undertaking radical internal reform.[97] Devotees' lack of interest in dialogue also results from what Robert Baird has documented as a kind of religious and intellectual isolationism advocated in certain Vaiṣṇavite texts and in Prabhupāda's commentaries upon them.[98] It may also be a function of an overly simplistic, self-serving view of Christianity as hopelessly mired in materialism, an attitude that deflects attention away from the spiritual riches that lie at the heart of that tradition.

There are, however, some hopeful signs. On the Christian side, the World Council of Churches along with the Lutheran World Federation have recently issued a substantial position paper calling for dialogue with members of "new religious movements," including ISKCON, as has the Vatican.[99] It remains to be seen whether the churches, and individual Christians, will respond to that call and in what manner.

On the ISKCON side, there is also some cause for optimism. Several years ago theologian Harvey Cox expressed hope that the Krishna consciousness movement might begin to develop "intellectually sophisticated yet still spiritually authentic," interpreters of Vaiṣṇava tradition sufficiently aware of developments in Hindu-Christian dialogue to contribute to and enrich that dialogue in America.[100] In his paper examining Prabhupāda's response to religious pluralism, Robert Baird wonders "to what extent the more ameliorating principles [of Prabhupāda's critique of other religions] will be brought to the fore by the movement now that the founder has died and as the movement becomes more acceptable."[101] There is increasing evidence that disciples of Prabhupāda are willing—impelled by scholarly and/or dialogical interests—to study Christian tradition and to enter into sustained dialogue with its representatives.[102] This author feels confident that through the serious study of Christian doctrine and spirituality, through experiencing direct contact with that profoundly rich tradition, and through entering into empathetic dialogue with conscientious and devout Christians, the Western devotees of Krishna inevitably will want to search the Vaiṣṇava scriptures (and their own Vaiṣṇavite tradition)—as Christians have done within theirs—for those theological principles that would allow and encourage a respectful and appreciative attitude toward those forms of spirituality that exist beyond the conceptual and linguistic boundaries of their own chosen tradition. I believe that that search is already underway and that valuable treasures have already been recovered. One major figure in modern Caitanya-Vaiṣṇava history, Bhaktivinoda Ṭhākura (1838–1914), for instance, seems to have begun to construct a theological basis for a new Vaiṣṇavite pluralism:

> Lord Caitanya has specifically ordered that we should execute our own service to the Supreme Lord ... and at the same time refrain from ridiculing the religious codes of others. ... Each [religious] community should, of course, properly honor its own spiritual masters, but simply for the sake of gaining followers, no one should try to establish that the instructions given by one's own spiritual master are better than the instructions of spiritual masters everywhere else....
>
> If one happens to be in another's temple at the time of his worship, one should think, "Here my Lord is being worshiped in a different form. ... The Supreme Absolute Truth is one without a second. Therefore, as I offer my obeisances to the form which I see here, I pray to my Lord, from whom this form comes, that this Deity will help me expand my love for Him.

> Those who do not behave in this way, but who exhibit malice, envy, or ridicule toward other religious processes, certainly deviate from true religion due to a lack of intelligence. If such people actually loved their own Supreme Lord, they would not be attracted to such useless disputes.[103]

I believe that if we truly have lived and understood our own religious traditions—not merely subscribed and acquiesced to, studied and interpreted, supported and defended them, but really plumbed their spiritual depths and imbibed their deepest truths—we could not help but have developed the kind of spiritual sensitivity, insight, charitas and empathetic compassion that allows us to sense the presence of the Spirit, the presence of divine grace, wherever and in whomever it may reside. I believe this is true no less for the Krishna devotee than it is for the Christian.

NOTES

1. *Walden and Other Writings by Henry David Thoreau,* ed. J. W. Krutch (Toronto: Bantam, 1962), p. 325, from the section "The Pond in Winter."

2. Recent works on the Krishna consciousness movement include Steven J. Gelberg, ed., *Hare Krishna, Hare Krishna: Five Distinguished Scholars on the Krishna Movement in the West* (New York: Grove Press, 1983); E. Burke Rochford, Jr., *Hare Krishna in America* (New Brunswick, N.J.: Rutgers University Press, 1985); and Larry D. Shinn, *The Dark Lord: Cult Images and the Hare Krishnas in America* (Philadelphia: Westminister, 1987).

3. For an exhaustive, six-volume biography by a disciple, see Satsvarūpa dāsa

Goswami, *Śrīla Prabhupāda-līlāmṛta* (Los Angeles: Bhaktivedanta Book Trust, 1980-83), condensed to one volume in Goswami's *Prabhupāda* (same publisher, 1983). For a view of Prabhupāda by a historian of religion, see "Interview with Thomas J. Hopkins," in Gelberg, pp. 126-51.

4. Though often used interchangeably, perhaps some distinction should be made between the Krishna consciousness (or Hare Krishna) movement and ISK-CON. ISKCON is a specific organization having local incorporations throughout the world but with a central governing body. The Krishna consciousness movement, once synonomous with ISKCON, now more properly refers to the wider movement of mostly-Western Vaiṣṇavas, consisting of current members of ISKCON, spiritually-active former members, lay adherents, sympathizers, schismatics and various other non-institutionally-affiliated practitioners of *bhakti*-yoga as taught by Prabhupāda.

5. For an elaboration on this theme, see my interview with the late, respected indologist A.L. Basham. Gelberg, pp. 163-67, 175-180.

6. Klaus Klostermaier, "Will India's Past Be America's Future?" *Journal of Asian and African Studies* 15.1-2 (1980): 94-103.

7. Shinn, pp. 61-62.

8. Thomas Merton, "The Significance of the *Bhagavadgītā*," in A. C. Bhaktivedanta Swami, *The Bhagavadgita As It Is* (New York: Collier Books, 1968), pp. 18-22.

9. Ibid. p. 18.

10. Edward McCorkell, O.S.C.O., "A Monastic Encounter," *Back to Godhead* 14.12 (December 1979): 20-21.

11. Ibid.

12. Ibid. p. 21.

13. Klostermaier, pp. 94-103.

14. Ibid. p. 99.

15. Ibid. p. 100.

16. Ibid. p. 94.

17. John A. Saliba, S.J., "Christian and Jewish Responses to ISKCON: Dialogue or Diatribe?" *ISKCON Review* 2 (1986): 76-103.

18. Ibid. p. 93.

19. Ibid. p. 94.

20. Ibid. pp. 93-94.

21. Ibid. p. 92.

22. Ibid. p. 93.

23. Philip Lochhaas, *How to Respond to the Eastern Religions* (St. Louis: Concordia, 1979), p. 28.

24. Ibid. pp. 27-28.

25. Philip Lochhaas, "International Society for Krishna Consciousness," St. Louis: The Commission on Organizations, Lutheran Church—Missouri Synod, (January 1978), pp. 3-4.

26. Ibid. p. 4.

27. "The Commission on Organizations: The 'New Religions,' Brainwashing and Deprogramming," St. Louis: The Commission on Organizations, Lutheran Church—Missouri Synod, n.d., pp. 4-5.

28. Gary Leazer, "Hare Hare, Hare Krishna." *Missions USA* (September/October 1981): 56.

29. A. L. McDaniel, Jr., "Hare Krishna," in *Beliefs of Other Kinds* (Atlanta: Home Mission Board, Southern Baptist Convention, n.d.), p. 136.

30. Robin H. S. Boyd, "Statement," in *An Appeal to Reason: Please Don't Lump Us In* (Melbourne: International Society for Krishna Consciousness, 1980), p. 32.

31. "Interview with Harvey Cox," in Gelberg, p. 27.

32. Ibid. pp. 27-28.

33. Ibid. p. 31.

34. Harvey Cox, "A Christian Tribute to Krishna Consciousness," *Back to Godhead* 12.6 (June 1977): 22. For a similar perspective from the Anglican Bishop of Tasmania, Australia, the Rt. Rev. Phillip K. Newell, see "What Is the Bishop Saying?" *Church News* (Tasmania) (October 1983): 3-7. For another, more formal theological assessment, see Kenneth Rose, "Has ISKCON Anything to Offer Christianity Theologically?" *ISKCON Review* 2 (1986): 64-75.

35. "Mantras, Sikhas & Krsna" (Chicago: Jesus People U.S.A., 1978). For a more elaborate treatment of conservative Christian views of ISKCON, see Saliba.

36. Harris Langford, *Traps: A Probe of Those Strange New Cults* (Philadelphia: Great Commission Publications, 1977), pp. 113-27.

37. Ibid. p. 114.

38. Ibid. p. 126.

39. Ibid. p. 118.

40. Ibid. p. 119.

41. Ibid. p. 120.

42. William Wood, "Who's this 'Harry' Krishna?" *Covenanter Witness* (November 19, 1975): 6-8.

43. Ibid. p. 8.

44. Ibid.

45. Josh McDowell and Don Stewart, *Understanding the Cults* (San Bernardino, CA: Here's Life Publishers, 1982), p. 54.

46. Two previous articles have reviewed Prabhupāda's views of other religions in general, including Christianity: Robert D. Baird, "Swami Bhaktivedanta and the Encounter with Religions," in Harold Coward, ed., *Modern Indian Responses to Religious Pluralism* (Maryknoll, NY: Orbis Books, 1987); and Graham M. Schweig, "*Bhakti*, 'The Living Religion of the Day': A Study of the ISKCON Vaishnava View of Other Religions," presented at a conference on "Krishna Consciousness in the West: A Multi-Disciplinary Critique," New Vrindaban, WV (July 1985). The present article focuses on Prabhupāda's particular views on Christianity in substantially greater detail than either of those sources, though I've found both of them helpful in clarifying my own reading of Prabhupāda's position.

47. *dharmaṁ tu sāksād bhagavat-pranītaṁ* (*SB* 6.3.19).

48. A. C. Bhaktivedanta Swami Prabhupāda, *Śrī Caitanya-caritāmrta* (hereafter referred to as *CC*) (Los Angeles: Bhaktivedanta Book Trust, 1973-75), *Madhya-līlā*, vol. 4, p. 262.

49. A.C. Bhaktivedanta Swami Prabhupāda, *Śrīmad-Bhāgavatam* (hereafter referred to as *SB*) (Los Angeles: Bhaktivedanta Book Trust, 1975-78), canto 3, vol. 2, p. 141.

50. *SB*, canto 2, vol. 2, pp. 110-11.

51. *SB*, canto 5, vol. 1, p. 132.

52. *CC*, *Madhya-līlā*, vol. 7, p. 325.

53. A. C. Bhaktivedanta Swami Prabhupāda, *Bhagavadgītā As It Is*, Complete

Edition (Los Angeles: Bhaktivedanta Book Trust, 1983), p. 227.

54. A. C. Bhaktivedanta Swami Prabhupāda, *The Science of Self Realization* (hereafter referred to as *SSR*) (Los Angeles: Bhaktivedanta Book Trust, 1977), p. 135.

55. *Letters from Śrīla Prabhupāda* (hereafter referred to as *LSP*) (Los Angeles: The Vaiṣṇava Institute, 1987), vol. 4, p. 154.

56. *SSR*, pp. 135-36.

57. *LSP*, vol. 2, p. 1076.

58. *CC, Ādi-līlā*, vol. 3, p. 347.

59. *SSR*, p. 135.

60. A. C. Bhaktivedanta Swami Prabhupāda, *Perfect Questions, Perfect Answers* (Los Angeles: Bhaktivedanta Book Trust, 1977), p. 94.

61. *harer nāma harer nāma harer nāmaiva kevalum/kalau nāsty eva nāsty eva nāsty eva gatir anyathā*: "In this age of Kali there is no alternative, there is no alternative, there is no alternative for spiritual progress than the holy name, the holy name, the holy name of the Lord." *Bṛhan-nāradīya Purāṇa* (cited in *CC, Ādi-līlā*, vol. 2, p. 61).

62. A. C. Bhaktivedanta Swami Prabhupāda, "Transcendental Broadcast," *Back to Godhead*, no. 56 (c. late 1973): 6.

63. A. C. Bhaktivedanta Swami Prabhupāda, *Rāja-vidyā, The King of Knowledge* (Los Angeles: The Bhaktivedanta Book Trust, 1973), p. 15.

64. *SSR*, p. 131.

65. *CC, Madhya-līlā*, vol. 9, p. 363.

66. *CC, Madhya-līlā*, vol. 7, p. 99.

67. A. C. Bhaktivedanta Swami Prabhupāda, *The Path of Perfection* (Los Angeles: Bhaktivedanta Book Trust, 1979), p. 118.

68. A. C. Bhaktivedanta Swami Prabhupāda, *The Teachings of Queen Kunti* (Los Angeles: Bhaktivedanta Book Trust, 1978), p. 136.

69. A. C. Bhaktivedanta Swami Prabhupāda, *The Teachings of Lord Kapīla* (Los Angeles: Bhaktivedanta Book Trust, 1977), pp. 5-6.

70. *vedaiś ca sarvair aham eva vedyo*: "By all the Vedas, I am to be known" (*Gītā* 15.15). *Vāsudeva-parā vedā*: "In the revealed scriptures, the ultimate object of knowledge is Srī Kṛṣṇa" (*SB* 1.2.28).

71. *SB*, canto 4, vol. 1, p. 57.

72. A. C. Bhaktivedanta Swami Prabhupāda, "Can We Keep Society from Going to the Dogs?" *Back to Godhead* 12.1 (January 1977), p. 6.

73. Prabhupāda, *The Path of Perfection*, p. 118.

74. *LSP*, vol. 3, p. 1390.

75. Excerpt from a letter by Prabhupāda, cited in "Christ and Krishna," a two-page unpublished compilation of statements on Christianity.

76. *LSP*, vol. 2, p. 1076.

77. Ibid.

78. *kali-kāle nāma-rūpe kṛṣṇa avatāra*: "In this age of Kali, the holy name of the Lord . . . is the incarnation of Lord Kṛṣṇa" (*CC, Adi-līlā* 17.22).

79. *CC, Madhya-līla*, vol. 4, p. 105.

80. Ibid. p. 262.

81. *SB*, canto 1, vol. 1, p. 40.

82. A. C. Bhaktivedanta Swami Prabhupāda, "The Aim of All Faiths" *Back to Godhead* 15.1-2 (January/February 1980), p. 3.

83. A. C. Bhaktivedanta Swami Prabhupāda, "The Secret of Real Religion," *Back to Godhead* 11.6 (June 1976), p. 5.

84. Ibid. p. 4.

85. *LSP*, vol. 2, p. 769.

86. *SSR*, p. 135.

87. A. C. Bhaktivedanta Swami Prabhupāda, "Rascals, Bluffers and Show Bottle Spiritualists," *Back to Godhead* 14.2-3 (February/March 1979), p. 4.

88. A. C. Bhaktivedanta Swami Prabhupāda, *The Matchless Gift* (Los Angeles: Bhaktivedanta Book Trust, 1974), p. 71.

89. *SSR*, p. 134.

90. *SB*, canto 6, vol. 2, p. 167.

91. *SB*, canto 8, vol. 1, pp. 304-5. Cf. Mt. 22:39: "You shall love your neighbor as yourself."

92. Ibid.

93. *SB*, canto 6, vol. 2, p. 167.

94. Satsvarūpa dāsa Goswami, "Secretary to a Pure Devotee." *Back to Godhead*, no. 68 (December 1974), p. 27.

95. Ibid. p. 134.

96. Prabhupāda, *Perfect Questions, Perfect Answers*, p. 94.

97. For more on ISKCON's internal upheavals since the death of Prabhupāda, see the author's "The Fading of Utopia: ISKCON in Transition," forthcoming in the *Bulletin of the John Ryland's University of Manchester*.

98. Baird, pp. 7-9 (ms.).

99. Both these documents have been published in Allan R. Brockway and J. Paul Rajashekar, eds., *New Religious Movements and the Churches* (Geneva: WCC Publications, 1987), pp. 171-97.

100. "Interview with Harvey Cox," in Gelberg, pp. 34-35.

101. Baird, p. 27 (ms.).

102. One devotee, for example, a doctoral candidate at Harvard, is working on a dissertation comparing elements of "bridal mysticism" in the Caitanya Vaiṣṇavite tradition with that in St. John of the Cross. Another, the author, has for a number of years been a keen student of and active participant in Hindu-Christian dialogue, and recently prepared a lengthy response to the Vatican report on new religious movements (Steven J. Gelberg, "The Catholic Church and the Hare Krishna Movement: An Invitation to Dialogue," *ISKCON Review* 2 [1986], pp. 1-63), which attempts to establish the groundwork for an informed, mutually-respectful dialogue between Catholics and Krishna devotees. Others have, in recent years, engaged in friendly, non-polemical dialogue with major figures within the Christian community including Dom Helder Camara (Archbishop of Recife, Brazil), Jaime Cardinal Sin of the Philippines and Fr. Bede Griffiths of Shantivanam Ashram, Tamil Nadu, India.

103. Śrīla Bhaktivinoda Ṭhākura, "The Nectarean Teachings of Śrī Caitanya," trans. by Gopīparāṇadhana dāsa, *Back to Godhead* 11.2 (February 1976), pp. 13-14.

10

Hindu Views of Christ

RONALD NEUFELDT

For anyone who has visited Hindu homes and shrines both in India and the West, it is obvious that Christ has been and is an important religious figure and inspiration for Hindus. It is not unusual to find pictures of Jesus in Hindu shrines and in the *pūjā* rooms of Hindu homes. On the basis of first-hand experience in India Klaus Klostermaier reports:

> The most devout among the Hindus call him an "incarnation"—one of Vishnu's avataras such as Rama, Krishna or Chaitanya. Others venerate him as a great teacher of righteousness, as a saint whose selflessness and spirit of sacrifice are a model to men. Others again consider him a great miracle-worker, like the yogis in ancient times, or like Ramakrishna or Sai Baba nowadays. In many a Hindu home and even in many a temple there is a picture of Jesus—mostly a picture of the Sacred Heart of Jesus, of Italian origin—and many a guru illustrates his upadesha, his religious instruction, with parables from the New Testament and with incidents from the lives of Christian saints.[1]

Devaraja distinguishes between Vaiṣṇava, intellectual and popular images, pointing out that variously Christ will be seen as an incarnation, as a god, or simply as a teacher.[2]

The importance of the story of Jesus for the Ramakrishna Mission has been reported more than once. The birth of Christ and Good Friday are celebrated regularly at Mission centers. Stewart reports that the Mission was born on a Christmas Eve in 1886 in conjunction with the telling of the story of Jesus by Vivekananda, and that the monks pledged themselves to be Christs in the sense of being responsive to human needs.[3] The architecture of the temple in Calcutta is supposed to represent a combination of Hindu, Muslim and Christian components.

This does point out that at least from the time of Francis Xavier there has been not only an awareness of the figure of Christ, but on various levels an incorporation of this figure into the religious preoccupations of Hindus. This incorporation was carried forward and heightened during and after the period of the Hindu Renaissance. The images dealt with in this chapter are taken solely from the nineteenth and twentieth centuries, beginning with figures usually associated with the Hindu Renaissance. Consequently these images are taken from the intellectual rather than the popular world of Hinduism. It will become apparent that there is no single image of Christ among the intellectuals. However, the various images will, in some cases, overlap, and it is not uncommon for a variety of images to be found in a single representative thinker. What will become clear, I hope, is that regardless of the various images, the figure of Jesus, is, for all intensive purposes, made into an Asiatic or Oriental, in some cases explicitly and in other cases implicitly. The approach taken for this study is a topical one. In other words, rather than dealing in consecutive fashion with various thinkers in case-study fashion, the approach here will be to discuss the ideas of representative figures under two main headings: Christ as incarnation, and Christ as an ideal.

CHRIST AS INCARNATION

If one begins with the Brāhmo Samāj, it is clear that for the most part Christ will not be seen as an incarnation, as God-become-man in any sense. Rather, Christ is seen as a reformer, prophet and teacher among other reformers, prophets and teachers like Muhammad and the Buddha. While at times he may be placed above others as a universal model because of the simplicity and power of his teachings, he was, for most Brāhmos very much human. For the most part notions of an atoning sacrifice and trinitarian theology are rejected as fabrications developed by mistaken disciples and early church fathers. An exception to this may be Keshab Chunder Sen.

Keshab's attitude to Christ is a complex one. On the one hand, like Rāmmohun Roy, he was not drawn to Christological formulations. On the other hand, he was quite willing to utilize, in a Hindu sense, the symbolism surrounding the birth and death of Jesus. Celebrating the Eucharist, for example, meant becoming informed by the spirit of Jesus.[4] The crucifixion suggested a yogic posture in which Jesus, incapable of movement, had died to the flesh.[5] But this would mean that crucifixion had happened many times in history in heroes like Gotama, who had achieved a similar death.

But was Christ an incarnation? There are those who claim that Keshab reverted to the traditional Hindu view of *avatāras* with respect to Christ. But this is too simplistic for two reasons. First, there is no single notion of "avatarahood" in Hinduism. Parrinder, for example, points out that Gandhi, Ramakrishna, Vivekananda, Radhakrishnan and Aurobindo all understood something different when speaking of the concept of *avatāra*.[6] Das points out that Keshab had at least an implicit notion of incarnation, but not one that necessarily made Jesus superior to other great men, all of whom were in a sense God's manifestations and therefore divine.

> True incarnation, according to Keshab, is not "the absolute perfection of the divine nature embodied in mortal form: it is not the God of the Universe putting on a human body—the infinite becoming finite in space and time, in intelligence and power. It simply means God manifest in humanity—not God made man, but God in man." Here again Keshab differs from the Hindu view of incarnation as contained in the Gita and also the Christian doctrine as contained in the Nicene Creed and in the Athanasian Creed. Keshab Chundra considers Great Men above ordinary men but not above natural laws, thus he rejects the possibility of miracles.[7]

This view of Jesus as a type of incarnation is apparently not consistent in the thought of Keshab. Scott points out that Keshab, before 1866, had seen Jesus as a great man, but following 1866 he proclaimed Jesus as "one with God and humankind," stressing his "divine humanity," his "absorption in God," Vedantic style.[8] Keshab is, however, consistent in his notion of Jesus as a great man among other great men. He is to be seen as one among other similar types who are superior to the rest of humankind by virtue of their "divine" nature and the good they do. This obvious superiority has at times, as in the case of Jesus, caused these figures to be exalted to the status of divinity and exclusive carriers of the truth.[9] However questionable such exaltation may be, this superior endowment and God-consciousness on the part of great men certainly entitles them to reverence.

> Great men are sent by God into the world to benefit mankind. They are his apostles and missionaries, who bring to us glad tidings from heaven; and in order that they may effectually accomplish their errand, they are endowed by Him with requisite power and talents. They are created with a nature superior to that of others, which is at once the testimonial of their apostleship, and the guarantee of their success. ... It is God's light that makes them shine, and enables them to illumine the world. He puts in their very constitution something superhuman and divine; hence their greatness and superiority. ... Though human, they are divine.[10]

Jesus is the greatest of these great men and more deserving of reverence because he has done more wonders and greater good than they have.[11]
The notion of divinity with respect to Christ is clearly stated by Keshab

in an 1879 article, "Who Is Christ?" Here he reiterates the theme of divine humanity asserting that it is an eminently Hindu idea since it has its basis in Jesus' declaration that, "I and the Father are one." This, for Keshab, is simply the principle of self-abnegation, which must precede the filling of the individual with the divine presence.

> He destroyed self. And as self ebbed away, Heaven came pouring into the soul. For as you know, nature abhors a vacuum, and hence as soon as the soul is emptied of self—Divinity fills the void. So it was with Christ. The Spirit of the Lord filled him, and everything was thus divine within him.[12]

The fundamental understanding of incarnation then appears to be that of God-in-man, not God-as-man.

The issue is, however, complicated somewhat by Keshab's assertion that Christ, in a sense, came down from heaven to earth to accomplish a particular mission—to manifest the "divine in man as no other man has ever done before."[13] There was therefore a spiritual pre-existence for Christ. Does this mean that Keshab waffles, that at times he sees Jesus as human and at other times as Godhead? The key to the language of preexistence is Keshab's distinction between Christ as an abstract idea existing in the mind of God—as indeed the whole economy of God has always existed in the mind of God—and Jesus as an actual human being. In this way Keshab attempts to preserve the view that incarnation means God-in-man, not God-become-man.

> How then and in what shape did he exist in heaven? As an Idea, as a plan of life, as a predetermined dispensation, yet to be realized, as purity of character, not concrete but abstract, as light not yet manifested. . . . His earthly life had certainly a beginning, but the divine life in him could not possibly have had a beginning; wisdom has no beginning; love can have none; truth can never commence to exist. For these existed through all eternity in God Himself. . . . Before the world was, the Eternal God existed, and in His bosom slept Jesus, or rather the Ideal Jesus.[14]

In the person of Christ we have the manifestation of the ideal of filial sonship that has existed in God from time immemorial and which is given flesh for the salvation of humankind.[15] Keshab joins this idea of manifestation to the idea of union with the Godhead. This he claims is nothing but Vedantic or Hindu pantheistic teaching. The pantheism of Christ, however, is superior to that practiced in India in that it is fully conscious, an active self-surrender of the will, while that practiced in India is unconscious quietism and trance.[16]

Trinitatian formulations, according to Keshab, are to be understood within the context of his view of God-in-man, or God manifesting himself within his own creation. In an article on the Trinity, he places the teaching of the Trinity within the context of involution and evolution, claiming that the Trinitarian formulation is nothing but God manifesting himself in his own creation and drawing this creation back up to him. It is simply the logos developing through ever-advancing stages of life.[17] The traditional Christian formulation of Father, Son and Holy Spirit is then nothing more than an expression of God's self-manifestation or creation. The Son is the symbol for divinity coming down to humanity and pervading the whole of the world, while the Holy Spirit is simply the evolution, or progressive realization of this divinity in creation, "carrying up humanity to heaven." This, Keshab claims, is not different from the meaning of *Sat* (Being), *Chit* (Consciousness), *Ananda* (Bliss).[18]

In this understanding Christ is not an incarnation if by that is meant something other than and separate from humanity. Like the rest of humanity he is human nature in which divinity dwells, but in him this nature is "perfected by true affiliation to the Divine nature."[19] Christ is an incarnation, but of brotherhood, not God-as-man, but God-in-man. In him was manifested and realized the ideal of sonship. In this sense he is our own divine brother. He is the logos but it is the same logos that is lodged in all creation, in all stages of life, only in Christ it has been realized to perfection.[20]

> Scattered in all schools of philosophy and all religious sects, scattered in all men and women of the East and the West, are multitudinous Christ-principles and fragments of Christ-life — one vast and identical Sonship diversely manifested.[21]

The key in Keshab's discussion of Christ as *avatāra*, the perfect realization of God-in-man, is the idea of the achievement of union but not identity. One finds in thinkers following Keshab the same terminology with respect to the *avatāra*, or Jesus as *avatāra*, but not the same meaning. In thinkers like Radhakrishnan, Aurobindo, and Vivekananda, the dominant term for the discussion of *avatāra* is the advaitin term, identity. For Radhakrishnan Jesus is an *avatāra* in the sense that he recognized the divine within, freed himself from all imperfection, took refuge in God, and attained to divine status. Thus he could say quite literally that he and God were one.[22] The resurrection of Jesus is not to be understood as a bodily resurrection but as the resurrection of the divine within, the growth of consciousness that he was essentially divine.[23] Jesus was an *avatāra* in the sense that he is a model of the perfect union of his will with the divine, although this perfection is available to all since we are, at bottom, all essentially divine. However, Jesus had to learn to overcome self to the point where he gave up his separate existence and identified himself solely with the will of God.[24] In the sense that Jesus is both an awakened one and shows others the way of the awakening, Radhakrishnan retains notions of Jesus as mediator and divine manifestation, but not as someone separate from the rest of humankind. For,

> The divine manifestation is not an infringment of man's personality. On the contrary, it is the highest degree of man's natural self-expressions since the true nature of man is divine.[25]

Like Rāmmohun Roy, Radhakrishnan recognizes that Jesus has been raised to the rank of God by his followers. Unlike Roy, Radhakrishnan sees this as a positive development in that it corrects the one-sided Old Testament view of God as infinite majesty, rather than the immanent principle of the world process (the Holy Spirit).[26] He rejects, however, the pietistic aspect of this development, which sees Jesus as a decisive act of God, somehow breaking into history. Jesus is special only in the sense that he reveals more than the ordinary person the eternal within the temporal and in the sense that he does so because the time demanded someone to restore the moral equilibrium. He is not an *avatāra* if this means that his relationship to God cannot be replicated in the lives of other human beings.[27]

For Radhakrishnan, then, Jesus is not so much an incarnation as one who incarnates God's love or develops God within himself. Any adoptionist Christologies or preexistence theories are untenable because they place a gulf between God and man and make it impossible for the human being to achieve that which Jesus achieved. In *The Recovery of Faith* he says:

> The Incarnation is not an historical event which occurred two thousand years ago. It is an event which is renewed in the life of everyone who is on the way to the fulfilment of his destiny.[28]

This leads to certain rather important conclusions concerning issues like saviorhood and mediatorship. Like any other *guru* Jesus is a savior in that he quickens divine life in us through his words and example.[29] But there is no such thing as propitiation or atonement for sin through the death of Christ. The redemptive significance of Christ's death is not in its power to atone but in its power to show us what is necessary and possible for the achievement of perfection.[30] There is in Radhakrishnan's thought a distinction similar to the one found in Keshab, the distinction between the historical Jesus and Jesus as the ideal representation of the eternal reality within. Whenever the world gets bogged down in error there is a necessity for an *avatāra*, for truth to take on human garb with clarity. Each such manifestation is a second coming.[31] It is the eternal within, not the historical Jesus, that mediates salvation. The historical Jesus is a life-giver only in the sense that he helps open our eyes to see the eternal reality within.[32]

A similar distinction can be found in Aurobindo. God is born in humanity in the sense that in each person *is* the divine nature. This is the eternal *avatāra*. The spiritual or second birth is one's becoming divine through one's growing consciousness of the divine nature within.[33] The historical *avatāra* is simply a clear manifestation of this fact.

> The divine manifestation of a Christ, Krishna, Buddha in external humanity has for its inner truth the same manifestation of the eternal Avatar within our own inner humanity. That which has been in the outer human life of earth, may be repeated in the inner life of all human beings.[34]

Trinitarian and incarnational formulations must then be seen as symbolic expressions of the oneness of the divine and the human. The Father is the representative of the divine, the Son of the divine within the mortal body, and the Holy Spirit is that pure consciousness through which we know our essential unity with the divine.[35] It is only where such knowledge has not yet been awakened that we construct imperfect notions of the Godhead, divinize figures such as Jesus and worship these constructions of ours.[36]

Incarnational theology figures rather prominently in the thought of Vivekananda and the Ramakrishna Mission. From the time of Ramakrishna, the belief in incarnations, both with respect to Jesus and Ramakrishna has been an important part of the movement. The consistent teaching has been that there have been many incarnations and that there will continue to be many, as long as these are necessary for the divinization of the world. However, any discussion of *avatāras*, as in the case of Radhakrishnan and Aurobindo, is controlled by the belief in the essential divinity of the human being. Jesus is different from the rest of humanity only with respect to actual achievement, not with respect to potential. Vivekananda points out that one's energy, if controlled and developed, "will tend to produce a mighty will, a character which makes a Christ or a Buddha."[37] Popular belief notwithstanding, Christ represents a status that can be achieved by anyone through many years of discipline.[38]

If, according to Vivekananda, Jesus attained to his status over many years of discipline, and if that status is open to us as well, then in what sense is it possible to speak of Jesus as a divine incarnation? Jesus could speak of himself as God in the sense that he was clearly aware of the divinity within him, but this is an awareness that is open to everyone.[39] While not different from us in that we are all sons or daughters of God, at least in potential, Jesus is one of the greatest in that in him this realization was perfected. It is proper, therefore, to worship figures like Jesus, for they are the most perfect manifestations of the eternal.[40] But such worship is not to be limited to Jesus, for to do so is to limit God and to engage in rank superstition.[41] The power of the Christ-figures lies, not in being able to save people, but in pointing beyond themselves to that which lies within.

Every Prophet is a creation of his own times, the creation of the past of his race; he himself is the creation of the future. The cause of today is the effort of the past and the cause for the future. In this position stands the Messenger. In him is embodied all that is best and the greatest in his own race, the meaning, the life, for which the race has struggled for ages; and he himself is the impetus for the future, not only to his own race but to unnumbered other races of the world.[42]

To speak of Jesus as an incarnation is therefore, in the first instance, to speak of him as one among many. In the second instance, as in the case of Keshab, it is to speak of God manifested in the human being, not God-become-man. But this does not separate Jesus from the rest of humanity. That we are all God, Vivekananda claims, is the teaching of Jesus.[43] That which separates him from us and makes him an incarnation is his perfect realization of the divine within, the level to which he makes actual the potential within every human being.

The Atman is pure intelligence controlling and directing Prana. But the intelligence we see around us is always imperfect. When intelligence is perfect, we get the Incarnation—the Christ. Intelligence is always trying to manifest itself, and in order to do this it is creating minds and bodies of different degrees of development.[44]

Properly understood, an incarnation, according to Vivekananda, is not one who is born that, but one who becomes that by realizing fully his essential divinity. And to be a Christ is simply to be a type that recurs about every five hundred years in a great person who typifies that toward which the age has been moving.[45]

In this understanding of *avatāra* or incarnation, the Trinitarian notions of Christ are not accepted and reinterpreted as they were by Keshab, Radhakrishnan and Aurobindo. Rather, they are rejected because they elevate Jesus too far above us. Similarly, unitarian notions of Jesus simply as a moral human being are rejected because there is nothing special or divine in such a figure. It is the Jesus who has not forgotten his divinity, but who has realized his essential divine nature who is an incarnation and who can help us, for we are like him in that we are also divine.[46] Indeed, Vivekananda looks for a time when the number of Christs and the number of sentient beings will be the same. "In time to come Christs will be in numbers like bunches of grapes on a vine; then the play will be over and will pass out."[47]

CHRIST AS IDEAL

Much less but still significant coverage is given to the notion of Jesus as an ideal of sorts. This is obviously an element in the discussion of Jesus as an incarnation. At issue there is the notion of Jesus as an ideal for the perfection of the divinity within. Vivekananda, for example, never tires of reiterating that the vision of Jesus was that we are soul, not body, and that in Jesus we have the realization of this in all its fullness.

> You are all sons of God, immortal spirit. "Know," he declared, "the Kingdom of Heaven is within you." "I and my Father are one." Dare you stand up and say, not only that "I am the Son of God," but I shall also find it in my heart of hearts, that "I and my Father are one"? That was what Jesus of Nazareth said.[48]

The controlling theology in such a view is Advaita. The key phrase or *mahāvākya* of Jesus' sayings is "I and my Father are one." The whole of the message and life of Jesus is to be understood through this sentence. His life is to be seen as a progressive realization of this truth. By life is meant not only the life recorded in the gospels, but also the preceding lives leading up to this grand realization. The key phrase itself is to be understood in Advaitin terms. Vivekananda claims that "there is very little difference between the pure religion of Christ and that of Vedanta."[49]

A similar emphasis on God-consciousness, but without the emphasis on identity or *avatāra* theology, can be seen in the literature of the samajes. Clearly in the speeches and writings of Keshab, Jesus is the ideal for the cultivation of God-consciousness, but the language is that of surrender to the will of God, of being controlled by the spirit of the God rather than achieving complete identity.

But there is much more to the image of Jesus as an ideal. In many respects the life of Jesus becomes the focus for speaking of a number of Hindu ideals relating to practical aspects of life and human relationships. While on the issue of Jesus as incarnation there is strong disagreement, with some accepting the idea of *avatāras* and others rejecting it, on the issue of Jesus as an ideal for living there is almost complete agreement.

This is, perhaps, crystallized most clearly by the pledge of the monks of the Ramakrishna movement on Christmas Eve 1886, the birth date of the movement. They pledged themselves to become Christs.[50] Vivekananda gives expression to the service orientation in the pledge through his emphasis on Jesus as the unselfish one who struggled and gave up his life for other human beings.[51]

The ethical or service orientation may have its roots in the Brāhmo Samāj emphasis on the ethical teachings of the historical Jesus and the perfection of these ethical ideals in his own life. Jesus becomes the ideal for complete trust in God, self-sacrifice and sympathy for the less fortunate. Keshab writes, "Jesus is identical with self-sacrifice, and as he lived and preached in the fullness of time, so must he be preached in the fullness of time."[52] For Keshab, the greatness of Christ lay in his exercise of two fundamental ethical teachings of the New Testament, forgiveness and self-sacrifice.[53] The great symbol of Jesus' devotion to suffering humanity was his death on the cross.

> His death on the cross affords the highest practical illustration of self-sacrifice. He sacrificed his life for the sake of truth, and the benefit of the world. . . . And surely, there is deeper meaning in the fact that even the orthodox attach to it, that the death of Christ is the life of the world. Fellow-country-men, it is your duty to follow these precepts and imitate this example of self-sacrifice in the cause of truth.[54]

The cross in this perception is not significant for its power to atone or to propitiate a just God who demands a sacrifice for sin, rather it becomes a symbol for the ideal of self-denial in the interests of service to the rest of humanity. Jesus' sacrifice is a redemptive one, but not in the terms in which this is usually understood. Rather, it is redemptive because it serves as an example to the rest of us.[55]

The achievement of the perfection of self-denial is based firmly on the perfection of other virtues or disciplines such as meditation, prayer and asceticism. Self-denial was not to be had without effort. For God-consciousness to become a reality self had to be destroyed in progressive fashion to the point of complete eradication. The wisdom, faith and piety of Jesus was a product of his meditation and prayer,[56] and his practice of true asceticism. For Keshab this was not self-mortification or a union sought through quietism and trance; rather, it was an active self-surrender of one's will to the divine, a commitment to seeking first the "Kingdom of God and His righteousness."[57] Keshab says of Jesus:

> He will come to you as self-surrender, as asceticism, as Yoga, as the life of God in man, as obedient and humble sonship. For Christ is nothing else.[58]

Similarly Vivekananda says:

> Christ was a Sannyasin, and his religion is essentially fit for Sannyasins only. His teaching may be summed up as: "Give up"; nothing more — being fit for the favoured few.[59]

Radhakrishnan, too, emphasizes the ideal of self-surrender in the life of Jesus in his commentary on the *Gītā*:

> Though conscious of his imperfections, Jesus recognized the grace and love of God and willingly submitted himself entirely to Him. Thus delivered from all imperfection and taking refuge in Him, he attained to a divine status.[60]

Accordingly, for Radhakrishnan, it is precisely the temptations to pride, self-conceit, cupidity, hatred and brutality that Jesus overcame in the wilderness.[61] In overcoming these temptations through the perfection of submission to the divine nature, rather than the demonic, Jesus becomes the ideal for all to follow. The actualization of this ideal in the life of Jesus was necessary, and in terms of *avatāra* theology, will be necessary again in order to preserve the moral equilibrium and aid the evolutionary process of life. Jesus and others like him are manifestations of spiritual values we are to cultivate if we are to realize the potentialities within us.[62]

The achievement of the ideal of self-surrender in Jesus' life culminates in two things, in direct knowledge of God and in death on the cross. Radhakrishnan speaks of a profound spiritual change in Jesus prior to his journey to Jerusalem. This change was the attainment of direct knowledge, the culmination of thirty years of preparation and discipline. In raising "himself through battling with inner discords, doubts and temptations he is the supreme example for us."[63] Jesus' death on the cross is not a sacrificial atonement but a symbol and ideal applicable to the life of all human beings.

> Suffering for the world out of love is the price which every son of man has to pay, if he is to be redeemed from evil and manifest himself as a son of God. The cross is not an offence or a stumbling block to the Hindu, but is the great symbol of the redemptive reality of God. It shows how love is rooted in self-sacrifice.[64]

In his discussion of *avatāras* Aurobindo places the emphasis on the *avatāra* as exemplar. The *avatāra* shows us how suffering and sorrow can become a means of redemption and how the divine soul in human nature can overcome suffering. Suffering, in this view, is redemptive, not because someone is suffering for us but because it is our own suffering. Christ merely shows us how this is possible.[65]

CONCLUSION

Whether one looks at the issue of Christ as *avatāra* or Christ as an ideal, there is a single thread that runs through Hindu views of Christ. This thread is the depiction of Christ as an Oriental or Asiatic. One might even be more specific and say that it is the depiction of Christ as the quintessential Hindu, the one who lives Hindu ideals as they ought to be lived and teaches the essence of Hindu truth as it ought to be taught. The emphasis on Christ as Oriental is found in Rāmmohun Roy, is made prevalent by Keshab Chunder Sen and is reiterated forcefully by Vivekananda. While the explicit notion of Christ as Oriental may not be prevalent in writings of more recent figures such as Radhakrishnan and Aurobindo, it is certainly there by implication. The purpose of proposing Christ as Oriental is twofold — to claim Christ and the teachings of Christ, however these may be interpreted, as indigenous to India, and to attack Eurocentric notions of Christ.

For Rāmmohun Roy, the insistence that Jesus was Asiatic comes in his disputes with Protestant missionaries over their assertions that Christianity is superior to Hinduism and that Asiatics are effeminate. In tongue-in-cheek fashion he states:

> Before "A Christian" indulged in a tirade about persons being "degraded by Asiatic effeminacy" he should have recollected that almost all the ancient prophets and patriarchs venerated by Christians, nay even Jesus himself, a divine Incarnation and the founder of the Christian Faith, were Asiatics, so that if "A Christian" thinks it degrading to be born or to reside in Asia, he directly reflects upon them.[66]

The term Asiatic is used here primarily in a geographic sense, although it is also clear that, for Rāmmohun Roy, the message of Jesus was Hindu inasmuch as it was at the heart of Hinduism properly understood. Such a view is made quite explicit by Mazumdar in his attacks on Eurocentric notions of Jesus in his "Oriental Christ."[67]

Keshab Chunder Sen explicitly stated that Jesus is Asiatic in every respect. He is Asiatic in race and dress and therefore not foreign to the Hindu in his appearance.[68] But he is also a brother to the Hindu in that his teachings and way of life are essentially Hindu.

> You will find on reflection that the doctrine of divine humanity is essentially a Hindu doctrine, and the picture of Christ's life and character I have drawn is altogether a picture of ideal Hindu life. Surely the idea of absorption and immersion in the Deity is one of those ideas of Vedantic Hinduism which prevail in Hinduism. . . . The doctrine of absorption in the Deity is India's creed, and through this idea I believe, India will reach Christ. Will he not fulfil the Indian scripture?[69]

In the later thinkers the notion of Jesus as Asiatic by race or birth ceases to be so much of an issue. Jesus as Oriental or Hindu in his teaching, however, is a notion that is maintained, if not explicitly, at least implicitly. This is clearly at the bottom of the view that Jesus exhibits in his life the fulfillment of Hindu ideals, that he is the ideal Yogi, ascetic, *sannyāsin*, that he fulfills the ideal of perfect union with the divine. Thus Radhakrishnan can say that "there is not much serious difference between Hinduism and Christianity on the question of the nature and means of salvation."[70] Vivekananda can assert that Jesus is an Oriental of Orientals in his vision of the essential divinity of the human being and the practical application of this experience to human life.[71]

NOTES

1. Klaus Klostermaier, *Hindu and Christian in Vrindavan* (London: SCM Press, 1969), p. 107.

2. N. K. Devaraja, *Hinduism and Christianity* (New Delhi: Asia Publishing House, 1969), pp. 71-72.

3. William Stewart, *Indian Religious Frontier* (Philadelphia: Fortress Press, 1964), p. 87.

4. David Kopf, *The Brahmo Samaj and the Shaping of the Modern Indian Mind* (Princeton, NJ: Princeton University Press, 1979), p. 273.

5. Ibid. p. 276.

6. Geoffrey Parrinder, *Avatar and Incarnation* (New York: Oxford University Press, 1982), pp. 99-115.

7. Sisir Kumar Das (New Delhi: Munshiram Manoharlal, 1974), p. 83.

8. David C. Scott, ed., *Keshab Chunder Sen* (Madras: The Christian Literature Society, 1979), pp. 34-35.

9. Ibid. p. 95.

10. Ibid. p. 80.

11. Ibid. p. 96.

12. Ibid. p. 205.

13. Ibid. p. 206.

14. Ibid. p. 208.

15. Ibid. p. 209-10.

16. Ibid. p. 214-15.

17. Ibid. p. 226.

18. Ibid. p. 228.

19. Ibid. p. 230.

20. Ibid. p. 237.

21. Ibid. p. 238.

22. S. Radhakrishnan, *The Bhagavadgita* (Bombay: Blackie and Son, 1982), p. 31.

23. Ibid. p. 36.

24. Ibid. p. 381.

25. S. Radhakrishnan, *Indian Religions* (New Delhi: Vision Books, 1979), p. 52.

26. Ibid. p. 133.

27. Ibid. pp. 137-38.

28. S. Radhakrishnan, *The Recovery of Faith* (Delhi: Hind Pocket Books, 1967), p. 117.

29. S. Radhakrishnan, *Indian Religions*, p. 39.

30. Ibid. p. 156.

31. S. Radhakrishnan, *The Recovery of Faith*, p. 117.

32. Ibid. p. 118.

33. Sri Aurobindo, *Essays on the Gita* (New York: The Sri Aurobindo Library, 1950), p. 132.

34. Ibid. p. 143.

35. Ibid. p. 145.

36. Ibid. p. 252.

37. *The Complete Works of Swami Vivekananda*, Mayavati Memorial ed. (Calcutta:Advaita Ashrama, 1966-71), 1, p. 33. (Hereinafter referred to as *Works*.)

38. *Works*, 1, p. 444.

39. *Works*, 1, p. 439.

40. *Works*, 3, p. 9.

41. *Works*, 4, p. 106.

42. *Works*, 4, pp. 141-42.

43. *Works*, 6, p. 122.

44. *Works*, 6, p. 128.

45. *Works*, 6, p. 134.

46. *Works*, 7, p. 4.

47. *Works*, 7, p. 7.

48. *Works*, 4, p. 146.

49. *Works*, 2, p. 353.

50. Stewart, p. 87.

51. *Works*, 4, p. 152.

52. Scott, p. 17.

53. Ibid. p. 67.

54. Ibid. p. 70.

55. On this issue see Scott, p. 72 for Keshab, and B. N. Dasgupta, *Life and Times of Raja Rāmmohun Roy* (New Delhi: Ambika Publications, 1980), p. 242 for Rāmmohun Roy.

56. Scott, p. 49.

57. Ibid. pp. 215-16.

58. Ibid. p. 217.

59. *Works*, 6, p. 109.

60. Radhakrishnan, *Bhagavadgita*, p. 31.

61. Ibid. p. 338.

62. Radhakrishnan, *Indian Religions*, p. 137.

63. Radhakrishnan, *The Recovery of Faith*, pp. 115-17.

64. Radhakrishnan, *Indian Religions*, pp. 154-55.

65. Aurobindo, p. 147.

66. Dasgupta, *Life and Times*, p. 257.

67. Kopf, pp. 20-21.

68. Scott, p. 201.

69. Ibid. p. 214.

70. Radhakrishnan, *Indian Religions*, p. 144.

71. *Works*, 4, pp. 142-46.

11

Christian Views
of Hindu *Bhakti*

A. FRANK THOMPSON

As an inter-subjective relationship or an indescribable emotional state ("like a taste which a dumb man enjoys"),[1] *bhakti* may declare itself by a variety of evidences, but is resistant to analysis. The term *bhakti,* commonly translated "devotion," has had a variety of meanings, and the range of these nuances and significations is still being explored — as, for example, in the contemporary phenomenological assessment of "emotional Kṛṣṇa bhakti" by F. Hardy.[2]

Such recent studies remain pretty much within the domain of the specialist indologist. This chapter addresses rather the question of Christian views of Hindu *bhakti* as they have developed over the last two hundred years — since the translation into English by Charles Wilkins of the *Bhagavadgītā* began to bring to the notice of Christians "a theology accurately corresponding with that of the Christian dispensation, and most powerfully illustrating its fundamental doctrines" (as Warren Hastings put it in a letter of 1784).[3] Christian views will be examined as developing through four stages. There was, first, a protracted period when an often uncomfortable awareness of similarities to Christianity in Indian theism raised questions for Christians. One may distinguish, second, a stage in which Christian scholars developed a more-or-less self-assured critique of Hinduism in general and *bhakti* religion in particular. Third, one may point to an attempted theological recognition of an engagement with distinctive doctrines of Indian *bhakti* religion, particularly on the part of Rudolf Otto. Fourth, one may discern a closer encounter of Christians with Hindu *bhakti* in the writings of A. J. Appasamy and C. F. Andrews; their writings reflect a sense of mutuality between the traditions. The chapter will conclude by raising some questions about the present status of *bhakti* religion in Christian eyes.

Three principal questions must be at issue in this survey. First, of course, is the question of the adequacy to Indian realities of the views represented — although, as indicated, it may not be possible to answer that question definitively within the scope of this chapter. Second, there must be the question of the sense in which the views represented are Christian. The authors chosen for study are the obvious ones since they deal at length with Hindu *bhakti*, yet they represent in fact a rather narrow range of Christian backgrounds.[4] Are the positions they take *vis-à-vis* realities of Indian religion well-supported by the foundational theology of what is, in some way, a centered tradition? One has also to consider that these authors were men of their respective times, subject to a variety of conditionings.[5] In assessing their judgments one must attempt a kind of pathology of the Christian tradition — just as, in a consideration of Christian attitudes to Jews one would discover a Christian anti-Semitism and be forced to reassess Christian thought as it has developed over long periods of time. Both of these principal questions lead to a third: What indications arise from this survey for a view of future relations between Christianity and Hinduism?

Two principal factors must then be mentioned as raising the question of Hindu *bhakti* for Christian assessment. One was scholarship, beginning from the signal contributions of the Orientalists[6] of the eighteenth century and continuing in a number of major developments in the nineteenth century, among which, so far as India is concerned, the labors of Max Müller[7] have pride of place. The Vedic hymns and Upaniṣads, the Laws, the Epics and the vernacular literatures unfolded a long history of religious expression; the *gītā* provided a doctrine of divine self-disclosure. Responses to these discoveries on the part of Protestant missionaries in India tended to be governed by a set of judgmental attitudes, prominent among which was a rather narrow soteriology, as Eric Sharpe has shown.[8] Sharpe sees two Christian views of Hinduism emerging side by side in the early nineteenth century:

> By the 1830s . . . the encounter of Christianity with Hinduism . . . was taking on two contrasting characters. A minority among Christians had begun to look for, and to find, common ground. . . . For the majority, Christianity was still a matter of personal salvation obtained only through the direct operation of the grace of God in Jesus Christ, and encounter with other religions could only be seen as a meeting of truth with falsehoods.[9]

A search for common ground is evident in works by Monier-Williams, a scholar of evangelical persuasion. In *Indian Wisdom* in 1876 he cited parallels between the *gītā* and the gospels,[10] sketched "points of contact" between Christianity and Hinduism,[11] and recognized in Vaiṣṇavism a religion governed by conceptions of grace:

It was as Vishnu, then, that the Supreme Being, according to the Hindus, exhibited his sympathy with human trials, his love for the human race, his respect for all forms of life, and his condescension toward even the inferior animals as integral parts of his creation.[12]

The second factor in raising for Christians the issue of faith and grace in Hinduism was the experience of converts. Conversion did not always involve an utter rejection of the parent tradition. Even Nehemiah Goreh (1825-95), remembered largely for a Christian apologetics directed against his background tradition, found in the *gītā* a profound and instructive element.

Most erroneous as is the teaching of such books as the *Bhagavadgītā,* the *Bhagavta* etc., yet they have taught us something of *ananyabhakti* (undivided devotedness to God), of *vairagya* (giving up of the world), of *namrata* (humility), of *ksama* (forbearance), etc., which enables us to appreciate the precepts of Christianity.[13]

More positively, Christian poets such as H. A. Krishna Pillai (1827-1900) and Narayanan Vaman Tilak (1862-1919) represented not only a lively contact with indigenous *bhakti* traditions but also a Christian adaptation of those traditions.[14]

Thus the question emerged, what recognition could Christians give to the teaching and apparent experience in Hinduism of a life of grace in communion with a "personal" God?

A conscientious exploration of Indian religious tradition with a focus on this question was undertaken in a series of works under the general title, "The Religious Quest of India," developed after 1910 under the leadership of J. N. Farquhar.[15] Each author undertook to work "in the sincere and sympathetic spirit of science."[16] At the same time, each author attempted a critique of Indian religion on a Christian basis and in consonance with the "fulfillment" theory first adumbrated by F. D. Maurice,[17] definitively stated by J. N. Farquhar in 1903[18] and widely accepted among "liberal" Christians in the period before and after the 1910 World Missionary Conference in Edinburgh.

In this series and in related works J. N. Farquhar, Nicol Macnicol and Sydney Cave offered a substantial treatment of Indian religious history and a genuine — if qualified — recognition of Indian spirituality. J. N. Farquhar in *The Crown of Hinduism*[19] traced the concept of *bhakti*, first in the *Svetāśvatara Upaniṣad*[20] and then in the *gita*, in the poems of devotees within the "Great Sects"[21] and in the teachings of Srī Rāmānuja.[22] Nicol Macnicol in *Indian Theism from the Vedic to the Muhammadan Period* covered the same ground with a particular focus on *bhakti* religion and went far to acknowledge the expression of an authentic spirituality in his sources. Thus he found the Tamil saint Māṇikka-vāśagar "giving utterance to such experiences as are common to all devout souls who have sought God sincerely and in some measure found Him."[23] In the saint's poems he found "the essential note of a truly ethical theism."[24] He noted in connection with the thought of Srī Rāmānuja the development indicated by the term *prapatti,* a devotion which did not "find the old word sufficient to express all that is in the heart of the worshipper who resorts to Krisna as his refuge."[25] He applauded the attainment of Śaiva Siddhānta, declaring that the South Indian philosophy had "grasped the basal conception of Theism that God is a moral being, governed from first to last by a purpose of compassion."[26] For Sydney Cave, in *Redemption Hindu and Christian,*[27] Tukaram's fervent poems "carry the mind back to the *Fioretti* and the 'little brothers' of St. Francis,"[28] and he finds in poems of the Śaivite saints of South India the expression of a "warm and living faith."[29]

These writers acknowledged also a social impact of *bhakti* spirituality. "The *Gītā* opened the doors of spiritual religion to women and to Śūdras (the servant caste); and the bhakti sects opened them to Outcastes," declared Farquhar.[30] Macnicol agreed and pointed particularly to the movement associated with the name of Srī Caitanya (1486-1534):

> It broke through the restrictions of caste ... permitted in its lower ranks the remarriage of widows and ... opposed much of the formal ritual of the Shastras [authoritative texts].[31]

Hindu *bhakti* is deficient however, these writers teach, by reason of its inadequate foundation and incomplete integration into a historically-grounded and morally-adequate religious system. Hindu *bhakti* was ineffective, according to Farquhar, because it failed to bring any real changes to the Indian social system. The principal reason for this failure has been, in Farquhar's view, the dominant influence in Indian religion of the concept of an "actionless Brahman," which could not intervene or declare its will in history: "The ethical character ascribed to Brahman, being shut up in his transcendental nature, and never made manifest among men in action, was utterly impotent."[32] What was essentially, then, the absence of a special and definite revelation, in this view, made possible in India a plethora of sects and modes of worship, a prevailing practical polytheism. In this connection Farquhar declares that "the *bhakti* of the Hindu, whether villager or saintly poet, is usually a passionate devotion to a single idol."[33] Without subscribing to this particular judgment, Macnicol agrees in the main with Farquhar's assessment. After describing the fervor of Tulsī Dās, Macnicol finds that "it is a somewhat wistful sense of need that creates this Theism."[34] He asks at a later point in his book, "What stable theology and enduring social order can be built upon what is after all only a 'feeling fond and fugitive'?"[35] Hinduism has, Macnicol declares, "no concrete and complete moral ideal."[36]

A criticism of the ethicis of *bhakti* religion on the part of these authors extends markedly to what is seen as an ungoverned eroticism. The very notion of *bhakti*, Macnicol writes, citing Hopkins, may be deficient in morality:

> Bhakti leans to love very perceptibly, even to erotic passion, but it expresses affection of a pure sort as well as that of a sensuous nature; which latter is to be found, however, and cannot be ignored.[37]

The sect of Vallabhāchārya (1479-1563) is then pointed out as having been dominated by an "erotic love" symbolized in the devotion of Radha to Krishna.[38] "From such a conception of the relation of worshipper to worshipped," Macnicol adds, "it was inevitable, in the sensuous atmosphere of Krishnaism, that gross abuses should result."[39] Sydney Cave also deplores some expressions of Krishna *bhakti,* declaring that "the *Gītā* has suffered much from the fact that the Krishna it proclaims is inevitably confused in the popular mind with the freakish vicious Krishna of the Purāṇas."[40]

The judgments of these writers, in retrospect, appear to be flawed in at least two ways. Common to them all appears to be a failure through literalism in their treatment of Hindu myths. They convey, secondly, a commendation of Christianity that must be seen as ideological.[41] They struggle against this! Farquhar, for example, disclaims the intention to "impose imperiously the whole of (the missionaries') religious, civil and social life unchanged upon the people of India."[42] His ideological bias appears, however, in his one-sided analysis of the ills of Hindu culture and in his usually implicit commendation of Christian religion. Macnicol in *Indian Theism* also commends Christianity in essentially ideological terms in his presentation of it as the "standard Theism,"[43] the measure by which Hinduism is to be judged. Cave writes of Christianity as the "absolute religion,"[44] justifying the term by the assertion that Christianity is the most adequate religion, integrating within itself emphases that tend to differentiate traditions on either side of it: the "legal" Western religions of Judaism and Islam on the one hand, and the Eastern mystical religions of "deliverance" on the other.[45] These writers raise very necessary questions about the role of religious and ethical concepts in social life. There is indeed a terrible poignancy, from a standpoint in the late twentieth century, about this quest for a social theory that will genuinely support "equality, freedom and justice."[46] One senses here, however, a set of commendations that, however good in themselves, have the effect of disguising moral realities in "Christendom." Sydney Cave, writing toward the end or in the aftermath of World War I, offered, however, a somewhat chastened sense of the failings of Western Christendom, for example, that the church "has been acquiescent in social conditions which make the freedom and joy of the kingdom almost impossible for many."[47]

Two later figures move away from a comparison of religions toward an encounter, as they intend, on a more profound basis. Thus Rudolf Otto acknowledges at the beginning of his well-known book, *India's Religion of Grace,*[48] the existence of a plurality of religions, but states his intention to compare Christianity and Hinduism in depth, in respect to doctrines expressive of a faith[49] that is at the heart of religious experience. He finds, then, profound resemblances between doctrines of grace held in the two religions.

> Beginning in the profound verses of the *Bhagavad-Gītā* passing through times of obscuration and reformation, as with us, this doctrine of grace rises till it gains at last positions which dumbfound us Protestants by their analogy to our fundamental ideas—*sola gratia, per fidem solam, sine omnibus propriis viribus, meritis, aut operibus*— and which led to like harshness and "offence" in India as with us.[50]

Otto recognizes in Indian theism, and especially in the writings of Srī Rāmānuja, a "struggle for God, a real God, not such a god as philosophical speculation gives us, but such as the heart and soul need and ask, a God to inspire personal trust, love, reverence and loyal self-surrender."[51] He traces out, then, similarities in salvific experience between reformed religion in Europe and *bhakti* religion in India: emphases on spiritual experience, preachings and insistence on the necessity of choice, experiences of "election," illumination and restoration, as well as practices conducive to these experiences, sacramental and community observances.[52] He goes on to show how divisions arose in India in the attempt to understand the workings of God's grace, which were "a double of our special Protestant problems of grace."[53] *Bhakti* came to be seen as a method, a human accomplishment or "work," and was then replaced, for some "by what in India is called simple 'approach' (*prapatti*) . . . to leave oneself just as he is in the hands of the Lord."[54]

It seems appropriate to mention at this point Sabapathy Kulandran's more recent work, *Grace in Christianity and Hinduism,* since it carries out in a more extended fashion the comparison instituted by Otto, particularly in accounts of Northern and Southern Vaiṣṇavism and Southern Śaivism. In the "relentless passion for grace" of Pillai Lokāchāri (1264-1327) of the Southern School of Vaiṣṇavism, Kulandran finds "echoes of Paul and Luther."[55]

Both Otto and Kulandran insist that such similarities must be seen in their respective contexts, thus reintroducing a comparison of religions. Otto puts forward the now-familiar notion that there is a central *axis* in each tradition, in Christianity "the Idea of the Holy" and in Hinduism the idea of *ātmasiddhi.*[56] Kulandran takes over and expands the notion of a central axis as designating "a basic spirit" governing "the atmosphere, the tradition and the long history" in which the doctrines have grown.[57] Similarities may then be misleading—as Kulandran emphatically asserts[58]—as disguising fundamental issues unresolved between the traditions. Otto points out that while both religions aim at "rescuing the lost," both lostness and rescue tend to be differently understood by the traditions. Thus "rescue" in India typically implies the removal of bonds or imperfections, while in Christianity it involves dealing with the spiritual and moral problems of sin and guilt, the burden of which on the conscience is the necessary reaction of the soul to a holy God. Both Otto and Kulandran understand grace to be confirmed to Christians in objective, historical events. The cross is "the self-surrender of God on man's behalf"[59] writes Kulandran. "India has no expiator, no Golgotha and no Cross," concludes Otto.[60]

These differentiations have important implications for *bhakti* in the view of these Christians. *Bhakti* in Hinduism is seen by them as an essentially individualisitic response to God, a response, moreover, which is unlikely to be morally adequate. *Bhakti* in a Christian context would convey for them not only the experience of divine forgiveness, but also anticipation of God's "kingdom" in a new solidarity governed by grace. "There is truly a service to God when the soul is alone with God" writes Otto,[61] but for the Christian, "the world of men and things external to himself and about him is *indispensable* as the sphere of his service."[62]

Otto and Kulandran, then, explore the teachings of "India's religion of grace" at a greater depth, but end by asserting a profound and—at least for Kulandran—irreducible contrast between the traditions. Kulandran, following Hendrik Kraemer and expressing the latter's judgment on Christian theological liberalism, affirms a Hindu sense of the being of God[63] but denies to Hinduism an effective revelation.[64] Otto, however, does attest the reality of revelation in India. It takes place, he suggests, in the encounter of "seers" with a noumenal reality understood as making "its inexplicable peremptory demand for the religious idea of an active, self-revealing announcement from above to the experience of the primeval mind."[65] Otto's thought clearly belongs to an earlier, pre-Barthian strain of Christian theology in the tradition of Schleiermacher. It affords ground for the interesting suggestion on Otto's part that such disclosures of sacred reality inaugurate distinct darśanas.[66] Otto makes the further suggestion that the fundamental difference between Christianity and Hinduism is that the former represents "another *darśanam,* another *vision,* another *eye.*"[67] He adds, "If a change is to come, another eye must first be opened."[68]

Does one feel the opening of eyes in the writings of A. J. Appasamy and C. F. Andrews? They share in a more positive, yet also in a more traditional, Christian approach to an understanding of Hinduism. They make their assessments on the basis of a broadly Trinitarian theology.[69] This involved, for both, the conception of a universal divine Fatherhood and a universal work of the divine Spirit. "Everyone is breathing the same air, so everyone, Christian or non-Christian, is breathing the Holy Spirit, though they do not call it by that name," wrote Andrews, adding, "The Holy Spirit is not the property of some special people."[70] Appasamy, to the alarm of some Christian colleagues,[71] found evidence for this address of the divine Spirit to the human spirit in Hindu sources[72] and declared that this belief in God's immanence was "dear to the heart of India."[73] Appasamy employed the traditional notion of general and special revelations. He held that God's special revelation in Jesus provides "a clear manifestation of God's purpose for mankind," and continued, "But that is not to say that all other religions are merely men's blind gropings in the dark. To them God has shown Himself, but not so clearly."[74] It may be noted that these notions of divine self-disclosure beyond the boundaries of the Christian churches had appeared in conclusions of the World Missionary Conference in 1910.[75] Such disclosure by the divine Spirit has also been claimed to be the traditional teaching of the Orthodox churches.[76]

Both Appasamy and Andrews are warmly appreciative of Hindu *bhakti* in many of its expressions. Appasamy explored in his major writings what he conceived to be the "intimate relation between the inner spirit of Christianity and the inner spirit of India's religious thought"[77] — further identified as *bhakti.* Appasamy acknowledged the "rich and complex" meaning of the term but affirmed that "the only English word that can adequately render *bhakti* is love."[78] He found, then, experience of the love of God to be a living reality in Indian tradition — as might be seen, in his view, in the hymns of the Tamil saints.[79] Not only there, however: selecting according to his own doctrinal agenda and quoting extensively, Appasamy draws from Indian religious texts not merely evidence of a sense of God but also a variety of insights that can be represented doctrinally, into the Fatherhood of God,[80] for example, or the Motherhood of God, which he terms "a beautiful way of thinking of the tender, devoted, unselfish love of God."[81] He illustrates from the *Bhāgavata Purāṇa* the conviction of a divinely-given ministry and takes as instances of this calling the examples of Debendranath Tagore, Rabindranath Tagore and Mahatma Gandhi, the latter termed, "perhaps the greatest social servant in the world today."[82]

The engagement of C. F. Andrews with Hindu *bhakti* was primarily through personal involvement rather than scholarship. Friendship, Andrews wrote,

has enabled me to realize, as nothing else could do, the currents of spiritual devotion which flow within the heart of the East. I came out to teach, but I have humbly to confess that I found myself a learner at the feet of saints whose life-surrender to the will of God was far more whole-hearted than my own.[83]

The saints to whom Andrews here makes reference were, of course, mainly Hindu and Muslim. They included Zaka Ullah (1832-1911), who was "like a father"[84] to Andrews in his early days in Delhi, as well as Munshi Ram, Rabindranath Tagore and Mahatma Gandhi. Concerning the latter and his wife, Andrews reports the declaration of "sincere and earnest Christians" in South Africa that "these good people are better Christians than we are."[85] Andrews was led to believe that in the age-long village culture in India as well as in these examples, "far beyond the boundaries of Christendom the pure in heart, who seek God, find Him with serene joy according to His good promise."[86]

Both Appasamy and Andrews continued to express a sense of the distinctiveness of Christianity, however. This sense, at least as spelled out by Appasamy, appears again as a set of reservations about the experience of God in Hindu *bhakti*. Thus Appasamy finds a moral depth in Christian experience not to be found, he believes, in Hinduism. At the center of Christian faith, for both of them, is a mysticism and morality that is also a practical commitment. "The Christian must identify himself with the suffering Lord,"[87] writes Appasamy. Moreover,

> This experience imparts a unique character to Christian mysticism which becomes a distinctly moral fact. Communion with our Lord is made possible not by emotional fervour, nor by flights of speculation, or even of intuition, but rather by the difficult but joyous discipline of walking along His path of suffering.[88]

By contrast, Appasamy writes that Hindu *bhaktas* "are inclined to make religious experience a highly emotional thing."[89]

A related reservation, for Appasamy, appears in the consideration of questions of human and religious solidarity. Many Hindu *bhaktas,* he writes, "regarded normal human relationships as hindrances to the perfect worship of their God."[90] A strong feeling for fellow devotees is indeed recognized as an element in Hindu *bhakti;* however, for him, the fellowship of *bhaktas* as evident in Hindu tradition offers only a "glimpse of the profound truth which lies at the bottom of the Christian belief about the Church."[91] In thus commending his ecclesiology Appasamy is forced to criticize not just Hindu spirituality but also a strong sentiment among some Indian Christians of his time. Against attacks on traditional Christian understandings of the church, which had appeared in *Re-Thinking Christianity in India,*[92] Appasamy declared, "To suppose that there cannot be real spirituality where there is organized religion is to ignore the clear, abundant and indisputable evidence of history."[93]

It was against the limitations that had seemed to be intrinsic to a traditional Christian ecclesiology, however, that Andrews had made his protest in leaving the Cambridge Mission to Delhi in 1914: "Henceforth I was prepared to abandon all sectarian restrictions."[94] Andrews had also encountered with pain the involvement of Christian communities in what he perceived to be the great social evils of his time, "Capitalism, Militarism and Imperialism."[95] The implicit ecclesiology of Andrews' later teaching was therefore much more open and might be termed functional. It recognized the church in loving service, service that rejected involvement with oppressive structures. Such service had its own center, however, its own distinctive concerns, and therefore also its characteristic operations and structures. These were spelled out by Andrews in the series of lectures on pastoral theology he gave at Cambridge in 1937.[96] Conspicuous among his concerns was what a later generation was to call a "preferential option for the poor."[97]

With this brief look at the attitudes to Hindu *bhakti* of Appasamy and Andrews, it may be possible to draw some tentative conclusions from this survey.

In the first place, one has to see in the works considered the extension of a sympathetic awareness, on the part of Christians, of Hindu *bhakti*. One must expect this awareness to be further enriched by contacts between persons and communities and by further contributions from scholarship. One finds an exemplary empathy and discernment in recent major works: Mariasurai Dhavamony's *Love of God According to Śaiva Siddhānta*,[98] for example, and John Braisted Carman's *Theology of Rāmānuja*.[99] Both of these authors are well aware of the potential significance of their respective works for relations between the religions. The former aims to show how "the values contained in an Eastern religion like Hinduism have relevance to contemporary problems of religious pluralism";[100] the latter subtitles his work "An Essay in Interreligious Understanding." Klaus Klostermaier might also be mentioned in this connection as the author of an experiential essay in interreligious understanding: *Hindu and Christian in Vrindavan*.[101] Klostermaier has offered also a scholarly assessment of *bhakti* traditions in India, which includes the judgment that insistence on "the cultivation of high moral virtues" is found among almost all of the *bhakti* poets.[102] Such positive assessments of the spirituality of non-Christian religious traditions have received a clear sanction from Christian councils in recent years.[103]

Where might such understandings lead? C. F. Andrews in 1924 set forth a theory of the interrelatedness of the great religious traditions.

> The patient study of the great religions makes it more evident that each has been both a "borrower and a lender." . . . This mutual indebtedness has been altogether denied in the past, owing to the special interests of proselytizing passion obscuring the sane vision of mankind. But whenever the organic conception of religious development takes the place of the earlier idea of separate, hostile faiths, then the consideration that no religion has ever stood alone becomes more and more a settled conviction of the mind. . . . Therefore, instead of seeking to deny this mutual indebtedness it becomes the essence of truth and justice to affirm it.[104]

Appasamy's work contributed illustrations for Andrew's thesis: his deliberate use of Hindu sources and perhaps also his reflection of Hindu appropriations of Christian emphases.[105] Thus while there may be truth in the assertion of Otto and Kulandran that there are distinct *axes* along which, in accordance with central convictions, the great religious traditions develop, there may appear also a path of "convergence," as Appasamy and Andrews suggest, through selective assumptions or assimilations.

Some assessment of Christian critiques of Hindu *bhakti* is necessary as a second tentative conclusion from this survey. The critiques represented in this chapter were developed on the basis of a variety of related Christian teachings, which will not be recapitulated here except through the observations that it is possible to observe, in the sequence of authors considered here, an increasing adequacy in the deployment of a foundational Christian theology *vis-à-vis* Hindu *bhakti*, and at the same time a diminishing ideological inflation of Christian claims. The ethical concern, which has been central in one way or another for all of these Christian authors, is founded in a fundamentally relational Christian theology, a theology classically outlined as Trinitarian. That a good deal of Christian devotion has lacked a Trinitarian or even ethical dimension should be obvious to anyone with a knowledge of Christian history; indeed, a Roman Catholic writer of the present generation has assailed a classical Catholic piety as "spiritual hedonism."[106] An ethical concern is intrinsic to Christian belief, however. Engagement with precisely the subject of this chapter has led some Indian Christian theologians to radically stress the immanence of God in the universe of moral relations.[107] The emergence of liberation theologies in several parts of the world, with the cultural critiques carried through by theologians of this sort,[108] tends to illustrate the same concern. Movements toward the reassessment and criticism of traditional devotion should increasingly be seen, however, as participation in a spiritual engagement that transcends traditional boundaries.

NOTES

1. Nārada's *Bhakti Sūtra*, in *Sources of Indian Tradition* 1, ed. Wm. Theodore DeBary (New York: Columbia University Press, 1958), p. 329.

2. Friedheim Hardy, *Viraha Bhakti, The Early History of Kṛṣṇa Devotion in South India* (Delhi: Oxford University Press, 1983). Hardy offers a comparison of Krishna *bhakti* with the Christian devotion of Ramon Lull, St. John of the Cross and St. Ignatius Loyola, pp. 569-75.

3. Quoted in Eric J. Sharpe, *The Universal Gītā* (London: Duckworth, 1985), p. 8. Sharpe surmises that the *gita* was understood by Hastings in essentially deist terms.

4. Farquhar was Congregationalist-Evangelical (he came to India with the London Missionary Society). Cave was Congregationalist; Macnicol was United Free Church of Scotland; Otto and Kulandran were Lutherans—although Kulandran became a bishop in the Church of South India. C. F. Andrews and A. J. Appasamy were 'Anglican' or, of the Church of India, Pakistan, Burma and Ceylon in the 1930s. The largest elements in world Christianity, Orthodoxy, and Roman Catholicism, are not represented.

5. Assessments of these conditionings are to be found in books by Eric Sharpe:

a study of Farquhar, *Not to Destroy But to Fulfill* (Uppsala: Swedish Institute of Missionary Research, 1965); also *Comparative Religion, A History* (London: Duckworth, 1975); and *Faith Meets Faith* (London: SCM Press Ltd., 1977).

6. See David Kopf, *British Orientalism and the Bengal Renaissance* (Berkeley and Los Angeles: University of California Press, 1969).

7. Max Müller was general editor of the Sacred Books of the East (1878-1910) and was influential in generating more positive attitudes on the part of English Christians to non-Christian religions. See Sharpe, *Not to Destroy But to Fulfill,* pp. 43-44 and *Comparative Religions,* pp. 36-46.

8. Sharpe, *Faith Meets Faith,* pp. 1-18.

9. Sharpe, *Faith Meets Faith,* p. 12.

10. Monier-Williams, *Indian Wisdom* (London: W. H. Allen and Co., 1876), pp. 149-50.

11. Ibid. pp. xxxvi-xxxviii: "the Hindu conception of original sin," "the Hindu theory of Incarnation and the need of a Saviour," etc.

12. Ibid. p. 329 (an account of the ten *avatars* follows).

13. Nehemiah Goreh, *Christianity Not of Man But of God,* 1888, as quoted in Robin Boyd, *An Introduction to Indian Christian Theology* (Madras: The Christian Literature Society, 1969), p. 55.

14. See J. C. Winslow, *Narayanan Vaman Tilak, The Christian Poet of Maharashtra* (Calcutta: Association Press, 1930), and A. J. Appasamy, *Temple Bells* (Calcutta: Y.M.C.A., 1930).

15. The genesis of the series is described in Sharpe, *Not to Destroy But to Fulfill,* pp. 269-70, 298-309.

16. As stated in the editorial preface to Nicol Macnicol, *Indian Theism from the Vedic to the Muhammedan Period* (London: Oxford University Press, 1915), p. iv.

17. Sharpe, *Faith Meets Faith,* pp. 13-15

18. "Christianity is the only faith in all the world which is purely spiritual and essentially ethical on the one hand, and on the other offers us historical facts of the largest significance and the mightiest emotional power. . . . The belief, that Jesus, the Son of God, died for our sins on Calvary, produces a religion which satisfies the modern mind, and which also proves to be the fulfillment and goal of all the religions of the world."

19. J. N. Farquhar, *The Crown of Hinduism* (London: Oxford University Press, 1913). Reprinted by Oriental Books Reprint Corporation, New Delhi, 1971 (second edition).

20. Farquhar, *The Crown of Hinduism,* p. 242.

21. Ibid. p. 384.

22. Ibid. pp. 385-86.

23. Macnicol, p. 173.

24. Ibid. p. 173.

25. Ibid. p. 209.

26. Ibid. p. 216.

27. Sydney Cave, *Redemption Hindu and Christian* (London: Oxford University Press, 1919).

28. Ibid. p. 118.

29. Ibid. p. 125.

30. Farquhar, *The Crown of Hinduism,* p. 203.

31. Macnicol, pp. 132-33.

32. Farquhar, *The Crown of Hinduism*, p. 400.

33. Ibid. p. 327.

34. Macnicol, p. 119.

35. Ibid. p. 219.

36. Ibid. p. 251.

37. Ibid. p. 207.

38. Ibid. p. 211.

39. Ibid. pp. 211-12.

40. Cave, p. 114.

41. On the "ideological taint" see Reinhold Niebuhr, *Christian Realism and Political Problems* (London: Faber and Faber, 1954), p. 76.

42. Farquhar, *The Crown of Hinduism*, p. 61.

43. Macnicol, p. 211.

44. Cave, pp. 4, 12.

45. Ibid. pp. 17-18.

46. Farquhar, *The Crown of Hinduism*, p. 191.

47. Cave, p. 12.

48. Rudolf Otto, *India's Religion of Grace and Christianity Compared and Contrasted* (London: SCM Press, 1930).

49. Otto, p. 13.

50. Ibid. p. 18.

51. Ibid. p. 29.

52. Ibid. pp. 44-51.

53. Ibid. p. 51.

54. Ibid. p. 55.

55. Sabapathy Kulandran, *Grace in Christianity and Hinduism* (London: Lutterworth Press, 1964), pp. 252-53.

56. Otto, pp. 94ff.

57. Kulandran, p. 225.

58. Ibid. p. 255.

59. Ibid. p. 241.

60. Otto, p. 108.

61. Ibid. p. 78.

62. Ibid. p. 79.

63. Kulandran, pp. 232-33.

64. Ibid. pp. 230-31. "The Christian faith is built round the belief in God's revelation. This is the primary difference between Christianity and Hinduism."

65. Otto, p. 119.

66. Ibid. p. 120.

67. Ibid. p. 110.

68. Ibid. p. 110.

69. This is questioned, so far as Andrews is concerned, in Hugh Tinker's biography, *The Ordeal of Love* (Delhi: Oxford University Press, 1979), p. 96: "In his perception of God and the Divine Will, he was not satisfied with the Trinitarian concept of God. He did not doubt that Christ was divine, the Son of God, but he had come to believe that God's divinity also filled Gautama, the Buddha—and indeed he believed that God was in all humanity—all men were divine, all men also lived out the agony of Christ in their own lives." Three considerations support the view that Andrew's theology was Trinitarian: i) his background in an English "lib-

eral Catholicism" as demonstrated by Daniel O'Connor in *The Testimony of C. F. Andrews* (Madras & Bangalore: CISRS & CLS, 1974), pp. 10-14; ii) his resumption of his function as an Anglican priest in 1936—he had ceased functioning as one in 1914; and iii) the shape of all his later works in which his faith in "Father, Son and Spirit" is abundantly clear.

70. C. F. Andrews, *Sadhu Sundar Singh* (London: Hodder and Stoughton, 1934), p. 59.

71. Appasamy is roundly criticized in a document published in 1966 by the Gurukul Theological Research Group of the Tamilnad Christian Council (*A Christian Theological Approach to Hinduism* [Madras: C.L.S.]) for confusing, in their view, "the Biblical doctrine of God's indwelling with the Hindu doctrine of God's immanence in man" (p. 13).

72. A. J. Appasamy, *The Gospel and India's Heritage* (London and Madras: SPCK, 1942), pp. 85-86.

73. Appasamy, p. 74.

74. Ibid. p. 16.

75. The major religions "in their higher forms . . . plainly manifest the working of the Spirit of God," according to the Report of the Commission on the Christian Message of Edinburgh, 1910: *Report of Commission IV* (New York: Fleming H. Revell Co., n.d.), p. 267.

76. In Demetrios J. Constantelos, "An Orthodox Perspective," in *Christ's Lordship and Religious Pluralism,* ed. G. H. Anderson and Thomas F. Stransky (Maryknoll, NY: Orbis Books, 1981), pp. 187-88.

77. Appasamy, p. 21.

78. A. J. Appasamy, *Christianity as Bhakti Marga* (Madras: Christian Literature Society for India, 1926), p. 23.

79. Appasamy, *The Gospel and India's Heritage,* p. 10: "Hundreds of these hymns still exist and are sung daily by devotees both in temples and homes . . . . The hymns make it clear that the poets had a real experience of God and came to know something of His grace and reality and power."

80. Ibid. pp. 67-68.

81. Ibid. p. 73.

82. Ibid. pp. 146-47.

83. C. F. Andrews, *What I Owe to Christ* (London: Hodder and Stoughton, 1932), p. 20.

84. C. F. Andrews, *Zaka Ullah of Delhi* (Cambridge: Heffer, 1919), p. xix.

85. Andrews, *What I Owe to Christ*, p. 258.

86. C. F. Andrews, *Christ in the Silence* (London: Hodder and Stoughton, 1933), p. 215.

87. Appasamy, *Christianity as Bhakti-Marga,* p. 111.

88. Ibid. p. 112.

89. Ibid. p. 98.

90. Ibid. p. 99.

91. Appasamy, *The Gospel and India's Heritage,* p. 188.

92. "Re-Thinking Group," *Re-Thinking Christianity in India* (Madras: 1938).

93. Appasamy, *The Gospel and India's Heritage,* p. 196.

94. Andrews, *What I Owe to Christ,* p. 23.

95. C. F. Andrews, *The Good Shepherd* (London: Hodder and Stoughton, 1940), p. 180.

96. Andrews, *The Good Shepherd*: consideration of pastoral work passes, in this book, from the "personal dimensions of ministry" to "practical work" in a variety of social ministries.

97. Andrews, *The Good Shepherd,* pp. 164ff. Here termed a ministry to "the multitude."

98. Mariasusai Dhavamony, *Love of God According to Śaiva Siddhānta* (Oxford: Clarendon Press, 1971).

99. John Braisted Carman, *Theology of Rāmānuja* (New Haven and London: Yale University Press, 1974).

100. Dhavamony, p. vii.

101. Klaus Klostermaier, *Hindu and Christian in Vrindavan* (London: SCM Press, 1969).

102. Klaus Klostermaier, *Mythologies and Philosophies of Salvation in the Theistic Traditions of India* (Waterloo: Canadian Corporation for Studies in Religion, 1984), p. 119.

103. See the positive assessment of non-Christian religions in the Declaration on the Relationship of the Church to Non-Christian Religions in *The Documents of Vatican II,* ed. Walter M. Abbott, S.J. (Chicago: Follett Publishing Co., 1966), pp. 660-68.

104. C. F. Andrews, "The Body of Humanity," in *Visvabharati Quarterly* (1924), printed in O'Connor, pp. 210-12.

105. As he understands Hindu expositions of sacrificial service: *The Gospel and India's Heritage,* pp. 237-38.

106. Leslie Dewart, *The Future of Belief* (New York: Herder and Herder, 1966), p. 29.

107. V. Chakkarai, *The Cross and Indian Thought* (Madras: C.L.S., 1932) and C. S. Paul, *The Suffering God* (Madras: C.L.S., 1932). The former assails Western piety as follows: "The West has reduced it (divine law) to a scheme of happiness, as if God's duty was to provide automobiles and *ladus* to the *bhaktas*" (p. 77).

108. For example, by Tissa Balasuriya in *Planetary Theology* (London: SCM Press, 1984; Maryknoll, N.Y.: Orbis Books, 1984).

12

Hindu-Christian Worship Settings in South India

PAUL YOUNGER

The theory of Hindu-Christian dialogue must in some sense be related to the practices of Hindu and Christian worshippers. To some extent theory may think of itself as informing the practice of the future, but in another sense it must begin from the practice of the past and the present, for it is in such practice that one sees the patterns of human religiosity set forth. It is these patterns that set the framework in which any new patterns in our religious life will be worked out, and in that sense they are the basis — but, of course, not the limit — of our theological hopes and theoretical considerations.

Christianity and Hinduism have co-existed in South India now for almost two millennia. In the lives of families, villages and the region as a whole this co-existence has often involved very close mutual awareness and as a result an extensive borrowing of religious practices, symbols and values. This chapter will not attempt to trace the overall history of that co-existence, but will look closely at three ostensibly Christian worship centers where Hindus worship and where the worship atmosphere reflects the long-standing, intimate and largely unconscious blending of Hindu and Christian patterns of worship. The first example is the Jacobite church in the village of Mannarkat in central Kerala. The second example is the Roman Catholic shrine of Velankanni on the seacoast of south Tamilnâtu. And the third is of the Pentecostal-like worship center of Pastor Sundaram in Madras.

MANNARKAT

Mannarkat is a village region of central Kerala about ten miles west of Kottayam, the commercial city that has served as the base of the St. Thomas

Christians, who have been a major factor in Kerala society probably since the reputed visit of the Apostle Thomas himself in the first century. Christians make up about one-third of the population in the region of Mannarkat. The social structure in the area is rather rigid with Nairs and wealthy Christians owning about equal amounts of the land (a mixture of paddy or rice planting and coconut and rubber plantations cover the area) and comprising about twenty percent of the population. The other eighty percent of the population are poor Christians or "untouchable" caste people who work for the landowners. In recent years the pattern has become somewhat less rigid as members of all groups leave the area for education and outside employment, but the general pattern is still easy to recognize.

There were traditionally four sacred centers in Mannarkat. A Visnu temple was built during the eighteenth century when there was a resurgence of Nair religious interest linked to the actions of Martanda Varman, the Raja of Trivandrum. It was Martanda Varman who organized the state of Travancore by bringing together all the petty râjas of south Kerala, and it was also he who tried to give the state a religious tone, especially by using the Padhmanabhavan (Visnu) temple in Trivandrum as a religio-political center. In the spirit of that development a petty râja near Mannarkat built the local Visnu temple, but it has since fallen down and a revivalist effort to rebuild it is currently being undertaken by the Rashtraya Swayamsevak Sangh and some of the Nair youth in the region. The natural rival of the Visnu temple was the much older Siva temple in the northeast of Mannarkat, which has a high wall around it and has for centuries been owned and served by a Nambiar family. This Nambiar family belongs to a caste that considers itself both a landlord and a priestly caste. This family continues to be the most prominent landlord family in the area and to perform most of the daily temple rituals. In deference to newer religious trends and government pressures to employ Namboodri brahmans in temples wherever possible, the Nambiar family now employs a young Namboodri brahman to do certain rituals, but they insist that this is a new arrangement and that he has no traditional rights in the temple. Very few worshippers now visit this temple.

Clearly the two oldest and most important worship centers of Mannarkat are the temple of the goddess Bhagavati (Kali) and the Jacobite church of Mary. Local legend claims that the two deities (Bhagavati and Mary) are sisters, and worshippers in each place claim that they worship in both these sacred places. The two centers are less than a mile apart, and during their respective festivals the festival processions stop at the other's sacred center. Worshippers at festival time often make a supplementary stop at the other worship center as a part of their festival worship.

The Bhagavati temple is operated by the Elayathu family, which is a low-status brahman family in the sense that they are not Namboodris but from a priestly lineage usually associated with Bhagavati temples popular primarily with worshippers from the lower status castes. The priestly family lives in a large and very old priest-styled house behind the temple. The temple itself is relatively small, but its grounds include a thick, untouched forest for the sacred snakes, a shrine for the *yaksis* or much-revered demonesses, a bathing tank, and a large field and podium for outdoor festival worship. The temple is considered to be directly linked with the main Bhagavati temple in Kotunkallur, a hundred miles to the north, and a door on the northern side is reserved for the goddess to be able to go off to the north. The temple is very popular with the poorer sections of society in this region and large crowds frequently gather for the regular worship and for healing and exorcisms with the temperamental goddess and with her snake grove and *yaksis* as well.

The Jacobite church of Mary in Mannarkat seems to be one of the oldest churches in this area, and may well be older than the Bhagavati temple. The earliest settlements of St. Thomas Christians were a hundred miles to the north very near the present-day Kotunkallur temple of Bhagavati, whose bell, incidentally, is marked by a cross and was probably originally a church bell. Because they were dominant in the field of trade, and because trade from the mountains to the east tended to concentrate in Kottayam, Christian settlements spread to this central Kerala region fairly early. A series of splits in the church occurred as the St. Thomas Christians later made contact with Western churches. The details of these splits need concern us only in the sense that we know that the Jacobite branch of the church, represented in Mannarkat, has been the one least involved with Western churches and therefore least concerned about "purifying" itself of its links with the local culture. About half of the St. Thomas Christians remained in the Roman Catholic Church after the dramatic sixteenth-century negotiations between the local church officials and the Portuguese clerical authorities were concluded. Among the non-Roman Catholics another group was influenced by Protestant missions in the nineteenth century and became the Mar Thoma Church. When the remaining local church split in recent years the Orthodox with their base in Kottayam became heavily involved in the worldwide Ecumenical Movement and made contact with the Orthodox churches in other lands. The Jacobites with their loose traditional ties to Syria continue to have their traditional base in the older Christian areas in the northern part of Travancore and Cochin, but some older churches, such as the one in Mannarkat, have also kept to the Jacobite tradition largely due to strong family ties.

The annual festival in the Mannarkat church is a major religious event in central Kerala. Attended by probably a hundred thousand, it has all of the sociological features of a Hindu temple festival in that people bring generous offerings of animals, fruits, spices, oil and money, sleep on the grounds for a week, bathe in the tank, participate in recreational activities and engage in fasting, prayer and processions (a special feature is the thousands of colored umbrellas carried in procession). The popularity of the festival among families of both Hindu and Christian background is related partly to the colorful ceremony, but is also linked to the healings and exorcisms that are reputed to be associated with the latter days of the festival. Special power is associated with the fragment of the scarf left by Mary at the time of her assumption. The most important focus of the entire festival is the moment on the concluding day when the window high above the altar is opened for only a few seconds and a visionary glimpse of Mary is provided to the surging ecstatic crowd for the only time during the year. During the latter phases of the festival, when the crowd approaches a hundred thousand, clearly a majority of the worshippers are not from Christian backgrounds. The eucharistic services, sung by a host of clergy in the central sanctum, are full orthodox Christian services, but the expectations associated with the visionary glimpse of Mary and the other activities of the festival represent wider patterns of worship with which all present are familiar.

VELANKANNI

The main festival of Velankanni now attracts more than a million worshippers and is therefore the most popular annual religious event in all of India. A very small percentage of the worshippers on these occasions are from Christian backgrounds, and the worship patterns used reflect the backgrounds of the worshippers.

The shrine of Velankanni is not a church related to a local community, but is a shrine on the seacoast adjoining a small fishing village and about five miles from the port town of Nakapattinam on the east coast of deep South India. The legends connected with the site associate the holy Mother with visions of shepherd boys and sailors lost at sea, but the most important concern of the extremely poor people (the majority of the worshippers) who make the pilgrimage to this place is healing. Following the local (Hindu) worship patterns, these worshippers take vows months before, bring offerings of cocks, shave their heads, push around the flagstaff to touch the ropes and induce trances, take their offerings of coconuts, bananas and garlands and push into the tiny East-facing shrine for a glimpse of "the goddess." Many either compare or confuse the deity with their local goddess, Mâriyamman, with whom they have both a stormy and healing relationship, which they have transferred onto Velankanni.

Behind the East-facing shrine is a large West-facing church where orthodox Roman Catholic masses are said regularly. The crowds in this area are relatively small and priests have a difficult time explaining to people who wander in what is going on. (While I was there a worshipper went to the altar and loudly demanded to know where the goddess was.) Most worshippers come from considerable distances in the stream of buses that pour in without stop over the ten days. Because of the vast sea of people, each cluster of worshippers tends to stay together and to camp somewhere on the sand with communication with others in the worshipping community rather limited. Nevertheless some communication obviously does take place and some sharing of worship experience is a part of the pilgrimage.

PASTOR SUNDARAM'S

For the past thirty years a company of a thousand or more leave their shoes outside and sit on the roof of a rambling old house in Madras for three- or four-hour Pentecostal-style services led by Pastor Sundaram and his staff. Pastor Sundaram himself is of the Nadar community, which was in traditional Tamilnâtu, the major community at the southern tip of India where they cultivated palm trees. Late in the nineteenth century large numbers of that community became Christian and immediately started demanding higher status than they were accorded in traditional society, where as relative outsiders they were given a relatively low standing. Pastor Sundaram's assistant is a convert from the landlord Velâla caste, and the two pastors have married sisters of a Sri Lankan Christian family. The congregation, like the pastors, is made up of people who have arrived in Madras during the present generation and are taking advantage of new opportunities in employment and in changing social identity. All services are bilingual in Tamil and English, and an elaborate translation system is used even in small midweek services where all participants are familiar with a common language. Only a few in the congregation are English-speaking Anglo-Indians, but the bilingual format appeals to other South Indians (from Kerala, Karnataka and Andhra) newly arrived in the largest city of South India, and it appeals even more to the large number in the congregation who aspire to high status English-speaking jobs in government service.

Most weeks a dozen or so Hindu converts are publicly baptized in the tank and are introduced to the congregation, indicating that among the regular worshippers are a fair number of Hindu observers. Like the rest of the congregation, the Hindu participants are relatively well-educated, recently urbanized members of middle- and upper-caste backgrounds.

At first glance the doctrinal stance of Pastor Sundaram seems to exclude links with Hindu worship patterns; he puts a heavy emphasis on an exclusive commitment to Christ and on a lifestyle of holiness. There are, however, many features of the worship Hindus and former Hindus find familiar and in harmony with Tamil religious tradition. One of the features of the worship mentioned in this regard is music. Two-thirds of the worship time is taken up in congregational singing, and many of the hymns are sung so often that they become part of conversations and homilies whenever members of the congregation meet elsewhere in the city. One of the knowledgeable former Hindus compared this hymn-singing with his childhood, when the hymns of the Medieval Śaiva saints were constantly on his lips. A second link with Tamil religious history is the intensity of the personal experience of both sin and grace. Testimonies are a central part of the worship pattern at Pastor Sundaram's, and those accounts of religious experience reflect the classic pattern found in Śaiva biographies where people struggle with God by taking vows, performing them, making a claim on God for healing or improved employment and then go through experiences of both failure and surprising encounters with grace. The third link with Tamil religious practice in the worship at Pastor Sundaram's is the role given to the religious *guru* and the strong sense of group obedience to a saintly personality. Pastor Sundaram has little churchly authority in a form familiar to Western Christians, but the fascination of the congregation with his saintliness and their willingness to accord him authority over their daily lives is a pattern that has a strong tradition in Tamil religious history.

CONCLUSION

What can be learned about Hindu-Christian worship patterns from the three examples of Mannarkat, Velankanni and Pastor Sundaram's? The main lesson learned, of course, is that in all three sites many worshippers are either unaware of, or indifferent to, the labels attached to different worship centers. Worshippers seek the experience of healing, exorcism, forgiveness or holiness depending on their need and the reports of earlier experiences they have heard from others. In Kerala, where there is a millennia-old tradition of distinctive religious communities, the worshippers recognize the plurality of options, but also affirm the importance of cultivating more than one. In Tamilnâtu, where the craze for one pilgrimage site after another has developed, many worshippers are quite unaware that Velankanni is different in an important way because of its Christian associations. In Madras, where Pastor Sundaram acknowledges no tradition and makes an exclusive commitment so central, both former Christians and former Hindus are in an important sense placed in the same camp. The new worship patterns are new to all, and yet in some unconscious sense they seem more familiar to some Hindus than they do to Christians raised in Westernized worship settings.

If worship patterns are as readily interwoven on the empirical plane as this evidence would seem to indicate, perhaps the question of Hindu-Christian relations needs to be rephrased. *Dialogue* was a word initially used to describe the rationalistic discourse engaged in by Plato and others. In the eighteenth and nineteenth centuries it came to be used in a wider context as whole cultures discovered one another for the first time and "negotiations" began to take place as European powers slowly relinquished political power and nations spoke up and demonstrated their cultural and economic viability. Within Indian society there has long been another kind of cultural situation, and by analogy I think it is now possible to say that something like that situation is found throughout the world. That situation is that a society with strong bonds in realms such as economics, language, and so on nevertheless had a variety of religious options. (This is not the place to explain why that was the case in India except perhaps to suggest that it was made possible by the fact that the early stages of India's development turned away from the monocultural "tribal" model to the multicultural "caste" model.) What is important to us is that post-World War II society throughout the world has in an analogous way developed strong bonds in the realms of economics and communication while at the same time affirming its multicultural multireligious nature.

If our microscopic look at what takes place in the multireligious contexts of Mannarkat, Velankanni and Pastor Sundaram's has anything to teach us about what might take place in the future in a much wider arena, it is that worshippers do not "dialogue" so much as they "share." Wherever the bonds of economics and language make communication possible, a sharing in the search for those things that ultimately concern people will take place. The theological interests of the leaders who organize the three worship centers studied have little in common, and yet the worshippers of differing backgrounds are able to communicate effectively with one another and to articulate a common concern with that which is ultimate. Theories about the wider patterns of communication will have to take into account many additional factors, but the rich experience of worshippers in these South Indian centers is at least one model of what sharing religious tradition is like, and it is one from which much can be learned.

13

Hindu Influence on Christian Spiritual Practice

MURRAY ROGERS

How I wish that I could convey through a few strokes of the brush or a few notes on a pipe the gift that the Hindu revelation has been to me, a Christian, in my spiritual life and experience! Words, however, must suffice, so I will begin my tale by asking you to travel with me in imagination to the temple of Tungnath, the highest shrine on the inner Himalayan range lying between two of the sources of the Ganga, Kedarnath and Badrinath. One year I was on the pilgrim path to Tungnath with a multitude of Rajputana pilgrims. We had already walked more than sixty miles from the railhead in Rishikesh and now, approaching the twelve thousand foot mark, we were nearing the goal of our journey, the place of that *darśana*[1] of the mystery of the One beyond all name and form who draws the soul beyond, beyond . . . to the very Source. Few words were spoken, other than the omnipresent murmur of OM,[2] that ineffable sound taken up by the pilgrims and echoed by stream and mountain and forest.

There, high up in the Himalayas whose unattainable summits ever beckon one upward, as also down on the broad Ganges plain where one walks among India's poorest people, the strongest influence of Hinduism comes not through concepts or philosophies, not through words and even less through "religion," but through life lived, through breathing a common air, sharing the work and suffering and joys of God's poorest children. The kernel of the faith of the poor comes seldom from what is said; it does not pass from mouth to mouth, from mind to mind, but rather is transmitted from heart to heart, at the level of perception, in smiles or tears or silence. At that level love is shared and there emerges a "way" deeper than any religious form, whether of ritual or of word.

There is in India, among the poor and oppressed, an exposure to life in all its stark reality, evidence most clearly perhaps on the ghats of Varanasi or in the slums of Calcutta[3] or Bombay, or, for me, in the villages of northern India that I know best. There the most basic existence is threatened daily and, as a Japanese friend of mine after years of life in India, wrote: "The naked destination of man's existence comes to sight without any kind of veil. It is powerfully shocking and provoking for outsiders."[4] In such circumstances of radical poverty faith is in fact "naked faith"; in the presence of such faith our schools and seminaries, with their trends and scholasticisms, are seen to be what they are: the theater of the world's privileged, a tiny minority of human beings. That is indeed a painful and deeply disturbing discovery for us Christian people who are accustomed to privilege; it is also a deep and healing experience.

In an encounter with this India there opened up for me what, in a review of Laurens van der Post's book *A Walk with a White Bushman* has been described as the "rediscovery of the soul's country . . . the opening of the door of the soul too long enclosed in our materialist civilization."[5] I, as a Christian and, at that time, as a Christian missionary, had learned to see myself as a teacher of a better way, the Way. As a preacher of the gospel of Christ I hoped and prayed that Hindu people might be converted to him, as I myself had been a few years earlier. It seemed self-evident to me and to my colleagues that we went to India full of thoughts and dreams of far-reaching results and benefits accruing to Indian friends. The relationship between education and humility had escaped us.[6] It took us years to discover that we ourselves can learn, we can even help others to learn, but as Vinoba Bhave has pointed out, we cannot "teach." It is not for nothing that in the Hindi language the only word that exists for teach is "cause to learn," and I am told that the same is true in all the main languages of India.[7]

The break in the Christian Western encapsulated way of living and seeing life came for us when I was blessed to meet and know a close colleague of Mahatma Gandhi, A. V. Thakkar Bapa, and when, as a result of this friendship, my wife and I were invited to live and work at Sevagram, Gandhiji's headquarters and ashram for the last fifteen years of his life. Subsequently, and as a sort of follow-up, an invitation came from another Gandhian, Banwari Lal Choudhri, to live for a year in his village, in a one-room mud hut, closely related to his Hindu joint family.

During that time in Gandhian circles and later during our seventeen years of ashram life in Jyotiniketan, Kareli village, U.P., it was Hindu friends, often close and respected friends, whether the path they followed was the one of action, of devotion or of spiritual knowledge (karma, *bhakti, jñāna*), who silently compelled me to re-think and to "re-feel" my original "Christian" understanding of their spiritual path, and consequently of my own. It began simply by being puzzled, by wondering what makes such dear, loving and gentle people. From what deep Source does their spiritual depth arise? Slowly I came to see that in the first place I needed—unless I were to call white black—to place their Way at a genuinely spiritual level, at the level of the Spirit. I was in the presence of a mystery, a spiritual experience that could only be approached with the deepest reverence. This reverence, whatever else it might come to mean, involved a refusal to judge, a refusal to stand against either the life or the truth of my neighbor,[8] and, concomitantly a disinclination to analyze and dissect according to my usual Western, "Christian" categories. If, consciously or unconsciously, a Hindu friend allowed me to glimpse a tiny corner of the mystery by which he lived, it was for me to listen humbly, to try to understand, often more with heart than with head, and to give him what Dr. Jacques-Albert Cuttat—a dear and respected friend in Hindu-Christian dialogue—used to call "the credit of his own beauty."[9]

The more I observed this mystery, which accompanied our Hindu friends both in life and in death, and the deeper I delved into their Hindu scriptures, the more my conscience struggled with the dilemma: What of my fundamental loyalty to Christ, what of my self-understanding as one who was there in India primarily to share his gospel? Far from being a liberal Christian I was—dare I say, am?—an evangelical Catholic holding closely both to the Christian scriptures and to the church and her sacraments. Yet here, in personal experience I could not deny, was a spiritual and human reality, a path concerning which all I had known hitherto had been intellectual formulations and notions given by specialists—both Western and too often Indian—who were content to present Hinduism in terms of concepts acceptable to Western ways of thought. Clearly the spiritual phenomenon that was being shared with me could not be approached and understood with the equipment with which I had arrived in India.

If I were to understand more deeply the heart of this experience I began to sense in our Hindu friends, I had to free myself from my own mental and spiritual conditioning; I had to resist judging from *my* theological or philosophical positions. Rather, it was a matter of throwing myself into the stream, entrusting myself to it, allowing it to do what it would with me. There were some sincere Christian people who saw great danger in this; we might easily lose our Christian faith and bearings and become, if not outwardly then inwardly, Hindu. We ourselves knew what it meant to tremble before such a venture of the spirit, but we believed then, as we do now, that if the Lord were not able to hold us himself and in himself, no matter how deeply we might plunge into this "other" spiritual way, then it would be clear that he is not the Lord we believe him to be.

Looking back down the years, I now see that the Hindu reality began to merge with my Christian reality before I realized it was happening through friendship, the sharing of faith experiences, the bearing together of suffering and joys. From that inner beginning came the practice of Upaniṣadic meditation, often led by that friend and guide Swami Abhishiktananda (Dom Le Saux), whose recently published journal is the intimate account of his personal Hindu/Christian "meeting point."[10] It was in those times of sitting at the feet of the ṛṣi, the vedic seers, and also in times of silence and solitude that must accompany any serious listening to that call, that the need to go beyond the *dvandva*,[11] the dualities, became clear. The resonances within our own "Christian" souls made it impossible any longer to judge this deep Hindu source as being "outside," another source than ours. Whether it was that extraordinary mystical document, the Katha, or some other Upaniṣad, or the *Bhagavadgītā* that has sustained countless Hindu men and women on their pilgrimage through life, we were slowly becoming aware that these were our spiritual sustenance as well as theirs. When during those years of the 1960s we began in our daily eucharistic celebration to read a passage from the Hindu scriptures before reading the epistle and gospel from the Bible, the converging streams flowed together, as they still do, as a part of our daily spiritual nutrition.

Thus in the insights of the Vedas, discovered not primarily as material for intellectual scrutiny but as food for the soul, we rejoiced to find many links with the spiritual food provided by our own Christian sources: the Bible, the Fathers of the Church, and the great Christian mystical writers such as Meister Eckhart, St. John of the Cross, St. Teresa of Avila, and a host of others. We found it natural and good to collect what we sometimes call our Hindu Prayer Book. Whether from the ancient Vedas themselves, from the Purāṇas, from the spiritual gems of Srī Sankaracarya, from Tulsidas or from some other source, we continue to discover unending enrichment.

Sometimes these are voiced by us as prayer together or singly, while at others we use whole Vedic hymns as "psalms" through which we too would offer our praise and gratitude to God:

> Homage to him who presides over all things,
> that which was and that which shall be;
> to that all-powerful Brahman be homage!
> Atharva Veda 10, 8[12]

or, for example, the prayer from the Sukla Yajur Veda 36, 18

> O God, Scatterer of ignorance and darkness,
>   grant me your strength.
> May all beings regard me with the eye of a friend,
>   and I all beings!
> With the eye of a friend may each single being
>   regard all others![13]

Time forbids that I share more of these beautiful verses, samplings, as it were, of some ancient vineyard, but I cannot resist sharing one Tamil lyric that somehow sums up for us this spiritual treasure, this "way" we long to travel, though as yet our steps falter and we have far to go before reaching the goal:

> O You, who have come into the depth of my heart,
> > enable me to concentrate solely
> > on this depth of my heart.
> O You, who are my guest in the depth of my heart,
> > enable me also to penetrate
> > into this depth of my heart.
> O You, who are at home in the depth of my heart,
> > enable me to sit peacefully
> > in this depth of my heart.
> O You, who alone belong in the depth of my heart,
> > enable me to dive deep and lose myself
> > in this deepest depth of my heart.
> O You, who are quite alone in the depth of my heart,
> > enable me to disappear into You
> > in this depth of my heart.

Words, however deep and appealing though they may be, can so easily remain on the conceptual level, on the ε'ίδος level. As pointers, icons beckoning to us to dare to go beyond, these Hindu scriptures and prayers are an invaluable gift for us Christians in our own spiritual practice. It has been in sharing, furthermore, many of the symbols and gestures of our Hindu friends that the mysterious inner meaning of words becomes real. I refer here to the offering of fire, the *āratī* whether performed in the great evening *puja*[14] at Har ki Pauri in Hardwar or evening by evening in our own small ashram chapel. Then there is the greater or lesser prostration, the lying full-length on the ground with hands together above the head or the simple touching of the ground with one's forehead. Equally meaningful can be the various *mudrās*, or gestures of the hand, the *anjali*, or joining of the hands in greeting, or the offering of flowers in worship with a sentence of praise — *OM namah* — sung as each of the eight flowers is offered. Each of these signs and a multitude more, and the actions they enjoin, are, properly speaking, calls to the Within, a silent beckoning to those who practice such actions to meet the Divine Mystery within, his image, his presence. Never may they truly be considered as ends in themselves, but rather as ways in which the person may "pass over" to the experience of that same Mystery. Alas for the intellectual, either Christian or Hindu, who despises these outer signs of the Spirit within — to do so is to invite alienation to grow in our worshipping communities.

I see a village farmer placing with great reverence a lump of gur or molasses in the earth before the planting of the first sugar cane, for how dare we human beings take sweetness from the earth without ourselves offering sweetness in return? I see myself present on the banks of the

Ramganga at a *yajña*[15] or sacrifice of grain that the atmosphere between heaven and earth may be purified, for without such purification how can our leaders hope to lead wisely, as the officiating priest explains to me. I remember the young bride, lonely for her first family but promising firmly to perform daily *pūjā* that her husband may be blessed.

More mysteriously and far more hidden—for not all are *adhikāri*, spiritually prepared, have "eyes to see"—it is the inner pull of the Absolute felt by a multitude of Hindu friends that affects us Christians most deeply. Whether they are among the great souls, known to millions, or tailor, a simple *sādhu* (holy man), a village woman, a young boy—a modern Nachiketas[16]—they are drawn irresistibly toward the Source and to that experience of unitive love that takes place once the chasm of separateness has been overcome.

Such an inner pull leads for some to the *tapas*[17] of years of silence and spiritual struggle. For others—businessman, workers, housewives—this persistent urge results in their burning up time and effort on the endeavor. This will take the form of a steady and disciplined concentration on silent meditation as a part of each day and, once or twice a year, a visit to their spiritual guide or *guru* for a week of more intensive *sādhanā*, spiritual practice and training. Such a time, taken perhaps from their yearly leave, will send them back strengthened for the daily struggle with the little self, the ego, without the mastery of which the sages of all spiritual paths know that there can be no growing consciousness of the Presence within.

This search/pilgrimage of countless Hindu people, whether it be expressed in prayer, silent meditation and yoga, or in the most radical ascetic practice (*sannyāsa*),[18] has for many Christian people a strong attraction and pull. It is generally lived out in a most hidden way and demands a most radical conversion. We say, and we say truly, that we have our Christian spiritual giants, St. Francis of Assisi, Julian of Norwich, Hildegard of Bingen, John of the Cross and countless others, men and women down the ages who have been athletes of the Spirit. We know too that the Lord Jesus challenges us to daily dying in order truly to live,[19] that our calling is in the words of the Greek Orthodox Hieratikon, "to participate in thy Godhead," but few accept in practice, in the daily giving of time and human resources, that this is the fundamental call to every person.

Having lived for almost a decade in the Old City of Jerusalem, the heart of the three so-called monotheisms—Jewish, Christian and Muslim—I can bear personal witness to our mistaken sincerity in claiming that each of our faiths is full and complete, that we have no need of teachers from elsewhere. Tragically I cannot bear testimony to very many in each of these spiritual families in that place whose daily practice and subsequent public and private lives bear the hallmark of the spirit of either Moses, Jesus or the Prophet. It is, I believe, from the East, not least from the *Sanātana Dharma*[20] of India, that we Christians have very much to learn, not, maybe, so much from the schools of philosophy as such as from the daily practice and experience of countless spiritual practitioners—whether philosophers or not!

Perhaps they too, at certain points, may receive God's gifts through us. For myself, I see a greater need for us to learn than for us to teach, for us to discover the interdependence and mutuality that link us together in our spiritual paths to a degree and to an extent infinitely higher and wider than we are as yet prepared to accept.

I begin to see—seemingly against much of my original upbringing and teaching—that the fundamental message of any of our religions, including my own, lies deeper and beyond the framework in which that message may have been given to the world. The Lord Jesus Christ was not a Christian! True, his message, his work of salvation, was lived out and revealed in a Jewish setting, but it was too strong a message to be confined within that spiritual and cultural packaging.[21] It outgrows every framework in which we out of love and devotion enshrine it. Similarly with the message of the Upaniṣads; it comes to us encased in its Vedic and Brahmanic clothing, but the message itself lies beyond those outer manifestations.

On 14 December 1971, nearly two years before his crossing to the further shore, Abhishiktananda, Christian monk/Hindu *sannyāsi*, wrote in his personal diary:

My message has nothing to do with any *dharma* whatever. That is the same with every fundamental message. The message of the Upanishads, as regards its formulation, still depends on its Vedic-Brahmanic roots, but it is self-luminous—*svaprakāśa*; it reveals the depth in its proper light. It reflects it.

Similarly, the Gospel message is no more bound to the Jewish world in which it was revealed. Its universal value consumes and melts the wax vessels of the Judaeo-Greek world in which this honey was deposited. It echoes the very depths of the human heart; the message of love, of mutual giving, of relationship. The message that mankind's condition is divine. The Upanishadi message has molded the Indian mind, and the Gospel message that of the West, though passing through channels that are further and further removed from the Source, and with waters more and more adulterated.

We have to recover the Source, and place humanity face to face with itself, with its own depth. To make man discover "that he is" at a level deeper than any external identity or any analysis of himself, even existential.[22]

The great gift of the Hindu experience to Christian people is to point us to that ultimate awakening of the human spirit, an awakening to which Jesus Christ himself also calls us, calling us to surrender every desire, however natural, to cling to externals, to the label level, the level of "name-and-form" whether Eastern or Western. That awakening, so wonderfully experienced by the Lord Jesus Christ, has nothing to do with any one religion. It is the awakening to the glory of transfiguration for which we and the whole cosmos were created.[23]

How can one but echo St. Paul: "O depth of wealth, wisdom, and knowledge in God! . . . Source, Guide, and Goal of all that is—to him be glory for ever! Amen."[24]

NOTES

1. *Darśana*: sight, vision, of God, a saint, an image, a holy place.

2. OM: primordial sacred syllable, symbolizing Brahman, the Ultimate Reality.

3. Cf. Dominique Lapierre, *City of Joy*, trans. Kathryn Spink (London: Century, 1986).

4. Dr. Minoru Kasal, an unpublished paper.

5. Kathleen Raine, *Resurgence* (March/April 1987): 46.

6. Cf. Vinoba Bhave, *The Intimate and the Ultimate*, ed. Satish Kumar (U.K.: Element Books, 1986), p. 21. "In our ancient books *vidya* (education) is equated with *vinaya* (humility); *vinaya*, in Sanskrit, is a synonym for education, and a student who had completed his studies was called *vinit*—perfected in humility. This humility is the fruit of true education.

7. Bhave, p. 20.

8. Translated from the French of Eloi Lerclerc, *Exil et tendresse*, Editions Franciscaines, Paris, no. 12, Présence de St. François, p. 83. "Because unity exists already, said Francis, it is something beyond our contriving. It is the most profound reality in creation. But our life is short and usually does not penetrate below the surface of things. We want to arrange things in our own way. I just simply know that authentic unity between persons will never be able to come into being against anything, by raising barriers. Unity is not made against, but with: with all that is, with all that God has willed into being. The one who regards thus all that exists little by little comes to perceive the deep truth of the world. He opens himself to unity; he discovers it at that deep level where all things dwell fraternally in the hand of God. He discovers it and enters into it."

9. Jacques-Albert Cuttat, *The Encounter of Religions* (New York: Desclée Company, 1960).

10. Abhishiktananda (H. Le Saux, O.S.B.), *La Montée au fond du coeur (le journal intime du moine chrétien-sannyāsi hindou)* (Paris: O.E.I.L., 1986).

11. *Dvandva*: pair of opposites such as heat and cold, pleasure and pain.

12. Cf. R. Panikkar, *The Vedic Experience, Mantramañjāri, An Anthology for Modern Man and Contemporary Celebration* (Pondicherry, India, and University of California, 1977), pp. 824, 342 (alternative translation).

13. Author unknown, quoted in Dom Le Saux (Swami Abhishiktananda), *Guru and Disciple* (London: SPCK, 1974), p. 100.

14. *Pūjā*: ritual worship, which may include *arat*; act of worship with oil or camphor flame being waved from side to side or in a circle.

15. *Yajña*: sacrifice (from the root *yaj*, "to offer").

16. Nachiketas is a young hero of ancient India who goes to Yama, king of death, to learn the meaning of life. He is immortalized in the Katha Upaniṣad.

17. *Tapas*: literally "heat"; hence inner energy, spiritual fervor, austerity, asceticism.

18. *Sannyāsa*: total renunciation.

19. Mark 8:34-37.

20. *Sanātana Dharma*: the traditional name of the religion that springs from the Vedas, the eternal religion or law.

21. For a Jewish perspective see Alfons Rosenberg, *Jesus der Mensch: Ein Fragment* (Kösel, 1986).

22. Abhishiktananda, *La Montée au fond du coeur (le journal intime du moine chrétien-sannyāsi hindou)* (translated into English by the Abhishiktananda Society, Delhi, in *Occasional Bulletin* no. 10, April 1987).

23. Cf. St. Hilary, quoted by Henri de Lubac, *Amida*, p. 307: "The rays of the Word are eternally ready to shine wherever, in all simplicity, the windows of the soul are opened."

24. Romans 11:33-36.

14

Christian Influence on Hindu Spiritual Practice in Trinidad

ANANTANAND RAMBACHAN

This chapter will focus on some of the ways in which the Christian tradition has influenced Hindu spiritual life and practice on the island of Trinidad in the West Indies. After an introductory historical account of the Hindu presence in Trinidad, I describe some specific examples of Christian influences on Hindu practices. I conclude with a personal reflection about the enrichment of my own spiritual outlook through this encounter.

HISTORICAL BACKGROUND

The Genoese sea captain Christopher Columbus, in quest of the riches of Asia, was firmly convinced that the way to the East was through the West. Hoping to win against the Portuguese in the race for the East, the Spanish monarchy agreed to support his venture, and on 3 August 1492 Columbus set sail from Palos. About two months later, with his crew on the verge of a mutiny, Columbus luckily sighted the island of San Salvador in the Bahamas. He explored the northern coast of Cuba and founded a settlement at Hispaniola (modern Haiti). Convinced that he had reached the East, Columbus wrote with great enthusiasm to the Spanish rulers of islands that promised "as much gold as their highnesses may need, spice and cotton, and mastic and aloes-wood and a thousand other things of value." He named the islands "las Yndias" (the Indies). Only in 1502 did he add "occidentales" to make them "West Indies." Three subsequent voyages were made by Columbus to these islands during the years 1493-1502.

Christopher Columbus died in dishonorable circumstances, firmly convinced that he had found a route to the East. He had not reached the East by sailing westward, but, in one of those intriguing paradoxes of history, the East was later to establish itself in the West. In an unusual way his dream was realized.

On 31 July 1498, Columbus stumbled on the island of Trinidad, lying just off the northeastern coast of Venezuela. The original inhabitants, the Caribs and Arawaks, were part of a large family of people known as Amerindians, who inhabited North and South America. The evidence of Spanish colonization can be found in many place names, such as Port of Spain and San Fernando, and in the musical traditions, festivals and cuisine of Trinidad. The native Amerindian population was virtually exterminated by forced labor and European diseases, and by the time the British took the island in 1802 there were very few left. In the eighteenth century considerable numbers of French planters came to Trinidad, and there has also been a French influence in the shaping of the island's life and history. Africans were brought as slaves from West Africa to work on the sugar plantations from as early as the seventeenth century, and they constituted the basic population, along with the British, until 1838, when slavery was abolished.

The abolition of slavery meant the virtual collapse of the plantation economy on which the economic life of the island was based. Africans refused to work on the sugar plantations, preferring instead to become small independent farmers. The harsh memories of slavery and its association with sugar cultivation were not easy to erase. The planters in most colonies, especially British Guiana (now Guyana), Trinidad and Jamaica, where the labor problems were desperate, looked elsewhere for workers. They turned to contracted immigrants to provide a source of cheap labor. Portuguese and Chinese immigrants were tried, but they drifted into business or private cultivation as soon as, or even before, their contracts expired.

In 1837 John Gladstone, the owner of two plantations in Guyana, applied to the Secretary of State for the colonies for permission to import Indian workers.

In 1838 three hundred ninety-six arrived. The scheme was considered a success, but investigations by the Anti-Slavery Society revealed that many of the immigrants had died quickly. Some had been flogged and unjustly imprisoned, while others had not been paid promised wages. In July 1839 the Indian government suspended immigration to the West Indies while conditions were investigated. The need, however, was great, and immigration resumed officially in 1844. Its termination came as a result of the work of the supporters of the Indian Nationalist Movement, who attacked the whole policy of emigration because they were disturbed by the condition of Indian workers in Fiji and Natal. In 1916 the Indian Legislative Council passed the Abolition of Indenture Act, and in 1918 the Secretary of State for India refused to reopen emigration under indenture. In roughly eighty years 548,000 Indians journeyed to the West Indies under the official immigration scheme. Of these, the majority (239,000) went to Guyana and Trinidad (134,000). The main port of embarkation was Calcutta, and the vast majority of Indian immigrants came from the districts of the United Provinces and Bihar.

The reasons for emigration were many. In several instances force was used and misleading information provided by recruiting agents. Some migrated out of a love for adventure, while others were fleeing the hands of British law for their involvement in the 1857 uprising. In the main, however, emigrants were seeking escape from the effects of frequent famines in the provinces of Agra, Oudh and Bihar.

Indian immigrants to the West Indies came under a system of indentureship. The labor contracts were generally for a period of five years in the case of males and three for females. At the end of this period the immigrant could reindenture himself or herself, return to India or assume an independent occupation. Most elected to stay, and today the Indians of the Caribbean constitute one of the largest groups outside India, existing for the longest period of time. There were some Muslims and Christians (from the Malabar coast), but more than eighty-five percent of the immigrants were Hindus. In an environment that was alien and often hostile to the persistence of Hindu traditions, the immigrants sought to establish the basic elements of their religion and way of life. While Hindu traditions in the Caribbean are continuously subject to challenge and change, these have survived with remarkable persistence during the past one hundred fifty years.

CHRISTIAN INFLUENCES

For a number of reasons Trinidad is an excellent location for observing the ways in which the Christian tradition has influenced Hindu spiritual practices. The complex mixture of peoples and religions — from Africa, Asia and Europe — enhances the significance of religious and cultural contact, change and mutual influence. In addition, the smallness of the island has ensured an intensity of contact among peoples of different traditions that might not be possible in a larger setting. Beginning in 1968 with John Morton, a Canadian Presbyterian minister, the Hindu community has continuously been subjected to the evangelization efforts of different Christian denominations. Until the 1940s good educational opportunities at the primary and secondary levels were available only in Christian mission schools. At these institutions Hindus who sought mobility through education were subject to Christian religious instruction. Even when conversion was not accomplished, they imbibed many Christian patterns of thinking and believing. Several generations of Hindus have been educated at institutions founded by missionary bodies.

It is useful to begin by pointing to a visually prominent influence. The traditional Hindu temple, in India, is primarily conceived as the abode of the particular deity to whom it is dedicated. The central feature of a Hindu temple, therefore, is the inner sanctuary or womb-room (*garbhagṛha*) where the icon (*mūrti*) of the deity has been ritually installed. This inner shrine is usually covered by a pyramidal canopy or roof (*śikhara*) denoting honor and eminence. Traditional Hindu temples were not constructed to accommodate congregational worship and are meant primarily for individual worship. The main purpose for visiting a temple is to obtain the sight (*darśana*) of the deity. *Darśana*, however, is much more than a physical view of the deity. It is an entry from the mundane into the presence, atmosphere and mystery of the sacred.

While the Hindu temples in Trinidad have preserved these conventional features, noticeable innovations have been made for congregational accommodation and worship. The *garghagṛha*, which in the traditional Hindu temple is not openly visible or easily accessible, is generally connected to a larger assembly hall and presents an altarlike appearance. Like the pulpit or communion table of a Christian church, the *mūrti* is always visible from any point within the assembly hall. Pews or benches are provided for seating worshippers during services.

These innovations point to the fact that congregational temple worship, while not mandatory in Hinduism, is a vital feature of Hindu spiritual life in Trinidad. The influence of Christianity is obvious in this regard, but the impetus to adopt community worship patterns also came from Hinduism finding itself in a minority situation and in a colonial environment that was not favorably disposed to its beliefs and practices. The sympathetic and uniform cultural base that could be taken for granted was unavailable, and the impact of Westernization, often indistinguishable from Christianity, was much greater than it had been in India. Private and individualistic devotional practices were no longer the only appropriate forms. Christian influence on Hindu temple worship in Trinidad is recognizable in many ways. Like their Christian neighbors, Hindus set aside Sunday, "the Lord's Day," for congregational worship in temples, and commonly refer to these as "Sunday morning services." The choice of Sunday as a day of worship for Hindus has, in fact, been determined by the dominant Christian influence on the structure of the work week. In recent times there has been a debate about allowing business and other secular activities on this day.

In structure these services also bear resemblances to Christian ones. The main ingredients are hymns, usually led by a temple choir, scriptural readings from texts such as the *Rāmāyaṇa* and *Bhagavadgītā*, prayers and a sermon. Numerous ecumenical events in Trinidad, usually hosted in Christian churches and involving participants from the major religious traditions, provide opportunities for observing Christian liturgy. Temple worship in Trinidad, however, still preserves many of the orthodox elements and procedures (*pūjā*), performed in honor of God visibly embodied in the *mūrti*. Among these are the offering of flowers (*puṣpa*), the burning of incense (*dhūpa*), the waving of lights (*āratī*), and the distribution of consecrated food (*prasāda*). In all areas of influence new elements have been incorporated without relinquishing anything vital and unique to the Hindu tradition.

The structure of temple services is usually clearly defined, and there is an orderly and disciplined progression with a high level of congregational participation. My experience of the practice of Hinduism in India has convinced me of the progress made in Trinidad in the evolution of congregational forms of worship, and the role of these in fostering a sense of community. These forms will be vital to the survival and adaptation of Hinduism in religiously plural and secularized societies where Hinduism exists as a minority tradition. In terms of utilization, the Hindu temple in Trinidad is much more than a center for private devotional practices. Like the Christian church, it is often the location for the performance of rituals connected with life-cycle events, particularly marriage; it serves as a place for the religious instruction of the young; and is the home for many community-related groups and activities. In all these respects, the Christian influence has been positive in assisting the successful adaptation of Hindu devotional practices to a new environment.

In addition to its general impact on the development of congregational forms of worship, Christianity has influenced Hindu devotional practices in other specific ways. In the town of Siparia, located in the southern part of Trinidad, is the well-known Roman Catholic Church of La Divina Pastora. The popularity of this church is associated with the presence in it of a black, wooden image of the Virgin, probably Spanish in origin. The second Sunday after Easter is the designated day for venerating La Divina, and the image is usually taken out in a procession through the streets. On the evening of Holy Thursday and into Friday, however, Hindus from various parts of the island congregate in the church for prayer and in order to make traditional *puja* offerings to the image. It is also customary for male children to have their hair cut for the first time on the steps of the church. The latter is not an unusual practice, for some Hindu parents regard it as obligatory to perform life-cycle rituals (*saṃskāras*) in honor of the deity from whom the child is seen as a gift. Here it is significant to note that the Virgin is often resorted to by childless Hindu women desirous of progeny.

One can only speculate about the adoption of these worship practices associated with the Virgin. While it generally points to the Hindu orientation of recognizing and acknowledging the divine in a plurality of forms, it is also conceivable that the Virgin was associated with the mother-goddess, and specifically, because of her black color, with the figure of Kali. The Virgin is commonly referred to as *mai* (mother) by Hindus, and this term is a suffix to the name of the goddess Kali (*Kālīmai*). It is also possible that the Catholic method of expressing homage to the deity by keeping and parading her image through the streets reminded Hindus of similar practices in larger Hindu temples. These are the occasions on which the deity, in a royal manner, allows itself to be seen. As will be evident from other examples, the worship rituals of the Roman Catholic Church are the ones that have most influenced Hindu devotional practices. This is so in spite of the fact that most Hindu converts to Christianity belong to the Protestant branches. The obvious similarity may be found in highly ritualized patterns of worship.

The influence of Christianity on Hindu religious life is also evident in several practices. The Roman Catholic monastery of St. Benedict is a popular site for pilgrimage among Hindus. This is probably related to the fact that the monastery is located in the northern hills of Trinidad and occupies a similar geographical relationship to the rest of the island as the Himalayas do to India. On the occasion of Good Friday, in particular, many Hindus visit the monastery location. The traditional Hindu desire for the sight (*darśana*) of a sacred place and to be part of a sacred order is an important motive for pilgrimage in India, and I am certain that it is also operative here. Hindus in Trinidad are generally familiar with the events of the Christ story and understand the significance of his life through the *avatār* concept. It is common to find images of Jesus along with those of Hindu deities in homes. While Hindus do not attend traditional church services to celebrate Christmas, they have imbibed many other practices associated with the occasion. It is an event for family gatherings, exchanging gifts and mailing cards with inscriptions and illustrations pertaining to the Christ child. I am also aware of services in some Hindu temples dedicated to reflecting on the teachings of Jesus.

A most interesting practice adopted by the Hindus, again reflecting the influence of Roman Catholicism, is the religious ritual of honoring the dead of "All Hallows' Eve." While cremation is customary in India, it was legally forbidden in Trinidad until 1936. Hindus, therefore, adopted and became accustomed to burial as the means of disposing the dead. In the evening prior to All Saints' Night family members congregate in the cemeteries; the graves are illumined with tiny earthen lamps. It is an intriguing sight to observe members of different faiths united in a common act of remembering loved ones. Having adopted the practice of burial, Hindus would have felt a sense of guilt about neglecting the sites on a day when Christian families tended theirs. In addition, the practice of honoring departed relatives is congenial to Hinduism, since a special ancestral fortnight (*pitṛpakṣa*) is set apart each year for this purpose.

CONCLUSION—A PERSONAL NOTE

Having described some of the ways in which Christianity has influenced practices among the general Hindu population in Trinidad, I wish to conclude by reflecting on the manner in which my own spiritual outlook and practice has been affected by this encounter. As a Hindu I have never found it difficult to identify with the person of Jesus. The symbols and images, parables and examples used by Jesus in talking about the spiritual life do not appear, in my view, to be entirely different from those employed in the Hindu tradition. From my Hindu viewpoint he embodies the ideals and values of the authentic spiritual life.

The dimension of Jesus's person, however, that continues to shape my spiritual practice is his outstanding demonstration of what genuine spirituality means in the process of living in the world. I think that he has provided some of the most concrete and challenging examples of practical spirituality, or what the spiritual life means when it is translated into human relationships. He has given us some of the finest instances of the fruits of the spiritual life in action. As a Hindu I find no difficulty in deriving guidance and inspiration from these, since I think that any authentic spirituality cannot but translate itself into this mode of relating, not only to human beings, but to all life.

In this context I think particularly of the many examples of his spontaneous and limitless compassion. I think of his unconditional love, tenderness and humility. I think of his capacity for suffering and self-sacrifice and his effortless forgiving. I have often reflected on the source and strength of his boundless compassion, which, even when life itself is being cruelly and painfully snatched away, choicelessly forgives. If authentic spirituality is to bear any fruits, there is no doubt that it must consist of the qualities that were reflected in Jesus's relationships. The source of a spirituality that is not characterized by an active compassion, unconditional love, gentleness, humility, self-sacrifice and non-retribution must always be suspect and questionable.

The practical spirituality of Jesus has acted as a stimulus to the exploration of my own tradition. I have felt the necessity to ask more urgently about its implication for life in society, and motivated to draw out the meaning of its vision when converted into terms of daily living and the problems of human beings in societies. Any worthy claim about the nature of ultimate reality must also be realized in terms of values and attitudes that contribute to the resolving of the fundamental struggles of our life in the world. There is a pressing need for contemporary Hinduism to gather and emphasize the practical implications in society of its profound realizations about the nature of ultimate reality. Hinduism has evinced a great and legitimate concern with metaphysics, especially in those traditions that emphasize the importance of wisdom (*jñāna*) as the means of attaining spiritual freedom (*moksha*). This concern, however, always needs the corrective balance provided by a stress on its significance of our human relationships and life in society. The actual and vivid examples of Jesus, and my contact with his followers, have intensified my awareness of the necessity and importance of this task.

It is in the challenge of developing a spiritual practice meaningfully oriented to life in the world that Hinduism can be most enriched by the best strands of Christianity. Hinduism's vision of its future, and the ways in which it sets about realizing it, is directly influenced by the impact of the past and the self-perception that has resulted from it. The experience of colonialism is the most important event in the recent history of the Hindu past, both in India and abroad, and continues to influence Hindu self-understanding. The colonial inheritance has conferred a very low sense of self-esteem and value in the Hindu identity. The recognition of this tendency toward self-rejection and denial resulted in a concern among many Hindu movements from the late nineteenth century onward to restore pride and self-respect in the Hindu identity and heritage. It is a concern that still dominates Hindu thinking and organizational strategies.

While the focus on pride is justified in the context of a continuous struggle with colonial values, it also needs to be approached with caution. Even as a justifiable objective, Hinduism has to recognize it as one dictated by the colonial past. In other words, it is a reaction to a set of circumstances, and not an ideal chosen in freedom. Its emphasis is an expression of the colonial impact. Because it is a constrained reaction and one that might not be necessitated in different historical circumstances, Hinduism ought not to allow the concern with pride-building to dominate its thinking about the future. This is a choice of self-determination that must be exercised in freedom. The concern must be a search for the values and ideals that constitute the heart of Hinduism and reflects its affirmation of the unity of all existence. These might be found in an inclusive, active and self-sacrificing love. It is in the search for a transformative way of living in the world that Hindu spiritual practice can be most enriched by genuine Christian experience.

PART THREE

Future Perspectives
on Hindu-Christian Dialogue

15

Hindu-Christian Dialogue and the Academic Study of Religion

ROBERT D. BAIRD

The issue I intend to address is the extent to which the academic study of religion is able, within the limits imposed by its method, to handle the religious phenomenon of Hindu-Christian dialogue. But the precise nature of this issue will not be clear until I have indicated precisely what I mean by the "academic study of religion" and "Hindu-Christian dialogue." As is the case with many, if not most, terms in the study of religion, these are ambiguous. Verbal ambiguity means that, lexically speaking, such terms have referred to more than one thing. The way to eliminate verbal ambiguity is through stipulation.[1] To stipulate a specific meaning for the designations "Hindu-Christian dialogue" and the "academic study of religion" is to indicate how these designations will be used in the present discussion, even though it must be recognized that the terms have been and will probably continue to be used in other ways in other discussions. Stipulation is a formal activity that has to do with the use of words rather than with the meaning of things.

While stipulation has to do with the meaning of words rather than the significance of things, it is also clear that one uses such words to point to things. Stipulation is not a word game, but a means of clarifying precisely what thing it is to which a given word points. In offering stipulative definitions of "Hindu-Christian dialogue" and the "academic study of religion," I am not, then, creating a set of relationships that are purely logical. That to which I am pointing with each stipulative definition does exist in the real world, even though the real world contains a great deal more than that.[2] Furthermore, a great deal more than that, or something quite different, might be intended when these same words are used in other discussions. The definitions that I am using, then, do not limit the range

217

of reality, but only the present range of meaning for certain terms.

Stipulation is also a neutral activity. The meaning of the "academic study of religion" used in this discussion should not be seen as suggesting what can legitimately be pursued within the confines of the university or how departments of religion should be organized. Nor should it be taken to suggest that one such identified activity is somehow superior to others. Stipulation is no more than a means of clarifying the meaning of certain words in a given discussion.[3]

CLARIFICATION OF TERMS OF DISCOURSE

By "the academic study of religion," I mean a study that not only proceeds with all the scholarly tools required of the subject matter, that is, languages, knowledge of history and culture, and so on, but also with a spirit of detachment or epoché, logical precision and verbal clarity.

The academic study of religion, then, is only one form of the study of religion. Religion may be studied for the purpose of *spiritual enrichment* by attending to upaniṣadic texts in Sanskrit or biblical texts in Greek or Hebrew. And one may study Greek or Latin texts with the purpose of arriving at a true view of the nature of Christ. A doctrinal system that one is prepared to believe in and act upon may even be one's purpose for the *scholarly* study of religion. But the *academic* study of religion, as I am using the term, has no such spiritual or theological purpose. It seeks to understand religious persons and phenomena on its level of inquiry, recognizing that its tools do not permit it to exhaust the religious phenomena. One might be quick to point out that there is no single level on which religious phenomena are exhausted.

The academic study of religion is willing, even eager, to study myth but not mythologically, poetry but not poetically, ambiguity but not ambiguously. It places a high premium on clarity of analysis and is uncomfortable with contradictions. While it recognizes that believers frequently express themselves in ways that violate the law of contradiction, an exposition of those expressions by the academic study of religion would not embody such contradictions (even though the believer may consider them as paradoxes). The epoché that it embodies is not merely a preliminary attitude which enables a person to hear another before appropriation takes place. In *dialogue*, epoché is sometimes seen as "a *temporary* suspension of the consideration of our own tenets, convictions and opinions (emphasis added)."[4] In this view it is a stage in the process, for "when the aim is reached, everything which had been put aside in the process of dialogue will be recovered."[5] In the academic study of religion, when one puts epoché aside, one is no longer engaged in the academic study of religion.

The term "dialogue" is also ambiguous. Richard W. Taylor distinguishes "Socratic dialogue," "Buberian dialogue," "Discursive dialogue" and "Pedagogic dialogue."[6] All forms of "Hindu-Christian dialogue," however, regardless of how discursive or scholarly they may be. are also religious. Interreligious dialogue in general and "Hindu-Christian dialogue" in particular, at least as I am using the term here, presuppose at least two people who meet as equals to advance their experience of God, to come to a more satisfying theological system, or to solve a human problem together. They must be open to the other, and willing to change and appropriate something from the other's experience or ideas.

Certain forms of "religious dialogue," whose practitioners claim exclusive right to the term, feel that the result of their endeavor is beyond language and is not to be subjected to such superficial analysis. Some hold that in dialogue theological contradictions are often resolved. This resolution is not a logical resolution, but a satisfying and apparently self-authenticating experience that is beyond logic and dissolves the logical problem by dissolving logic itself. "Niels Bohr once pointed out that, besides the 'simple truths' whose opposite could not be defended, there are also 'deep truths' of which the opposite also contains deep truth!"[7] This "real dialogue" is also seen as synonymous with "dialogue in depth."

> By dialogue I do not mean any talk about religion, which can be mere gossip — and often is. Nor do I mean the exchange of views between theologians of different religions. Interesting and necessary as it is, it is not "dialogue" but "comparative religion." The real dialogue is an ultimate personal depth — it need not even be a personal talking about religious or theological topics.[8]

When this is coupled with the assertion that dialogue is not a means, but an end in itself, it becomes clear that this level of dialogue is not merely a method that produces religious results, but that the very act of dialogue is a religious act and that dialogue itself is a religious experience. "Strictly speaking, dialogue has no goal: like love, dialogue is an end in itself, it is the full expression of our human experience."[9] That dialogue in general and Hindu-Christian dialogue in particular has no goal outside of itself is also affirmed by Klostermaier:

> Dialogue has no ulterior or extrinsic purpose. We cannot use it for private ends or manipulate it without destroying the spirit of dialogue. But we appreciate the fact that there is a built in purpose in all dialogue, insofar as we share in and through it what God is and what He gives to both the participants. It is in this sense an experience of our deepest oneness in God and of our being men for other men even in our differences.[10]

The history of religions encounters believers in almost any cumulative tradition who denigrate the intellectual or discursive level of religion and who seek to place their position or experience beyond the jurisdiction of logic. It is also familiar with believers who seek to say that one should not subject to analysis religious experiences one has not experienced, an assertion that is also common in the context of Hindu-Christian dialogue. One even finds articles written which, if they do not disparage the mere academic approach, do seem to suggest that they are more beneficial since they grow out of experience.[11] While some scholars might return the favor and denounce such blatant anti-intellectualism, the academic study of religion should not. It accepts this witness to a self-authenticating experience as an object of study, and it does not censure it any more than it approves it or participates in it. Nor, on the other hand, does it apologize for the differing rules that govern its own discourse. The fact that it simply *asserts* logical clarity as part of the rules of its game is seen in the fact that any argument for or against logic must use logical categories or it will not be taken seriously. Within the academic study of religion, even the argument that really cannot be exhausted by logical categories would have to proceed logically to be taken seriously. Logic is not argued for, but assumed, and any attempt to refute it must proceed logically, which makes the argument circularly destructive.

Understanding, then, that "Hindu-Christian dialogue" and the "academic study of religion" operate on two different levels (neither higher nor lower) and that there has been suspicion on both sides, we now turn to two scholars who have attempted to narrow the gap.

ATTEMPTS AT CONVERGENCE

Just as Hindu-Christian dialogue has been initiated predominantly from one side, that is, the "Christian" side,[12] so attempts to narrow the gap have come more from the side of participants in dialogue than from the academic study of religion. In each of the two instances cited below the individuals are serious scholars of religion, but scholars engaged in dialogue, who seem to have a religious stake in the matter but who do not want to be considered unscholarly in their endeavor.

John Carman seeks to minimize the conflict between dialogue and the academic study of religion by proposing that the academic study of religion is a preparation for a more existential dialogue, that it can provide an environment (as at the Center for the Study of World Religions at Harvard University) in which dialogue can take place, and that it actually creates a new form of dialogue.[13] In support of his last point, Carman describes one facet of the academic program at the Center which requires that the student not only have a minimal theological grounding in his own tradition, but also in a major "second tradition." "The relation of the student's 'first tradition' and 'second tradition' is the heart of our conception of comparative religion."[14]

However, the extent to which this issues in dialogue, Carman admits, is dictated not so much by the disciplines involved as by the interest (or lack of it) of the students themselves. Some may seek to interpret the "second tradition" in the light of the "first tradition"; others may treat the second in a more existential manner; while still others might simply do comparative religion. And comparative religion is not necessarily dialogue.[15]

To seek to bring the two approaches together by placing them in a common environment may succeed if there are students of the academic study of religion who are also interested in engaging in dialogue. But there is nothing in either approach to religion that requires that the one lead to the other. As we have defined the two terms, it might be quite possible for a single scholar to engage in the academic study of religion as well as to participate in Hindu-Christian dialogue. But when he or she does so, he or she will be doing two distinct things that cannot be done *simultaneously*. One simply cannot be detached and engaged simultaneously. Carman's lament and Wilfred Cantwell Smith's admission that little dialogue in fact takes place at the Center would seem to support this observation.[16]

Klaus Klostermaier pleads that dialogue be considered a legitimate method for the study of religion. He, too, recognizes the potential animosity on both sides, but urges the reader to agree that engaging in dialogue is a necessary human activity, which cannot be avoided, and which is essential to the study of both science and religion.[17] He is aware that "dialogue" has been used to describe a variety of activities, but here and elsewhere in his writing he pleads that "real" dialogue or "serious" dialogue takes place in depth when individuals open themselves existentially to each other, when they come together as equal partners and expect to learn from each other. A "sensitive" study of religion should proceed on the same principle. He holds, for example, that one cannot explain the beginning of Buddhism by examination of the cultural setting in which the Buddha lived, but only by attention to his message, the four noble truths and dependent origination. He goes on to propose that without the proper spiritual experience one cannot hope to understand a religious position:

> Similarly, Vedānta is not "explained" by describing the socioeconomic conditions of India in 1000 B.C.E., but it requires an *extensive meditational practice* and familiarity with the texts of the upaniṣads and their commentaries throughout the ages to understand what a contemporary Advaitin wishes to say when entering into a dialogue [emphasis added].[18]

An appeal is made to modern physics to support his position on dialogue in depth. "The impossibility of cutting out the subject from a description of reality has been recognized by modern physics: deep subjectivity is a necessary component of all in-depth dialogue."[19] The study of religion cannot any longer proceed with integrity if it concentrates only on one tradition. It is obvious to Klostermaier that the historical, sociological, psychological and other types of study of religion do not exhaust the pos-

sibilities of the study of religion, for "the issues of enlightenment and justification, of self-realization and salvation are not entered into by any of
the other methodologies."[20]

Klostermaier is correct in noting the limits of academic method. It is
true that it does not exhaust the study of religion and that dialogue can
surely be considered another method for the study of religion. But the
goal(s) of dialogue are still distinct from the academic study of religion. As
Carman's language points out, while Klostermaier's does not, the academic
study of religion is more restricted than the study of religion. While that
does *not* make it superior, it *does* make it different. The academic study of
religion is not only more restricted than the study of religion, but as I am
using the terms, it is also more restricted than the *scholarly* study of religion.
One may be competent in the relevant languages, well-versed in the history
and culture of an area, produce learned commentaries on sacred texts and
not be engaging in the *academic* study of religion. For the academic study
of religion operates on agreed-upon principles regarding what kinds of
questions one asks and what counts as evidence or constitutes an argument.
In the academic study of religion, private (or personal) experience, no
matter at what depth, or revelation as held within a particular tradition,
simply does not count.

> No veridical proposition can be generated on the basis of mystical
> experience. As a consequence it appears certain that mystical expe-
> rience is not and logically cannot be grounds for *any* final assertions
> about the nature or truth of any religious or philosophical position
> nor, more particularly, for any specific dogmatic or theological belief.
> Whatever validity mystical experience has, it does *not* translate itself
> into "reasons" which can be taken as evidence for a given religious
> proposition."[21]

Hence, for the academic study of religion, one can determine the belief
of Sankara by quoting from his *bhāṣyas*, but such a quote will not settle a
dispute regarding the actual status of the world. The academic study of
religion does not always engage the whole person. It is not required that a
person believe or not believe, have certain experiences or not. The only
requirement is that one have the necessary academic training, the critical
faculties and the desire to apply them to the study of religion. Hence the
practice of meditation is *not* a prerequisite for the understanding of Advaita
on this level any more than one must pray or respond to an altar call to
understand Billy Graham.

Since "dialogue in depth" takes place on an interior and spiritual level,
it is not methodologically compatible with the academic study of religion.
The latter will be interested in such dialogue as a religious phenomenon,
but participation in interreligious dialogue will not be part of the academic
discipline. Whether some academics engage in dialogue as Christian or

Hindus is another matter. If they do so they will do so as Hindus or Christians and not as academics, regardless of how much their academically derived information contributes to the dialogue. That is why we call the enterprise *Hindu-Christian* dialogue. The participants are identified in a religious, not an academic way, and that is the way they participate.

What about dialogue on the discursive level? Again, I would submit that it is not the academic study of religion. The reason for this is that in "discursive dialogue" as well, the two partners come together as equals, open to each other and willing to change. When an academic engages in discussion with a believer, it is not as equals. We have already pointed out that this is not an assertion of superiority or inferiority, but of difference. They have different goals. The Hindu or the Christian, even on the level of discursive dialogue, will be open to an amendation or perhaps even radical change of his or her doctrinal systems. But the academic is interested in understanding the believer's doctrinal system, not in searching for a viable one for himself or herself. The academic as academic always stops short of appropriation. If, as John Carman suggests is possible, the academic may later appropriate some of the material for his own doctrinal system, that is nevertheless beyond the academic study of religion. To include interreligious dialogue, then, in the forms of "deep dialogue" or "discursive dialogue" in the academic study of religion, is to turn the latter into a form of religion, and thereby dissolve it as a distinct level of inquiry. So, while it may be true that under certain circumstances and with particular goals in mind, "engaging in structured interreligious dialogue on these issues is certainly an eminently sensible and fruitful way of studying religion,"[22] it is *not* appropriate for the *academic* study of religion. I must conclude that the desires of Carman and Klostermaier notwithstanding, Hindu-Christian dialogue and the academic study of religion operate on two distinct levels.

ACADEMIC STUDY AND THE PHENOMENA OF DIALOGUE

To what extent, then, is the academic study of religion interested in Hindu-Christian dialogue, and to what extent can it handle the phenomena of dialogue within the limitations of its method?

Even with discursive dialogue, which operates on a propositional level, the goals, the questions that are asked and the types of data that count as evidence, all differ from the academic study of religion. The academic and the partner in discursive dialogue are simply not on the same quest. But, the academic study of religion will find the dynamics and results of such dialogue exceedingly fruitful for its investigations. In discursive dialogue the academic study of religion is dealing with a phenomenon within its frame of reference in the sense that it operates on the propositional level. And, to the extent to which candid discussion transpires, the academic will come to a more precise, more complete and more profound understanding of the Hindu or Christian systems being articulated. Of course, no Hindu or Christian can do more than articulate or clarify his or her Hinduism or Christianity.[23]

But to what extent can the academic study of religion achieve an understanding of a phenomenon that claims to go beyond, or even in some instances cancel out, conflicting propositions? In interreligious dialogue the form designated "dialogue in depth" or "interior dialogue" would appear to be most removed and hence of least interest to the academic study of religion. But if the academic study of religion is interested in studying all religious forms and expressions, then it is interested in this form as well. Nevertheless, the participants in this form of dialogue frequently claim that their experience transcends logical contradictions and is an interior spiritual experience. How would the academic study of religion handle such claims?

First we must document this position more fully. "Interior dialogue" or "dialogue in depth" centers in a mystical or contemplative experience. "A basic (though not always acknowledged) assumption is that all intellectualization, doctrinal or otherwise, is of limited relevance, useful only as a means of approach to the divine mystery."[24] Swami Abhishiktananda states that "the most essential qualification for a fruitful interreligious dialogue is not so much an acute mind, as a contemplative disposition of the soul."[25] The Bombay Consultation on the Theology of Hindu-Christian Dialogue (1969) urges that one pay more attention to negative theology in dialogue since,

> it is more a spiritual discipline than an intellectual exercise. It negates the primacy of logic and conceptual knowledge and relies on experiences, intuition and contemplation. It agrees with the unique character of advaitic experience.[26]

Dialogue in this spiritual and mystical sense lies beneath theological formulations and indeed may lie beneath several propositionally conflicting theological formulations.

> Dialogue thus proves to be not only an encounter of one intellect with another intellect, but a meeting of faith with faith. A theological discussion between Hindus and Christians conducted in terms of propositions and logical arguments will soon come to a dead end, and there is no end to the list of examples. Dialogue does however continue when it is based on a meditative approach to the word rather than an analytical one, finding a common basis in a certain awareness of an inner dynamism of reality communicating itself to the seeker.[27]

It is for this reason that Klostermaier finds promising the practice of meditation on parallel upaniṣadic and biblical texts. Christians must learn in this context to read the upaniṣads to find Christ in them as he was found in the Old Testament. This is not to misread these texts, but to find "their true inner meaning."[28] The point of this is to probe beneath the discursive to the "level of spirituality," which is the only level on which actual encounter can take place.[29] Dialogue, then, is not merely the only authentic encounter between human beings, but is where God encounters human beings as well.

> Dialogue is an end in itself—it is not preliminary to the traditional methods of proselytizing. In dialogue the essential encounter of God and man takes place—far more than in the mass-attacks from pulpits and raised platforms.[30]

In response to C. Murray Rogers, Sivendra Prakash quotes approvingly from the "Report on Dialogue with Other Religions" issued at the All-India Seminar on the Church in India Today (Bangalore, 1969): "Dialogue at its highest level is spiritual and religious communion, the experiencing in common of the religious reality."[31]

Not only, then, does this take place at a level other than theology, but it is an experience of truth in distinction from the truth of propositions. And since it is an experience of truth in distinction from the truth of propositions, it is an experience that breaks the "barrier of words," for it speaks of "the possibility of a communion and exchange of experience that go beyond and behind words."[32] Included as a characteristic of this level of dialogue is "ineffability."[33]

This experience of God in "dialogue in depth" is not only beyond words, inexpressible in words, and deeper than words, but includes silence as well as utterances. "It may be either spoken or silent—and seems usually partly both."[34] Klostermaier reiterates in a variety of places that those who learn dialogue only from books tend to distort it,[35] and C. Murray Rogers calls the experience an experience of "supernatural complementarity."

> At this point the difference and contrast between Christian and pre-Christian have to be stressed and seen in their clear light. Rationally these contrasts will be seen to be insoluble while at a deeper level we will begin to perceive a "supernatural complementarity," a coming together in Christ of all that is genuine in non-Christian spirituality and experience.[36]

The question before us is whether, since the academic study of religion is so far removed from this experience, it is simply incapable of handling it and should therefore refrain. It is to be conceded that the academic study of religion does not have access to the "ineffable" or to "supernatural complementarity" or any other experience of a mystical nature that is personal, private or reserved for a religious few. But the academic study of religion is interested in pursuing its understanding of religion as far as its methods will permit. It should also beware lest it become reductionistic by implying that when its methods are no longer applicable, what is said to be left simply does not exist.

Fortunately for the academic study of religion, those who engage in this activity of "deep dialogue" do not remain silent, do indeed speak, and seem to write an ample supply of books and articles on the topic. If the reading of their books and articles inevitably distorts the reality to which they seek to point, it is hardly the academic's fault. But, the academic study of religion is interested in these writings, even when they claim that about which they are writing or speaking goes beyond the words that are being written or uttered. And this *can* be understood academically.

Furthermore, it is not new in the history of religions. It is a claim that mystics have repeatedly made. And if the academic study of religions does not participate in the mystical experience, it has increasingly been interested in analyzing the statements made about that experience by those who claim to have had it. That an art historian does not work with oils does not make him or her any less an art historian. When the statements of the believer contradict each other, the academic cannot appeal to "supernatural complementarity," but he or she can note that such an appeal is made.

If the only response to the experience of "dialogue in depth" is silence, there is little the academic study of religion can do with that. *Silence is ambiguous.* It may point to a lack of understanding of the question, to inability to offer an appropriate answer, or to enlightenment, to suggest a few possibilities. The Buddha's "Flower Sermon" is interpreted by Zen as a non-verbal transmission of the satori experience. But without some verbal explanation, the smile of Mahakasyapa at the silent holding of a flower communicates nothing definite. The silence of the Buddha in the face of certain questions of a metaphysical nature has been the subject of considerable discussion. The *avyākṛta* and their interpretations are discussed by T. R. V. Murti at some length.[37] Although silence is of itself uninterpretable, it takes on meaning within Madhyamika when it is interpreted in the context of the transcendent nature of the real and that the real transcends all thought. In that context the erroneous nature of all metaphysical views of the real is communicated through silence. Fortunately, as Taylor points out, the response is usually a mixture of silence *and* words. To that extent the academic study of religion can understand, but it reaches its limit in the face of pure silence.

Partners in "deep dialogue" sometimes want to affirm in spiritual experience something which, when put in propositional form, is in conflict with other propositions to which they also give assent. A preliminary attempt has been made by James D. Redington to give an account of how one can affirm in "deep dialogue" the truth of an experience while different and sometimes conflicting statements may be made about the experience. He appeals to Bernard Lonergan's distinction between faith and beliefs, and similar distinctions made by Raimundo Panikkar and John A. T. Robinson. For Lonergan, as interpreted by Redington, a faith is a dimension of the human being by which a person relates to his or her destiny. Beliefs are the formulations a person makes for oneself and others of that faith.[38]

> Once again, then, a distinction between faith and beliefs is seen as essential for a world in dialogue. The immediate intention of Lonergan's distinction may be to render intelligible how two very different sets of beliefs stem from a faith and love whose Source is the same. But the belief seems applicable to our present problem too: the question of whether another religion's belief, now seen as stemming from that profound faith and love that grounds beliefs, can be affirmed as in some way true for *all* who see it.[39]

Another well-known attempt to distinguish the interior experience from the external manifestation is that of Wilfred Cantwell Smith. Smith uses the term *faith* to refer to "an inner religious experience or involvement of a particular person."[40] "Cumulative tradition" refers to

> the overt mass of objective data that constitute the historical deposit, as it were, of the past religious life of the community in question: temples, scriptures, theological systems, dance patterns, legal and other social institutions, conventions, moral codes, myths and so on; anything that can be and is transmitted from one person, one generation, to another, and that an historian can observe.[41]

The difficulty with both of these formulations for the academic study of religion is that "faith" is inaccessible. The academic study of religion can only work with Smith's "cumulative tradition." "Theology is part of the traditions, is part of this world. Faith lies beyond theology, *in the hearts of men*. Truth lies beyond faith, in the heart of God."[42] One can grant that for the believer these external phenomena merely point beyond themselves and one can draw inferences and surmise what that to which they point might be. But the inferences are seldom necessary (as distinct from possible), and the fact is that surmise is not sufficient evidence for conclusions within the academic study of religion. And so, one who engages in academic study must limit himself or herself to the "cumulative traditions," the beliefs and other data that can be used by the historian. That is not to deny the "reality" to which they point—nor is it to affirm it. There is a sense in which the academic study of religion is going too far when it states either that the conflicting words that purport to point to an experience beyond themselves actually point to a uniform or similar experience *or* that they point to differing ones. They certainly say things differently. But if we have no access to the thing itself, how do we verify if the experience itself is the same (though *variously* described) *or* different (*as* described)? Perhaps the believer will want to say more, and the participant in Hindu-Christian dialogue will want to say more, and that more will be duly noted. But noting it does not constitute either assent or dissent.

The academic study of religion, then, operates within limits. It is difficult to see how one engaged in dialogue can object to that so long as it does not claim that its level of investigation exhausts reality. And it is equally difficult to see how the academic study of religion can justify ignoring Hindu-Christian dialogue, which is a prominent religious phenomenon in the modern world.

NOTES

1. For an analysis of the nature of stipulative definition see Richard Robinson, *Definition* (Oxford: Oxford University Press, 1954), and for an application of these distinctions to the study of religion see Robert D. Baird, *Category Formation and the History of Religions* (The Hague: Mouton & Co., 1971).

2. This means that there are *in fact* those who see the "academic study of religion" and "Hindu-Christian dialogue" as I am using these terms, even though they do not comprise all who study religion or all those who engage in dialogue.

3. If the reader still has doubts about this, a careful reading of Richard Robinson on the distinction between stipulative, lexical and real definitions will be invaluable.

4. Swami Abhishiktananda, "The Way of Dialogue," in *Inter-Religious Dialogue*, ed. Herbert Jai Singh (Bangalore: Christian Institute for the Study of Religion and Society, 1967), p. 86.

5. Ibid. p. 87.

6. Richard W. Taylor, "The Meaning of Dialogue," in *Inter-Religious Dialogue*, pp. 55-64. For other helpful analyses see Eric J. Sharpe, "The Goals of Inter-Religious Dialogue," in *Truth and Dialogue in World Religions: Conflicting Truth-Claims*, ed. John Hick (Philadelphia: Westminster Press, 1974), pp. 77-95; Arvind Sharma, "The Meaning and Goals of Interreligious Dialogue," *Journal of Dharma* vol. 8, no. 3 (July-September 1983): 225-47; and Anand Nayak, "Hindu-Christian Dialogue in India," *Pro Mundi Vita Bulletin* 88 (January 1982): 1-30.

7. See Klaus Klostermaier, "Interreligious Dialogue As a Method for the Study of Religion," *Journal of Ecumenical Studies* 21:4 (Fall 1984): 757.

8. Klaus Klostermaier, "Dialogue—The Work of God," in *Inter-Religious Dialogue*, p. 119. Cf. also Klostermaier, *In the Paradise of Krishna: Hindu and Christian Seekers* (Philadelphia: Westminster Press, 1969), p. 102.

9. Nayak, p. 27.

10. Klaus Klostermaier, "Hindu-Christian Dialogue," in *Dialogue Between Men of Living Faiths*, ed. S. J. Samartha (Geneva: WCC, 1971), p. 20.

11. Cf. Monika Konrad Hellwig, "Bases and Boundaries for Interfaith Dialogue: A Christian Viewpoint," in *Interreligious Dialogue: Facing the Next Frontier*, ed. Richard W. Rousseau, S. J. (Scranton, PA: Ridge Row Press, 1981), p. 68, where the author commences by saying: "This paper is written directly from experience."

12. Nayak, p. 2.

13. John Carman, "Inter-Faith Dialogue and Academic Study of Religion," in *Dialogue Between Men of Living Faiths*, pp. 81-86.

14. Ibid. p. 85.

15. There is a tendency on the part of those engaged in Hindu-Christian dialogue, in an attempt to gain the support of history, to see dialogue in almost any exchange between "Hindus" and "Christians," or any historical influence of the one upon the other. This is an extremely elastic use of the term and does not qualify as "dialogue" as I have defined the term above.

16. Carman, p. 86.

17. Klostermaier, "Interreligious Dialogue As a Method for the Study of Religion," p. 757.

18. Ibid. *(emphasis mine)*.

19. Ibid.

20. Ibid. p. 759.

21. Steven T. Katz, "Language, Epistemology and Mysticism," in *Mysticism and Philosophical Analysis*, ed. Steven T. Katz (New York: Oxford University Press, 1978), p. 22.

22. Klostermaier, "Interreligious Dialogue As a Method for the Study of Religion," p. 759.

23. Cf. Wilfred Cantwell Smith, *The Meaning and End of Religion* (New York: Macmillan, 1962), chap. 5; and Baird, pp. 134-152.

24. Sharpe, "The Goals of Inter-Religious Dialogue," p. 87.

25. Abhishiktananda, p. 85.

26. Quoted by Sharpe, p. 88.

27. Klaus Klostermaier, "Hindu-Christian Dialogue: Its Religious and Cultural Implications," *Sciences Religieuses/Studies in Religion* (1971), p. 89.

28. Klaus Klostermaier, "Hindu-Christian Dialogue," p. 12.

29. Ibid.

30. Klostermaier, "Dialogue – The Work of God," p. 125.

31. *Dialogue Between Men of Living Faiths*, n. 13, p. 26.

32. Matthew John, "The Biblical Basis of Dialogue," in *Inter-Religious Dialogue*, p. 72.

33. Richard W. Taylor, "The Meaning of Dialogue," *Inter-Religious Dialogue*, p. 56.

34. Ibid., p. 58.

35. "Dialogue – The Work of God," p. 121.

36. C. Murray Rogers, "Hindu and Christian – A Moment Breaks," in *Inter-Religious Dialogue*, p. 113.

37. T.R.V. Murti, *The Central Philosophy of Buddhism* (London: George Allen & Unwin, 1955), pp. 36-54.

38. James D. Redington, S. J., "The Hindu-Christian Dialogue and the Interior Dialogue," *Theological Studies* 44 (1983): 601-2.

39. Ibid. p. 602.

40. Smith, p. 156.

41. Ibid. pp. 156-57.

42. Ibid. p. 185.

16

The Experience of Scripture in Hinduism and Christianity

HAROLD COWARD

Many who look do not see [*vāk*, the word], many who listen do not hear it. It reveals itself like a loving and well adorned wife to her husband.

When mind's intuitions are shaped in the heart, when brahmins perform rites together as friends, some are wittingly eliminated, others emerge on account of the manifest excellence of the power of [*vāk*].

Rig Veda 10.71, verses 4 & 8[1]

> For the heart of this people has grown dull.
> Their ears are hard of hearing,
> And their eyes they have closed,
> Lest they should see with their eyes
> and hear with their ears,
> Lest they should understand with their
> heart and turn,
> So that I should heal them.

Matthew 13:15[2]

In each of these passages scripture is said to give understanding and to have healing or transforming power. For Hindus and Christians the word of scripture plays a powerful role in spiritual experience — indeed, for both scripture is necessary for release or salvation. Yet there are some definite differences in the way the word functions that must be noted at the outset.

Whereas the word of the Bible has definite beginnings, as reported in Genesis and in Luke-Acts, the Hindu scriptures are held to be beginningless — just as in the Hindu view the whole of the universe has existed without beginning as a series of cycles of creation going backward into time infinitely. Although the Hindu scripture is spoken anew at the beginning of each cycle of creation, what is spoken is identical with the scripture spoken in all previous cycles, without beginning. The very idea of an absolute point of beginning for either creation or the scripture is simply not present in Hindu thought. A close parallel to this Hindu notion of the eternal presence of scripture[3] is perhaps found in the Western idea of logos, especially as expressed in the gospel of John, "In the beginning was the Word, and the Word was with God, and the Word was God" (Jn. 1-1).

Another difference in the Hindu view is that its basic scripture, the Veda, is held to be authorless. The idea of an authorless scripture is of course logically consistent with the claim of its eternality, in that the identification of an author would indicate a historical point of beginning. Another consideration is that authors are human and thus capable of error. Being authorless, it is argued, safeguards Hindu scripture from the possibility of human error. While the majority of Hindus are satisfied to think of their scripture as in some sense identified with or authored by God, one school, the Pūrva Mīmāṃsā, goes to the extreme of denying the existence of God as author to ensure that the errorless nature of the scripture cannot be called into question.[4] God is seen by some philosophers as being a human personification and thus also open to error. If even God is open to question as author, certainly humans cannot be seen as composers of scripture. The *ṛṣis* or seers identified as speakers of particular Vedas are understood to be mere channels through which the divine word passes to make itself available to humans at the start of each creation cycle. Thus, the same *ṛṣis* are said to speak the Vedas in each cycle of creation.

For the Hindu, the spoken scripture of the tradition is the Divine Word (*Davī Vāk*) descending and disclosing itself to the sensitive soul.[5] The "sensitive soul" was the seer or *ṛṣi* who had purged himself or herself of ignorance, rendering his or her consciousness transparent to the Divine Word. The *ṛṣi* was not the author of the Vedic hymn, but rather the seer (*draṣṭā*) of an eternal, impersonal truth. As the modern Hindu scholar Aurobindo Ghose explains, the language of the Veda is "a rhythm not composed by the intellect but heard, a Divine Word that came vibrating out of the Infinite to the inner audience of the man who had previously made himself fit for the impersonal knowledge."[6] The *ṛṣi's* initial vision is of the Veda as one, which is then broken down and spoken as the words and sentences of scripture. In this Vedic idea of revelation there is no suggestion of the miraculous or supernatural. The *ṛṣi*, by the progressive purifying of consciousness through the disciplines of yoga, had simply removed the mental obstructions to the revelation of the Divine Word. While the Divine Word is inherently present within the consciousness of all, it is the *ṛṣis* who first reveal it and in so doing make it available to help all others achieve the same experience. The spoken Vedic words of the *ṛṣi* act powerfully upon us to purify our consciousness and give to us that same full vision of the unitary Divine Word which the *ṛṣi* first saw. This is the enlightenment experience, the purpose for which Hindu scripture exists.

In this enlightenment experience yet another difference may be seen — for most Hindus once the direct experience of the Divine Word is realized, the manifested forms (the words and sentences of the Veda) are no longer needed.[7] The Vedic words and sentences function only as the "ladder" to raise one to the direct, intuitive experience of the complete Divine Word. Once the full enlightenment experience is achieved the ladder of scripture is no longer needed. The very idea that scripture can be transcended is heresy to orthodox Christians. For them the obstructions of human limitations are such that even the most saintly person would get only part-way up the ladder — scripture, the Bible, could never be transcended in the sense that most Hindus accept.

But Christians and Hindus agree that for the full power of the word to be experienced it must be spoken aloud. The Hindu Grammarian devised rules for prosody, phonetics, accentation (*Prātiśākayas*) and *sandhi* to ensure that the speaking of the scripture would be preserved and passed on with little loss or distortion.[8] For the Hindu it is in the context of the *guru-*student relationship that the correctly spoken word of scripture has the most power to purify consciousness. In the Christian context the word is to be spoken aloud in the form of preaching. Jesus preached in parables that brought new meaning and changed peoples lives. Taking from Greek culture the techniques of rhetoric, the New Testament Christians and their successors spread the word through powerful preaching. For Augustine, Luther, the Puritans and Martin Luther King, it was the ability to preach the word in the context of public worship that yielded powerful results. A similar practice is seen in the preaching (*kathā*) of the Hindu Rāmāyaṇa by a *vyāsa* or professional expounder in India today.[9]

With these initial observations in mind let us now proceed to a more detailed analysis of how scripture is experienced as a transformer of lives first in Hinduism and then in Christianity. Finally, we will ask the question, What can Hindus and Christians learn from each other's experience of scripture?

THE HINDU EXPERIENCE OF SCRIPTURE

Unlike Christianity with its set canon, Hindu scripture embraces an enormous variety of texts touching upon individual, family and public life in India and increasingly throughout the world. Since the Hindu religion has no institutional or church basis, these texts are the heart of Hindu life. They provide Hindu "religion with its substance, with its principal assumptions, art with its themes, literature with its topics, and music and dance with their souls."[10] It is through the speaking and hearing of scripture that the Hindu rediscovers eternal truth and realizes its presence in everyday life.

It is not our intention to present a complete description of Hindu scriptures. This has been ably done by J. A. B. van Buitenen in his recent Encyclopaedia Britannica article, "Hindu Sacred Literature."[11] Suffice it to say that in addition to the *śruti* or primary texts (Veda, Brāhmaṇa and Upaniṣad) there exists the vast and open-ended category of *smṛti* or secondary scripture. A word or two about this second category might prove helpful, since it is the *smṛti* scriptures that in practice evoke spiritual experience for the vast majority of Hindus.[12]

Smṛti designates all Hindu scripture other than the Vedas. *Smṛti* often takes story form as in the epic poems, the *Mahābhārata* (which includes the *Bhagavadgītā*) and the *Rāmāyaṇa*. *Smṛti* texts are said never to add any new revelation but simply to represent the teaching of *śruti* in a form more suited to a wider audience in its own particular age. *Smṛti* thus provides for a continual updating of the scriptural revelation and, in practice, the Hindu acquires his or her knowledge of religion almost exclusively through *smṛti*.

Smṛti post-Vedic scripture is extremely voluminous and may be summarized under the following headings: epics, purāṇa, *tantra* and others. The two main epic texts, the *Mahābhārata* and the *Rāmāyaṇa* were likely compiled around 400 B.C.–A.D. 200. The term *compiled* is especially appropriate to the *Mahābhārata*, which is a vast library into which new material was constantly added over many years. Perhaps the most significant insertion into the *Mahābhārata* is the *Bhagavadgītā*. The *Bhagavadgītā* is significant as a scriptural form in that it contains the idea of revelation occurring through incarnation (*avatāra*). God (Vishnu) incarnates himself in the human form of Krishna, a chariot driver, to teach people (symbolized by Arjuna, the warrior whose chariot Krishna drives) divine truth. Although orthodox tradition maintains that no new content is being revealed, it is certainly true that the form in which the teaching is presented, and the response required, is new. In particular there is a stress on devotion (*bhakti*) as a relationship between the devotee and a personalized God, which is open to all regardless of caste or sex. None of this was evident in the Veda. This same kind of *bhakti* emphasis is found in the *Rāmāyaṇa*, which to this day continues to be one of the most powerful pieces of Hindu scripture in its impact upon people. Unlike the *Mahābhārata*, the *Rāmāyaṇa* has a unitary style suggesting a single author, Vālmīki. The idea of God becoming incarnated in Rama is also present in the *Rāmāyaṇa*. Especially appropriate for the modern period is the extension of the divine incarnation to include Rama's wife Sita, thus providing a female form through which God may be approached.

Purāṇa which literally means "ancient story" is a general name given to a long series (traditionally 18) of voluminous texts that contain myths and legends as well as genealogies of gods, heroes and saints. As in the epics, the stress is on devotion (*bhakti*). Purāṇas can loosely be divided into three groups: those exhalting the god Brahmā, those devoted to the god Viṣṇu, and those devoted to Śiva. However, many deal with similar materials. The most important Purāṇas are the *Viṣṇu*, *Linga*, *Bhāgavata* and the *Skanda*. The Purāṇas are dated from A.D. 300 to 1600. "This puranic literature continues with Upapurāṇas ("sub-Purāṇas") and *Māhātmyas* (glorifications) of temples and sacred places."[13]

Tantras (literally "looms") are texts presenting Hindu religion on a more popular level, and dealing mainly with mantras (chants), temple ritual and mandalas (drawn symbols for use in meditation). There are *Tantras* for the worship of Viṣṇu, Śiva and the goddess Śakti. They focus on practical techniques for spiritual practice rather than metaphysical ideas. In some of the Śākta *Tantras* evidence of the "left-handed" practices (esoteric, magical and sometimes sexual) is found, but the incidence of such material is relatively infrequent. The *Tantras* are dated from A.D. 500-1800. They seem to have arisen outside the literate Brahmin tradition. Although they often criticize established religious practices and the brahmins who preside over them, the *Tantras* largely support the central Hindu ideas and practices. Basic to the *Tantras* is the assumption that the individual is a microcosm of the cosmos and that by learning to unite the pairs of opposites within one's being, the goal of spiritual fulfillment may be achieved. Tantric techniques include the chanting of mantras, meditation on maṇḍalas and yogic practices, sometimes to the exclusion of traditional Vedic rituals. It is argued that Tantric methods are more suited to the present decadent era in which people are less likely to follow the elaborate Vedic rituals of an earlier age.[14]

Other sacred texts came to be composed in the many regional languages found throughout India. Of these non-Sanskrit sacred texts mention may be made of the devotional hymns authored by the South Indian Tamil poet-saints from the seventh century A.D. on in worship of Śiva and Viṣṇu. These Tamil hymns have provided the basis for a rich and fervent devotional Hindu practice in South India over the past thousand years. In the North Hindi language became dominant and there the devotional poems of Kabir, ca. 1500, the princess poetess Mīrabaī, ca. 1550, and Tulsī Dās, ca. 1600, were influential. Translations of both the *Rāmāyaṇa* and *Bhagavadgītā* have been made into most of the regional languages of India. Devotional poems in Bangali are worthy of special mention. One of the best examples of these poems in which divine love is symbolized by human love is Govinda Dās's *Gita Govinda*. Tagore's English poem *Gitanjali*, which won a Nobel prize, must also be considered a great Hindu devotional work from Bengal.

Hindu sacred books embrace an enormous collection of texts of startling antiquity and variety. While the canon of the *śruti* texts is well set, the *smṛti* collection is massive and continues to expand. These sacred texts are put to a wide range of uses. Vedic texts continue to function in the formal rituals presided over by the brahmins in temples, and at key points in family life. The later parts of the Vedas, the Upaniṣads became the basis for various philosophical schools, each with its own method of exegesis. The epics, pūraṇas and *Tantras*, on the other hand, established a widespread popular devotion in the many regional languages of India and the changing eras right up to the present day. Hindu texts are used in private devotions in the home (for example, the chanting of mantras morning and evening), and on public occasions (such as during temple festivals). In some temples professional reciters have their own booths in which they patiently set forth day after day texts such as the *Bhagavadgītā*. Perhaps the most dramatic use of a sacred text is that of Tulsidā's *Rāmāyaṇa*. At the Rām Līlā festivals in Northern India that epic is acted out with the whole city becoming involved — much like the Oberammmergau re-enactment of Christ's passion in the West. Similar dramatic use of various Hindu texts takes place all over India. Today the texts are also travelling with the "Hindu diaspora" to all corners of the globe. Mantra chanting of sacred scriptures occurs in North American homes; Vedic rituals to Agni in Arya Samāj ceremonies take place throughout the Western world; and enactments of the *Rāmāyaṇa* have long been a high point in Pacific islands like Bali. Many educated English homes have a copy of Tagore's *Gitanjali*, and the *Bhagavadgītā* in translation is read around the world.

Unlike the modern Christian experience of the Bible, Hindu experience of its vast array of scriptures is dominantly oral. In the conduct of religious rituals individual devotees chant verses of scripture (mantras) from memory or after the priest. Individual devotions morning and evening consist in the chanting of scripture passages or reciting of a divine name like Rama or Krishna. In Hindu spiritual experience the chanting of such mantras puts one in direct touch with divine power. In "The Indian Mantra" Gonda points out that mantras are not experienced as products of discursive thought or poetic fantasy, but as "flash-lights of the eternal truth, seen by those men who have come into supersensuous contact with the Unseen."[15] By concentrating one's mind on such a mantra, through repeated chanting, the devotee invokes the power inherent in the divine intuition and so purifies consciousness.

Mantras are experienced as having not only intellectual meaning but also power (*śakti*). Mantras have the power to remove ignorance (*avidyā*), reveal truth (*dharma*) and realize release (*moksha*).[16] In Vedic practice the importance of mantra *śakti* is recognized in the careful attention given to the correct speaking of Vedic verses so as to avoid distortions and corruptions. In view of the Tantric perception of mantra as "the sonic reverberation of divine power, it is hardly surprising that quality control of its components cannot be left to the caprices of the individual reciter."[17] In both Vedic and Tantric ritual, mantra chanting is the catalyst that allows the sacred potential of the ritual setting to become a reality.

In the Indian experience, then, the repeated chanting of mantras is an instrument of power. The more difficulties there are to be overcome, the more repetitions are needed. Bhartṛhari in *Vākyapadīya 1-14* makes clear that repeated use of correct mantras removes all impurities, purifies all knowledge and leads to release. The psychological mechanism involved is described by Bhartṛhari as a holding of the scriptural revelation (*sphoṭa*) in place by continued chanting. Just as from a distance or in semi-darkness it takes repeated observations of an object before one sees it correctly, so also concentrated attention on the *sphoṭa* by repeated chanting of the mantra results in the revelation finally being perceived in all its fullness.[18] Maṇḍana Miśa describes it as a series of progressively clearer impressions until a clear and a correct apprehension takes place in the end.[19]

As the above discussion of the Hindu experience of mantras makes clear, it is the vibrating, spoken word that has power, that is heard (*śruti*) and remembered (*smṛti*) and transforms human consciousness. For the Hindu scripture is truly powerful and most fully experienced only in its oral form. The written word is secondary, useful for teaching purposes and as an aid for those too dull to remember the important texts by heart. For Hindus, the criterion form of scripture is not written but oral, and the *Prātiśākhyas* play the important role of keeping the oral form disciplined and pure in its presentation. Thus knowledge of the Hindu scriptures includes memorization and the ability to speak the words with correct accent and meter. Rather than the notion of scripture as something written—the Latin *scriptura*—in Hindu experience scripture is the pure spoken word, which is awesome in its power and eternality.

It has been argued that the writing down of a scripture democratizes it and frees it from the elite for the masses.[20] Something like this may have happened in Hinduism with the Purāṇas, which developed a strong tradition of written scripture. In a recent article Mackenzie Brown argues that the writing down of the Purāṇas, perhaps as early as the beginning of the Christian era, freed scripture from control of the priestly class[21] and so democratized Hindu scripture in a move parallel to Luther's translation of the Bible into German so as to take it away from the control of the priests and make it widely accessible to the German common people. Brown shows how the copying and giving of Purāṇa books even becomes a religious act. Scriptural texts become objects of worship or *pūjā* for some Hindus. The sacred word is transformed from sound to image, from mantra to *mūrti*.[22] But even though they encompass a written textual tradition, for the Purāṇas it is still the oral telling of the story which has remained primary, as can be seen in the *Kathā* preaching tradition. Now, however, the story can be read and told by anyone, not just a priest.[23]

The continued strength of oral scripture within the Hindu tradition may be due to its scholarly sophistication. Oral forms of technical grammars and dictionaries were developed very early along with a high quality oral corpus of poetry, prose and drama. Complex philosophical commentaries along with free philosophical speculations were composed orally and passed down through chains of teachers and students from the classical Hindu period 200 B.C.E.-700 B.C.E. right up to the present day. Although writing was available very early in India and there were evidently large temple libraries — a few written Sanskrit texts are available which date back to 1000 B.C.E. — the rigors of the Indian climate meant that few texts survived for long periods.

Today, as in the past, the well-trained Hindu scholar depends on memorized text learned early in life rather than upon books. Even if a written version of a text is used today, it will be studied not alone at one's desk, but with a teacher who will read it aloud and explain the text in dialogue. For Hinduism, it is still the oral tradition, within the *guru*-student context, that gives real knowledge. At the popular level, it is through the folksingers, storytellers and professional reciters that the majority of Hindus continue to experience their scriptures. For the modern well-off Hindu, especially those living in diaspora in the modern West, audio and video cassettes of such oral performances of the favorite texts are increasingly used as substitutes for the real thing.[24]

A brief comment on techniques of exegesis will serve to conclude this survey of the Hindu experience of scripture. Hindu exegesis or interpretation is premised upon the idea that the full revelation is given originally in the Veda. Later works, both *smṛtis* and commentaries, serve only to bring out more clearly meaning that is already present in the Veda. An earlier truth may be represented in a way that is easier for a later generation to understand, or hidden meanings implicitly present in the original revelation may be explicitly developed. Throughout, however, continuity is maintained. Already in the later portions of the Veda itself the exegetical process can be seen at work. The original Vedic hymns, the Saṃhitās, are poems that contain a variety of meanings. The Brāhmaṇas commentaries bring out the outer ritual aspects, while the later Upaniṣadic dialogues focus on the deeper spiritual insight of the original poems, yet, always there is continuity. The intuitive vision (*dhi*) of the Vedic *ṛṣi* is still very much present in the Brāhmaṇas and Upaniṣads. As Aurobindo puts it:

> They [the Upanisadic Rsis] used the text of the ancient *mantras* as a prop or an authority for their own intuitions and perceptions; or else the Vedic Word was a seed of thought and vision by which they recovered old truths in new forms. What they found, they expressed in other terms more intelligible to the age in which they lived. In a certain sense their handling of the texts was not disinterested. . . . They were seekers of a higher than verbal truth and used words merely as suggestions for the illumination towards which they were striving.[25]

As we move from the exegesis within the Veda itself to the commentaries written within the Classical and Medieval periods, we find that the same basic pattern continues. Older commentaries add nothing new but simply bring out insights present in seed form in the original Vedas, and only partially made present by earlier authors. Thus it is a process of commentaries written upon commentaries. Following the Upaniṣads, the next major works were in *sūtra* style—pithy aphorisms which summarized a great deal of content in "shorthand" form, and designed for the oral instruction of students by a teacher. Each of the major schools of Hindu thought claims to be based upon the Veda, but really begins from a *sūtra* composed by a founding master. For example the Sankhya-Yoga schools depend upon the *sūtras* of Patanjali,[26] the Pūrva-Mīmāṁsā school on the *sūtras* of Jaimini,[27] the Vedanta school on the *sūtras* of Bādarāyaṇa,[28] the *Nyāya* on the *sūtras* by Gautama and the Vaiśeṣikas on the *sūtras* of Kaṇāda.[29] Because of their absolute economy and conciseness, these *sūtras* are not intelligible without a prose commentary, called a *bhāṣya*. In the teacher-student context, this *bhāṣya* would ordinarily be given orally. Later it may have been written down and attached to the *sūtras* by a senior student.[30] As the generations passed, a need may have been felt within the teacher-student lineage of the school for more commentaries to be added—so as to better bring out the intended meaning of the earlier commentary, the *sūtra*, and so on back to the Veda. Thus the process of commentaries being written upon commentaries continues open-ended, yet with a thread of continuity running right back to the Veda. In this way the classical commentaries are able to update the exegesis of the texts, just as the *smṛti* represents in a fresh way the original *śruti* through new versions of epic, story and drama.

THE CHRISTIAN EXPERIENCE OF SCRIPTURE

Christians began with a scripture, the Hebrew Bible and its synagogue tradition of public reading in worship followed by a sermon. To this Christians added the life and teachings of Jesus Christ, known not through biblical texts but in the oral tradition of missionary preaching and charismatic experience. Whereas in Judaism the oral Torah provided the criteria for the interpretation of the written Hebrew Bible, in Christianity it was the teaching of Jesus and the testimony of the apostles that filled this same function. Both Judaism and Christianity start from the same basic Bible, but use different oral means of interpretation to develop the truth of the Hebrew Bible. Thus for Christians the Hebrew Bible is described as the Old Testament or "Old Covenant" with God, which prepares the way for the "New Covenant" with God in Jesus Christ. Originally, then, Christian scripture included just the Hebrew Bible, which was read in public worship. Later the oral traditions, including the sayings of Jesus and the writings of the apostles, were added and gradually became canonized as the New Testament over a five-hundred-year period.

Jesus and the Oral Tradition

Jesus left no writings. Our knowledge of his teaching comes from his immediate followers. At first this information circulated orally. Later it was written down and finally some of it was canonized. Jesus was born into a culture that was strongly oral in nature. There was the oral Torah of the rabbis and the Greek tradition of oral rhetoric. His sermons were not written in advance, but were spoken to suit the occasion. His followers listened and remembered his teachings. His word had a spontaneous quality that seemed to directly engage the situations he encountered. Jesus did not use a sacred or learned language; rather he used the language and idioms of Aramaic, the popular language of the day. Jesus also used an economy of speech, as did his followers. The New Testament is very brief when compared with other scriptures. Jesus spoke in short aphorisms and tightly-knit parables, which were easy to remember and retell.[31] Three forms of speech are found in the New Testament: gospel, letter, and apocalypse or vision.

The gospels begin from an oral basis. The teachings of Jesus and the events of his life were transmitted orally for over thirty years until the compilation of the gospel of Mark. Selecting from the various oral and written materials that had been circulating in the churches, Mark created a connected narrative of the life and ministry of Jesus for evangelistic purposes. The oral nature of many of these materials is indicated by their storytelling form. The aim of their retelling is to make Jesus come alive in the imagination of the audience of hearers.[32] The oral nature of the parable, for example, is shown in its repetition, its use of patterns of threes for easy remembering, its use of everyday events, which are clearly "true to life" yet with surprising aspects added to make them memorable (for example, the use of the adjective *good* with Samaritan, the despised foreigner).[33] The parable is also an open-ended speech act, which is dependent on the oral context of the speaker and hearers. In that sense the parable lacks both an original form and an original meaning.[34] Every time a parable is told or retold it is a new event and therein lies its spiritual power. Each new context will produce different hearings of the revelation. In the oral context of retelling or preaching the parable is always fresh and possesses potential to speak with transforming power.

Jesus' parables point beyond themselves. They invite hearers into the story and take them, by surprise, to a special awareness (a revelation) that lies hidden beyond the story. Thus the closing admonition of many parables, "He who has ears to hear, let him hear." As metaphors, parables suggest but withhold meaning. This open-endedness makes parables particularly dependent on the oral context. The parable, when told, engages the hearer to complete the process begun by the story. This often does not happen effectively when a parable is frozen into a written text and read in the abstract. Because the parable is not self-explanatory "but intent on transcending what it says literally, it needs all the help it can get to carry out this delicate transaction."[35] Nuances of voice, the use of gestures, eye contact and a shared environment between the speaker and hearers are all crucial aids in conveying the meaning without saying it. The reader of a written parable lacks these aids and thus may be unable to enter into the revelation it carries. In the modern context the power of the parable may show itself only in the situation that is sufficiently sensitive to the words so as to bring them to life in the speaking and hearing of worship or teaching. The language of the parables is like that of the native North American Indian who said to the white man, "Our language is not at all like yours. In our language, we talk about something and never mention it. But everybody knows what is meant. We understand from the context."[36] Those who understand the meaning of the parables become insiders, and their newly shared experience brings them together in an intimate communion (Mk. 4:10-12).

While the gospels contain other forms in addition to the parable, it is the parable that was most characteristic of Jesus' teaching, and it is the parable that seems to have had the greatest power in Christian experience through the ages. Thus our emphasis on the parable.

In addition to gospels, letters make up the other major source of the New Testament. In the New Testament we find both actual letters and discourses composed in letter form (for example, Romans and Hebrews). In conformity with the practice of the day, these letters were written to be read aloud in public. For Paul there is an identity between the spoken word (or the letter being read aloud) and the power of the Spirit to enliven Christian fellowship. In writing to the Corinthians Paul admonishes them to be living letters from Christ "to be known and read by all men . . . written not with ink but with the Spirit of the living God."[37] Unlike a merely written text, the speaking of the letter—the content of which for Paul is always a re-presentation of the gospel—enters the hearts of individuals and joins speakers and hearers together into a fellowship of the word, a logos of giving and receiving (Phil. 4:15; Gal. 6:6). We see in this Christian experience of the word an emphasis that is somewhat different than in Hinduism. Whereas in Hinduism it is frequently the individual chanting the word to remove *karma* and purify consciousness, in the New Testament it is the individual being brought into fellowship through the word.

If Paul is so committed to the spoken gospel, why then does he write letters? There is of course the practical reason. He was often away from his congregations. But it is also quite likely that he used letters to compensate for his own weakness in speaking. In 2 Corinthians 10:10 we read that Paul's opponents say, "His letters are weighty and strong, but his bodily presence is weak and his speech is of no account." By sending his letter with a follower who was an accomplished speaker, Paul would be able to compete with the polished performances of other rhetoricians (who were appealing to the Corinthians) more successfully than if he spoke himself.[38] Although written, the real life of Paul's letters in the early church seems to have been in their oral performance. What is true of Paul's letters would also appear to hold for the writers of other New Testament letters. Although conceived in written form, they were written to be read publicly in the various Christian churches of the day.[39]

To summarize, we have seen that Jesus taught orally, that his teachings were remembered and passed down orally, that at some point thirty or forty years after his death these various oral collections of his teachings were edited and written down as systematic life stories. These written gospels, along with the letters of the apostles, continued to function in the life of the New Testament church as scripts for oral performances in congregations.

The Written New Testament

If it is true that the stress was on the oral in the early Christian experience, then why was there a transition to the written? No clear answer presents itself. The deaths of original apostles such as Peter and Paul in Roman persecutions may have placed the written text in higher profile as a safeguard against loss of the oral. Or it may be, as Kelber suggests, that the oral alone did not allow for a synoptic presentation of Jesus' life.[40] As Christianity assumed a more established position in Roman culture, there was also an attempt to improve the status of the gospels and letters by presenting them as classical writings.

The process that led to the collection of written items from the oral tradition into one book, and its designation as the canon, was a gradual one. The period that saw the collecting of the letters of Paul and the four gospels (about 70-150 C.E.) also saw the production of a large number of other Christian writings—histories or "acts," letters, homilies, apocalypses, and soon some of these achieved favorable enough status to be included in the eventual canon: Acts, the three pastoral letters (1 and 2 Timothy and Titus), the letters of James, John, Peter and Jude, Hebrews and Revelation. By the end of the second century the books of Matthew, Mark, Luke and John were accepted as the gospels everywhere except in Syria.[41] Even then, however, there appear to have been some Christians who attached greater weight to an oral chain of testimony that could be traced back through teachers to apostles and to Jesus. In their view authority still rested in the living transmission of the words of Jesus, not in any of the books containing his words.[42]

A major push toward collecting these writings into a single authoritative book was provided by Marcion in the middle of the second century. Before Marcion the tendency was to add new writings to the Hebrew Bible to make up the Christian scriptures. Due to his Gnostic attitudes Marcion rejected the Hebrew Bible as representing an inferior deity to the God revealed by Jesus. Marcion's new Christian scripture contained only the gospel of Luke and the letters of Paul. Marcion's success in Rome forced the other Christian churches to develop their own definition of Christian scripture. Against Marcion they retained the Hebrew Bible or Old Testament and added to Luke and Paul's letters the other gospels and letters mentioned above, and this collection was gradually accepted as the final canon.

Exegesis

Once the New Testament was canonized, exegesis or interpretation was required for two reasons: (a) interpretation was required to harmonize or explain internal differences in this diverse collection of texts, which now, due to canonization, had the status of being "inspired writing"; (b) once the canon was closed, the oral development of teaching and texts was halted and interpretation was therefore required to make the fixed texts of the canon relevant to changing conditions.

Over the years Christian exegesis has been marked by openness, flexibility and a rich diversity of interpretation. The basic question asked in Christian exegesis has been, How many meanings may a given passage have, and what are they? Allegory, which dominated the first thousand years of Christian interpretation, went beyond the literal meaning of the passage to find deeper meanings for spiritually advanced persons. In eleventh-century Europe, however, emphasis began to be placed on the literal or "plain sense"of the passage, and on the need to read the text in the original Hebrew or Greek language. Luther and the other reformers continued this same thrust, but added that the natural person must first be transformed by the action of the Holy Spirit—only then could the text be understood. For the Reformers, all church authorities must submit themselves to the voice of God in scripture, thus the motto, *sola scriptura*, scripture alone. In the Roman Catholic Church, *tradition*, as "the mind of the Church" that had been handed down in unbroken succession from the apostles, was placed above scripture. Part of this Roman Catholic stress on tradition comes in response to the Protestant emphasis on scripture alone. In the Eastern Orthodox Church interpretation is aimed at conveying the historical or narrative sense as opposed to the allegorical meaning of the text. The Orthodox approach is based on the activity of God's Holy Spirit in history.

Two modern approaches to interpretation go against the openness and flexibility that have been the hallmarks of Christian exegesis down through the centuries: the historical-critical and the fundamentalist approaches. Both close off openness by claiming to be "the true interpretation." The historical-critical approach claims to recover the *original meaning* of the text and represents this as the "true meaning." The fundamentalist approach, stressing the *inerrancy* of the Bible, directs interpretation to harmonizing different passages that appear to conflict so that the doctrine of the inerrancy of the text is safeguarded.

Functions of Scripture in Christian Life

Following Jewish synagogue practice, scripture is read and preached in worship following a lectionary system so that over a period of time all of the scriptures are covered. Up to and including the King James Version, the stress was on preservation of the oral character of scripture. Translations were made for reading aloud and care was taken to train readers in rhetoric so that the full power of the word would be made present in the hearing of the congregation. The sermon aimed at making scripture "come alive" in the experience of the congregation and the church itself. It is through preaching that tradition has been formed and influenced. Therefore the relationship between scripture and tradition has been one of mutual reciprocity under the Holy Spirit.[43] This process has been hampered at times by doctrinal pronouncements of theology (such as inerrancy of Bible), by the fixing of truth in the pope and by the attempt of modern biblical scholarship to produce a fixed historical meaning. Scripture has been powerful in Christian experience when it is freed from fixed dogmas and allowed to function dynamically as the oral word under the guidance of the Holy Spirit.

Luther emphasized the need for the written word to be preached to be alive. But even when orally encountered, said Luther, it is the action of the Holy Spirit within that allows the Good News of the spoken word to take possession of a life and be understood.[44] In the *Kirchenpostille* of 1522 Luther makes clear that the reason the gospel must be experienced through preaching is not just the speaking aloud—it is the context of personal relationship, present in the oral experience of the word, that is essential to its transforming power.[45]

The Puritans of England followed Luther's lead, giving further emphasis to the presence of the Holy Spirit in preaching. They saw printed and mechanically read sermons, the Anglican practice of the day, as "killing" the living word. Preaching of the "lively word," as the Puritans called it, required freedom from a printed text so that the inspiration of the Holy Spirit within both the preacher and hearers could take possession of the process.[46] The presence of large amounts of memorized scripture in the consciousness of the hearers and the preacher paves the way for spontaneous functioning of the word through the Holy Spirit. The lack of power in many modern sermons may be due, in part, to the lack of this reservoir of scriptural knowledge held in common by both preacher and congregation.

In addition to the preaching of the word, scripture also appears in other parts of the worship service. Psalms are read responsively and provide lyrics for powerful hymns. In Orthodox liturgy one is constantly "washed" in scripture. As the liturgy puts it, "Thine of Thine own we offer to Thee."

Private devotional reading of scripture has also had a long history in the Christian tradition. For this to be effective, however, Bibles in the vernacular had to be generally available and people had to be literate. Thus this practice did not become widely rooted until after the development of the printing press and the production of translations during the fifteenth and sixteenth centuries. Many Protestants read the Bible daily for both devotion and guidance. For the Protestant, the power of the word and its truth come through the activity of the Holy Spirit within each person. Biblical criticism can help one understand the historical content and meaning of a passage, and the traditions of the church can enable one to perceive the range of biblical truth. But the written word comes alive only when the Spirit illumines the mind and convicts the heart that God is speaking directly to one through the words of scripture.[47] For this to happen requires sincerity, openness of mind and a fundamental reverence from the reader. As C. H. Dodd puts it, "For those who approach the Bible in this spirit (which Jesus described as that of a child), it is capable of awakening and redirecting the powers of mind, heart and will."[48]

WHAT CAN EACH LEARN FROM THE OTHER?

We have shown that both Hinduism and Christianity are fundamentally grounded in an experience of scriptural revelation. For dialogue to be successful, each will have to gain an understanding of the experience of scripture of the other. Such a mutual understanding will highlight both similarities and differences. Once the differences, such as those outlined at the outset of this chapter, are recognized and respected, it will be possible for study of the many similarities to produce a deepened experience of scripture for both.

What Christians Can Learn from the Hindu Experience of Scripture?

Our study has shown that in both religions it has been the oral experience of the word that has had the greatest power to transform lives. Christianity in the modern West has tended to lose touch with this fact due to the domination of the written form and the academic approach to scripture. Exposure to Hindu practice, which is still strongly oral in nature, can re-sensitize Christians to the importance of recovering and maintaining the oral experience of their own scripture.

The strong Hindu emphasis on memorization of texts during childhood will remind many Christians that, until recently, such memorization was also practiced in their own tradition. Christians seem to have uncritically followed modern secular thinking, which has judged such memorization during the early years to no longer be necessary. Contact with adult Hindus, who know their texts by heart for both devotional and analytical purposes, can cause Christians to question this change in educational policy. A deeper analysis of the psychological function of the memorized and repeated Hindu mantra may well demonstrate to Christians that early memorization and disciplined repetition are crucial to the devotional power of the word in later life. Such an analysis might well prove helpful to current debates over "modernizing" and changing the words used in the Anglican and Roman Catholic liturgies. Liberal Protestant churches, with a tendency to supplant scripture with the latest in secular word use, might also gain valuable insight. Leaving the devotional and moving to the analytical study of scripture, the Hindu experience again argues strongly for early memorization of the key texts. The point would seem to be that in memorizing such texts the child has embedded the central contents of the tradition firmly within consciousness. Although these texts may not be fully understood when learned at a young age, their presence in consciousness allows the remainder of life to be spent in appropriating their meaning—through both conscious and unconscious processes. Rather than operating on emptiness or on a lack of content, analytic study in adolescence and adulthood has the primary scripture of the tradition immediately before it. Christian education teachers should carefully study this process, as it occurs in Hinduism, and critically compare it with current curricular approaches in Christian education. Preachers, too, might ask whether preaching to a congregation which has in mind the scriptures of the texts being exposited might not render their preaching more powerful. Here the practice of the Hindu *kathā* tradition might be usefully examined. All of this might prove not to be "learning new things" but being resensitized to the importance of previous Christian practice that is no longer strongly functioning.

The need for a *guru* or teacher and a regular devotional discipline is emphasized in the Hindu experience of scripture. This is attractive to many Christians who sense the need for a teacher and a discipline in their own lives. Here again the Hindu experience can sensitize Christians to search within the Christian tradition and recover resources that need to be developed. One aspect of Hindu devotional practice—the repeated chanting of a mantra of scripture—is particularly puzzling to many modern Christians. To many it smacks of brainwashing. For others it is a mindless repetition guaranteed to produce a dulling rather than a deepening of experience. To the modern rational mind such chanting is a manifestation of primitive prayer practice, which touches neither heart nor mind and should be rejected in favor of the creative use of scripture.[49] This assessment needs to be critically tested against Hindu experience, which offers both practical experience and theoretical analysis to support the opposite conclusion.

Both Hinduism and Christianity are rooted in oral traditions in which exegesis exhibits an open-ended continuity. Recent Christian developments within fundamentalism, biblical criticism and the Catholic papal function have tended toward a "fixing of the word" as the truth. This "closing off" of flexibility within scriptural exegesis might be helpfully examined against the Hindu experience, which claims both an eternal unchanging word and a constantly evolving commentarial tradition. Here again the result may well be a sensitizing of Christians away from modern errors and back to traditional approaches.

Within Hinduism there has been considerable sophistication in the analysis of the various levels on which the word is experienced, from the uttered literal word to the word of thought and the word as mystically "seen" (*pratibhā*). Perhaps modern Christian experience, which tends to focus on the literal and the rational, can be sensitized to the poetic and mystical levels through study of Hindu experience. This might well prove especially helpful to Christian biblical scholars who are struggling to break free from encapsulation in seeing scripture as historical to an awareness of the word as narrative and poetic.

What Hindus Can Learn from the Christian Experience of Scripture

As modernity influences Hinduism, both in India and in the Indian diaspora, more and more attention will likely be given to Hindu scripture as written. Christianity has in many ways "specialized" in written scripture, especially in the last few centuries. From this Christian experience Hindus can learn how to preserve and study written text through the techniques of higher and lower criticism. Indeed, the application of such techniques to Hindu texts was already underway at the turn of the century and has been a positive force in Hindu Renaissance movements like the Arya Samāj. When Hindus move from the oral culture, which still dominates much spiritual experience within India, out into the diaspora of the highly literate world of the West, the availability of Hindu scriptures in carefully edited, clearly translated and well bound books may well be essential to continued Hindu vitality. In all of these areas Christianity has thoroughly tested expertise to offer.

In addition to knowing how to put scripture into written form effectively, Christianity, partly perhaps through its encounter with Hinduism, is becoming aware of the danger of giving too much place to the written word. In struggling toward a balance between oral and written scripture, Christianity may gain insight that will be useful to Hinduism in its coming struggle with modernity—both at home and abroad.

Whereas Hindus in India have dominantly experienced their scripture at home in devotion, the Christian tradition has a rich history of the use of scripture in congregational settings. As Hinduism modernizes, especially in diaspora settings, such knowledge might provide helpful leads for Hinduism, as to how its scripture might be adapted to new conditions. As was the case for Christians, Hindus would not likely import Christian practice as such, but use Christian practice to sensitize Hindus to aspects of their own tradition that could be relevant to contemporary experience (such as *kathā* preaching of the *Rāmāyaṇa* as a model for the use of scripture in congregational worship). Hindus may also discover that, as our study has shown, the Christian experience of scripture has traditionally been open and flexible, not literal and fixed as some missionaries have led Hindus to believe. As an open and flexible word, Christian scripture has the capacity to reach out and embrace other scriptures, much in the way that Hindu scripture has been used to embrace Christian scripture in the past. Christian scholars such as Karl Rahner, Krister Stendahl and Raimundo Panikkar have found resources in Christian scripture that enable the grace of Jesus Christ to be seen as functioning through the Veda.[50] Awareness of this could help Hindus to see that Christianity is no more exclusivistic than is Hinduism. Each embraces the other by superimposing its own scriptural norms on the other, thereby enabling a limited positive acceptance of the other. Just as Hindus may embrace Jesus Christ as an *avatār* of Brahman, so Christians may see in Hindu scripture a manifestation of the grace of the Father of Jesus Christ. Neither is a correct perception of the other from its own perspective. But what is achieved is a way of giving positive valuation to the other tradition by an extrapolation and superimposition of one's own scriptural norms. Hindus have to learn that Christians can also do this, that it provides a basis for Christian tolerance of Hindus just as it does for Hindu tolerance of Christians. Both Christian and Hindu scriptures are exclusivistic (that is, only through Veda or Christ is salvation or release possible). Yet in the heart of each scriptural exclusivism there exists a basis for tolerance and dialogue.

NOTES

1. As translated by Frits Staal in *Revelation in Indian Thought*, ed. Harold Coward and Krishna Sivaraman (Emeryville: Dharma Publishing, 1977), pp. 5-6.

2. As translated in *Holy Bible: The New King James Version* (New York: Thomas Nelson, 1982), pp. 944-45.

3. See for example, the Pūrva Mīmāṁsā view of eternality of the word: Ganganatha Jha, *Purva Mimamsa in its Sources* (Varanasi: Banaras Hindu University, 1964), pp. 133, 156.

4. Ibid. p. 157.

5. T.R.V. Murti, "The Philosophy of Language in the Indian Context," in *Studies in Indian Thought*, ed. Harold Coward (Delhi: Motilal Banarsidass, 1983), p. 361.

6. Aurobindo Ghose, *The Secret of the Veda* (Pondicherry: Sri Aurobindo Ashram, 1971), p. 8.

7. The Pūrva Mīmāṁsā school is a significant exception to this doctrine. The Pūrva Mīmāṁsā reject the suggestion that the Vedic words and sentences could ever be transcended because that would remove scripture as the one certain, unchanging ground of *dharma* (rules of behavior and duty). The Pūrva Mīmāṁsā could be described as "scriptural fundamentalists" within Hinduism.

8. Satykam Varma, "Importance of the Prātiśākayas" in *Studies in Indology* (Delhi: Bharatiya Prakashan, 1976), pp. 35-52.

9. Phillip Lulgendorf, "The Life of a Text: Tulasīdāsa's *Rāmacaritamanasa* in Oral Exposition." Unpublished paper presented at the American Academy of Religion, December 1984. While Lulgendorf gives a good description of the Hindi *Kathā* of Tulasīdās's *Rāmacaritamanasa*, much older and more widespread is the training in *Kathā* of the Sanskrit *Bhagavatam Purāna*. In Vrindaban, India, for example, there is a school in which Kathā-singers are trained in a three-year course.

10. J.A.B. van Buitenen, "Hindu Sacred Literature" in *Encyclopaedia Britannica III*, Macropaedia, vol. 8, p. 940.

11. Ibid.

12. The following summary is based on van Buitenen's Britannica article and "The Ancient and Classical Literatures," in *The Literatures of India: An Introduction*, ed. Edward C. Dimock, Jr. (Chicago: University of Chicago Press, 1974), pp. 15-46.

13. Van Buitenen, p. 935.

14. David Kinsley, *Hinduism* (Englewood Cliffs, NJ: Prentice Hall, 1982), pp.19-20.

15. J. Gonda, "The Indian Mantra," *Oriens* 16 (1964): 247.

16. Bhartṛhari's *Vākyapadīya* 1:5. *Vṛtti* states it clearly: "Just as making gifts, performing austerities and practising continence are a means of attaining heaven. It has been said: When, by practising the Vedas, the vast darkness is removed, that supreme, bright, imperishable light comes into being in this very birth." Translation by K.A. Subramania Iyer (Poona: Deccan College, 1965).

17. A.S.C. McDermott, "Towards a Pragmatics of Mantra Recitation," *Journal of Indian Philosophy* 3 (1975): 290.

18. *Vākyapadīya* 1:89.

19. *Sphoṭasiddhi of Maṇḍana Miśra*, tran. K.A. Subramania Iyer (Poona: Deccan College, 1966), *Kārikā* 19-20. A technical description of this purification process is offered in *The Yoga Sutras of Patanjali*. (See *sūtras* I:27-28, 42-44 and II:32.) Special symbolic scriptural words, such as OM, are judged to have particular power. They are said to be the "seed forms" or fundamental sounds out of which all others arise. Thus, chants such as OM are taken as symbolically including within themselves, in potential form, all other scriptural sounds. The repetition of OM, then, provides a "shorthand" technique of chanting all scripture in one syllable. The vibration produced by chanting OM is seen to equate with the primal manifestation of *Davī Vāk*, the divine Word, in its descent from the noumenal into the phenomenal realm.

20. See E. A. Havelock, *The Literate Revolution in Greece and Its Cultural Consequences* (Princeton: Princeton University Press, 1982).

21. C. Mackenzie Brown, "Purāṇa as Scripture: From Sound to Image of the Holy Word in the Hindu Tradition," *History of Religions* 26 (1986): 76.

22. Ibid. p. 82.

23. One account of the writing down of Hindu scripture appears in the *Mahābhārata* 1:1:53 ab. The passage tells how Vyāsa, having composed the great epic, wonders how he might teach it to his disciples. The God, Brahmā, the teacher of the world, approaches Vyāsa.

After the appropriate ceremonies of greeting, Vyāsa complains to Brahmā that, despite the great honor the epic has received, no writer (*lekhaka*) for the work can be found on earth. Brahmā then recommends Gaṇeśa to be the scribe, who indeed soon fulfills the task of transcription.

The story does suggest a motivation for writing down the epic—to make it available to all people regardless of caste or sex.

24. See David Goa, Harold Coward and Ronald Neufeldt, "Hindus in Alberta: A Study in Religious Continuity and Change," *Canadian Ethnic Studies* 16 (1984): 96-113.

25. Ghose, p. 12.

26. For translation see J.H. Woods, *The Yoga System of Patanjali* (Delhi: Motilal Banarsidass, 1966).

27. See Ganganatha Jha, *Pūrva Mīmāṁsā in Its Sources*.

28. See S. Radhakrishnan, *The Brahma Sūtra* (London: George Allen & Unwin, 1960).

29. See *Indian Metaphysics and Epistemology*, ed. Karl H. Potter (Princeton: Princeton University Press, 1977).

30. A good example of this *sūtra* commentarial process of exegesis may be seen in the discussion of *Yoga Sūtra* I: 24-25 where the beginningless relationship between Iśvara and the scripture he speaks at the start of each creation cycle is examined in terms of the epistemological and psychological implications involved. See my article "Agama in the Yoga Sutras of Patanjali," *Indian Philosophical Quarterly* 12 (1985): 341-359. This example shows the relation between reason and scripture in Hindu exegesis. Reason is employed to remove doubts and contradictions thus clearing the way for scriptural words to evoke immediate knowledge of the Divine. For an excellent article on the Hindu (specifically Vedānta) view of reason and revelation see T.R.V. Murti, "Revelation and Reason in Vedānta," in *Studies in Indian Thought*, ed. Harold Coward (Delhi: Motilal Banarsidass, 1983), pp. 57-71.

31. Amos N. Wilder, *Early Christian Rhetoric: The Language of the Gospel* (Cambridge: Harvard University Press, 1978), p. 27.

32. See Werner Kelber, *The Oral and Written Gospel* (Philadelphia: Fortress Press, 1983). Kelber identifies four kinds of stories in Mark: healings, exorcisms, ethical teaching stories and parables. Each of these he finds display oral characteristics.

33. John Dominic Crossan, "Parable and Example in the Teaching of Jesus," *Semeia* (1974): 76. As Crossan puts it, the whole thrust of the story demands that Jesus "say what cannot be said: Good & Samaritan." The hearer is put into a condition of cognitive dissonance by the putting together of what, for the hearer, are contradictory words.

34. Kelber, p. 62.

35. Ibid.

36. As quoted by Kelber, p. 76.

37. 2 Corinthians 3:2-3, Revised Standard Version.

38. Richard Ward, "The Apostle Paul and the Politics of Performance at Corinth." A paper read at the Annual Meeting, Society of Biblical Literature, Anaheim, California, 24 November 1985.

39. This also appears to hold for the book of Revelation. David Barr has recently argued that in the early churches Revelation was read completely through as a dramatic oral performance. Indeed Revelation 1:3 says, "Blessed is he who reads aloud the words of prophecy, and blessed are those who hear." David L. Barr, "The Apocalypse of John As Oral Enactment." A paper read at the Annual Meeting, Society for Biblical Literature, Anaheim, California, 24 November 1985. To be published in *Interpretation*.

40. Kelber, p. 220.

41. F. W. Beare, "The Canon of the N.T." in *The Intepreter's Dictionary of the Bible*, vol. 1 (Nashville: Abingdon Press, 1962), p. 521.

42. Ibid., p. 524.

43. Bruce Vawter, *Biblical Inspiration* (Philadelphia: Westminster Press, 1972), p. 154.

44. Willen Jan Kooiman, *Luther and the Bible*, trans. John Schmidt (Philadelphia: Muhlenberg Press, 1961), p. 52.

45. Martin Luther, *Works*, ed. Jaroslav Pelican (St. Louis: Concordia Publishing House, 1958), vol. 7, p. 526.

46. Ronald Bond, "The 'Lively Word' and the Book of Homilies: The Preaching and Reading Ministries in Tudor and Stuart England," unpublished paper, p. 2.

47. Bernard W. Anderson, "The Bible," *A Handbook of Christian Theology* (New York: Meridian Books, 1958), p. 40.

48. C. H. Dodd, *The Authority of the Bible* (London: Fontana, 1920), p. 269.

49. See Friedrich Heiler, *Prayer: A Study in the History and Psychology of Religion* (New York: Oxford University Press, 1958), p. 65. Heiler describes ritual chanting as no longer being the free outpouring of the heart. "It becomes a fixed formula which people recite without feeling or mood of devotion, untouched both in heart and mind."

50. See H. G. Coward, *Pluralism: Challenge to World Religions* (Maryknoll, NY: Orbis Books, 1985), chap. 2.

17

A World Council of Churches' Perspective on the Future of Hindu-Christian Dialogue

S. WESLEY ARIARAJAH

INTRODUCTION

Dialogue literally means a thorough conversation. In such an exchange it is not so much the words spoken but the persons involved that are at the center of the enterprise, for words simply perform the function of facilitating communication, contact and relationship. When the World Council of Churches first organized the dialogue program it was decided that it should be called the program on "Dialogue with *people* of living faiths." This concern to keep the people at the center has continued to influence the way the program has developed over the years. In a recent workshop organized by the World Council of Churches to create a community of pastors who would promote the dialogue concern in South India, Dr. Stanley J. Samartha again emphasized this understanding:

Dialogue is not a matter of discussion but of relationships. It has more to do with people than with ideas. Dialogue is a spirit, a mood, an attitude towards neighbours of other faiths. In a multi-religious country like India where the destinies of different religious communities are intertwined and where people of different religious persuasions and ideological convictions face the same human problems in the life of the nation we need to remove suspicion, and build up confidence and trust between people. Thus, in a community where people of different faiths live and work together, dialogue can become an expression of Christian neighbourliness and part of the Christian ministry in a pluralist world.[1]

I, therefore, welcome the topic that has been assigned to me — "A World Council of Churches' Perspective on the Future of Hindu-Christian Dialogue." What we want to discuss here has to do with the future of the Hindu-Christian dialogue "on the ground," as it were, in actual situations of life. Or, to use the word employed by Dr. Samartha, what we want to examine has to do with how Christians and Hindus would and could live as neighbors in the years ahead.

This, however, is not a matter on which one could give predictions. We are dealing here with two religious communities that exhibit great diversity in their own self-expression and have adherents with vastly different attitudes and understandings of other religious traditions. The socio-political realities, and the increased pressure of modernity on these religious communities, keep these traditions in a state of flux. Surely no one today can guess what changes Christianity and Hinduism themselves will have to undergo in the modern world.

Also of significance are the different types of relationships into which Hindus, who were at one time seen predominantly as Indians, have entered during the last decades. There are at least four different types of situations that seem to have influenced the development of Hindu-Christian relations in recent years.

First, of course, is the situation in India where, as the predominant religious community, the Hindus are seeking ways to live and relate to neighbors of other faiths. There are a number of developments and problems here that deserve serious attention, and to which we should return.

Second, there are countries like Sri Lanka, Fiji and Trinidad where Hindus have settled for a long time, and where they are faced with the task of dealing with other religious communities — often in the majority — in seeking ways of participating in national life.

Third, Hindus now live in significantly large numbers in the Western nations as neighbors of Christians, who have a different culture and orientation to life; and fourth, Hindus are in constant contact with Christians through the new religious movements and spiritual expressions that continue to challenge and affect the assumptions of Western civilization and the predominant lifestyle that it has produced.

I recognize that this is not a comprehensive list. But it is important to note these differences because, at least at the level of the Council's work, we are approached for expertise, which we often do not have, to help in these different situations. "Can the Council do something about Christian-Hindu relations in Fiji?" "What resources have you to help Christians to relate to the Hindus who are now here in Germany?" "Do you have any advice on dialogue with the Hare Krishna Movement?" — these are concrete questions we are often asked, witnessing to the manifold ways in which the

Christian-Hindu encounter is taking place in the world.

In dealing with the future of Hindu-Christian dialogue in this chapter, therefore, one can only hope to speak in general terms, pointing to some of the areas where much more needs to be done in the years ahead.

THE SEARCH FOR COMMUNITY—THE UNFINISHED TASK

In the early years the primary goal of the dialogue between Christians and Hindus was described as the search for community. The word *community* itself however came under pressure because it is in use both in exclusivistic and inclusivistic ways. The relationship then of "a community" to a larger community became a serious issue. The importance of belonging to a specific community, which was the spiritual home base, was emphasized. This led some to speak of the goal of dialogue as the creation of "a community of communities," or "of a community of heart and mind," or "a community of conversation" across the religious barriers. There were voices in favor of a "world community," and others that were justly afraid of the presumptions involved in such a concept and the inherent dangers.[2]

The word *community*, however, was used to express the desire that the goal of dialogue should be to strengthen relationships, so that persons who belong to different religious communities might discover the common life they have as neighbors and grow together into a group of persons who hold mutual responsibility for one another. These thoughts were expressed rather boldly by the multifaith meeting that the World Council of Churches organized in Colombo.

Acknowledging the "real common links" that bound them together, and accepting the sense of "the universal interdependence and responsibility of each and every person with and for all other persons," the dialogue group affirmed "the fundamental unity of human beings as one family." Recognizing that all religious communities have from time to time compromised this ideal and have acted with lack of responsibility, the group committed itself to "strive and, if necessary, to be ready to pay a price to realize the equality and dignity of all human beings."[3]

This certainly is a vivid way to speak about the goal of the dialogue relationship between religious communities. It might even sound rather idealistic. But as we look into the future, nothing less can be set as the goal of all dialogue, except the promotion of the sense of belonging to the one human family where we hold responsibility for one another, and together for all persons.

The future of Hindu-Christian dialogue in actual life situations depends on our willingness to find ways in which actual meetings take place between Christians and Hindus that will remove misunderstandings and misconceptions, and open the way for common action in the struggles against the evils that dehumanize people in our societies.

Some years back we brought together some Christians and Hindus at

Rajpur, India, to ask how the future of Hindu-Christian relations could be built at local levels so that the dialogue would relate to daily life. The common answer given dealt with several practical steps. There was an attempt to identify specific areas where concrete collaboration was seen as the way of community.

At a regional and local level, dialogue may take many forms:

1. *Talking together.* We need to discuss with one another the problems we share in common in our communities: the oppression of harijans; the corruption of institutions of justice; the outbreaks of violence between castes or religious groups; the suffering and exploitation of many women.

2. *Working together.* One of the most profitable and powerful forms of dialogue is working together with our neighbors in concrete projects of social action. This might mean joining together in flood relief projects or joining together to call the community's attention to victims of violence or injustice. At a more ambitious level, this might mean joining together to establish those hospitals, educational projects, and social agencies which Hindu and Christian groups have hitherto established separately. Working together in intentionally undertaken joint projects, large or small, will also mean reflecting upon our work together. Such active and socially-conscious dialogue may especially serve to attract the energies and engage the commitments of young people who have drifted away from their religious traditions.

3. *Living together.* We hear how Hindus and Christians live together in cities, towns and villages not only in India, but in Indonesia, South Africa, Kenya, Trinidad, the United Kingdom, the United States of America, and many other countries. However, living together should not be merely an accident of geography which places us in proximity to but not in relation to our neighbors. Our living together should be intentional — that we intend to create a community in which we all participate. One way we might begin to develop that awareness and appreciation of our neighbors is to undertake retreats together. For example, Hindu and Christian doctors, or teachers, or social workers, might spend a weekend or a week living together at a conference or retreat center discussing their professional work in relation to their religious commitments.

4. *Celebrating together.* On national or regional holidays, Hindus and Christians might join together in their programs and celebrations. During appropriate religious festivals, Hindus and Christians might invite one another to visit, taking advantage of these occasions to become educated about and appreciative of the traditions of the other. On a more daily level, Hindus and Christians might arrange for mutual visits in temples, churches, ashrams, and homes. In all

these cases, Christians and Hindus should prepare for such visits through programs of education and reflect on such visits in discussion.[4]

* Behind these suggestions lies the conviction of the Hindu-Christian group that met in Rajpur that community, harmony, relationships, and so forth, do not happen automatically; that they cannot be taken for granted; that relationships have to be built, fostered, preserved and celebrated.

I suggest that the future of Hindu-Christian dialogue in most of our societies will depend very much on persons who are willing actually to "work at it" by creating the opportunities that become occasions of dialogue.

In the early stages of the ecumenical movement the churches attempting to be in dialogue evolved what is commonly called the "Lund principle" (after the place in which the commitment was made), which stated that the churches "should not separately do what they can do together." At a later stage they also evolved the principle that the unity of the church should be sought in *each* place and in *all* places. I believe that these principles can today be also applied to the relationship between religious communities. The dialogue that we should seek to promote in the future is not a general Hindu-Christian dialogue, but a relationship that matures in each place and in all places. It should be based on a common commitment that despite the fact that we are different and would continue to do many things separately, we should not do separately what we can do together. There is much more that needs to be done before we can move to this stage; I here highlight three areas for emphasis in the coming years.

The Threat to Community — The Rise of Fundamentalism and Militant Religious Expressions

No one concerned with the future of Hindu-Christian dialogue can afford not to be deeply concerned with the rising tide of fundamentalistic and militant forms of religious expression all over the world. On the Christian side a sizable section is today prepared to abandon some of the dominant presuppositions of eighteenth- and nineteenth-century missionary enterprise that sought to displace the other faiths and to "conquer the world for Christ." A number of Christian theologians are struggling to come to terms with religious plurality and are seeking to reinterpret the Christian faiths in ways that promote dialogue and co-existence. The attempt to preserve the particularity of a religious tradition in the context of an affirmation of plurality, the desire to defend the rights of religious persons to witness to their faiths in the context of also striving to preserve the integrity of religions as authentic communities, and so on, presents issues that are being studied at some depth. But the new awareness of plurality has made and is continuing to make a significant impact on the Christian church. At the same time, however, there are also other sections of the church that are unrepentant in their desire to conquer the world. One of the matters that should deeply concern Christians is the rising number of churches and missions that act in ways that totally deny the spiritual foundations of the Christian faith, and also seriously impair the emerging dialogical relationship between the Christians and Hindus. Time has come when Christians who are concerned with the future of Hindu-Christian dialogue should join the Hindus who have condemned triumphalistic presentations of Christianity, distorted presentations of Hinduism, exploitation of the poverty of persons for conversion and proselytism of every kind. What have crusades to do with Christ? As Kosuke Koyama has put it so well, what the Christians need is a "crucified" mind and not a crusading mind.

On the Hindu side, again one is greatly encouraged by the considerable sections of the Hindu community that, despite deep reservations about some of the negative aspects of Christian and Muslim missions, have maintained a creative attitude to plurality. Also of deep interest are the ways in which Hinduism is being interpreted to throw light on some of the contemporary concerns such as peaceful ways of resolving conflicts, of humanity's relation to nature, the developing of the spiritual potential in the human, and so on. There are also, however, militant and aggressive forms of Hinduism that are at least by implication becoming intolerant of pluralism. Often these expressions are reactions to the negative features of other missions. But they can have the effect of checking some of the ways in which other missions have challenged some of the inherent social evils that continue despite the attempts of Hindu reformers to deal with them with the resources within their tradition.

This is of course a very sensitive subject, and one cannot hope to deal with it without sooner or later misrepresenting one or another of the religious traditions. But the underlying issues raised by the rise of conservatism and militancy on all sides have a serious bearing on the future of Hindu-Christian dialogue. Many issues such as plurality, the rights of religions to witness, the rights of individuals to change religious allegiance, the rights of communities to protect their religion and culture, the relation between religion and state, and so on, are involved. There was a time when Hindu-Christian dialogue was unrelated to these developments. But we will not be able to avoid them in the future, for many of the common perceptions about Christians and Hindus in each other's community are being shaped by these militant elements, causing serious damage to relationships and creating an atmosphere conducive to interreligious conflict.

This is a complex subject also because the political forces in the world are ever willing to use religious sentiment to their advantage. Very often religious sentiment is deliberately used to heighten tension and religious coloring is given to conflicts whose causes are socio-political or economic. Also at stake here are the relationships linking religion, culture, nationalism, state. The future health of Hindu-Christian dialogue will depend very much on our willingness to face some of these hard questions, and more important, on our willingness to face them together.

Religious Formation — The Way toward Community

The foregoing consideration leads me directly to the next concern I wish to raise on the future of Hindu-Christian dialogue, namely education.

Our experience in the World Council of Churches of attempting to promote interfaith dialogue has shown that the lack of widespread interest in dialogical relations has little to do with people's willingness. Much of the problem of interreligious relations has to do with the theological, spiritual and social formation of individuals. Christian identity, for example, in addition to the positive sides, has often been established negatively as "non-Hindu," "non-Buddhist," and so forth, leading Christians to speak also of others not so much as Hindus or Buddhists but as "non-Christians." Theologically, the religious formation has been exclusivistic, leading a Christian quite naturally to assume that he or she has the right or true or saving religion even long before the religious faith has been intellectually owned or spiritually experienced. Such a theological formation naturally closes the person to any consideration of other ways or even any active interest in the faith of others. One interesting observation is that many Christians who read secular authors and poets generally do not read scriptures of other faiths or the writings of those considered as enlightened within other religious traditions. The way that the Christian faith is taught in the Sunday schools is in itself often prejudiced, offering little or no way for a child to attain an informed understanding and appreciation of the faith of his or her neighbors.

The dialogue sub-unit of the World Council of Churches extended this exploration into the theological seminaries where those who have leadership in Christian formation as pastors and teachers are themselves trained. We explored the way Christian theology is taught, the reasons why other religions are taught and the way a pastor is prepared to work in a multifaith society. What has emerged is a rather dismal picture.[5] Neither the children nor the pastors today are equipped to live in a religiously plural world. In the Hindu-Christian context, the Christian has little or no information or knowledge of the Hindu as a religious person. The primary attitude that is fostered is missiological: the intention, about which nothing much is often done, is that one has to influence the other to become as he or she is.

I have here stayed with the Christian side of the story, for the Hindus are the best judges of their own situation. But my suspicion is that almost all religious communities have enabled their people to grow in mutual isolation, and our only hope ever to create a truly pluralistic community depends on our willingness to do something about it.

It is for this reason that the World Council of Churches' sub-unit launched a study process in the churches entitled: "My Neighbor's Faith —

and Mine, Theological Discoveries through Interfaith Dialogue." This study guide, now being translated into over twelve languages (including the Indian languages of Hindi, Marathi, Urudu, Tamil, Telugu, Malayalam and Sinhalese in Sri Lanka) is not intended to give information on other faiths; nor is it an attempt at comparative religion. What it seeks to do is to raise awareness in the Christians of the Hindu, Buddhist, Sikh, and others, as believing and praying people, who have a spiritual history and life. Raising that awareness alone can bring much difference in the Christian attitude toward the Hindu. Education and the formation it brings will have much to contribute to the future of Hindu-Christian dialogue.

Growing Together — The Marks of a Community

What does the future hold for Hindu-Christian dialogue? I am glad that there is another presentation, from a theological perspective, for we will have then an opportunity to consider the different visions. Some wish to see the Christian and the Hindu as deeply and firmly rooted in their respective traditions, but in truly mutual relationship and partnership. Others wish to see this relationship essentially as a transforming friendship where the two traditions would interpenetrate and transform each other. Still others may wish to see only relative value in the historical expressions of religious life and see the emergence of an authentic religious life for contemporary society that has the imprint and input of the spiritual resources of the different traditions.

At the level of the concrete life situations, however, there is much pressure to give greater guidance of the ways Hinduism and Christianity could share at the spiritual level. There are, of course, numerous examples of individual persons who have transcended the religious boundaries and have entered into the spiritual disciplines and practices of another tradition. But is this possible at a more popular level? A good example is the increasingly frequent multifaith prayer services for peace, justice and others.

The Prayer for Peace at Assisi, for example, raised numerous questions in the preparatory meetings. Can persons of different religious traditions pray together? How much agreement on symbols, images and theological constructs are necessary before people can engage in common prayer? Or is there a meeting of persons at the deep spiritual and personal level where there is the genuine possibility of common prayer?

The Assisi event was made possible by a distinction that was made between "coming to pray together" and "coming together to pray." The organizers insisted that what happened was the latter, thus warding off any charges of syncretism. However one might assess the Assisi event itself, it points to situations where Hindus and Christians are called to make a response. These are likely to be on the increase in the future. This, however, is not only a question of practical situations. On a more positive note, one is often asked whether common prayer should not be a way forward in our growing together. This question was so real in so many situations that the Committee for Relations with People of Other Faiths of the British Council of Churches had to prepare a booklet, "Can We Pray Together? Guidelines on Worship in a Multi-Faith Society" to give some practical guidelines to Christians, Hindus and others who were ready to grow together in their search for community. The fundamental issue here is how one can be rooted in one's own spiritual tradition and yet benefit from the spiritual traditions of humanity, which are a common heritage to all. This matter will need detailed attention in the future from those who have had the courage to move further afield in this area.

The World Council of Churches brought together (December 1987) twenty-five Christians who ventured into using spiritual disciplines not particular to their own tradition in their search for spiritual enrichment. The questions were:

What is your story?
What have you learned from it?
What does it say to the spiritual life of a wider community?
Is there a future for the Christian-Hindu dialogue at the spiritual level? Or are we here entering an area where much more clarity is needed?

Growing together, however, is not only a matter of praying and worshipping. Much of the ongoing Hindu-Christian dialogue at local levels happens between people who are engaged in the struggles for justice and human rights, in places where persons, both Christians and Hindus, have come out in solidarity with the poor and the oppressed in society. In most situations, however, those who have been drawn together in this way have either shed their religious identity or at least become reluctant to interpret their commitment in religious symbols. Conversations with these groups suggest that this reluctance has sometimes to do with a fear that any emphasis on religion would lead to division and disruption; more often it involves a belief that religious systems are often themselves oppressive and subject to exploitation by those who wish to protect their own privileges. It is not my intention here to examine the truth of such a belief, for all of us are aware that all religions are constantly in danger of being used by forces that care little for the people and their destiny.

One should point out that one of the most significant areas where there can be a genuine growing together of Christians and Hindus lies not so much at the level of the recognition of doctrinal excellence, of belief systems or even of the depth of piety, but at the point of the recognition of the liberating potential of religions. Where religious beliefs are related to human liberation, where religions have had the function of effecting genuine reconciliation, and where religious persons have on the basis of their profound convictions striven for the cause of justice and peace, there has been a growing together that bears the mark of genuine dialogue. One of the challenges that faces the Hindu-Christian dialogue of the future is how this reality can become as true of the wider community as it is now of small sections of Hindus and Christians, who are themselves often on the margins of their own communities.

One reason why this is important is that it is in this area that Christianity could be said to have had its deepest engagement with the Hindu community. Christians have often claimed that their message has a liberating potential that makes it attractive to the oppressed sections of Hindu society, insisting that the success of Christian mission among the Hindu outcasts has not stemmed from the exploitation of their poverty, as has frequently been suggested, but from the liberation that it brings. Hindus, on the other hand, have constantly argued that their own understanding of reality can provide this liberation and that the Hindu tradition is strong enough and diverse enough to furnish both the symbols and the energy required for the social transformation that will free all persons from social degradation.

The Hindu-Christian dialogue of the future should enable us to move away from such false polarization and polemics, for both religious communities are deeply concerned with the total liberation of human life from all that is alien to truth. This is an area where there is room for much mutual enrichment and correction, if only it can be done in the context of a trusting relationship where the Christian and the Hindu advance together into a fresh discovery of what it means to be human in our times.

CONCLUSION

Aloysius Pieris of Sri Lanka sees the Christianity shaped by the Semitic and Greco-Roman civilizations, and the Hindu-Buddhist-Taoist traditions shaped by Asian civilization, as two distinct impulses in human history. He calls these the agapeic and gnostic idioms.

Pieris claims that here there are two religious models that, "far from being contradictory, are in fact, incomplete each in itself and, therefore, complementary and mutually corrective." He holds that in dealing with the Hindu/Buddhist traditions and the Christian tradition, often characterized as Eastern and Western, we are actually dealing with two poles of tension that are not so much geographical but psychological. "They are two instincts," says Pieris, "emerging dialectically from within the deepest zone of each individual, be he Christian or not. Our religious encounter with God and man (*sic*) would be incomplete without this interaction."[6]

Here is a view that perceives the Christian-Hindu/Buddhist encounter of the future not as an option but as a necessity, for it sees the Christian and the Hindu as needing each other to become complete in themselves. There is a mutual complementarity and correction that each brings to the other simply by who they are and the impulse that drives them, and this complementarity accounts for a fuller understanding of life itself.

The Hindu-Christian dialogue of the future, therefore, is pregnant with promise. But this promise can never become a reality unless persons like you and me are convinced that the promotion of this encounter is an essential part of our own ministry. The future of Hindu-Christian dialogue depends on a number of Hindus and Christians in many situations taking concrete steps to ensure that the ongoing dialogue of life also becomes a conscious encounter between persons of faith. If it fails, it will have done so because those who believed in it did nothing about it. For I believe, despite some signs to the contrary, that the Hindu and the Christian in the ordinary situations of life are more ready for this dialogue at depth than we imagine.

In one of the gospel stories the disciples who had gone into town to buy food returned to find Jesus in a deep conversation with a Samaritan woman, breaking the barrier that stood between women and men, Samaritans and Jews. To the disciples who were still surprised Jesus said:

> You have a saying: "Four more months and then the harvest." But I tell you, take a good look at the fields; the crops are now ripe and ready to be harvested! (Jn. 4:35).

In the field of dialogue too, "the harvest is plenty but the laborers are few."

NOTES

1. S. J. Samartha, "Christian Concern for Dialogue in India," *Current Dialogue*, no. 9, December 1985, World Council of Churches, Geneva.

2. Some of these issues have been discussed in detail at the World Council of Churches' multifaith dialogue on "Towards World Community," published as *Towards World Community — The Colombo Papers,* World Council of Churches, Geneva, 1975. See memorandum from pp. 115f.

3. Ibid. p. 116.

4. *Religious Resources for a Just Society, A Hindu-Christian Dialogue*, Report of the Rajpur Meeting, World Council of Churches, Geneva, 1981, pp. 17-18.

5. For a full report of this study see: *Ministerial Formation in a Multi-faith Milieu: Implications of Interfaith Dialogue for Theological Education*, ed. Sam Amirtham and S. Wesley Ariarajah, World Council of Churches, Geneva, 1986.

6. Aloysius Pieris, "Western Christianity and Asian Buddhism, A Theological Reading of Historical Encounters," *Dialogue*, New Series, vol. 7, no. 2 (1980).

18

The Future of Hindu-Christian Dialogue

KLAUS KLOSTERMAIER

A basic prerequisite for such future dialogue is that all participants have accurate information about each other's religions. Fulfilling this prerequisite is probably the single largest obstacle to the success of religious dialogue. The majority of people today are illiterate of their own religion as well as the religion of others. The academic study of religion has a major role to play in overcoming this problem.

—Harold Coward[1]

INTRODUCTION

My first and only excursion into futurology so far took place about ten years ago. A colleague from history teaching a course on futurology asked me to speak about "The Future of Religion." I accepted with some hesitation and made the usual excuses before the class, saying that I was neither a futurologist nor a visionary and that anyhow future could not be predicted with certainty, least of all the future of religion. Nevertheless, when pressed for some details, I hazarded some guesses as regards the future of religion. I reread these with some curiosity after I had received Harold Coward's invitation to speak about the "Future of Hindu-Christian Dialogue." Here are some of the things that ten years ago seemed to me to be in the future of religion.

In the West I predicted a further polarization between "traditionalists" and "progressives." I also foresaw a growing antagonism between intellectuals and an increasingly irrational mass-religion. I guessed that there would be an outward movement toward ecumenism coupled with an inward emptying of content. I also ventured to predict an increase in fundamentalist and sci-fi-faith groups.

For the East I predicted a further emphasis on nationalism in conjunction with religion and more attempts to equate nationhood with religion. I thought there would be a massive Muslim missionary movement based on petrodollars. I predicted a lessening of opposition of communism toward religion and vice versa: Communism as the most conservative social movement at present would ultimately be considered as savior also of conservative religions. What I did not foresee were important events such as the election of Pope John Paul II and the rise of Ayatollah Khomeni, the Iran-Iraq war and Sikh extremism, the election of Reagan as president of the United States and of Gorbachev in the USSR, the Tammy and Jimmy Bakker story, the Waldheim affair . . .

Thus, venturing for a second time into futurology, I am conscious of the fact that a) it is possible to extrapolate from existing situations developments that are likely to occur and to continue, b) it is impossible to predict events and the role new actors on the scene are going to play. The latter may well cancel out much of what could be assumed on the basis of the former.

The English language has three moods that are future oriented:[2]

1) The future mood assumes that a certain event is going to occur, and that its occurrence can be anticipated with some confidence.

2) The subjunctive mood leaves alternatives open and attributes a certain probability to the occurrence of a future event.

3)The imperative mood expects a certain event to occur as the result of a command given or an order executed.

While in our daily use of the language we form future forms of verbs with ease and regularity, from a logico-epistemological viewpoint future-talk is quite problematic. Can meaningful and true statements be made about future events? Can the rules of thought that were developed on the basis of past experience be extended into the future? Must we not assume an unproven homogeneity of time when doing so? Things become even more problematic when we address the ontological status of future events. There are theories that assume all future events are already located in an eternal present. The *Bhagavadgītā* maintains such a view,[3] and it could also be extrapolated from certain biblical passages.[4] Classical Galilean-Newtonian science operated with a similar concept: It did assume that all events were predetermined by the immutable eternal laws of nature, operating in a uniform, infinite space and time, that a complete knowledge of these laws would unfailingly allow us to predict all future events. The power of accurate prediction was seen as the greatest strength and proof for the validity of the scientific method.

Modern science, as well as modern religion, has become more careful. The acknowledged irreversibility of time, the asymmetry introduced by it into the universe, the relativity of space and time, both conceived as finite, the fact of "negentrophy" and other such phenomena have lead to an acceptance of indeterminacy, which at the very least, would (fundamentally) restrict our power to predict the future, because of our inability to know simultaneously all the factors necessary for doing so.[5] The role of prophets and seers, shamans and yogis has been greatly diminished in the major religions of our time in comparison to former ages.

Nevertheless, the future still plays a major role in religion. Not only are there books like the *Bhaviṣya Purāṇa* and the *Apocálypsis*, but religions quite literally live by predicting and anticipating an absolute future, the *páraloka*, the *éschaton*, the future beyond earthly life. The threat of unpleasant re-births motivates millions of Hindus to practice *sādhanas* of many kinds and the prospect of a divine judgment after death is the major incentive for Christians to practice the commandments.

Since by its very nature the future is open, and since I have no claim to a special knowledge of future events, let me use grammar as the organizing principle of my presentation and thus address the future of Hindu-Christian dialogue in the three future-oriented moods the English language offers.[6]

WHAT WILL BE THE FUTURE OF HINDU-CHRISTIAN DIALOGUE?

The Essential Hindu-Christian Dialogue Will Largely Take Place in India

In spite of the presence of some twenty million Hindus worldwide out-side India and in spite of the establishment in the West of genuine Hindu movements (such as ISKCON), Hinduism is, by its nature and its history, closely identified with the political-geographic reality of Bharat. I need not demonstrate the importance of Ganga and Yamuna, Himalaya and Arun-acala, Kasi and Kanci, Vrindaban and Srirangam, and countless other places, the irreplaceable function of *melās* and *Yātrās* and of *śrāddha* cer-emonies performed in India. In order to enter into a genuine dialogue with Hindus, Christians need an extensive knowledge of, and an empathy with, the reality that is Bharat Mata. A Christian who has not grown up in India or who has not been exposed at length to the living Hindu reality should normally not expect to be taken seriously in Hindu-Christian dialogue. Yes, one can and one should read books about Hinduism, one can study Mī-māmsā and Vedanta, one can practice yoga and meditation, one can look at pictures of gods and goddesses, one can even participate in Hindu cer-emonies in North America. Yes, I would encourage all students of Christian theology to also study Hinduism, to inform themselves about the genuine piety and the deep religious thought of Hindus. But I would not encourage anyone to engage in Hindu-Christian dialogue unless prepared to live for at least a couple of years in India and to seek contacts with Hindus there. Doctrinally Hinduism outside India is very liberal; the openness for new ideas of modern Hindus in the West is so great that dialogue is almost pointless. In India itself Hindu-Christian dialogue will imply a facing up to present-day socio-political realities. Conversion is one such major real dialogue issue, so is the possession of holy places, the openness for mixed worship, and the joining in festivities.

The Future of Hindu-Christian Dialogue Will Largely Depend on Future Mutual Interest

There are many Hindus who are familiar with the New Testament and who are in sympathy with the ideals of the Sermon on the Mount. There are few Hindus who are interested in (contemporary) Christian theology, and there are fewer still who have a desire to enter into a dialogue with their Christian counterparts. There is a growing interest among Christians in India for Hinduism. Several Christian training institutions now have courses in Hinduism, and a fair number of good studies of specific aspects of Hinduism are appearing, often authored by Christian clergy.[7] There have been seminars and conferences in India (and abroad) where Hindus and Christians actually met and exchanged ideas. That there is a certain amount of mutual interest today is certain. Whether that interest is going to increase is uncertain. I notice a certain stagnation. Celebrations and affirmations of dialogue notwithstanding, there seem to be few new ideas; there seems to be little progress. I may be wrong. But let me report one little anecdote, which I find telling. One of the handful of Hindu scholars who had shown an interest in Hindu-Christian dialogue over the past decades read a very good address at the 1986 Interfaith Seminar in Tambaram/Madras. The thoughts sounded somewhat familiar to me. When checking up I found that it was word by word the same address the same scholar had delivered at the WCC Interfaith Meeting in 1970 in Ajaltoun/Lebanon, at which I also happened to be present.

Hindu-Christian Dialogue Will Require the Affirmation of the Role of Scholars in Religion

Hindu-Christian dialogue at the level of theology is by definition a scholarly affair. While not wishing to see living religiosity reduced to mere intellectualism, I attribute an important role within major religions to the activity of scholars, to thought and reflection. R. Boyd has rightly said, "For the modern educated man in India religion is philosophy or it is nothing."[8] Intellectuals are not the favorite children of Mother Church in our time and age. Not only does one often have the impression that church leadership is not intellectual itself, it often comes through as anti-intellectual. There is a tendency to equate church membership with blind obedience to authority, faith with repetition of traditional formulae, theology with language regulation. There are true scholars within the church—but more often than not they feel repressed, unwanted, under suspicion. In contemporary organized Hinduism too the trend appears to be toward the political rather than toward the intellectual, toward agitation more than toward reflection.[9] Hindu-Christian dialogue is a frontier for both Hinduism and Christianity. It requires new thought and new articulations. It requires the honest work of true intellectuals. It is the perception of many of those working in this area that the institution is not behind them.

WHAT MAY BE THE FUTURE OF HINDU-CHRISTIAN DIALOGUE?

Hindu-Christian Dialogue May Be Linked to the Future Development of Hinduism and Christianity[10]

I believe I am not exaggerating when saying that as institutions both Hinduism and Christianity are today in a severe identity crisis. It is very obvious in many areas, less so in others. For an institution an identity-crisis arises out of a crisis of legitimacy. The institutional crisis is more radical than the crisis in individual lives. I believe that Christianity as a contemporary institution cannot (and should not) establish its legitimacy on the words of Jesus, nor Hinduism on the word of the Veda. Both institutions must seek legitimacy for their present and future structures from elsewhere and develop along lines for which there are no clear instructions in the documents they refer to. Institutions, Hindu or Christian, represent concrete interests, which have much to do with their own past and which they must legitimate. They have institutional rights to defend, a historically-grown identity to preserve, rules to enforce; they aim at self-sufficiency and ideally at an impersonal way of functioning.[11] The church used to be terribly fast with its anathemas when it encountered new ideas, and so were caste-pañcáyats with excommunicating members. As an institution the church was all that the individual Christian was not supposed to be:[12] it made a show of its charities; it had no patience with its dissenters; it was vain and self-seeking, tough and suspicious, avaricious and unscrupulous in pursuing its supposedly divine mission. There is a Hindu counterpart to this too in many a *sampradāya* and many a temple board, which flatly contradict the lofty ideals of the Upaniṣads or the exalted image of a Vaiṣṇava as depicted, for example, by Caitanya.

As long as the institutions have not come to terms with their identity crisis they cannot meet as institutions. Some individuals in them may be able to dialogue as private persons, but it will not be an institutional Hindu-Christian dialogue, nor will it have any repercussions on the majority of Hindus or Christians. There also may be not much future for Hindu-Christian dialogue if the prevalent right-wing, conservative and fundamentalist factions in both Hinduism and Christianity take over.[13]

The Future of Hindu-Christian Dialogue May Be Endangered by an Institutional Misunderstanding of Its Nature [14]

From my own experience of dialogue with Hindus I would surmise that a statement like the following from the pen of Cardinal Arinze, president of the Vatican Secretariat for Non-Christians, in the opening lines of the latest official declaration on "Urgency of Dialogue with Non-Christians" would not be found very helpful for dialogue: "Jesus Christ, the Son of God, made man, is our saviour. . . . He ascended to heaven but not before he had carefully prepared his apostles to bring salvation to all men, of all times, in all places."[15] While a Hindu might not have difficulty accepting such a statement qualified by a "we Christians believe. . ." — in its naive dogmatism it not only offends non-Christians but also more thoughtful Christians. Hindus, I suspect, would take this as an expression of the church's missionary intentions rather than as an invitation to dialogue. Even less reassuring, I fear, are some lines on the next page: "Interreligious dialogue would be unnecessary if all men believed in Jesus Christ and practiced only the religion which he established." This time, I am afraid, also Christians in denominations other than Roman Catholicism might be pricked. Is it that easy to make out "the religion which Jesus Christ established"? Or would interreligious dialogue also be unnecessary if all men believed in Buddha and the religion he established? Or in Mohammed, or . . . or . . .? Is the very mention of a possible single-religion Christian world not a sign of lack of realism, a revelation of a profound ignorance of history and uncalled-for Christian triumphalism? It does not save the statement from being totally beside the point when at a later stage quotations from papal statements on dialogue made during the last twenty years are brought in. It only helps to support the claim that people without personal dialogue experience can do more harm than good in this area.

Hindu-Christian Dialogue May Have To Be Placed into a Larger "Secular" Context

The secular, science-based modern culture of the West has become the background to contemporary intellectual life almost everywhere — or is fast becoming so. Hindu-Christian dialogue of the future may not only have to take place in the awareness of this situation, but it may have to incorporate it into its agenda. Most Hindus and most Christians know very little of the traditions they belong to; most have no interest in acquiring any extensive knowledge of the ritualism or the theologies of their faiths. The *de facto* emancipation of large populations in East and West from traditional religious domination has led to a great deal of independence *vis-à-vis* religious authorities also in matters where religions were traditionally thought normative. Hindu-Christian dialogue need not aim at preserving existing institutional structures or maintaining traditional beliefs. Largely unofficially as yet and not yet fully recorded, a massive shift has taken place in the understanding of key concepts of both traditional Christianity and Hinduism, much of it under the impact of modern science. Today's science is no longer the materialistic atheistic mortal enemy of religion science was in the nineteenth century, but it also has not become an ally of traditional

institutional religions. There is much deep spirituality and religious searching in some of the writings of twentieth-century giants of science and some
contemporary scientists are quite clear about their offering a "new religion"
in their thinking.[16] Hindu-Christian dialogue cannot bypass this development, especially since these scientists quite often enter into dialogue with
both Hinduism and Christianity, albeit in a somewhat eclectic and not
always scholarly fashion.

I may add that I was quite surprised how often the issue of nature and
science was brought up in the presentations by delegates to the major
Interfaith Seminar in Tambaram/Madras last year.

HINDU-CHRISTIAN DIALOGUE IN THE IMPERATIVE

Hindu-Christian Dialogue Is Inevitable. It Is an Imperative

Hindus and Christians in India share the same country and largely the
same laws. They interact every day on many levels, and they cannot ignore
each other's religions. Hindus and Christians must demolish the barriers
that have been set up between them by zealous ecclesiastics and by centuries of sectarianism.[17] While engaging in honest dialogue, both Hindus
and Christians will discover that the denominational fragmentation of their
traditions is against the true spirit of these traditions, and that they will
have to recover an identity beyond that of denominationalism. In a sincere
and open dialogue focused on the basics of religious life it will not be
possible for participants to retreat to the safety of their narrowly-defined
sectarian identities, to refuse to come out of their shells with references to
their "Lutheran tradition," their "Vaiṣṇava background," their "Catholic
identity," their "Śaiva faith." Hindu-Christian dialogue, if it has a future,
must be a radical questioning of traditions and an in-depth searching for
ultimates.[18] I cannot help feeling that denominational Christianity has nar-
rowed down what was meant to be a universal spirituality to a sectarian
doctrine, and that something similar has happened in sectarian Hinduism.
They apply to themselves exclusively—not only as Christians and Hindus,
but as Catholics and Rāmānandis, as Lutherans and Śrīvaiṣṇavas, as Men-
nonites and Saivasiddhāntins—what was meant for all humankind. They
disregard the majority of humankind and the most important aspects of
human existence in their efforts to claim salvation for themselves as fruit
of their sectarian practices and beliefs. They take no notice of the struggle
of so many who have over the ages sought to find truth, to lead moral lives,
to build communities. The sacred for them is not sacred unless it carries
their own trademark; the good is not good unless it is identified by sectarian
signs. In the process Christians and Hindus have lost the ability to see
goodness and truth where it appears and have been trained to look only
for the external signs of their traditions, regardless of whether these signs
are imprinted on the genuine article or on fakes. They have spent their

time and energy fighting over symbols and signs, over facades and legal points.

Hindu-Christian Dialogue Must Emphasize Jñāna

There is a strong trend in present-day Christian theology to replace systematic thinking and philosophical engagement by story and narrative, to dismiss the intellectual approach to religion as irrelevant and to cultivate only its emotional and pragmatic sides. This trend may be both symptom of a lack of intellectual substance and cause for an erosion of intellectual content of Christianity. I see a similar trend also in contemporary Hinduism, especially in the "new movements." When they were really strong, both Hinduism and Christianity were intellectually very vigorous. It hardly needs stating that the world today is neither governed by Christian nor by Hindu principles, and that both Hinduism and Christianity must fight hard to get a hearing.[19] While in their best times religions lead the intellectual life of a civilization, today they are trailing it.[20] While in former times the populations of Christian and Hindu countries may not have been more moral than they are today, they were prepared to consider the position of their religious leaders as the ideal standard and as desirable norm. Today religions are largely perceived as political lobby, as representing particular interests and as, generally, out-of-touch with the times. Hindu-Christian dialogue must recover the intellectual substance of Hinduism and Christianity and must contribute actively to the ongoing search for truth/reality in all spheres of life. The intellectual dimension of life has not lost its importance in our time.

Hindu-Christian Dialogue Must Exhibit More Continuity

All too many organizers of dialogue conferences and writers of dialogue books believe, and claim, that they are the first who have seen the light, and that they are the ones with whom serious dialogue really begins.[21] They often do not know about, or underestimate, the importance of the work of their predecessors. If a dialogue is to be fruitful it must continue what was said and done before. An amazing amount of constructive work has been done, and many ideas have already been tried out.[22] This work has to be taken into account in planning future dialogues. Today's Hindu-Christian dialogue cannot begin with a *tabula rasa*, but it adds on to a page of history on which much has already been written. It may not have been called dialogue in former times, but meetings, exchanges and encounters have taken place in India between Hindus and Christians for centuries, and both sides formed opinions of each other, which have to be taken into account. Western Christian missionaries often carried tension and dissension into India and separated not only Indian Christians from their Hindu neighbors but also brought about a split within Indian Christianity. Part of Hindu-

Christian dialogue in India must be devoted to the healing of old wounds, the expression of regret over what has happened in the past, and the admission that Christians have grievously misunderstood and misrepresented Hinduism. Hindus will not necessarily be reassured that all is well now if a Christian agency distributes pamphlets advocating dialogue or announcing that twentieth-century Christianity is so different from that of the nineteenth century.[23]

HINDU-CHRISTIAN DIALOGUE IN THE BENEDICTIVE MOOD

Over and above the three future-oriented moods of the English language, which we utilized, Sanskrit possesses a "benedictive" mood (*āśīrliḍ*) used to express wishes and blessings, hope and support. Our so-called hard-nosed modern world does not believe much in these things. But wishes and hopes have come true before, and blessings and supportive words have helped many. Why not use them in the context of Hindu-Christian dialogue?

May Hindus and Christians discover in each other's traditions insights and values and blend them with their own insights and values.

May Hindus and Christians open up in dialogue toward each other and toward that which they call — by different names — God, Brahman, Bhagvān, Śiva, Śakati. . .

May Hindus and Christians gain respect for each other and may they have the courage to change their institutions accordingly.

May Hindus and Christians make their communities aware of the presence of each other, as well as of the necessity to better know each other.

May dialogue become the normal way of communication between Hindus and Christians rather than the exception.

May Hindus and Christians (in conjunction with all others) regain the center needed to order our social and political, our economic and our ecological lives.

May Hindus and Christians in dialogue shed all pretensions and all claims of racial superiority or religious privilege. May they discover what it means to be human and what it is to be in the Presence.

May Hindu and Christian scholars not only talk about dialogue but enter into genuine dialogue for their own enlightenment as well as of those for whom they teach and write.

CONCLUSION

Let me conclude with a suggestion that reaches beyond the future of Hindu-Christian dialogue. A consequence of the encounter between Hinduism and Christianity (and other religions and ideologies) might be a certain alienation from the local and accumulated traditions in the same sense in which the discovery of new continents brought about — as Hanna

Arendt sees it[24] — an alienation of Europeans from their homelands, and the discovery of distant planetary systems through the telescope brought about an alienation of humankind from earth. The process is not likely to be stopped. The attempt to conquer foreign continents and alien religions, to missionize and to make them like one's homeland has ended in failure, and not only for reasons of strategy. Horizons have shifted and the point once considered the center has turned out to be on the periphery.[25]

John Archibald Wheeler, one of the most thoughtful astrophysicists of our time, ends a major essay with the remark that we only begin to understand the universe and to grasp how simple it is when we begin to see how strange, unexpected and different it is from what we had imagined.[26] This is true also of religion. Not only do we begin to understand in genuine, profound and personal Hindu-Christian dialogue how strange and different and also unsuspectedly familiar the "other's" religion is, but we also begin to understand something of the extraordinary strangeness of our own religion, which we believed we knew and were familiar with.

NOTES

1. Harold Coward, *Pluralism: Challenge to World Religions* (Maryknoll, NY: Orbis Books, 1985), p. 107.

2. Other languages have somewhat different arrangements.

3. *Bhagavadgītā*, 32ff.: "Time am I, world-destroying, grown mature ... by me alone are they slain already. Be thou merely the occasion ..." (trans. S. Radhakrishnan). Foreseeing the future is one of the *siddhis* Yogis are supposed to be able to acquire. Cf. *Yogasūtra* IV, 16.

4. Cf. Ps. 139:16: "You had scrutinized my every action, all were recorded in your book, my days listed and determined, even before the first of them occurred" (Jerusalem Bible). It was the sign of the "true" over against the "false" prophet to be able to accurately predict future happenings.

5. J. Bronowski, in *A Sense of the Future* (Boston: MIT Press, 1977) still seems to cherish the classical ideal when he writes: "The future is not already determined, but neither is it arbitrary. We know its possible states, and what weight to give to each; it has a defined area of uncertainty which we calculate and within which we can expect it with confidence" (p. 38). A rather interesting blend of traditional and scientific/modern ways of predicting the future has developed in India where some astrologers use computers to work out the horoscopes of their clients. See "Computer Kundlis" in *India Today* (April 30, 1987), pp. 165f.

6. I am trying what one might call "middle-range" forecasting, that is, for the next ten or so years. Short-term and long-term is far too risky for me. I claim no foreknowledge of the price of pork-bellies six months from now (which people playing the futures market need), and I do not intend to compete with writings in professional futurology like Herman Kahn's *The Next 200 Years: A Scenario for America and the World* (New York: William Morrow, 1976) with a great number of neatly-drawn graphs and statistics extending over the next two centuries. In a 1986 publication, *India 2000: The Next Fifteen Years*, J. R. Roach, ed., one chapter is dedicated to "The Puzzle of Religious Modernity" (L. A. Babb). It "puzzles" about

the future of Hinduism and uses as its data basis three so-called modern movements: the Radhasoami movement, the Brahmā Kumāris and the movement around Sathya Sāī Bābā. No mention is made of the great questions that arise from the juxtaposition of mainstream Hinduism with Islam and Christianity. I am afraid the approach to the future of Hinduism by looking at English pamphlets of some of the fringe of modern Hinduism does not yield workable results. Most Hindus do not speak and read English, and most Hindus do not belong to these three movements. Their future is not typical of the future of Hinduism.

7. The Institute for the Study of Religion and Society (formerly in Bangalore, now in Delhi) has published valuable studies of, and contributions to, Hindu-Christian dialogue for over twenty-five years. Recently a *Dialogue Series* (Madurai, Madras, Varanasi) has started publishing Monographs, and the Centre for the Study of World Religions at Dharmaram College in Bangalore publishes the dialogue-oriented *Journal of Dharma*.

8. R. Boyd, *An Introduction to Indian Christian Theology* (Madras: CLS, 1979), p. 262.

9. The quick rise of the *Viśva Hindu Parishad* and other organizations affiliated with and spawned by the RSS prompted *India Today* to devote the cover story of its May 31, 1986, issue to "Militant Hindu Revivalism." It editorialized: "Slowly, but surely, like a juggernaut gaining angry momentum, a palpable, resurgent, united and increasingly militant movement of Hindu revivalism—*Hindu Jagaran*—is sweeping across the land. Frenzied in pace, frenetic in character, the religious and communal combat vehicle is freewheeling across the collective Hindu consciousness."

10. Harold Coward, in the above-mentioned book, makes this link explicit in chapter 6, "Religious Pluralism and the Future of Religions."

11. Both Hinduism and Christianity (in its mainstream) are mass-religions, "national religions," to which one belongs automatically by the sheer fact of being born into a certain community (infant-baptism, at least as it used to be practiced, is the equivalent of being born into a religion, as is the case in Hinduism). What we see developing today, both in Hinduism and Christianity, is the forcing of identities in contrast to "the others"; the present Catholic Church is as good an example as the Viśva Hindu Parisad.

12. I am referring here to the portrait of a Christian drawn by Paul in 1 Corinthians 13.

13. Hindu communalists are reportedly challenging religious minorities with the battle cry: "We are sixty crore Hindus—we will break your bones," *India Today* (April 30, 2987), p. 66. The rhetoric of people like Golwalkar (*Bunch of Thoughts*) is also not designed to encourage Hindus to dialogue with Christians. Similarly the anti-dialogue statements coming from those who call themselves Evangelicals within Christianity are quite explicit; cf. Vinay Samuel and Chris Sugden, "Dialogue with Non-Christians: An Evangelical View" in *Sharing Jesus in the Two Thirds World* (Grand Rapids: Eerdmans, 1984), pp. 122-40.

14. One of the most stunning misrepresentations of dialogue was made by Cardinal Marella, the first president of the Vatican Secretariate for Non-Christians in an address to the Collegium Urbanum in Rome, printed in the English version of the *Osservatore Roman* on December 19, 1968 (also reprinted in the *Bulletin of the Secretariat for Non-Christians*, no. 10 (March 1969), pp. 3-19. In the address entitled "Nature, Presuppositions and Limits of Dialogue with Non-Christians," he referred

by name to virtually all Catholic scholars who were active in dialogue with Hindus in India at the time as "enemies of dialogue."

15. "The Urgency of Dialogue with Non-Christians" in *Origins* 39/14, Washington (March 14, 1985), pp. 641-50.

16. Douglas Hofstädter ends the preface to his widely acclaimed *Gödel, Escher, Bach: An Eternal Golden Band* (New York: Vintage Books, 1980) with these words: "In a way, this book is a statement of my religion. I hope that this will come through to my readers, and that my enthusiasm and reverence for certain ideas will infiltrate the hearts and minds of a few people. That is the best I could ask for" (p. xxi). See also Ken Wilbur, ed., *Quantum Questions: Mystical Writings of the World's Great Physicists* (Shambhala, 1984). Books like Siu's *Tao of Science* and F. Capra's *Tao of Physics* have become "bibles" for a generation of science-and-religion-interested youth.

17. The sociologist L. Dumont has said emphatically: "Cultures not only *can* be made to communicate, they *must!*" *Religion/Politics and History in India* (Mouton, 1970), p. 161.

18. Thomas Aquinas in *Summa Theologiae* II-II, 1, 2 c approvingly quotes Dionysius, *De divinis nominibus*, "Fides est circa simplicem et semper existentem veritatem" ("faith is about the simple and ever existing truth"). This must be the definition of faith adopted by both Christians and Hindus in order to enter into meaningful dialogue.

19. Neither Hinduism nor Christianity (nor religion as such) figures in prominent futurological works like Kahn's *The Next 200 Years* or Heilbronner's *Inquiry into the Human Prospect* (New York: Norton, 1975). Heilbronner suggests, however, that "it is possible that a post-industrial society would also turn in the direction of many pre-industrial societies—toward the exploration of inner states of experience rather than the outer world of fact and material accomplishment. Tradition and ritual, the pillars of life in virtually all societies other than those of an industrial character, would probably once again assert their ancient claims as the guide to and solace for life" (p. 140).

20. Where religions determine the course of public life, like in Northern Ireland and Iran, they certainly present a less-than-ideal condition of life.

21. Thus W. Strolz and S. Ueda, eds., *Offenbarung als Heilserfahrung im Christentum, Hinduismus and Buddhismus* (Collected Papers from a Dialogue Conference: Vienna, 1982) begin their preface with the sentence: "Christian theology has just now begun the dialogue with the great religions of Asia."

22. Just two major works—out of an impressive number—may be mentioned to substantiate the claim: R. Boyd, *An Introduction to Indian Christian Theology* (Madras: CLS, 1979) and M. M. Thomas, *The Acknowledged Christ of the Indian Renaissance* (London: SCM, 1969).

23. There appeared in 1900 the second edition of a book, published by the CLS Madras: *Indian Hindu and Indian Christian: Or What Hinduism Has Done for India and What Christianity Would Do for It: An Appeal to Thoughtful Hindus*, which is extremely embarrassing to read today for its brazen arrogance and ignorance. That this is not a single slip of a fanatic's pen but the expression of a prevailing mentality among Western Christians becomes clear from such documents as those referred to by Carl T. Jackson, *The Oriental Religions and American Thought: Nineteenth Century Explorations* (Westport, CT: Greenwood Press, 1981), pp. 85-102.

24. Hanna Arendt, *Vita activa oder vom tätigen Leben* (München: Piper, 1984).

25. I disagree with John Dunne, who in his widely acclaimed *The Way of All the Earth: An Encounter with Eastern Religions* (SPCK, 1973) describes the process of dialogue as "passing over" and coming home, affirming one's roots and one's traditions with greater firmness.

26. John Archibald Wheeler, "From Relativity to Mutability," in J. Mehra, ed., *The Physicists' Conception of Nature* (Dordrecht, 1973), pp. 202-47.

About the Authors

Anand Amaladass is Professor at Satyanilayam, Institute of Philosophy and Culture, Madras. Apart from a number of articles, he has published *Philosophical Implications of Dhvani* (1984), co-edited *Philosophy and Human Development* (1986) and edited *Jesuit Presence in Indian History* (1988).

S. Wesley Ariarajah is Director of Sub-unit on Dialogue with People of Living Faiths, WCC. In addition to numerous articles, he has published *Dialogue* (1980), *The Bible and People of Other Faiths* (1986) and *The Spirituality of Interfaith Dialogue* (with Tosh Arai) (1989).

Robert D. Baird is Professor of the History of Religion, University of Iowa, Iowa City, Iowa. In addition to numerous articles, he has published *Category Formation and the History of Religion* (1971) and edited *Religion in Modern India* (1981).

Harold Coward is Professor of Religious Studies and Director of the Humanities Institute at the University of Calgary, Calgary, Alberta. In addition to numerous articles and edited books, he has published *Bhartrhari* (1976), *The Sphota Theory of Language* (1980), *Pluralism: Challenge to World Religions* (1985), *Jung and Eastern Thought* (1985), *Sacred Word and Sacred Text: Scripture in World Religions* (1988) and *The Philosophy of the Grammarians* (1990).

Steven J. Gelberg is Director for Interreligious Affairs, International Society for Krishna Consciousness. In addition to numerous articles, he has published *Hare Krishna, Hare Krishna: Five Distinguished Scholars on the Krishna Movement in the West* (1983) and *The Hare Krishna Movement: A Bibliographic Survey* (1987).

David J. Goa is Curator of Folk Life, Provincial Museum of Alberta, Edmonton, Alberta. His publications include *Seasons of Celebration: Ritual in Eastern Christian Culture* (1986), "The Word that Transfigures," in *Silence: The Word and the Sacred* (1989), *Dying and Rising in the Kingdom of God: The Ritual Incarnation of the "Ultimate" in Eastern Christian Culture* (1986) and *Hindus in Alberta: A Study in Religious Continuity and Change* (1983).

Klaus Klostermaier is Professor and Chairman of the Department of Religious Studies, University of Manitoba, Winnipeg, Manitoba, Canada. In addition to numerous articles he has published *Hinduismus* (1965), *Hindu and Christian in Vrindaban* (1970), *Mahatma Gandhi: Freiheit ohne Gewalt* (1968), *Salvation, Liberation, Self-realization* (1974), *Mythologies and Philosophies of Salvation in the Theistic Tradition of India* (1984) and *A Survey of Hinduism* (1989). His publications include *Contemporary Conceptions of Karma and Rebirth among North-Indian Vaisnavas* (1986), *Indigenisation of Worship in India* (1986) and *Dharmamegha Samadhi* (1986).

Roland E. Miller is Professor of Religious Studies, Academic Dean of Luther College, and Coordinator of the Religious Studies Program of the University of Regina. The volumes, *The Mappila Muslims of Kerala — A Study in Islamic Trends*, and *The Sending of God* are among his numerous publications.

Ronald Neufeldt is Associate Professor and Head of Religious Studies at the University of Calgary, Calgary, Alberta. In addition to various articles he has published *F. Max Müller and the Rig Veda* (1980) and edited *Karma and Rebirth: Post Classical Developments* (1986).

Anantanand Rambachan is Assistant Professor in the Department of Religion, St. Olaf College, Northfield, Minnesota, U.S.A. He has contributed articles to several journals, including *Philosophy East and West*, *Religious Studies*, *Religion*, *Theology* and *World Faiths Insight*.

Murray Rogers, after a year's stay in Mahatma Gandhi's Sevagram in central India and a year in a Hindu joint-family in an Indian village, founded Jyotiniketan Ashram near Bareilly, U.P., where he lived from 1954-71. Jyotiniketan now continues under Indian leadership. After living the same ashram-style life for nine years in The Old City of Jerusalem, he and his small community moved to a hill-top house in the New Territories, Hong Kong, where under the name One Bamboo Hermitage they continue a simple lifestyle with emphasis on prayer, silence, and dialogue with visiting friends. He has written various articles on subjects related to interfaith dialogue.

Eric J. Sharpe is Professor of Religious Studies at the University of Sydney, Australia. In addition to many articles he has published *Not to Destroy but to Fulfill* (1965), *The Theology of A.G. Hogg* (1971), *Comparative Religion: A History* (1975; second, enlarged edition 1986), *Faith Meets Faith* (1977), *Understanding Religion* (1983) and *The Universal Gita* (1985).

Richard W. Taylor is Senior Associate Director (Research), Christian Institute for the Study of Religion and Society, New Delhi. He has written *The Contribution of E. Stanley Jones* (1971), *Jesus in Indian Paintings* (1975) and *A Remembered Parish* (1986) and contributed to and edited a number of books and the quarterly *Religion and Society*.

A. Frank Thompson is Associate Professor, Religious Studies, University of Waterloo. In addition to numerous articles he has published *The Splintered Glass: Painting and Religion in Modern India* (1981).

John C. B. Webster is Professor of History of Christianity, United Theological College, Bangalore, India. In addition to numerous articles he has published *The Nirankari Sikhs* (1979), *The Christian Community and Change in Nineteenth Century India* (1976) and *History and Contemporary India* (1971).

Richard F. Young is with the Presbyterian Church (U.S.A.) as Associate Professor of South Asian Studies in the Faculty of International Studies at Meiji Gakuin University, Tokyo, Japan. In addition to a number of articles on indological subjects, he is the author of *Resistant Hinduism: Sanskrit Sources on Anti-Christian Apologetics in Early Nineteenth-Century India* (1981).

Paul Younger is Professor, Department of Religious Studies, McMaster University. In addition to various articles he has published *Indian Religious Tradition* (1970), *Introduction to Indian Religious Thought* (1972) and *Hinduism* (1978).

Index

CONCORDIA UNIVERSITY LIBRARY

3 9371 00048 6738

BR 128 .H5 H55 1989

Hindu-Christian dialogue